SELECTIONS FROM

EXPERIENCING THE WORLD'S RELIGIONS

TRADITION, CHALLENGE, AND CHANGE
FIFTH EDITION

MICHAEL MOLLOY

T. L. HILGERS
PRINCIPAL PHOTOGRAPHER

REL III: EASTERN RELIGIONS

T.H.

Boston   Burr Ridge, IL   Dubuque, IA   New York   San Francisco   St. Louis
Bangkok   Bogotá   Caracas   Lisbon   London   Madrid
Mexico City   Milan   New Delhi   Seoul   Singapore   Sydney   Taipei   Toronto

Selections from
Experiencing the World's Religions: Tradition, Challenge, and Change
Fifth Edition
REL 111: Eastern Religions

1 2 3 4 5 6 7 8 9 0 WDD WDD 12 11 10 09

ISBN-13: 978-0-07-740460-4
ISBN-10: 0-07-740460-2

Learning Solutions Representative: Ann Hayes
Learning Solutions Representative: James Doepke
Production Editor: Jessica Portz
Printer/Binder: Worldcolor
Photo Credits: Buddha statue and fabric © 2009 JupiterImages Corporation

In memory of Sandra Minn, caring wife, mother, teacher; kind and gentle neighbor.

Contents

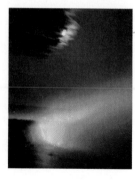

2 Indigenous Religions   **34**

3 Hinduism   **74**

4 Buddhism   124

5   Jainism and Sikhism   **188**

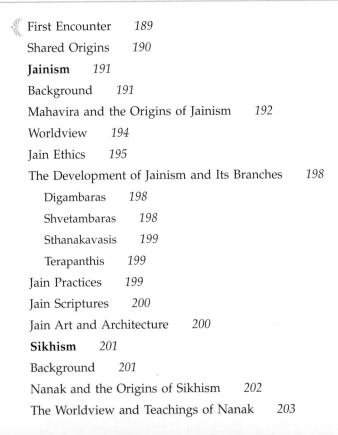

6 Daoism and Confucianism   **212**

7 Shinto   262

Boxed Features

RITUALS AND CELEBRATIONS

WOMEN AND RELIGION

Experiencing the World's Religions

ENCOUNTER

Learning about the religions of the world begins as an encounter. Students often encounter unfamiliar religions from faraway places, practiced by people whose culture is very different from their own. With *Experiencing the World's Religions*, this encounter is made accessible, inviting, and intriguing.

EXPERIENCE

Experiencing the World's Religions immerses students in the practices and beliefs of the world's major religions. This book, praised by instructors for its comprehensive, personal, and compelling approach, connects the concepts, systems of beliefs, and rites and rituals of these religions with the lived experience of the people who practice them every day. Art, architecture, music, literature, politics, and social issues—the culture of a religion's people—contribute to the student's intimate learning experience.

UNDERSTANDING

Over four editions of this text, students have told us they read more, retain more, and recall more with *Experiencing the World's Religions*. The inviting style, coverage, and organization pull readers into the unfamiliar landscape where they encounter, experience, and understand the most important and memorable elements of each religion.

Preface

Religions are not always easy to love. Like all institutions that span hundreds of years, the world's great religions have checkered histories. A friend of mine, active in religion, divides the details of these histories into two columns: "religion at its best" and "religion at its worst." Perhaps this is a realistic assessment, and the distinction is a wise one. We don't expect all people to be good all of the time. Why should we expect the same of religions?

In response to the religious tensions of today's world, books have appeared that are highly critical of religions. Some books speak of the cruelty done in the name of religion. Others speak of religious oppression of women, minorities, and nonmembers of a particular faith. Several promote nonbelief as the most rational course.

Perhaps influenced by these books, some readers have asked me to address the less rosy aspects of religion—the social pressures that religions can exert, their limitations, and their capacity to hurt as well as help. While I have thought often about this dark side of religion, I love so much about religions that I tend to focus on their beauties, not their blemishes. But I do agree that we must recognize and discuss the blemishes.

As I thought about the more dangerous aspects of religion, I remembered a conversation from my youth with one of my aunts. Noticing that she wrote an odd kind of backhand, I asked her, "Why does your handwriting slant to the left?" She told me that when she was a girl she had attended a religious elementary school. Though left-handed, she had been forced to write with her right hand. "If I tried writing with my left hand," she told me, "my teachers hit my hand with a ruler." But she said that she had never become completely used to writing with her right hand, and the result was her odd backhanded way of writing. As I recall the story now, it seems a small but thought-provoking example of how people and their institutions—including religious ones—may intend to do good but can cause harm instead.

There are many areas in which religions have done harm. Some religions have tolerated, condoned, or even justified slavery. Religions have crushed minorities. Religions have forced individuals to conform in thought and action, and people have sometimes been killed in the name of religion simply because they refused to conform. Religions have promoted, and often commanded, divisions based on gender. Religions have also tolerated and often justified social division. They have taken the side of the political establishment at least as often as they have opposed it. This edition of the textbook tries to look more closely at some of these issues, thereby inviting students to look at religions from multiple angles.

Perhaps the most exciting aspect of working on this edition, however, relates to something quite positive about religions today. In past editions, I treated environmentalism primarily in the final chapter and spoke of it in a few paragraphs as just one emerging religious development. But now, in only a few years, environmentalism has become a significant religious concern. Nowadays, nearly all the major religions have environmental movements within them. Reflecting on this fact, I can even begin to entertain the idea that some type of "Green Religion" is emerging as a new superreligion. Although religions tend to change slowly, this development shows that religions can also change quickly and can respond well to real needs within the world.

The theme of the cover remains flowing water. It symbolizes the purification, new life, and hope that religions promise. It also symbolizes the constant change that is an essential part of religions, as it is of everything. The flowing water should remind us of the possibilities of religions to renew both their followers and themselves.

This book is written for beginners. With each new edition, I have tried to remain true to those readers who are just starting their study of religions. Five aims have guided me:

1. *Offering the essentials.* What would a person seeking to be an informed world citizen want to know about the major religions? This book tries to present that essential content, but no more. But it also encourages further discovery by pointing to additional places, texts, and people of interest.

2. *Providing clarity.* Some years ago I heard this ironic axiom: "When you see the spark of ambition, water it!" I have learned that students come to a course in world religions with eagerness to learn. But their initial enthusiasm can easily be drowned by waves of details presented in overly academic language. I try to give only the essentials and to present them in the clearest language possible. Maps, photos, definitions, and timelines are incorporated into the text to provide additional clarity.

3. *Showing the multidimensional nature of religions.* A religion is not just a system of beliefs. It is also a combination of ways in which beliefs are expressed—in ceremony, food, clothing, art, architecture, pilgrimage, scripture, and music. This book tries to make the multifaceted expressions of religion clear, with photographs that have been carefully chosen to help achieve this goal.

4. *Encouraging direct experience.* Religions are better understood through firsthand experience. I hope here to encourage students to imagine and seek out direct experience of religions both at home and abroad. To illustrate the excitement of personal exploration, each chapter features "First Encounter" and "Personal Experience" sections.

5. *Blending scholarship and respect.* This book necessarily presents religions from a somewhat academic point of view. At the same time, it tries to show its empathy for the thoughts and emotions of people who live within each religious tradition.

In the small space of this single volume, much should be said that cannot be; therefore simplification and generalization are unavoidable. Also, no one person can know the entire field of religion, which is as full of facts as a galaxy is full of stars. But these shortcomings should invite professors and students to compensate for what is missing by adding their own insights and interpretation.

My overriding focus in this edition is what it has been in every other edition: to help students of religion to understand the often complicated content of the world's religions. In addition to providing fuller treatment of religious suppression and religion-based environmentalism, I have included an illustrative reading at the end of each chapter, along with lists of books, films, music, and Web sites of interest to students. In the chapter on Christianity, the new "First Encounter" draws attention to a little-known type of Christianity, ancient but still alive. The new "First Encounter" in the chapter on Islam considers contemporary developments within Islam in Malaysia—one of the most rapidly industrializing Muslim countries—developments that may be occurring in other Muslim countries, as well. New photos of Islam in Malaysia and Turkey give insights into how Islam is being transformed in these two modernizing nations. The "Personal Experience" at the end of the last chapter echoes some current criticism of religion. End-of-chapter resource lists have been expanded. (Instructors may want to suggest other Web resources, including relevant YouTube topics.) A "Test Yourself" quiz has been added at the end of each chapter. Although suggestions for intellectual exploration and physical travel have been moved to the Web site, those suggestions remain keys to understanding for great numbers of students.

This text offers a wealth of supplemental materials to aid both students and instructors. The Online Learning Center at www.mhhe.com/Molloy5e is an Internet-based resource for students and faculty members.

INSTRUCTOR'S RESOURCES

Instructor's Resources are password-protected and offer:

- **Instructor's Manual,** including an outline for each chapter, learning objectives, lecture supplements, notes on For Fuller Understanding feature, discussion starters, and video resources.
- **Test Bank,** including over 750 multiple choice and essay questions.

- **Computerized Test Bank.** McGraw-Hill's EZ Test is a flexible, easy-to-use electronic testing program. It accommodates a wide range of question types, and instructors may add their own questions. Any test can be exported for use with course management systems. The program is available for Windows and Macintosh.
- **PowerPoint slides** for each chapter, outlining key concepts and ideas.

STUDENT RESOURCES

The Online Learning Center at www.mhhe.com/Molloy5e is a robust study tool for students, providing a wide range of material to enhance learning and to simplify studying. Resources are keyed directly to this edition and include:

- **Student Quizzes** that allow students to check their understanding of the course material. The quizzes can be e-mailed directly to instructors.
- **Chapter Objectives and Chapter Summary** that guide and focus students' reading for each chapter.
- **Possible Paper Topics** provide suggestions for further research and deeper exploration of each chapter's topics.
- **Reflection Exercises** encourage students to explore and build on key chapter concepts through exercises incorporating their own ideas and thoughts.
- **Interreligious Comparisons** provide questions that aid students in drawing parallels between the religions discussed in each chapter.
- **"For Fuller Understanding" and "Religion beyond the Classroom"** features, previously included at the end of the textbook chapters, are now online and updated for the fifth edition.

ELECTRONIC TEXTBOOK

This text is available as an eTextbook at www.CourseSmart.com. At CourseSmart, students can take advantage of significant savings off the cost of a print textbook, reduce their impact on the environment, and gain access to powerful Web tools for student learning. You can view CourseSmart eTextbooks online or download them to a computer. CourseSmart eTextbooks allow students to do full text searches, add highlighting and notes, and share notes with classmates. Visit www.CourseSmart.com to learn more and try a sample chapter.

ACKNOWLEDGMENTS

Many great teachers have shared their insights with me—I am simply passing on the torch. I will always be especially thankful to Walter Daspit, Sobharani Basu, Abe Masao, Eliot Deutsch, Winfield Nagley, and David Kidd. It is a joy to recall the influence of their unique personalities. I remain grateful to the East-West Center in Honolulu for a grant that early on assisted my studies in Asia, and I encourage students and professors to apply for grants there and elsewhere. Several monasteries were kind in allowing me to share in their life: Songgwang-sa in South Korea, Engaku-zan in Japan,

Saint John's Abbey in Minnesota, and Saint Andrew's Abbey in California. I am indebted to the late Alden Paine, to Ken King, and to Jon-David Hague, whose editorial encouragement was a model of insight. Thanks to Mark Georgiev, my editor at McGraw-Hill, for his availability and help; to Brian Pecko for his photographic research; to Robin Mouat for her fine illustrations; to Cassandra Chu, who designed the cover; to Adam Beroud, my industrious developmental editor; and to Andrea McCarrick, my fine copy editor. Because so many people work on this project, and because we are spread from Honolulu to Boston, perfection is a difficult goal. Despite such challenges, it's wonderful to see how much turns out right. But the never-ending work of clearing typos and getting captions right is like trying to bathe your dog. I apologize if you find a flea.

Thanks also go to these teachers and scholars who offered their ideas for earlier editions: Nikki Bado-Fralick, Iowa State University; Lee W. Bailey, Ithaca College; Robert M. Baum, Iowa State University; Wendell Charles Beane, University of Wisconsin–Oshkosh; Ann Berliner, California State University–Fresno; Dan Breslauer, University of Kansas; Charlene Embrey Burns, Loyola University–New Orleans; Madhav M. Deshpande, University of Michigan; D. Kerry Edwards, Red Rocks Community College; Brett Greider, University of Wisconsin–Eau Claire; Rita M. Gross, University of Wisconsin–Eau Claire; George Alfred James, University of North Texas; Philip Jenkins, Penn State; Ramdas Lamb, University of Hawaii; Richard A. Layton, University of Illinois–Urbana-Champaign; Jared Ludlow, Brigham Young University–Hawaii; R. F. Lumpp, Regis University; Thomas F. MacMillan, Mendocino College; Mark MacWilliams, Saint Lawrence University; Robert J. Miller, Midway College; G. David Panisnick, Honolulu Community College; Robert Platzner, California State University–Sacramento; Kenneth Rose, Christopher Newport University; Lori Rowlett, University of Wisconsin–Eau Claire; Stephen Sapp, University of Miami; Gerald Michael Schnabel, Bemidji State University; John G. Spiro, Illinois Wesleyan University; R. C. Trussell, Pikes Peak Community College; David D. Waara, Western Michigan University; Ralph Wedeking, Iowa Central Community College; Brannon M. Wheeler, University of Washington; and Daniel Wolne, University of New Mexico.

To the reviewers and pedagogical advisors of the fifth edition, I am also indebted:

REVIEWERS	SCHOOLS
Richard Anderson	Oregon State University
Lulrick Balzora	Broward College
Harold Bruen	Wake Tech Community College
Dexter Callendar	University of Miami–Coral Gables
Lee Carter	Glendale Community College, Arizona
Ron Cooper	Central Florida Community College

Michele Desmarais	University of Nebraska–Omaha
Jonathan Ebel	University of Illinois–Urbana-Champaign
Tanya Erzen	Ohio State University–Columbus
Steven Fink	University of Wisconsin–Eau Claire
Mark Hanshaw	Richland College
Sarah McCombs	University of West Florida
Sarah Paulk	Okaloosa-Walton College
Lloyd Pflueger	Truman State University
Maria Selvidge	University of Central Missouri
Mark Stewart	San Joaquin Delta College

PEDAGOGICAL ADVISORS SCHOOLS

Lulrick Balzora	Broward College
Dexter Callendar	University of Miami–Coral Gables
Ron Cooper	Central Florida Community College
Steven Fink	University of Wisconsin–Eau Claire
Sarah McCombs	University of West Florida
Mark Stewart	San Joaquin Delta College

The book is far better as a result of their reviews. Although it is a truism, this book has also been influenced by hundreds of other people who are also owed my sincere thanks. They planted in me seeds that I hope have come to flower.

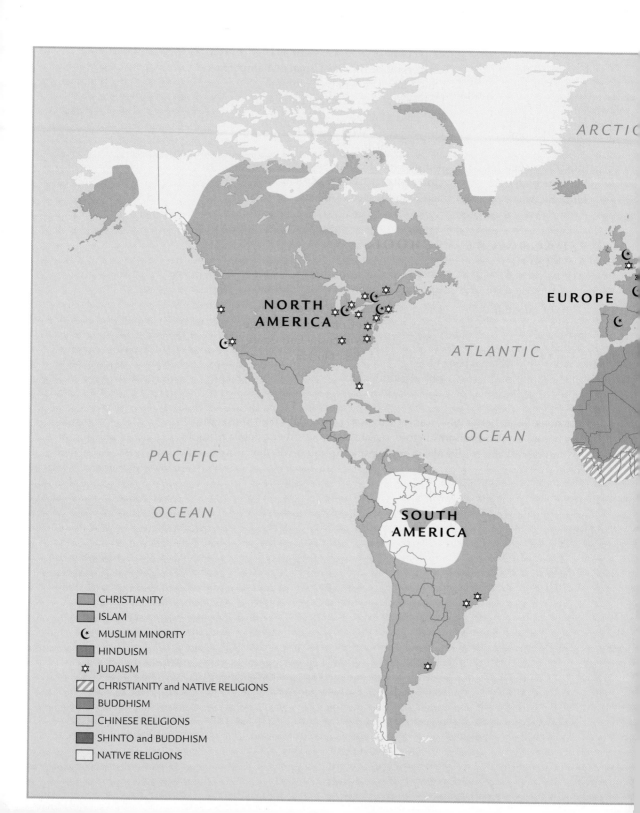

ARCTIC

EUROPE

NORTH
AMERICA

ATLANTIC

OCEAN

PACIFIC

OCEAN

SOUTH
AMERICA

CHRISTIANITY
ISLAM
☾ MUSLIM MINORITY
HINDUISM
✡ JUDAISM
CHRISTIANITY and NATIVE RELIGIONS
BUDDHISM
CHINESE RELIGIONS
SHINTO and BUDDHISM
NATIVE RELIGIONS

1

Understanding Religion

⟨ FIRST ENCOUNTER

For months you have wanted to take a break from work and everyday life, and recently some friends invited you to vacation with them at their mountain cabin. At first you hesitate. This is not the kind of trip you had in mind. After reconsidering, you realize that a remote getaway with friends is just the change of pace you need.

Now, three weeks later, you have been traveling all day and have just arrived at the cabin. It is late afternoon, and the air is so cold you can see your breath. Your friends welcome you warmly, and there's a nice fire in the living room. Your hosts show you to your room and give you a short tour. Soon you are all fixing supper together—pasta, mushrooms, salad. During the meal you discuss your work, your zany relatives, and your mutual friends. Everyone is laughing and having a good time. It's confirmed: coming here was a great idea.

After supper, your friends won't let you help with the dishes. "I think I'll go out for a walk," you say, putting on your heavy, hooded jacket. As the front door closes behind you, you step into a world transformed by twilight.

What strikes you first is the smell in the air. There is nothing quite like the scent of burning wood—almost like incense. It fits perfectly with the chill. You walk farther, beyond the clearing that surrounds the house, and suddenly you are on a path beneath tall pine trees. As a strong breeze rises, the trees make an eerie, whispering sound. It is not exactly a rustle; it is more like a rush. You recall reading once that the sound of wind in pines is the sound of eternity.

Moving on, you find yourself walking along the mountain's ridge. To your left, you see the evening star against the blue-black sky. To your right, it's still light and you see why you are cold: you are literally above the clouds. You sit down on a flat rock, pull up your hood, and watch the pine tree silhouettes disappear as darkness spreads its thickening veil.

It's difficult to pull yourself away. All around you stars begin to pop out, and soon they are blooming thick as wildflowers. Overhead, the mass of stars resembles a river—it must be the Milky Way. You get up and slowly turn full circle to take it all in.

You had almost forgotten about stars. You don't see them much back home, let alone think of them. Where you live, stars appear in movies. Here, though, stars are mysterious points of light. You remember what you once learned: stars are so distant that their light can take millions of years to reach earth. You realize that some of the stars you see may no longer exist. Only their light remains.

At last you begin to walk back to the cabin. A cluster of clouds emerges on the horizon, lit from behind by the rising moon. You see your friends' wooden cabin in the distance. From here it looks so small. The stars seem like the permanent, real world, while the house appears little and temporary—more like a question mark in the great book of the universe. Questions flood your mind. Who are we human beings? Do we make any difference to the universe? Are we part of any cosmic plan? Is there any point to the universe at all? What is it all about?

WHAT IS RELIGION?

The Starry Night, one of the world's most loved paintings, depicts a sky full of luminous, spinning stars. Painted near the end of its creator's life, the work summarizes the vision of Vincent van Gogh (1853–1890). Van Gogh was an intensely religious man who had planned to be an ordained minister in the Dutch Reformed Church, as was his father. But he struggled with his studies and had a falling-out with Church authorities. For a time, he lived as a lay preacher, working with poor miners in Belgium. When he was 27, his brother Theo, an art dealer, encouraged him to take up painting.

Despite his new career, van Gogh continued to think of himself as a minister. If he could not preach in words, he would preach in pictures. His subjects were the simple things of life: trees, sunflowers, a wicker chair, a bridge, his post-man, a farmer sowing seeds, peasants eating a meal, workers bringing in the harvest. His paint-ings express a quiet awe before the wonder that he sensed in everyday objects and ordinary people. It was his special sense of the sacredness he saw all around him that he wanted to share. Almost as a reminder, in *The Starry Night* van Gogh placed the little church tower below the night sky, pointing like a compass needle upward to the stars. The heavenly realm with its spinning fires illuminates van Gogh's vision of the sacred character of the entire universe.

Key Characteristics of Religion

Vincent van Gogh's *Starry Night* provides a startling perspective. A familiar and comforting earthly neighborhood is dwarfed by the vast, mysterious, even daunting, cosmos.

When people begin their study of religions, they bring ideas from the religion in which they were raised or from the predominant religion of their society. They may assume, for example, that every religion has a sacred book or that it worships a divine being or that it has a set of commandments. Indeed, many religions do share all these characteristics, but some do not. Shinto, for exam-ple, does not have a set of commandments, nor does it preach a moral code; Zen Buddhism does not worship a divine being; and many tribal religions have no written sacred scripture. Nevertheless, we call them all religions. What, then—if not a common set of elements—must be present for something to be called a religion?

An obvious starting point for many scholars is to examine linguistic clues: What are the linguistic roots of the term *religion?* Intriguingly, the word's Latin roots are *re-*, meaning "again," and *lig-*, meaning "join" or "connect" (as in the word *ligament*).[1] Thus the common translation of *religion* is "to join again," "to reconnect." If this derivation is correct, then the word *religion* suggests the joining of our natural, human world to the sacred world. In classical Latin, the term *religio* meant awe for the gods and concern for proper ritual.[2] We must recognize, though, that the term *religion* arose in Western culture and may not be entirely appropriate when applied across cultures; *spiritual path,* for example, might be a more fitting designation to refer to other religious systems. We will keep these things in mind when we use the long-established term *religion.*

Traditional dictionary definitions of *religion* read something like this: A system of belief that involves worship of a God or gods, prayer, ritual, and a moral code. But there are so many exceptions to that definition that it is neither comprehensive nor accurate. So instead of saying that a religion *must* have certain characteristics, it is more useful to list a series of characteristics that are found in what are commonly accepted as religions. We may accept as a religion whatever manifests a reasonable number of these characteristics.

> Religion [is] a way of life founded upon the apprehension of sacredness in existence.
> —Julian Huxley, biologist[3]

Scholars do note, however, that what we ordinarily call religions manifest to some degree the following eight elements:[4]

Belief system Several beliefs fit together into a fairly complete and systematic interpretation of the universe and the human being's place in it; this is also called a *worldview.*

Community The belief system is shared, and its ideals are practiced by a group.

Central myths Stories that express the religious beliefs of a group are retold and often reenacted. Examples of central myths include the major events in the life of the Hindu god Krishna, the enlightenment experience of the Buddha, the exodus of the Israelites from oppression in Egypt, the death and resurrection of Jesus, or Muhammad's escape from Mecca to Medina. Scholars call such central stories *myths.* We should note that the term *myth,* as scholars use it, is a specialized term. It does not in itself mean that the stories are historically untrue (as in popular usage) but only that the stories are central to the religion.

Ritual Beliefs are enacted and made real through ceremonies.

Ethics Rules about human behavior are established. These are often viewed as having been revealed from a supernatural realm, but they can also be viewed as socially generated guidelines.

Characteristic emotional experiences Among the emotional experiences typically associated with religions are dread, guilt, awe, mystery, devotion, conversion, "rebirth," liberation, ecstasy, bliss, and inner peace.

Religious rituals are often symbolic reenactments of a religion's key stories. Here, monks in Bhutan perform a dance that passes a story across generations.

Material expression Religions make use of an astonishing variety of physical elements—statues, paintings, musical compositions (including chants), musical instruments, ritual objects, flowers, incense, clothing, architecture, and specific locations.

Sacredness A distinction is made between the sacred and the ordinary; ceremonies often emphasize this distinction through the deliberate use of different language, clothing, and architecture. Certain objects, actions, people, and places may share in the sacredness or express it.

The Sacred

All religions are concerned with the deepest level of reality, and for most religions the core or origin of everything is sacred and mysterious. This sense of a mysterious, originating holiness is called by many names: Brahman, Dao, Great Mother, Divine Parent, Great Spirit, Ground of Being, Great Mysterious, the Ultimate, the Absolute, the Divine, the Holy. People, however, experience and explain sacred reality in different ways, as we shall see in the chapters that follow.

One familiar term for the sacred reality, particularly in the Western world, is *God,* and **monotheism** is the term that means a belief in one God. In some systems, the term *God* often carries with it the notion of a Cosmic Person—a divine being with will and intelligence who is just and compassionate and infinite in virtues. God is also called *omnipotent* ("having total power over the universe"). Although God may be said to have personal aspects, all monotheistic religions agree that the reality of God is beyond all categories: God is said to be pure spirit, not fully definable in words. This notion of a powerful God, distinct from the universe, describes a sacredness that is active in the world but also distinct from it. That is, God is **transcendent**—unlimited by the world and all ordinary reality.

In some religions, however, the sacred reality is not viewed as having personal attributes but is more like an energy or mysterious power. Frequently, the sacred is then spoken of as something **immanent** within the universe. In some religions, there is a tendency to speak of the universe not just as having been created but also as a manifestation of the sacred nature itself, in which nothing is separate from the sacred. This view, called **pantheism** (Greek: "all divine"), sees the sacred as being discoverable within the physical world and its processes. In other words, nature itself is holy.

Some religions worship the sacred reality in the form of many coexisting gods, a view called **polytheism.** The multiple gods may be fairly separate entities, each in charge of an aspect of reality (such as nature gods), or they may be multiple manifestations of the same basic sacred reality.

In recent centuries, we find a tendency to deny the existence of any God or gods (**atheism**), to argue that the existence of God cannot be proven

---

Note: Words shown in boldface type are listed and defined in the "Key Terms" section at the end of each chapter.

The mandala, according to Jung, illustrates "the path to the center, to individuation."

(**agnosticism**), or simply to take no position (**nontheism**). (Such tendencies are not strictly modern; they can also be found in some ancient systems, such as Jainism; see Chapter 5.) However, if one sees religion broadly, as a "spiritual path," then even systems based on these three views—particularly if they show other typical characteristics of a religion—can also be called religions.

Religious Symbolism

Religions present views of reality, and most speak of the sacred. Nevertheless, because religions are so varied in their teachings and because the teachings of some religions, when taken at face value, conflict with those of others, it is common to assert that religions express truth *symbolically*. A symbol is something fairly concrete, ordinary, and universal that can represent—and help human beings intensely experience—something of greater complexity. For example, water can represent spiritual cleansing; the sun, health; a mountain, strength; and a circle, eternity. We frequently find symbolism, both deliberate and unconscious, in religious art and ritual.

Symbols and their interpretation have long played an important part in analyzing dreams. It was once common to think of dreams as messages from a supernatural realm that provided a key to the future. Although this type of interpretation is less common nowadays, most people still think that dreams are significant. Sigmund Freud introduced his view of the dream as a door into subconscious levels of the mind; he argued that by understanding dreams symbolically we can understand our hidden needs and fears. For example, a dream of being lost in a forest might be interpreted as distress over losing one's sense of direction in life, or a dream of flying could be interpreted as a need to seek freedom.

Carl Gustav Jung extended the symbol-focused method of dream interpretation to the interpretation of religion. Some religious leaders have been cautious about this approach—popularized by the mythologist Joseph Campbell—lest everything be turned into a symbol and all literal meaning be lost. And specialists in religion oppose the view that two religions are basically the same simply because they share similar symbols.

Nevertheless, there are many scholars and religious leaders who recognize the importance of symbolic interpretation, because the use of religious symbols may point to some structure that underlies all religions. There is no doubt that many of the same symbolic images and actions appear repeatedly in religions throughout the world. Water, for instance, is used in all sorts of religious rituals: Hindus bathe in the Ganges River; Christians use water for

baptisms; Jews use water for ritual purification; and Muslims and followers of Shinto wash before prayer. Ashes also have widespread use among religious traditions to suggest death and the spirit world: ashes are used by tribal religions in dance ceremonies, by Hindu holy men to represent asceticism and detachment, and by some Christians, whose foreheads are marked by ashes in observance of Ash Wednesday. Likewise, religious buildings are placed on hills or are raised on mounds and reached by stairs—all suggesting the symbol of the holy mountain, where the sacred can be encountered.

We also see in various religions the recurrence of a symbolic story of transformation: a state of original purity degenerates into pollution or disorder; a battle to fight disorder culminates in a sacrificial death; and the result is a renewed sense of purity and order. Scholars point out, too, that religions frequently use words in a symbolic way; for example, the divine is often described as existing "up above," insight can be "awakened," a person can feel "reborn," and so on.

When viewed this way, religious symbols, myths, and terminology at times suggest a universal symbolic "language" that all religions speak. Those interested in religious symbolism hope that understanding the "language" of symbols will help uncover what is universally important in all religions.

Before entering this mosque in Istanbul, these men symbolically purify themselves with water. Behind the washing area stands what was the baptistery of a church, St. Sergius and Bacchus, where people once became Christians through baptism with water. The church was converted to a mosque after Ottomans captured Constantinople.

Speculations on the Sources of Religion

Why does religion exist? The most evident answer is that it serves many human needs. One of our primary needs is having a means to deal with our

A so-called Chac-Mool figure, used in sacrifice, sits in front of the ruins of the Pyramid of Kulkulkán in Chichén Itzá, Mexico.

mortality. Because we and our loved ones must die, we have to face the pain of death and the inevitable questions it brings about whether there is any soul, afterlife, or rebirth. People often look to religion for the answers. Religion can help us cope with death, and religious rituals can offer us comfort. Human beings also desire good health, a regular supply of food, and the conditions (such as suitable weather) necessary to ensure these things. Before the development of modern science, human beings looked to religion to bring about these practical benefits, and they often still do.

Human beings are also social by nature, and religion offers companionship and the fulfillment that can come from belonging to a group. Moreover, religion often provides a structure for caring for the needy.

Human beings have a need to seek out and create artistic forms of expression. Religion stimulates art, music, and dance, and it has been the inspirational source of some of the most imaginative buildings in the world. Religion not only makes use of multiple arts but also integrates them into a living, often beautiful whole.

Perhaps the most basic function of religion is to respond to our natural wonder about ourselves and the cosmos—our musings on a starry night. Religion helps us relate to the unknown universe around us by answering the basic questions of who we are, where we come from, and where we are going.

Issues relating to the origins of religion have engaged thinkers with new urgency ever since the dawn of the age of science. Many have suggested that religion is a human attempt to feel more secure in an unfeeling universe. The English anthropologist E. B. Tylor (1832–1917), for example, believed religion was rooted in spirit worship. He noted how frequently religions see "spirits" as having some control over natural forces and how commonly religions see those who die—the ancestors—as passing into the spirit world. Fear of the power of all these spirits, he thought, made it necessary for people to find ways to please their ancestors. Religion offered such ways, thus allowing the living to avoid the spirits' dangerous power and to convert that power into a force that worked for the good of human beings. Similarly, the Scottish anthropologist James Frazer (1854–1941), author of *The Golden Bough,* saw the origins of religion in early attempts by human beings to influence nature, and he identified religion as an intermediate stage between magic and science.

Sigmund Freud (1856–1939) theorized that belief in a God or gods arises from the long-lasting impressions made on adults by their childhood experiences, in which their parents play a major part; these adults then project their sense of their parents into their image of their God or gods. According to Freud, these experiences—of fear as well as of security—are the basis for adults' attempts to deal with the anxieties of a complicated present and an unknown future. Freud argued that since a major function of religion is to help human beings feel secure in an unsafe universe, religion becomes less necessary as human beings gain greater physical and mental security. Freud's major works on religion include *Totem and Taboo, The Future of an Illusion,* and *Moses and Monotheism.*

These grave markers in the middle of Istanbul remind passers-by that living according to religious teachings is the best way to prepare for death.

Another psychologist, William James (1842–1910), came to his ideas on religion via an unusual course of study. Although he began his higher education as a student of art, he made a radical switch to the study of medicine. Finally, when he recognized the influence of the mind on the body, he was led to the study of psychology and then of religion, which he saw as growing out of psychological needs. James viewed religion as a positive way of fulfilling these needs and praised its positive influence on the lives of individuals. He wrote that religion brings "a new zest" to living, provides "an assurance of safety," and leads to a "harmonious relation with the universe."[5]

The German theologian Rudolf Otto (1869–1937) argued in his book *The Idea of the Holy* that religions emerge when people experience that aspect of reality which is essentially mysterious. He called it the "mystery that causes trembling and fascination" (*mysterium tremendum et fascinans*). In general, we take our existence for granted and live with little wonder; but occasionally something disturbs our ordinary view of reality. For example, a strong manifestation of nature—such as a violent thunderstorm—may startle us. It is an aspect of reality that is frightening, forcing us to tremble (*tremendum*) but also to feel fascination (*fascinans*). The emotional result is what Otto called *numinous awe*.[6] He pointed out how often religious art depicts that which is terrifying, such as the bloodthirsty Hindu goddess Durga.[7]

Carl Gustav Jung (1875–1961), an early disciple of Freud, broke with his mentor because of fundamental differences of interpretation, particularly about religion. In his books *Modern Man in Search of a Soul, Psychology and Alchemy,* and *Memories, Dreams, Reflections,* Jung described religion as something that grew out of the individual's need to arrive at personal fulfillment, which he called *individuation.* According to Jung, many religious insignia can be seen as symbols of personal integration and human wholeness: the circle, the cross (which is made of lines that join at the center), and the sacred diagram of the mandala (often a circle within or enclosing a square), which he called "the path to the center, to individuation."[8] He pointed out that as people age, they can make a healthy use of religion to understand their place in the universe and to prepare for death. For Jung, religion was a noble human response to the depth of reality and to its complexity.

Some recent theories do not look specifically at religion, but their wide-ranging insights are applied in the study of the origin of religions, as well as in many other fields. Among these theoretical approaches are structuralism and post-structuralism, along with the technique of deconstruction. We will look at some of these ideas and applications later.

Various scholars have attempted to identify "stages" in the development of religions. Austrian ethnographer and philologist Wilhelm Schmidt (1868–1954) argued that all humankind once believed in a single High God and that to this simple monotheism later beliefs in lesser gods and spirits were added. The reverse has also been suggested, namely, that polytheism led to monotheism. Influenced by the notion of evolution, some have speculated that religions "evolve" naturally from **animism** (a worldview that sees all elements of nature as being filled with spirit or spirits) to polytheism and then to monotheism. Critics of this view feel it is biased in favor of monotheism, in part because it is a view originally suggested by Christian scholars, who presented their belief system as the most advanced.

Scholars today hesitate to speak of any "evolution" from one form of religion to another. To apply the biological notion of evolution to human belief systems seems biased, oversimple, and speculative. Even more important, such a point of view leads to subjective judgments that one religion is more "highly evolved" than another—a shortsightedness that has kept many people from appreciating the unique insights and contributions of every religion. Consequently, the focus of religious studies has moved from the study of religion to the study of religions, a field that assumes that all religions are equally worthy of study.

PATTERNS AMONG RELIGIONS

When we study religions in a comparative and historical sense, we are not looking to validate them or to disprove them or to enhance our own belief or practice—as we might if we were studying our personal religious tradition. Instead, we want to comprehend the particular religions as thoroughly as possible and to understand the experience of people within each religion. Part of that process of understanding leads us to see patterns of similarity and difference among religions.

Although we do look for patterns, we must recognize that these patterns are not conceptual straitjackets. Religions, especially those with long histories and extensive followings, are usually quite complex. Furthermore, religions are not permanent theoretical constructs but are constantly in a process of change—influenced by governments, thinkers, historical events, changing technology, and the shifting values of the cultures in which they exist.

> Religion is the substance of culture, and culture the form of religion.
> —Paul Tillich, theologian[9]

First Pattern: Focus of Beliefs and Practices

Realizing the limitations of all generalizations, we nonetheless might gain some perspective by examining the orientations exhibited by individual religions. When we look at the world's dominant religions, we see three basic orientations in their conception and location of the sacred.[10]

Sacramental orientation The sacramental orientation emphasizes carrying out rituals and ceremonies regularly and correctly as the path to salvation; in some religions, correct ritual is believed to influence the processes of nature. All religions have some degree of ritual, but the ceremonial tendency is predominant, for example, in most tribal religions, in Roman Catholic and Eastern Orthodox Christianity, in Vedic Hinduism, and in Tibetan Buddhism. Making the Catholic sign of the cross, for example, is done in a certain way: only with the right hand, beginning with a touch on the forehead, then on one's chest, and finally on each shoulder, left to right.[11]

Prophetic orientation The prophetic orientation stresses that contact with the sacred is ensured by proper belief and by adherence to moral rules. This orientation also implies that a human being may be an important intermediary between the believer and the sacred; for example, a prophet may speak to believers on behalf of the sacred. Prophetic orientation is a prominent aspect of Judaism, Protestant Christianity, and Islam, which all see the sacred as being transcendent but personal. The television crusades of evangelistic ministers are good examples of the prophetic orientation in action.

Mystical orientation The mystical orientation seeks union with a reality greater than oneself, such as with God, the process of nature, the universe, or reality as a whole. There are often techniques (such as seated meditation) for lessening the sense of one's individual identity to help the individual experience a greater unity. The mystical orientation is a prominent aspect of Upanishadic Hinduism, Daoism, and some schools of Buddhism. (Master Kusan [1909–1983], a Korean teacher of Zen Buddhism, described the disappearance of self in the enlightenment experience of unity with this memorable question: "Could a snowflake survive inside a burning flame?"[12]) Although the mystical orientation is more common in religions that stress the immanence of the sacred or that are nontheistic, it is an important but less prominent tendency in Judaism, Christianity, and Islam as well.

Any one of these three orientations may be dominant in a religion, yet the other two orientations might also be found in the same religion to a lesser extent and possibly be subsumed into a different purpose. For example, ceremony can be utilized to help induce mystical experience, as in Catholic and Orthodox Christianity, Japanese Shingon Buddhism, Tibetan Buddhism, Daoism, and even Zen Buddhism, which has a strongly ritualistic aspect of its own.

Second Pattern: Views of the World and Life

Religions must provide answers to the great questions that people ask. How did the universe come into existence, does it have a purpose, and will it end? What is time, and how should we make use of it? What should be our relationship to the world of nature? Why do human beings exist? How do we reach fulfillment, transformation, or salvation? Why is there suffering in the world, and how should we deal with it? What happens when we die? What should we hold as sacred? The questions do not vary, but the answers do.

Given the great variety in their worldviews, it is not surprising that each religion defines differently the nature of sacred reality, the universe, the natural world, time, and human purpose. Religions also differ in their attitudes toward the role of words in expressing the sacred and in their relations to other religious traditions. By examining different views on these concepts, we will have further bases for comparison that will lead us to a more complete understanding of the world's religions.

The nature of sacred reality Some religions, as we have seen, speak of the sacred as transcendent, existing primarily in a realm beyond the everyday world. In other religions, though, sacred reality is spoken of as being immanent; that is, it is within nature and human beings and can be experienced as energy or holiness. Sometimes the sacred is viewed as having personal attributes, while elsewhere it is seen as an impersonal entity. And in certain religious traditions, particularly in some forms of Buddhism, it is hard to point to a sacred reality at all. Such facts raise the question as to whether "the sacred" exists outside ourselves or if it is better to speak of the sacred simply as what people "hold to be sacred."

The nature of the universe Some religions see the universe as having been begun by an intelligent, personal Creator who continues to guide the universe according to a cosmic plan. Other religions view the universe as being eternal, that is, having no beginning or end. The implications of these two positions are quite important to what is central in a religion and to how the human being acts in regard to this central belief. If the universe is created, especially by a transcendent deity, the center of sacredness is the Creator rather than the universe, but human beings imitate the Creator by changing and perfecting the world. If, however, the universe is eternal, the material universe itself is sacred and perfect and requires no change.

The human attitude toward nature At one end of the spectrum, some religions or religious schools see nature as the realm of evil forces that must be overcome. For them, nature is gross and contaminating, existing in opposition to the nonmaterial world of the spirit—a view, known as **dualism,** held by some forms of Christianity, Jainism, and Hinduism. At the other end of the spectrum, as in Daoism and Shinto, nature is considered to be sacred and needs no alteration. Other religions, such as Judaism and Islam, take a middle ground, holding that the natural world originated from a divine action but that human beings are called upon to continue to shape it.

Time Religions that emphasize a creation, such as Judaism, Christianity, and Islam, tend to see time as being linear, moving in a straight line from the beginning of the universe to its end. Being limited and unrepeatable, time is important. In some other religions, such as Buddhism, however, time is cyclical. The universe simply moves through endless changes, which repeat themselves over grand periods of time. In such a religion, time is not as crucial or "real" because, ultimately, the universe is not moving to some final point; consequently, appreciating the present may be more important than being oriented to the future.

Human purpose In some religions, human beings are part of a great divine plan, and although each person is unique, individual meaning comes also from the cosmic plan. The cosmic plan may be viewed as a struggle between forces of good and evil, with human beings at the center of the stage and the forces of good and evil at work within them. Because human actions are so important, they must be guided by a prescribed moral code that is meant to be internalized by the individual. This view is significant in Judaism, Christianity, and Islam. In contrast, other religions do not see human life in similarly dramatic terms, and the individual is only part of much larger realities. In Daoism and Shinto, a human being is a small part of the natural universe, and in Confucianism, an individual is part of the family and of society. Such religions place less emphasis on individual rights and more emphasis on how the individual can maintain harmony with the whole. Actions are not guided by an internalized moral system but by society, tradition, and a sense of mutual obligation.

Words and scriptures In some religions, the sacred is to be found in written and spoken words, and for those religions that use writing and create scriptures, reading, copying, and using sacred words in music or art are important. We see the importance of words in indigenous religions

Young Vajrayana monks
in Bhutan study Buddhist
scriptures from old-
fashioned books of
"leaves."

(which primarily pass on their traditions orally), in Judaism, in Christianity, in Islam, and in Hinduism. Other religions—such as Daoism and Zen Buddhism, which show a certain mistrust of words—value silence and wordless meditation. Although Zen and Daoism utilize language in their practices and have produced significant literature, each of these religions finds language limited in expressing the richness or totality of reality.

Exclusiveness and inclusiveness Some religions emphasize that the sacred is distinct from the world and that order must be imposed by separating good from bad, true from false. In that view, to share in sacredness means separation—for example, withdrawal from certain foods, places, people, practices, or beliefs. Judaism, Christianity, and Islam are among the religions that have been generally exclusive, making it impossible to belong to more than one religion at the same time. In contrast, other religions have stressed inclusiveness. Frequently, such religions also have emphasized social harmony, the inadequacy of language, or the relativity of truth, and they have accepted belief in many deities. Their inclusiveness has led them to admit many types of beliefs and practices into their religions, to the point that it is possible for an individual to belong to several religions—such as Buddhism, Daoism, and Confucianism—simultaneously. Such inclusiveness has led to misunderstanding at times, as in the case of a Christian missionary having "converted" a Japanese follower only to find the new convert still visiting a Shinto shrine.

Multiple Images of the Female

Feminists and others have criticized traditional religions for the dominance of males both in religious leadership and in representation of the sacred. While there is truth to such criticism, scholarly attention helps us to note the multitude of female roles and images to be found among religions. Consider these examples:

- In India, the divine is worshiped in its female aspects as the Great Mother (also known as Kali and Durga) or as other female deities.
- In Catholic and Orthodox Christianity, Mary, the mother of Jesus, receives special veneration; she is held to possess suprahuman powers and is a strong role model for women's behavior.
- In the Mahayana Buddhist pantheon, Guanyin (Kannon) is worshiped as a female ideal of mercy.
- In Japan, the premier Shinto divinity is the goddess Amaterasu, patroness of the imperial family. In contrast to many other religious systems, the goddess Amaterasu is associated with the sun, and a male god is associated with the moon.
- In Korea and Japan, shamans are frequently female.
- In Africa, India, and elsewhere, some tribal cultures remain matriarchal.
- In Wicca, a contemporary restoration of ancient, nature-based religion, devotees worship a female deity they refer to as the Goddess.
- Symbolic forms of the female divine are still prominent in the rites of several religions. Common symbols include the moon, the snake, spirals and labyrinths, the

Easter, a springtime festival of fertility, is marked by these Easter eggs decorating a European shop window.

egg, *yoni* (symbolic vagina), water, and earth. These symbolic representations of the female suggest generation, growth, nurturance, intuition, and wisdom.

Third Pattern: Views of Male and Female

Because gender is such an intrinsic and important part of being human, religions have had much to say about the roles of men and women, both on earth and in the divine spheres. Thus, views of what is male and what is female provide another basis for comparing religions.

In many influential religions today, male imagery and control seem to dominate; the sacred is considered male, and the full-time religious specialists are frequently male. But this may not always have been the case. Tantalizing evidence suggests that female divinities once played an important role in many cultures and religions. The most significant female deity was particularly associated with fertility and motherhood and has been known by many names, such as Astarte, Asherah, Aphrodite, and Freia (the origin of the word

Friday). Statues of a Mother-Goddess—sometimes with many breasts to suggest the spiritual power of the nurturing female—have been found throughout Europe, as well as in Turkey, Israel, and the Middle East.

Is it possible that female images of the divine were once more common and that female religious leadership once played a more important role? It has been argued that male dominance in religion became more common as the result of the growth of city-states, which needed organized defense and so elevated the status of men because of their fighting ability. In Israel, worship of a female deity was stamped out by prophets who preached exclusive worship of the male god Yahweh and by kings who wanted loyalty paid to them and their offspring. We read passages like this in the Hebrew scriptures: "They abandoned the Lord and worshipped Baal and the Astartes. So the anger of the Lord was kindled against Israel" (Judg. 2:13–14).[13] The Christian New Testament contains words that sometimes have been interpreted to mean that women should not play a prominent role in public worship: "I do not allow them to teach or to have authority over men; they must keep quiet. For Adam was created first, and then Eve. And it was not Adam who was deceived; it was the woman who was deceived and broke God's law" (1 Tim. 2:12–14).[14] In Asia, Confucianism has been distrustful of women in general and has ordinarily refused them leadership roles. In Buddhism, despite recognition in scripture that women can be enlightened, in practice the great majority of leaders have been men.[15]

Nevertheless, changes—inevitable in religion, as in everything else—are occurring. In some societies, as women take leadership roles in business and civic life, they are assuming similar leadership roles in religion. The study

In many religions, the gender associated with positions of power is no longer exclusively male. Here, female priests lead a communion service.

of comparative religion has helped this process by opening people's eyes to those religions of the past in which goddesses were worshiped and women played leading roles. Students of art, literature, and the history of religion are finding abundant evidence of female mystics, poets, shamans, and prophets. This is nudging several religious traditions to accept women in areas where in earlier centuries they were not expected to have a role. Although there are many resultant tensions (those in Buddhism, Christianity, and Islam are currently receiving publicity), we can expect that women will be widely successful in receiving full acceptance in roles of leadership.

MULTIDISCIPLINARY APPROACHES TO THE STUDY OF RELIGION

Religion has influenced so many areas of human life that it is a subject not only of religious studies but of other disciplines, too. As we have seen, the social sciences, in particular, have long studied religion. More recently, linguistics, literary theory, and cultural studies have offered us new ways of seeing and interpreting religion.

There are other approaches, too. We can focus our study on a single religion or look at several religions at the same time. Believers may opt to explore their own religion "from the inside," while nonbelievers may want to concentrate on the answers that several religions have given to a single question, such as the purpose of human life. Following is a list of some common approaches to religion.

Psychology Psychology (Greek: "soul study") deals with human mental states, emotions, and behaviors. Despite being a fairly young discipline, psychology has taken a close look at religion because it offers such rich human "material" to explore. A few areas of study include religious influences on child rearing, human behavior, and self-identity; group dynamics in religion; trance states; and comparative mystical experiences.

Mythology The study of religious tales, texts, and art has uncovered some universal patterns. Mythology is full of the recurrent images and themes found in religions, such as the tree of knowledge, the ladder to heaven, the fountain of life, the labyrinth, the secret garden, the holy mountain, the newborn child, the suffering hero, initiation, rebirth, the cosmic battle, the female spirit guide, and the aged teacher of wisdom.

Philosophy Philosophy (Greek: "love of wisdom") in some ways originated from a struggle with religion; although both arenas pose many of the same questions, philosophy does not automatically accept the answers given by any religion to the great questions. Instead, philosophy seeks answers independently, following reason rather than religious authority, and it tries to fit its answers into a rational, systematic whole. Some questions philosophy asks are, Does human life have any purpose? Is there an afterlife? and How should we live? Philosophy is essentially the work of individuals, while religion is a community experience; philosophy tries to avoid emotion, while religion often nurtures it; and philosophy is carried on without ritual, while religion naturally expresses itself in ceremony.

Theology Theology (Greek: "study of the divine") is the study of topics as they relate to one particular religious tradition. A theologian is an individual who usually studies his or her own belief system. For example, a person who is in training to become a Christian minister might study Christian theology.

The arts Comparing patterns in religious art makes an intriguing study. For example, religious architecture often uses symmetry, height, and archaic styles to suggest the sacred; religious music frequently employs a slow pace and repeated rhythms to induce tranquillity; and religious art often incorporates gold, haloes, equilateral designs, and circles to suggest otherworldliness and perfection.

Anthropology Anthropology (Greek: "study of human beings") has been interested in how religions influence the ways a culture deals with issues such as family interaction, individual roles, property rights, marriage, child rearing, social hierarchies, and division of labor.

Archeology Archeology (Greek: "study of origins") explores the remains of earlier civilizations, often uncovering the artifacts and ruins of religious buildings from ancient cultures. When possible, archeologists translate writings left by these people, much of which can be religious in origin. Archeology occasionally sheds light on how one religion has influenced another. For example, the excavation of a cuneiform library at Nineveh 150 years ago revealed a story (in the *Epic of Gilgamesh*)

Much of what we know about ancient religions, such as the religion of Egypt's pharaohs, results from archeological study.

that is similar to—and may have influenced—the biblical story of Noah and the flood. Archeology can also reveal religious material that enables scholars to decipher an entire writing system. For example, the discovery in the early nineteenth century of the Rosetta Stone (which contained the same inscription in three different scripts) led researchers to unlock the meaning of Egyptian hieroglyphics.

Linguistics and literary theory The study of linguistics has sometimes involved a search for patterns that may underlie all languages. But linguistics has occasionally also suggested general patterns and structures that may underlie something broader than language alone: human consciousness. This interest in underlying patterns has brought new attention to the possible structures behind religious tales, rituals, and other expressions of religious beliefs and attitudes. Linguistics has also examined religious language for its implications and often-hidden values. (Consider, for example, the various implications of the religious words *sin* and *sacred*.) Literary theory, on the other hand, has studied the written texts of religion as reflections of the cultural assumptions and values that produced the texts. Literary theory has thus pointed out some of the ways in which religions have reflected and promoted the treatment of women and minorities, for example, as different from or inferior to more dominant groups. Literary theory has also shown that nonwritten material—such as religious statues, paintings, songs, and even films—can also be viewed as forms of discourse and can therefore also be studied in the same ways that written texts are studied.

The use of theory for the study of religion is not limited to the fields of linguistics and literature. In fact, increasing numbers of academic disciplines are studying religions as part of the human search for understanding. Thus a scholar in the field of art may see and interpret religions as forms of art. Specialists in psychology may interpret religions primarily as expressions of individual human needs. Sociologists may see religions as ways of shaping groups and of promoting and maintaining group conformity. The viewpoints of these and other disciplines can also be adopted by scholars of religion as keys to understanding the complexities of religions.

KEY CRITICAL ISSUES

As an academic discipline, the field of religious studies is now more than two hundred years old, and scholars have become increasingly aware of the complexity of their task. Among the questions they ask are, What should we study in order to properly understand religions? What attitudes should we have when we study the religions of others? How can researchers be objective?

Studying religions may seem a fairly straightforward, though time-consuming, endeavor: scholars read the scriptures of the various religions, talk with practitioners, visit or research the sacred sites, and experience the major ceremonies. We must keep in mind, though, that in the first century of comparative religious scholarship, scholars had little ability to travel. Their studies were often limited to what they could read. Scholars would read the scriptures of specific religions, read accounts by others who had experienced some of the sacred sites and rituals, make comparisons based on what they had read, and publish their conclusions. Moreover, because archeology and anthropology were only in their earliest stages as disciplines, they could not be utilized to enhance scholars' studies and conclusions. Among scholars who had to rely on such an approach—sometimes called "armchair scholarship"—were James Frazer and E. B. Tylor, mentioned earlier. But the limitations of that style of work soon became apparent.

Sometimes the texts of the scriptures were incomplete, or the translations that scholars might need to depend on were not accurate. Also, scriptures of many religions often contain *hagiography* (Greek: "holy writing" or "saint writing"). Hagiography is not objective history, written to present dry facts, but rather it is storytelling whose aim is to inspire devotion; some or all of the details might be pious elaboration. Again, outside help (from archeology and other sciences) was unavailable to check scriptural stories for historical accuracy.

Another large area of concern involved the study of religions that did not have written scriptures but had only oral traditions. Scholars of religion asked numerous questions: How should the oral traditions be studied properly? In the case of oral religions, are religious artifacts and ritual words the equivalent of scriptures? And how can we understand the meaning of religious rituals and artifacts for the people who actually use them?

In more recent times, scholarship in religions has increasingly been carried out by people trained in the behavioral sciences. This scientific tendency began seriously with the work of the French sociologist Émile Durkheim (1858–1917). Before Durkheim, it was commonly thought that each major religion was the creation of a "great founder." But Durkheim insisted on studying religions as group phenomena that were subject to social laws. He pointed out that religious behavior is relative to the society in which it is found, and that a society will often use a religion to reinforce its own values. Durkheim argued that societies, rather than great founders, create religions. Durkheim based his conclusions on research, and he urged thinkers to base their conclusions on evidence rather than mere speculation.[16]

The study of religion has been influenced more recently by other French thinkers. Their work is connected with the social sciences but involves many disciplines. Claude Lévi-Strauss (b. 1908), one of the most fertile thinkers, spent the early part of his career in Brazil, where he studied the cultures of tribal peoples. His experiences there led to a lifelong interest in mythology. Lévi-Strauss explored tribal stories of the Americas and recognized, despite differences in their details, some extraordinary structural similarities. This insight led to his exploration into the structures underlying kinship relations, social relationships, and language. He came to argue for an underlying structure-making process in the human mind, which helps all human beings give meaningful form to their experiences and languages. The influence of

Religion and Oppression

We know that religion does much to help people and improve their lives. But can religion also hurt people? The answer appears to be yes, according to cultural studies that identify forms of oppression carried out in the name of religion.

It is easy to find examples from the past. In the name of religion, "heretics" have been tortured and burned to death, "witches" have been killed, and religious sects have persecuted one another. Religious authorities have condoned slavery and have forced indigenous peoples to convert from their traditional faiths to the religions of outsiders. Even today, the dominant religion within a country may work hard, if subtly, to marginalize those who profess other faiths. All of these examples involve what most of us think of as oppression.

But can religion involve forms of oppression that are less obvious, where the bruises are not so visible? Is it child abuse to frighten children with images of hell and threats of damnation? Is it oppression to keep girls from going to school? Is it a form of cruelty to teach believers to follow a religious leader blindly?

The French thinker Michel Foucault showed religions to be social systems that maintain control through their use of authority, language, reward, and punishment. Religions are especially powerful because they shape our thinking, often in unconscious ways, from our earliest years. Religions, Foucault maintained, can control not only the believers' outer world but also their inner world of self-understanding and self-definition. Power

in religions, he pointed out, is sometimes obvious, as with that granted to authority figures and scriptures. But power can also come in less obvious forms, primarily as various social pressures to conform.

We now recognize more clearly the power of religion to influence individuals when they are most vulnerable—as children, when critical judgment is undeveloped, and as adults, when overwhelmed by fear or pain. The values of family and society, often influenced by religion, can shape the mind in ways that the individual does not recognize. Religions shape from within the ways that people feel about themselves and the outside world. Religions even shape the way that people think about their own thinking.

The power of religion to shape individuals and the organization of societies is potentially overwhelming. As we will see in the rest of the book, this power has been used for good and for ill, and often as a mixture of both. Although a religion may expressly speak to the transcendent, in practice it functions as a social institution and so is always wrapped up in the history and politics of its environment. This is why, despite its ideals, religion always manifests the same ills, abuses, and problems that beset secular social institutions.

Perhaps the goal of studying religions is to recognize the subtle forces of oppression and to help societies to minimize them. Even better, it may help us to eliminate oppressive forces and work instead to promote the welfare of all.

Lévi-Strauss's position, called **structuralism,** has been felt widely. In the study of religion, structuralism has been applied to varied questions, such as how taboos arise, how religions influence marriage practices, and how certain foods come to be considered "pure" or "impure."

The growing emphasis on finding structures everywhere brought a countermovement called **post-structuralism.** Its proponents questioned both the existence and interpretive value of grand structures. They argued not only that a belief in universal structures limits understanding, and hence new thought, but that it also can be used to justify imprisonment and oppression. Among the most influential of such thinkers was Michel Foucault (1926–1984), who had training in philosophy and psychology but was also well versed in history, sociology, medicine, linguistics, anthropology, and religion. Foucault particularly turned his gaze to minorities and alienated groups, analyzing how they are identified, viewed, and even "created" by societies. His major books considered prisoners, medical patients, those labeled insane, so-called deviants, and other marginalized groups. He pointed out how society has, over centuries, viewed these groups differently, according to its current view of the marginal group.

Jacques Derrida (1930–2004) continued this kind of multidisciplinary work. His primary training was in philosophy, but he was also intrigued by linguistics and the behavioral sciences. (In French academic practice, these disciplines are known collectively as the "human sciences," and they are seen as interconnected fields more so than in typical Anglo-American academic practice.) Although first known as a structuralist, Derrida moved away from grand theories to focus on issues of language, meaning, and interpretation.

Derrida is especially known for his efforts to go beyond and behind ordinary interpretations of texts and other cultural elements. He begins by rejecting any expected interpretation—a technique called **deconstruction.** In literature and film, for example, the practice of deconstruction encourages people to examine works in unexpected ways. In traditional literary studies, novels and films have been examined in terms of their plots and character development. In contrast, a deconstructionist approach may look at the unstated values that underlie behavior—values that often express and maintain a particular culture or period. Thus we can investigate novels and films for their attitudes toward indigenous people, women, children, the old, the young, the poor, the rich, immigrants, and many other groups. (To show how widely the technique can be applied, Derrida once said in an interview in a restaurant that even the surrounding restaurant, with its food and clientele, could be deconstructed.) The implications of deconstruction for religion have been important. For example, scriptural texts can be investigated for their cultural values and biases. Likewise, ceremonies, paintings, ritual objects, and religious buildings may also be viewed as "texts" that can be deconstructed for the attitudes and values that underlie them.

Increasingly, scholarly work in religions depends heavily on anthropological investigation in the field, done by specialists who have learned the necessary languages and have lived among the people they study. One anthropologist who became highly regarded for this type of research was E. E. Evans-Pritchard (1902–1973), who lived among the Azande and Nuer peoples in the Sudan. Another esteemed researcher was the American anthropologist Clifford Geertz (1926–2006), who lived in Bali, Java, and Morocco and wrote about the specific religious practices there. Geertz championed what he called "thick description"—a description not only of rituals and religious artifacts but also of their exact meaning for practitioners.

This research-based approach would seem to be a valuable way to study religions. But it raises its own problems and questions: Are we listening only to the opinions of the researcher, or are the voices of the people who are studied truly being heard? Can an outsider, no matter how sensitive, be truly objective? Doesn't a researcher automatically contaminate the research? And is it possible that informants might give deliberately false answers to questions that they consider inappropriate? (They do.)

There are also moral questions: Does the research arise from respect, or is the researcher's curiosity just another example of cultural domination—a new form of colonialism? (A *New Yorker* cartoon expressed this well. Two friends in a forest village are talking about a sad-looking foreigner nearby. The foreigner, dressed in a safari suit and sun helmet, is tied up and awaiting his fate. One villager asks, "Another missionary?" "No," says the friend. "It's another anthropologist.") A second moral question relates specifically to the study of native religions. Any researcher inevitably introduces new ideas and new objects (clothing, flashlight, camera, video recorder). But is it ethical to bring significant changes to a culture that may have been unchanged for thousands of years? (Of course, this problem is becoming less pressing, as modern life enters even the remotest areas around the globe.)

Researchers have turned their attention not only to indigenous religions but also to unique variants within major world religions. Just below the surface of some major religions are often older religions, still alive, sometimes in blended forms. These syncretic forms are common, for example, among Catholic Christians in Latin America, Muslims in Indonesia, and Theravada Buddhists in Southeast Asia. But greater awareness of the enormous variety among practitioners of major religions has raised new questions: Can we really talk anymore about a single "Christianity" or "Buddhism" or "Islam"? Do the so-called world religions really exist, or are they just useful fictions?

When a new business building is being erected, it is common for the site to be blessed. Here we see a Thai "spirit house," at which people make offerings for good fortune.

The scholar Wilfred Cantwell Smith has argued in his book *The Meaning and End of Religion* that the notion of monolithic world religions is a fiction that should be abandoned. He even argues that, ultimately, the only religion is that of each individual. Other scholars have enlarged his critical approach. Some have pointed out that the religious experience of women within a religious tradition may be quite different from that of men. (In Islam, for example, women's religious experience takes place at shrines and in the home, whereas men's religious experience is more centered on the mosque.) We should also recognize that within a single world religion, the personal religious experience of an individual will be quite different for a child, a teenager, or an adult. And the meaning of being a "Buddhist" or "Christian" or "Hindu" will differ, depending on the culture or historical period that the individual inhabits. (Think of the difference between being a Christian in the Roman Empire of the first century and being a Christian in North America in the twenty-first century.) Lastly, there is the fact that individuals in some societies, such as in China and Japan, practice forms of religion that effortlessly blend elements from several major religions.

Although this book obviously has not abandoned the category of world religions, it tries to show that religions are not separate, homogeneous, or unchanging. It sees world religions as grand patterns but recognizes that we are true to these religions only when we acknowledge the great diversity within them.

WHY STUDY THE MAJOR RELIGIONS OF THE WORLD?

Because religions are so wide-ranging and influential, their study helps round out a person's education, as well as enrich one's experience of many other related subjects. Let's now consider some additional pleasures and rewards of studying religions.

> Science investigates; religion interprets. Science gives man knowledge which is power; religion gives man wisdom which is control.
> —Martin Luther King Jr.[17]

Insight into religious traditions Each religion is interesting in its own right, as a complex system of values, relationships, personalities, and human creativity.

Insight into what religions share The study of religions requires sympathy and objectivity. While it is true that being a believer of a particular religion brings a special insight that an outsider cannot have, it is also true that an outsider can appreciate things that are not always obvious to the insider. This is particularly true of shared patterns of imagery, belief, and practice.

Insight into people Understanding a person's religious background tells us more about that person's attitudes and values. Such understanding is valuable for successful human relations—in both public life and private life.

Tolerance and appreciation of differences Because human beings are emotional creatures, their religions can sometimes allow inflamed feelings to override common decency. As we see daily, religions can be employed to justify immense cruelty. Examining the major religions of the world helps us develop tolerance toward people of varying religious traditions. In a multicultural world, tolerance of differences is valuable, but enjoyment of differences is even better. Variety is a fact of nature, and the person who can enjoy variety—in religion and elsewhere—is a person who will never be tired of life.

Intellectual questioning Religions make claims about truth, yet some of their views are not easy to reconcile. For example, doesn't the theory of reincarnation of the soul, as found in Hinduism, conflict

Travel and Pilgrimage

One of the most universal religious practices is pilgrimage—travel undertaken by believers to important religious sites. But you do not have to belong to a specific religion to benefit from this ancient practice. Travel to religious sites is a wonderful way to experience the varieties of human belief firsthand, particularly at times of religious celebration. Travel that is not specifically religious can also offer similar benefits, because it allows us to experience religious art and architecture in the places and contexts for which they were created.

Travel programs for young and old abound. Many colleges offer study-abroad programs, including summer courses that incorporate travel, as well as semester- and year-long study programs abroad. Scholarships and other financial aid may be available for these programs. Large travel companies also offer summer tours for students, particularly to Europe and Asia; these companies are able to offer affordable tours by scheduling charter flights and inexpensive hotel accommodations. Programs such as these often make an excellent first trip abroad for students. Young travelers touring on their own can also join the Youth Hostel Association of their country and make use of a worldwide network of inexpensive youth hostels, which is quite extensive in Europe but also exists in the United States and many other countries around the world. Senior citizens (people 55 years and above) can take advantage of Elderhostel programs. Elderhostel offers a wide variety of activities—educational courses, excursions, and service projects—all around the world, usually lasting from one to several weeks.

Information on travel, youth hostels, and home exchanges can be found in the travel sections of libraries and bookstores. The Internet is also a good source for travel information, including the dates of religious festivals in other countries.

with the teaching of several other religions that a soul has only one lifetime on earth? And how can the notion of an immortal soul be reconciled with the Buddhist teaching that nothing has a permanent soul or essence? We must also ask questions about tolerance itself. Must we be tolerant of intolerance, even if it is preached by a religion? Questions such as these arise naturally when we study religions side by side. Such study sharpens our perception of the claims of religions and invites us to examine important intellectual questions more closely.

Insight into everyday life Religious influences can be found everywhere in modern culture, not just within religious buildings. Politicians make use of religious images, for example, when they speak of a "new covenant" with voters. Specific religions and religious denominations take public positions on moral issues, such as abortion and war. Our weekly routines are regulated by the originally Jewish practice of a six-day work week followed by a day of rest, and the European American school calendar is divided in two by the originally Christian Christmas holidays. Even comic strips use religious imagery: animals crowded onto a wooden boat, a man holding two tablets, angels on clouds, a person meditating on a mountaintop. The study of religions is valuable for helping us recognize and appreciate the religious influences that are everywhere.

Appreciation for the arts Anyone attracted to painting, sculpture, music, or architecture will be drawn to the study of religions. Because numerous religious traditions have been among the most significant patrons of art, their study provides a gateway to discovering and appreciating these rich works.

Enjoyment of travel One of the great pleasures of our age is travel. Visiting the temple of Angkor Wat in Cambodia or a Mayan pyramid in Mexico is quite different from just reading about them. The study of world religions gives travelers the background necessary to fully enjoy the many wonderful places they can now experience directly.

Insight into family traditions Religions have influenced most earlier cultures so strongly that their effects are readily identifiable in the values of our parents and grandparents—even if they are not actively religious individuals. These values include attitudes toward education, individual rights, gender roles, sex, time, money, food, and leisure.

Help in one's own religious quest Not everyone is destined to become an artist or a musician or a poet, yet each one of us has some ability to appreciate visual arts, music, and poetry. In the same way, although some people may not be explicitly religious, they may have a sense of the sacred and a desire to seek ways to feel at home in the universe. Those who belong to a religion will have their beliefs and practices enriched by the study of the world's religions, because they will learn about their religion's history, major figures, scriptures, and influences from different points of view. Others who have little interest in traditional religions yet nonetheless have a strong interest in spirituality may view their lives as a spiritual quest. For any person involved in a spiritual search, it is extremely helpful to study a variety of religions. Stories of others' spiritual quests provide insights that we may draw on for our own spiritual journey.

THE JOURNEY

With open minds, eager for the many benefits of studying religions, we now begin an intellectual pilgrimage to many of the world's important living religions. We will first look at a sample of religions often associated with native peoples across the globe. We will then go on to study religions that emerged on the Indian subcontinent and then to the religions that arose in China and Japan. Next we will travel to the area east of the Mediterranean Sea—a generally arid region that nonetheless has been a fertile ground for new religious ideas. Finally, we will encounter some of the newest religious movements and will consider the modern religious search.

The journey begins.

Our journey, though academic and intellectual, may prompt strong emotions in some readers. For some it will be a prelude to an actual physical pilgrimage. For others it will be an intellectual pilgrimage that will provoke both doubt and insight.

We begin with the knowledge that at the end of every journey we are not quite the same as we were when we started. Ours is a journey of discovery, and through discovery, we hope to become more appreciative of the experience of being human in the universe.

READING

JUNG'S DREAM OF THE LIGHT WITHIN

By emphasizing the symbolic interpretation of dreams and religious images, psychologist Carl Jung enlarged our understanding of religions. Here he describes an early dream that was important to his self-understanding.

About this time I had a dream which both frightened and encouraged me. It was night in some unknown place, and I was making headway against a mighty wind. Dense fog was flying along everywhere. I had my hands cupped around a tiny light which threatened to go out at any moment. Everything depended on my keeping this little light alive. Suddenly I had the feeling of something that was coming up behind me. I looked back and saw a gigantic . . . figure that was following me. But at the same moment I was con-scious, in spite of my terror, that I must keep my little light going through night and wind, regardless of all dangers. When I awoke, I realized at once that the figure was . . . my own shadow on the swirling mists, brought into being by the little light I was carrying. I knew, too, that this little light was my consciousness, the only light I have. My own understanding is the sole treasure I possess, and the greatest. Though infinitely small and fragile in comparison with the powers of darkness, it is still a light, my only light.[18]

TEST YOURSELF

1. Religions manifest eight possible elements: belief system, community, central myths, ritual, ethics, characteristic emotional experiences, material expression, and _____.
   a. symbolism
   b. sacredness
   c. dualism
   d. deconstruction

2. The belief that all is divine is called _____.
   a. atheism
   b. monotheism
   c. pantheism
   d. agnosticism

3. _____ argues that the existence of God cannot be proven.
   a. Agnosticism
   b. Pantheism
   c. Monotheism
   d. Nontheism

4. Anthropologist _____ believed that religion was rooted in spirit worship.
   a. James Frazer
   b. E. B. Tylor
   c. Sigmund Freud
   d. Carl Gustav Jung

5. _____ theorized that belief in a God or gods arises from the long-lasting impressions made on adults by their childhood experiences.
   a. James Frazer
   b. E. B. Tylor
   c. Sigmund Freud
   d. Carl Gustav Jung

6. Rudolph Otto argued that religions emerge when people experience that aspect of reality which is essentially mysterious; while _____ believed that religion was a noble human response to the depth of reality and to its complexity.
   a. James Frazer
   b. E. B. Tylor
   c. Sigmund Freud
   d. Carl Gustav Jung

7. Religions express truth _____. For example, water can represent spiritual cleansing; the sun, health; a mountain, strength; and a circle, eternity.
   a. symbolically
   b. prophetically
   c. mystically
   d. structurally

8. In early religions, the most significant female deity was particularly associated with _____ and motherhood and has been known by many names, such as Asherah, Aphrodite, and Freia.
   a. strength
   b. wisdom
   c. the arts
   d. fertility

9. When we look at the world's dominant religions, we see three basic orientations in their conceptions and location of the sacred: sacramental, prophetic, and _____.
   a. mystical
   b. spiritual
   c. immanent
   d. animistic

10. As an academic discipline, the field of religious studies is now more than _____ years old.
   a. 10
   b. 25
   c. 200
   d. 2,000

11. Based on what you have read in this chapter, what are some benefits of finding patterns among different religions? What are some possible risks?

12. In this chapter we see attempts by numerous thinkers to answer the question, "Why does religion exist?" Whose idea do you think presents the most interesting insight into religious experience? Why?

RESOURCES

Books

Armstrong, Karen. *The Great Transformation: The Beginning of Our Religious Traditions*. New York: Knopf, 2006. An exploration of the evolution of the world's major religious traditions, written by a popular historian of comparative religion.

Campbell, Joseph, and Bill Moyers. *The Power of Myth*. New York: Doubleday, 1991. An investigation of myths, fairy tales, and religious symbols in readable style.

Dawkins, Richard. *The God Delusion*. New York: Houghton Mifflin, 2006. A book by an evolutionary biologist and atheist that argues the case against belief in God.

Foucault, Michel. *Religion and Culture*. Ed. Jeremy Carette. New York: Routledge, 1999. Writings of Foucault that show his lifelong interest in religious topics.

Juschka, Darlene, ed. *Feminism in the Study of Religion: A Reader*. New York: Continuum, 2001. A discussion by feminist scholars of religion from a multicultural perspective.

Kunin, Seth D. *Religion: The Modern Theories*. Baltimore: Johns Hopkins University Press, 2003. An introduction to modern social-scientific theories of religion.

Lévi-Strauss, Claude. *Tristes Tropiques*. New York: Penguin, 1992. A celebrated autobiographical account of Lévi-Strauss's anthropological work among indigenous Brazilian peoples.

Pals, Daniel L. *Eight Theories of Religion*. New York: Oxford University Press, 2006. A very readable survey of major theories of the origin and purpose of religion, including theories of Freud, Marx, Eliade, and Evans-Pritchard, with good biographical sketches of the thinkers.

Ward, Keith. *God: A Guide for the Perplexed*. Oxford: Oneworld Publications, 2002. A philosophical attempt to reconcile religion and science by explaining the shared interests of these two ways of understanding the universe.

Film/TV

Bill Moyers on Faith and Reason. (PBS.) A seven-part miniseries, first broadcast in 2006, that explores the tension between belief and disbelief in religion.

Freud. (Director John Huston; Universal International.) A classic film that sees the young Freud as a hero in a painful search for new understanding of unconscious motivations.

In Search of the Soul. (BBC.) An examination of Jung's vision of reality.

Joseph Campbell and the Power of Myth. (PBS.) A six-part presentation on mythology.

The Question of God: Sigmund Freud and C. S. Lewis. (PBS.) A four-part miniseries that examines belief in God through the context of the lives of Sigmund Freud and C. S. Lewis, two noted intellectuals with sharply divergent views on religious faith.

Internet

American Academy of Religion: http://www.aarweb.org/. Information about conferences, grants, and scholarships, presented by the primary organization of professors of religion in North America.

Internet Sacred Text Archive: http://www.sacred-texts.com/index.htm. An electronic archive of texts about religion, mythology, and folklore.

The Pluralism Project: http://www.pluralism.org/. An excellent resource for studying the many religions now present in the United States.

KEY TERMS

agnosticism: "Not know" (Greek); a position asserting that the existence of God cannot be proven.

animism: From the Latin *anima,* meaning "spirit," "soul," "life force"; a worldview common among oral religions (religions with no written scriptures) that sees all elements of nature as being filled with spirit or spirits.

atheism: "Not God" (Greek); a position asserting that there is no God or gods.

deconstruction: A technique, pioneered by Jacques Derrida, that sets aside ordinary categories of analysis and makes use, instead, of unexpected perspectives on cultural elements; it can be used for finding underlying values in a text, film, artwork, cultural practice, or religious phenomenon.

dualism: The belief that reality is made of two different principles (spirit and matter); the belief in two gods (good and evil) in conflict.

immanent: Existing and operating within nature.

monotheism: The belief in one God.

nontheism: A position that is unconcerned with the supernatural, not asserting or denying the existence of any deity.

pantheism: The belief that everything in the universe is divine.

polytheism: The belief in many gods.

post-structuralism: An analytical approach that does not seek to find universal structures that might underlie language, religion, art, or other such significant areas, but focuses instead on observing carefully the individual elements in cultural phenomena.

structuralism: An analytical approach that looks for universal structures that underlie language, mental processes, mythology, kinship, and religions; this approach sees human activity as largely determined by such underlying structures.

transcendent: "Climbing beyond" (Latin); beyond time and space.

Visit the Online Learning Center at www.mhhe.com/molloy5e for additional exercises and features, including "Religion beyond the Classroom" and "For Fuller Understanding."

2

Indigenous Religions

FIRST ENCOUNTER

As it is for most visitors, your first stop in Hawai`i is crowded Waikiki, on the island of O`ahu.* After four days of swimming, sightseeing, and viewing the sunsets, you fly to Maui for a few days, and then on to the much less populated island of Hawai`i—called the Big Island by local residents. From the airport in Hilo, you begin to drive upcountry, toward the little town of Volcano. The area around Hilo, on the rainy side of the island, resembles the tropical paradise of fantasy: the leaves of the trees are bright lime-colored flames, and the yards of the houses are planted with vanda orchids and fragrant white-flowered plumeria trees.

As you drive inland and upward, lawns and homes yield to fields of beige grass and clusters of dark brown rock. Banyan trees give way to small silver-leaved `ohi`a lehua bushes, as delicate as their

*Note: The `okina (glottal stop mark) is used throughout this book in the spelling of certain Hawaiian words. It is indicated by a backward apostrophe.

red flowers. Now you are closer to the volcanoes that are still producing the island. The land here is raw and relatively new. You check into the old lava-rock hotel near the volcanic crater and look forward to settling in for the night. After supper you listen to ukulele music in front of the big fireplace in the lobby and watch a man and two women perform a slow hula for the guests.

The next morning, after a good sleep, you walk out to the rim of the crater. You are a bit startled by the steam rising through cracks and holes in the rock. You hike down a trail that leads to a bed of old lava, passing yellow ginger and tiny wild purple orchids on the way. The lava in the crater at this spot is dry; it crunches underfoot. Here and there you see stones wrapped in the broad leaves of the *ti* plant and wonder why they're there.

On the way back up the trail, you fall in step with a woman who explains that she was raised on the Big Island but now lives on another island. She is here just for a few days, to visit the volcano area and to see old friends. She tells you about Pele, the goddess of fire, whose place of veneration is the volcano.

"When I was young I learned that Pele came from the island of Kaua`i to Maui, where she lived in Haleakala Crater before she moved to this island. Nowadays, people here are mostly Buddhist or Christian, but they still respect Pele. I know a man who says Pele once appeared to him. He told me she had long hair and was surrounded by fire. Other people have seen her on the road. Pele gets a lot of offerings—mostly ti leaves and food. But when the lava is flowing toward Hilo, people also bring out pork and gin," the woman says with a little grin, "and my friends tell me that the offerings work."

The lava, she explains, is active now at the other end of a series of craters, closer to the ocean. She suggests that you drive to the lava flow before dark and adds, "Be sure to have good walking shoes, as well as a flashlight in case it gets dark before you go back to your car. Be sure not to take any lava rock away with you. They say it brings bad luck, you know."

In midafternoon, you drive down the curving black asphalt road, past old lava flows, to the highway near the ocean. You stop and park near the cars of other lava watchers, then begin hiking with a few people across the fresh lava, toward the ocean. About half a mile in, you encounter yellow caution strips and overhear an officer warning one man to stop. "Further on it's just too dangerous. It looks solid on top, but you can slip through the crust." You and the others crowd up next to the barriers and see steam rising on the right up ahead. Through the rising steam you glimpse a bright orange band of molten lava underneath the dry crust as it falls into the ocean.

Sunset comes quickly, and even more people arrive, some with blankets around their shoulders. As darkness falls, the flowing lava becomes more visible, and the steam takes on a reddish glow. "Look over there," someone says. In the distance a bright stream of orange lava slides down a hill, a slow-motion waterfall of fire. You watch at least an hour as the sky becomes completely dark. Now the only light comes from the flowing lava and a few flashlights. It is, you think, like being present at the time of creation: this land is being born.

The next morning in the lobby you see the Hawaiian woman again. "Well, did you see Pele last night?" she asks, smiling. You smile back. For the rest of your stay you wonder about Pele, about what else might remain of native Hawaiian religion. Isn't hula, you ask as you think back over what you've read, an expression of Hawaiian beliefs? Why do people make offerings of ti leaves? How much of the ancient religion lives on?

DISCOVERING INDIGENOUS RELIGIONS

The practice of native religions takes place throughout the world. Among the Ainu in far northern Japan, the Inuit (Eskimo) in Canada, the aboriginal peoples of Australia, the Maori of New Zealand, and the many indigenous peoples of Africa and the Americas, religious teachings have been passed on primarily by word of mouth rather than through written texts. In some areas, the ancient religious ways of traditional peoples may not be easily apparent, but certain characteristics may live on in local stories and customs.

There is no agreement on how to speak of these ancient religious ways. Various terms include *traditional, aboriginal, indigenous, tribal, nonliterate, primal, native, oral,* and *basic.* Each term is inadequate. For example, although the word *native* is used frequently in the Americas, that term in Africa—with its memories of Offices of Native Affairs—can be offensive. The words *oral* and *nonliterate* describe correctly the fact that most indigenous religions were spread without written texts. But there have been exceptions: the Mayans and Aztecs, for example, had writing systems, and even many native religions without writing systems have had their sacred stories and beliefs written down by scholars at some point. The distinction between oral religions and others is also blurred by the fact that religions that have written texts are also, to a large degree, transmitted orally—for example, through preaching, teaching, and chanting. The term *traditional* would be suitable, except that all religions but the very newest have many traditional elements. Some terms, such as *primal* and *basic,* may be viewed as derogatory (like the older term *primitive religions*). The word *indigenous* has the advantage of being neutral in tone. (It means the same thing as *native,* except that it comes from Greek rather than Latin.) There is no easy solution. Although *indigenous* comes closest to capturing these ancient religions, we will use several of the preceding terms interchangeably throughout the text.

Indigenous religions are found in every climate, from the tropical rain forest to the arctic tundra, and some are far older than today's dominant religions. Because most of them developed in isolation from each other, there are major differences in their stories of creation and origin, in their beliefs about the afterlife, in their marriage and funeral customs, and so on. In fact, there is as much variation among indigenous religions as there is, for example, between Buddhism and Christianity. In North America, for instance, there are several hundred Native American nations and more than fifty Native American language groups. The variety among indigenous religious traditions is stunning, and each religion deserves in-depth study. But because of the limitations of space, this book must focus on shared elements; regrettably, we can barely touch on the many differences. (You can complement your study of basic patterns by making your own study of a native religion, especially one practiced now or in the past by the indigenous peoples of the area in which you live.)

Past Obstacles to the Appreciation of Indigenous Religions

Up until the early part of the twentieth century, scholars focused more on religions that had produced written texts than on those that expressed themselves through orally transmitted stories, histories, and rituals. This lack of attention may have been due in part to the relative ease of studying religions with written records. Religions with written records don't necessarily require travel or physically arduous research. Moreover, when scholars have mastered reading the necessary languages, they can study, translate, and teach the original writings either at home or to students anywhere.

There has also been a bias toward text-based religions because of a misconception that they are complex and oral religions are simple. Greater research into oral religions, however, has dispelled such notions of simplicity. Consider, for example, the sandpaintings of the Navajo people and the ceremonies of which the paintings are a part. "In these ceremonies, which are very complicated and intricate, sandpaintings are made and prayers recited. Sandpaintings are impermanent paintings made of dried pulverized materials that depict the Holy People [gods] and serve as a temporary altar. Over 800 forms of sandpaintings exist, each connected to a specific chant and ceremony."[1]

Indigenous religions have, of course, created much that is permanent, and sometimes even monumental. We have only to think of the Mayan pyramids in Yucatán and the great city of Teotihuacán, near Mexico City. But native religions often express themselves in ways that have less permanence: dance, masks, wood sculpture, paintings that utilize mineral and plant dyes, tattoo, body painting, and memorized story and chant. Perhaps we have to begin to see these transitory expressions of religious art as being equal in stature to more permanent sacred writings and artistic creations. In speaking of African art, one scholar has called it the "indigenous language of African belief and thought," even saying that African art "provides a kind of scripture of African religion."[2]

The Modern Recovery of Indigenous Religions

We know about native religious traditions through the efforts of scholars from a number of disciplines, particularly anthropology. One pioneer was Franz Boas (1858–1942), a professor at Columbia University and curator at the American Museum of Natural History in New York. Other notable contributors to this field include Bronislaw Malinowski (1884–1942), Raymond Firth (1901–2002), Mary Douglas (1921–2007), and E. E. Evans-Pritchard (mentioned in Chapter 1).

The ecological movement has also made our study of indigenous religions more pressing. Environmentalist David Suzuki argues that we must look to native peoples and religions for insightful lessons in the relationship between human beings and nature. In his introduction to the book *Wisdom of the Elders*, he writes that the earth is rapidly moving toward what he calls "ecocrisis." He quotes the ecologist Paul Ehrlich in saying that solutions will have to be "quasi-religious." Suzuki argues that "our problem is inherent in the way we perceive our relationship with the rest of Nature and our role in the grand scheme of things. Harvard biologist E. O. Wilson proposes that we foster *biophilia*, a love of life. He once told me, 'We must rediscover our *kin*, the other animals and plants with whom we share this planet.'"[3]

These masked dancers in Papua New Guinea celebrate spirits of their ancestors.

Some of this interest derives, of course, from a sometimes romanticized view of native peoples and their relationship with nature. We should recognize that some native peoples, such as the Kwakiutl of the Pacific Northwest, have viewed nature as dangerously violent, and others have seriously damaged their natural environment. Despite such cases, one finds in many indigenous religions extraordinary sensitivity to the natural elements.

The development of photography and sound recording has helped the recovery of native religious traditions. Photography captures native styles of life and allows them to be seen with a certain immediacy. Ethnomusicology involves the recording of chants and the sounds of musical instruments that might otherwise be lost. Gladys Reichard, a specialist who pioneered study of the ritual life of the Navajo (Diné), has written that chanters in the Navajo religion need to memorize an "incalculable" number—that is, thousands—of songs.[4] The fact that listeners can replay such recordings has no doubt added to the appreciation of this music.

Little Big Mouth, a medicine man, sits in front of his lodge near Fort Sill, Oklahoma. The photo dates to around 1900.

> All our histories, traditions, codes were passed from one generation to another by word of mouth. Our memories must be kept clear and accurate, our observation must be keen, our self-control absolute.
>
> —Thomas Wildcat Alford, Shawnee[7]

Artists in many cultures, trying to go beyond their own limited artistic traditions, have found inspiration in native wood sculpture, masks, drums, and textile design. Pablo Picasso (1881–1973), for example, often spoke of the strong influence that African religious masks had on his work. By the early 1900s, West African masks had found their way to Paris and the artists there. A scholar describes the effect of one African work on several artists who were close friends. "One piece . . . is a mask that had been given to Maurice Vlaminck in 1905. He records that [André] Derain was 'speechless' and 'stunned' when he saw it, bought it from Vlaminck and in turn showed it to Picasso and Matisse, who were also greatly affected by it."[5] French artist Paul Gauguin moved to Tahiti and the Marquesas to find and paint what he hoped was a fundamental form of religion there, and some of his paintings allude to native Tahitian religious belief.[6] Gauguin thereby hoped to go beyond the limited views of his European background. The work of such artists as Picasso and Gauguin helped to open eyes to the beauty produced by indigenous religions.

Of course, the religious art of native peoples needs no authentication from outsiders. And outsiders present a problem: they tend to treat native religious objects as purely secular works of art, while people within an indigenous religious tradition do not make such a distinction. Indigenous religions exist generally within **holistic** cultures, in which every object and act may have religious meaning. Art, music, religion, and social behavior within such cultures can be so inseparable that it is hard to say what is distinctly religious and what is not. Although we can find a similar attitude among very pious practitioners of the dominant world religions, for whom every act is religious, people in modern, industrial cultures commonly see the secular and religious realms as separate.

Fortunately, the bias that once judged native religions to be "primitive" manifestations of the religious spirit—as opposed to the literate, so-called higher religions—is disappearing. It is an inescapable fact that the span of written religions is relatively brief—barely five thousand years—yet scientists now hold that human beings have lived on earth for at least a million (and possibly two or three million) years. Although we do not know how long human beings have been manifesting religious behavior, we believe it goes back as long as human beings have been capable of abstract thought.

STUDYING INDIGENOUS RELIGIONS: LEARNING FROM PATTERNS

The study of indigenous religious traditions presents its own specific challenges. Happily, oral traditions are being written down, translated, and published. Yet our understanding of these religions depends not only on written records but also on field study by anthropologists, ethnomusicologists, and others.

It would be ideal if we could study and experience each native religion separately; barring that, however, one workable approach is to consider them collectively as "sacred paths" that share common elements. Thus, in this chapter we will concentrate on finding patterns in native religions—while keeping in mind that beyond the patterns there is enormous variety. The patterns we identify in indigenous religions will also enrich our encounter with other religions in later chapters. Three key patterns we will consider are the human relationship with nature, the framing of sacred time and space, and the respect for origins, gods, and ancestors.

Human Relationships with the Natural World

Most indigenous religions have sprung from tribal cultures of small numbers, whose survival has required a cautious and respectful relationship with nature. In the worldview of these religions, human beings are very much a part of nature. People look to nature itself (sometimes interpreted through traditional lore) for guidance and meaning.

Some native religions see everything in the universe as being alive, a concept known as *animism* (which we discussed briefly in Chapter 1). The life force (Latin: *anima*) is present in everything and is especially apparent in living things—trees, plants, birds, animals, and human beings—and in the motion of water, the sun, the moon, clouds, and wind. But life force can also be present in apparently static mountains, rocks, and soil. Other native religions, while more theistic, see powerful spirits in nature, which temporarily inhabit natural objects and manifest themselves there.

In an animistic worldview, everything can be seen as part of the same reality. There may be no clear boundaries between the natural and supernatural and between the human and nonhuman. Everything has both its visible ordinary reality and a deeper, invisible sacred reality. Four Oglala Sioux shamans, when asked about what was *wakan* ("holy," "mysterious"), said, "Every object in the world has a spirit and that spirit is *wakan*. Thus the spirit[s] of the tree or things of that kind, while not like the spirit of man, are also *wakan*."[8] To say that nature is full of spirits can be a way of affirming the presence of both a universal life force and an essential, underlying sacredness.

Among many peoples, particular objects—a specific rock, tree, or river—are thought of as being animated by an individual spirit that lives within. And in some native traditions, we find deities that care about and influence a whole category of reality, such as the earth, water, or air. Among the Yoruba of Africa, storms are the work of the deity Shangó, a legendary king with great powers who climbed to heaven (see Chapter 11). The Igbo (Ibo) pray to Ala, an earth-mother deity, for fertility of the earth. Women also pray to her for children, and men pray to her to increase their crops. In the Ashanti religion, Ta Yao is the god of metal. The work of blacksmiths and mechanics is under his charge.[9]

In a world that is animated by spirits, human beings must treat all things with care. If a spirit is injured or insulted, it can retaliate. Human beings must therefore show that they respect nature, especially the animals and plants that they kill to eat. Human beings must understand the existence and ways of the spirit world so that they can avoid harm and incur blessings. (We will revisit this spirit world later, when we discuss trance states and the spiritual specialist, the shaman.)

Native American religions are noted for their reverential attitude toward the natural world; human beings and animals are often pictured as coming into existence together, and the sun, moon, trees, and animals are all considered kin. Hehaka Sapa, or Black Elk, an Oglala Sioux, although he had become a Christian, explained the sense of relationship to nature that he had experienced when he was growing up among his people in South Dakota. In his autobiography, which he dictated in 1930, he points out that his community, which traditionally lived in *tipis* (circular tents made of animal skins and poles), arranges itself in a circle—as does all nature, which is constantly making circles, just like the sun, the moon, and the whirlwind.

Native American religions often express the kinship bond between human beings and animals in ritual. (To a lesser extent, some other religions do this, as well). Åke Hultkrantz, a Swedish scholar, clarifies with an example the meaning of many dances that imitate animals. "Plains Indian dances in which men imitate the movements of buffaloes . . . are not, as earlier research took for granted, magic rituals to multiply the animals. They are rather acts of supplication in which Indians, by imitating the wild, express their desires and expectations. Such a ritual tells us the Indian's veneration for the active powers of the universe: it is a prayer."[10]

Birds make their nests in circles, for theirs is the same religion as ours.

—Black Elk, Oglala Sioux[11]

In many Native American religious traditions, there is little distinction between the human and animal worlds; rather, there is a sense of kinship. To exploit nature mindlessly is even thought to be as sacrilegious as harming one's own mother. As Smohalla of the Nez Perce people said, "You ask me to plow the ground. Shall I take a knife and tear my mother's breast? Then when I die she will not take me to her bosom to rest."[12]

Native religions also frequently embrace an ethic of restraint and conservation concerning nature's resources. One is expected to take only what one needs and to use all the parts of an animal or plant. In traditional Hawai`i, for example, fishing in certain areas would be temporarily forbidden (*kapu*, or taboo) in order to allow the fish population to be replenished. Of course, the ideal is never universally maintained, and even native peoples have sometimes been unaware of the destructive effects of their actions. Consider, for example, the devastation of the beaver by native peoples in

North America who sold the pelts to European traders, or the cutting of most sandalwood trees by native Hawaiians for sale in China. Given examples like these, it is clear that native peoples who did not live in harmony with nature could not long survive.

It is difficult, perhaps, for urban human beings today to experience fully the intimate connection with the rest of nature that has been a common aspect of native religions. The predominant contemporary view sees human beings as fundamentally different from other animals. Perhaps this tendency is a result of our modern culture, which emphasizes the skills of writing and reading. We also have little connection with the origins of our food, and we live and work indoors. Electric light diminishes our awareness of day and night and obstructs the light of the moon and stars. Except for insects, rodents, and the most common birds, we seldom see wildlife firsthand. Traffic noise drowns out the sounds of wind, rain, and birdsong.

In contrast, consider the sense of kinship with animals found, for example, among the Haida people of the Pacific Northwest: "the Haida refer to whales and ravens as their 'brothers' and 'sisters' and to fish and trees as the finned and tree *people.*"[13]

Another example of contrast is apparent in the way the BaMbuti, forest dwellers of central Africa, perceive their forest. Outsiders might find the darkness and thick foliage frightening. But, as one anthropologist has written, for the people who live within it and love it, the forest "is their world. . . . They know how to distinguish the innocent-looking *itaba* vine from the many others it resembles so closely, and they know how to follow it until it leads them to a cache of nutritious, sweet-tasting roots. They know the tiny sounds that tell where the bees have hidden their honey; they recognize the kind of weather that brings a multitude of different kinds of mushrooms springing to the surface.... They know the secret language that is denied all outsiders and without which life in the forest is an impossibility."[14]

Sacred Time and Sacred Space

Our everyday lives go on in ordinary time, which we see as moving forward into the future. Sacred time, however, is "the time of eternity." Among the Koyukon people of the Arctic it is called "distant time," and it is the holy ancient past in which the gods lived and worked.[15] Among Australian aborigines it is often called "dream time," and it is the subject of much of their highly esteemed art.

Sacred time is cyclical, returning to its origins for renewal. By recalling and ritually reliving the deeds of the gods and ancestors, we enter into the sacred time in which they live. Indigenous religions even tend to structure daily lives in ways that make them conform to mythic events in sacred time; this creates a sense of holiness in everyday life.

Like ordinary time, ordinary space exists in the everyday. Sacred space, however, is the doorway through which the "other world" of gods and ancestors can contact us and we can contact them. Sacred space is associated

A solitary figure experiences the center of Ireland's Drombeg Stone Circle. In this sacred space, particular stones are aligned with the setting sun on the winter solstice (December 21 or 22).

with the center of the entire universe, where power and holiness are strongest and where we can go to renew our own strength.

In native religions, sacred space may encompass a great mountain, a volcano, a valley, a lake, a forest, a single large tree, or some other striking natural site. For Black Elk and his people, after the Lakota had moved west, it was Harney Peak in South Dakota. In Australian aboriginal religion, Uluru (Ayers Rock) has served as this sacred center. In Africa, Mount Kilimanjaro and other high mountains have been considered sacred spaces.

Sacred space can also be constructed, often in a symbolic shape such as a circle or square, and defined by a special building or by a boundary made of rope or of rocks, such as Stonehenge in England. It can even be an open area among trees or buildings, such as the great open space between the temples of Teotihuacán, near Mexico City.

Respect for Origins, Gods, and Ancestors

Origins Most indigenous religions have cosmic tales of their origins that are regularly recited or enacted through ritual and dance. Some tell how the world originated from a supernatural realm. According to other emergence stories, the earth rose out of previous earths or from earlier, more chaotic material forms. Often the land and creatures emerged from watery depths. In a Hopi creation story the earth, before it took shape, was mist.

Stories of the origin of a tribe may be connected with its story of the earth's creation. Among the Ácoma Pueblo, there is a story of two sisters who lived entirely underground. Eventually they climbed up the roots of a tree and into the sunlight through a hole in the ground, to become the first human beings on earth. One became mother of the Pueblo.[16]

Gods   Native religions frequently speak of a High God who is superior to all other deities and is considered to be wise, ancient, and benevolent. The Inuit speak of a Great Spirit living in the sky who is female and to whom all human spirits eventually return. In a few African religions, too, the High God is female, neuter, or androgynous; and in some religions there are two complementary High Gods, characterized as male/female, brother/sister, or bad/good. The BaKuta of central Africa speak of the twins Nzambi-above and Nzambi-below, although in their myths the lower twin disappears and Nzambi-above becomes the High God.[17]

In some African religions, stories of the High God, who is almost always the creator of the world, offer some explanation for the ills of the world or the distance between human beings and the divine. Many African religions tell how the High God created the world and then left it—sometimes out of dismay at human beings or simply for lack of interest. "Many people of central and southern Africa say that God (Mulungu) lived on earth at first, but men began to kill his servants and set fire to the bush, and so God retired to heaven on one of those giant spiders' webs that seem to hang from the sky in morning mists. In Burundi, however, it is said that having made good children God created a cripple, and its parents were so angry that they tried to kill God and he went away."[18] The High God in African religions, however, is not always remote. The Diola, for example, believe in direct, prophetic revelation from the High God, and the Igbo and Shona have oracles from the supreme being. While monotheism is common in African religions, it can express itself in many ways.

Although indigenous religions often revere a High God, altars and imagery dedicated to a High God are not common. Large temples, temple ritual, and priesthoods have been found in a few cultures, such as in Mexico and western Africa, but these elements are rare. Instead, in their prayer, ritual, and art many native religions tend to focus on lesser deities, especially those associated with the forces of nature. More commonly, ceremonies in indigenous religions are performed at small-scale shrines or meeting places. Sometimes the religious ceremonies occur indoors, such as in a sweat lodge or *kiva* (a submerged meeting hall). At other times they occur outdoors, at a river bank, beside a rock formation, or in a grove of trees.

Ancestors   Many indigenous religions make little distinction between a god and an ancestor. Both are important, because living people must work with both for success in life. Spirits of ancestors must be treated well out of love for them, but also out of respect for their power. Some native religions, such as the Navajo, have not wished closeness with the spirits of the dead, fearing them. But more commonly the dead are venerated. In African religions, ancestor spirits are commonly thought to bring health, wealth, and children if they are pleased, and disease and childlessness if they are not. The way to appease angry ancestors is through ritual, sometimes including sacrifice. The ancestors often are thought to live in an afterlife that is a state of existence much like earthly life. Belief in reincarnation is

Religion of the Pueblo Peoples

One of the great sights of the world is the group of multistoried buildings hidden high up in the cliffs at Mesa Verde, Colorado. Inhabited for more than 700 years, the now-empty buildings give an unparalleled view into the life of the Ancestral Pueblo peoples (also called Hisatsinom and Anasazi). Visitors can walk down from the top of the cliff, via narrow stone paths and stairs, to visit some of the houses and to experience the plazas that were once used for ceremonial dance. Visitors can then climb down a wooden ladder to enter a *kiva,* a dark and womb-like ritual chamber beneath the surface. There they can see the *sipapu,* the hole in the floor that is a symbol of the emergence of human beings into this world. The kiva and sipapu show how thoroughly oriented to the earth the religion practiced here was.

The cliff dwellings at Mesa Verde are only one site in what was—and still is—a wide-ranging culture. The territory of this culture includes large parts of what are now Arizona, New Mexico, Utah, and Colorado. Similar cliff dwellings may be seen at the Canyon de Chelly in Arizona and at Bandelier National Monument in New Mexico. In New Mexico one may also visit the great spiritual center of Chaco Canyon, once a flourishing city. Tens of thousands of pilgrims would come here regularly, and as many as forty thousand would be present at the time of the twice-yearly solstices. This site is sacred to the Pueblo peoples even today.

The religious life of the Ancestral Pueblo peoples is not fully known, but some evidence comes from traces of ancient roads and from archeology, petroglyphs, and paintings. Some of their buildings were oriented to coincide with the solstices and equinoxes. The presence of kivas suggests that ceremony took place there, and in some of the kivas the remains of wall paintings have been found. Remaining petroglyphs show elements from nature, including stars and the moon, and in the period from about 1200–1250 C.E. there was a profuse growth of the cult and imagery of *kachinas*—benevolent guardian spirits who are believed to appear among the people on ceremonial occasions (and whom we will discuss in a moment).*

When the large settlements, such as the one at Mesa Verde, were abandoned, their people moved to villages—primarily in modern-day northeastern Arizona and northwestern New Mexico—but they took with them

---

*Note: This text uses the time designations B.C.E. ("before the common era") and C.E. ("of the common era") in place of the Christianity-centered abbreviations B.C. ("before Christ") and A.D. (*anno Domini,* "in the year of the Lord").

The image on the previous page shows what remains of a kiva at Chaco, an important ancestral site for the Pueblo peoples. The image above, a reconstruction at the Aztec Ruins National Monument, shows how a functioning kiva may have looked.

their religious beliefs, images, and ritual, especially the cult of the kachinas. The traditional style of multistoried buildings continued, as well, suggesting to the Spanish colonizers the name by which the peoples are still commonly known: *pueblo* in Spanish means "village." (The Pueblo peoples who live in New Mexico are sometimes called the Eastern Pueblos; those in Arizona are called the Western Pueblos.)

Many mountains, lakes, and rivers in the region are sacred to the Pueblo peoples. Kachinas are believed to live there, and the souls of the dead are sometimes believed to travel there. The Taos Pueblos believe that Blue Lake is the home of their ancestors, and it is a place of pilgrimage.

The Pueblo peoples share many features of their architecture, governance, and religious practice, but there are also great differences among them in all these areas. Each of the more than two dozen pueblos governs itself independently, and multiple languages are spoken: Keresan, Zunian, three Tanoan dialects (Tiwa, Tewa, Towa), and Hopi. The independence of each pueblo may have actually been to its advantage, helping each unique culture to survive. Despite the pressures to change, the Pueblo peoples have kept their identities

intact—particularly through fidelity to their religious beliefs and practices.

Each pueblo has its own religious traditions. Here we will touch on just a few. The stories of human origins differ among the peoples and clans, but many tell of human emergence from a lower world, of assistance from supernatural beings in learning to live, of help from animals, and of wanderings before final settlement. Among the seven Keresan-speaking pueblos, for example, the story of origins tells of how people moved upward through four different-colored worlds. Standing in an eagle's nest on top of a tree, with the help of a woodpecker and a badger, they made a hole large enough to climb up into this world.

Religious traditions are passed on through initiation ceremonies, male and female secret societies, and special rites conducted by priests. We get a sense of the complexity simply by considering the religious societies of the Zuñis. The Zuñis have six religious societies (dedicated to the sun, rainmakers, animal deities, war gods, guardian spirits, and priests of the guardian spirits), and each society has its own calendar, ceremonies, and ritual objects. Religious symbolism is equally complex. Among the Zía, for example, four is a sacred number. It

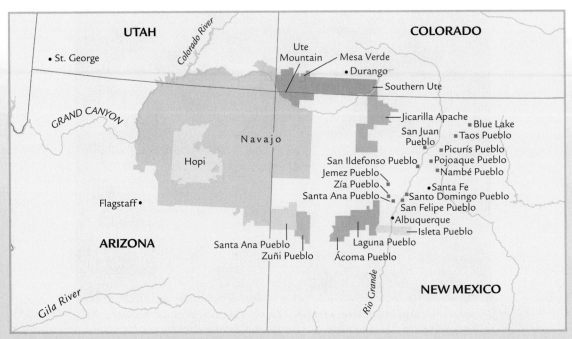

FIGURE 2.1 *The Pueblo peoples and other Native American tribes of the American Southwest.*

symbolizes the four seasons, four directions, and four stages of life (infancy, youth, adulthood, old age). It is used in many designs found in Zía art. (The state flag of New Mexico, which shows a crosslike symbol made of four lines in each of the four directions, is based on a Zía design).

Some of the Pueblo peoples, influenced by Christianity, are monotheists; but many retain a belief in the

found sometimes, as in native Tahitian religion and in many African religions, from the Diola of Senegal to the BaKongo of the Congo region. In traditional Hawaiian religion, it was believed that the spirits of the dead went to an underworld, while the spirits of cultural heroes ascended into the sky.

SACRED PRACTICES IN INDIGENOUS RELIGIONS

In native societies, everyday religious activity and practice are significant because their primary purpose is often to place individuals, families, and groups in "right relationships" with gods, ancestors, other human beings, and nature. Rituals are the basic way in which human beings ensure they are living in harmony with each other and with nature. Rituals are frequently devoted to major aspects of human life: key events in the life cycle, rules traditional deities, and they sense no disharmony. The Great Spirit, they believe, can take many forms. Among the Hopis, for example, more than thirty gods are recognized. Perhaps the most important are Tawa, the sun god, prayed to each morning; Mu-yao, the moon god, imagined as an old man; Sotuqnangu, god of the sky, who sends clouds and lightning; and Kokyang Wuuti, called Spider Woman in English, who is thought of as a loving grandmother.

Among all the Pueblo peoples there is a belief in guardian spirits, who play a role something like angels and patron saints. These are the kachinas. They are not gods, but are the spirits of ancestors, birds, animals, plants, and other beings. They are believed to have once lived among the people, then to have retreated to their own world; but they return yearly. They are represented by human beings when the human beings are dressed in specific masks and costumes.

One of the most complex systems of belief in guardian spirits is found among the Hopis, where traditional religion has been least affected by other cultures. From February through the summer, dancers represent the spirits, and more than two hundred different masked figures appear in the dances. In the Hopi language they are called katsinam (singular: katsina). Bird and animal spirits are based on many birds and animals, including the deer, badger, sheep, cow, horse, hummingbird, and eagle; and nature spirits express the rain cloud, rainbow, moon, and fertile earth. Some figures show human characteristics, such as warriors, corn-grinding maidens, guards, clowns, and children. There is also a wide variety of ogrelike figures. Each has a name, special costume, and specific mask. The Zuñi recognize similar guardian spirits, whom they called koko.

The Hopi and the Zuñi are also well known for their painted representations of these spirits, called tithu (singular: tihu). (Outsiders know the figurines as "kachina dolls.") They are re-creations in miniature of the masked kachina figures that dance in the villages. The tithu were originally created to be given as gifts from the masked dancers to girls in the villages—a form of religious teaching through images. But they have become collectors' items, cherished by outsiders.

Dances are an especially significant part of the life of all the pueblos. They retell the stories of creation, emergence, and migration, and they are performed throughout the year under the sponsorship of the religious societies. Dances also include practical purposes—to ensure rainfall, fertility of the earth, and good harvest, or to achieve a bountiful hunt and protection from danger. We get an idea of their purposes from some of their names, such as Corn Dance, Snake Dance, and Elk Dance. Visitors who have the privilege of observing these and other Pueblo ceremonies come away with a renewed appreciation for the variety of religious paths and a sense of amazement at the persistence through the centuries of such beautiful, ancient ways.

concerning certain kinds of behavior, sacrifice, and access to the spirit world. In addition, artifacts such as masks and statues are an essential part of specific rituals.

Life-Cycle Ceremonies

In indigenous societies, the human journey through life is aided and marked by rites of passage. In addition to being important to the individual, these rites also help hold the society together by renewing bonds and admitting new members to the community.

Rites of passage mark an important life event, such as the birth of a child. In some native religions, a woman about to give birth goes off by herself to bear her child at a sacred site or in a house built for that purpose. Birth is considered a powerful time for the mother and child, and the blood associated with it is believed to have dangerous power.

Read myths. They teach you that you can turn inward, and you begin to get the message of the symbols. Read other people's myths, not those of your own religion, because you tend to interpret your own religion in terms of facts—but if you read the other ones, you begin to get the message.

—Joseph Campbell[19]

Some indigenous peoples of western Canada erect a totem pole to honor an ancestor. Images on the totem pole are related to the ancestor's life story.

After the birth, the newborn is often celebrated with a public event that may occur immediately or anytime from a week to a year after the actual birth. In some parts of Africa, babies do not become members of the community until they receive their names in a special public ceremony that is accompanied by song, dance, and a meal. A name is chosen carefully because of the influence it is thought to have on the child's future.

Special rituals also mark a person's entry into adulthood. They may include a period of instruction in sex, adult responsibilities, and tribal history and belief. They often involve an initiation ritual that may be experienced in seclusion or in the company of other initiates. Rites can include a symbolic death—painful and frightening—meant to turn a boy into a man. Across Africa, circumcision for boys in their early teens is a common rite for entering adulthood.

In western Africa, initiation societies oversee coming-of-age rituals. "The Poro [a secret initiation society] is for boys, controlled by a hierarchy of elders, different in each village, which meets in a sacred grove where the clan founder was buried. The purpose of the initiation is the rebirth of the youths, who are said to be swallowed by the Poro spirit at the beginning and returned to their parents as reborn at the end of the initiation."[20] A parallel initiation society exists for girls, who receive sexual instruction and training in the skills necessary for marriage.

A girl's first menstrual period may also be marked publicly. For example, among the Apache, a four-day ceremony marks a girl's *menarche* (first menstruation). During the ceremony, which is elaborate, the girl performs a dance, receives a massage from her female sponsor, kneels to receive the rays of the sun, and circles repeatedly around a ceremonial cane.

In Native American religions, a common ritual of early maturity is the "vision quest," or "dream quest," which may involve prolonged fasting and some kind of preliminary cleansing, such as washing or undergoing a sweat bath. Details of the construction of the sweat lodge and the attendant ritual can include cutting willow branches, during which tobacco might be offered; gathering sticks, rocks, moss, and sweet grass; making an altar and heating a stone; rubbing smoke over the body; marking the ground; and saying appropriate prayers at each stage.

For years before the vision quest, the young person may receive training to prepare for the experience. Commonly, a tribal religious specialist will

The Igbo: An Indigenous Religion in Transition

Today, at least six million Igbo (or Ibo, pronounced *ee'-bo*) live in western Africa, mostly in the nation of Nigeria. While there are some variations among tribes, traditional Igbo people worship the goddess of the earth (Ala) and various spirits (*alusi*), such as the spirit of the river, the spirit of the yam, and the spirit of the hearth. Many Igbo worship a High God (Chukwu, or Chineke), conceived of as the creator. They also venerate the souls of ancestors, who are believed to have power over the lives of their descendants. The Igbo believe that each person has a unique spirit (*chi*), which plays a major role in determining the person's fate.

Within Igbo religion, special rituals mark significant life events. Daily ritual takes place in the home at a central shrine with wooden images of ancestors. These images receive regular offerings of food, drink, and sometimes the blood of sacrificial animals. Religious rites mark the naming of children, marriage, planting, and harvest. The most important and complex rituals occur at funerals, when the Igbo believe they must help the deceased enter the spirit world contentedly. For these ceremonies, the Igbo have developed elaborate masks for use in religious dances and masquerades.

This photo from the 1930s gives a sense of how masks play a role in traditional Igbo dance.

Christian missionaries began to work among the Igbo in the mid-nineteenth century. Throughout the British colonization of Nigeria in the nineteenth and the twentieth centuries, the Church of England, also known as the Anglican Church, sent many missionaries to the region. Catholic missionaries, who arrived after 1880, were also successful with conversions. As a result, Christian belief and practice have strongly influenced Igbo religion. Sometimes Christianity has displaced traditional beliefs and practices. But more commonly, in varied forms of religious syncretism (blending), the two religions have mixed and sometimes even produced new independent religions.

Many parallels between traditional Igbo faith and Christianity assisted the mixing of the two religions. The High God of the Igbo resembles the Creator Father God of Christianity. Igbo spirits of nature resemble Christian angels, and souls of Igbo ancestors intercede on behalf of the living, as do Christian saints. Igbo belief in an individual's spirit resembles Christian belief in the soul.

Although Christianity prohibits traditional Igbo polygamy, other elements of older practice remain. Igbo who worship at Christian churches on Sunday may visit traditional priests and shrines during the week in order to seek the advice and help of the spirits. And the souls of ancestors continue to receive veneration. Masquerades are used even for celebrating Christmas, a major national holiday in Nigeria.

What has happened among the Igbo is quite typical of what has happened throughout sub-Saharan Africa. Christianity is becoming the dominant religion, but its flavor is African.

create a sacred space by ritually marking the four directions of the compass and the center. The sacred space, set apart from the community, should be a place of natural beauty.

The seeker remains in the sacred space until a vision, or dream, comes. Although the vision quest is often a part of the coming-of-age ceremonies for males, among some peoples it is also employed for females. The vision quest may be used at other times, too—particularly when the individual or the group must make an important life decision.

In indigenous societies, as in many other cultures, marriage is a ritual that not only publicly affirms and stabilizes a union but also cements economic arrangements and, through the ceremony, ensures fertility. In both Africa and North America, however, marriage in tribal cultures often has been a practical arrangement. Among Native American peoples, marriage has frequently been celebrated simply as a social contract that is worked out by the families. Monogamy has been the norm, but divorce is acceptable when a marriage is not successful. In indigenous African religions, marriage is sometimes marked by rituals to unite the two lineages and transfer the power of fertility; but often its religious aspect "is not distinctive. It is regarded as the normal sequel to rites of adolescence, whose purpose was to prepare for this state."[22]

As the final passing from this life, death is accompanied by rituals that serve to comfort close relatives, assist the spirit of the dead person in moving on, and protect the living from bad influences that could come from an unhappy spirit. Because the spirit of the dead person may be sad to leave the family circle, it must be helped to make its trip to the spirit world. Relatives and friends assist by placing clothing, food, money, and favorite objects with the body. In the case of a chief or other notable person, the body may be embalmed or mummified for public display until a large funeral can be arranged. In the past, great African chiefs have had wives, children, and servants buried alongside them. Among Native American tribes, the sacrifice of relatives and attendants to accompany a dead leader has also occurred. For example, after the death of the Natchez leader Tattooed Serpent in 1725, two of his wives and six others, after preparation by fasting, were strangled as a part of the funeral ritual.[23] In Native American religions, bodies of the dead are usually buried, but sometimes they are placed on platforms or in trees.

> There, when I was young, the spirits took me in my vision to the center of the earth and showed me all the good things in the sacred hoop of the world.
> —Black Elk, speaking of his vision quest at age nine.[21]

Taboo and Sacrifice

A **taboo** is a rule that forbids specific behavior with regard to certain objects, people, animals, days, or phases of life. Taboos represent a codification of the social and religious order. In our language, *taboo* means, often negatively, something that is prohibited. This is essentially the viewpoint of an outsider. From inside native religions, a taboo is often better seen as a way of protecting the individual and of safeguarding the natural order of things.

The Vision Quest

Among the Ojibwa, who live in the northern plains and Great Lakes area of North America, fasting was often expected of children as preparation for a great fast upon reaching puberty. Girls were expected to make a special fast at menarche, but boys were expected, in addition, to undertake a vision quest. "The Ojibwa boy was led deep into the forest, where a lofty red pine tree was selected. In this tree, a platform of woven sticks covered with moss was placed upon a high branch as a bed upon which the youth was to conduct the fast. Perhaps a canopy of branches would be prepared to shelter him from the wind and rain. Left alone in this place, the youth was strictly warned not to take any kind of nourishment or drink. He was to lie quietly day and night on this platform in a patient vigil for his vision."[24] He might be checked secretly by elders and would be allowed to go home if he could not continue, but he would have to return the following year. "When visions rewarded the fast, they commonly took the form of a journey into the world of the spirits, a spiritual journey on a cosmic scale. During this journey the visionary was shown the path upon which his life should proceed. He was associated with one or more spirit beings who would serve as his guardians and protectors throughout his life."[25] The boy would also gather, or later be given, physical symbols of his guardian spirits, which he would keep for the rest of his life to remind him of his quest and the spirits' protection.

Taboos frequently relate to sex and birth. Blood, too, is always an element of mysterious power—both helpful and dangerous. For example, in some but not all groups, menstruating women are expected to remain separate from everyone else, since menstrual blood is considered powerful and dangerous. In contrast, a few cultures (such as the Apache) hail a girl's menarche as a time when she has power to heal illness.

Probably because of the blood involved during childbirth, a woman in some native cultures must remain alone or in the company of women only during the birth—not even the woman's husband may be present. In traditional Hawai`i, for example, women of high rank gave birth in isolation, at the site of special large stones used only for this purpose. Indigenous societies also frequently forbid a husband from resuming sexual relations with his wife for some time after childbirth—this period can even last until the child is weaned.

Like birth, death is also surrounded by taboos concerning the spirit of the dead person, who may seek to reward or take revenge on the living because of the way he or she was treated in life. The afterlife can be a shadowy, uncertain realm that the departing spirit is reluctant to enter, especially if the spirit is leaving a happy family circle. Proper rituals must be performed, accompanied by public mourning, to avoid angering the dead person's spirit.

A number of taboos regulate other social behavior. One common taboo relates to rank: people of high position, such as chiefs, nobility, priests, and shamans, must be treated with extraordinary care because of their special powers; taboos protect them from insult or inappropriate action. In traditional Hawaiian culture, for example, the shadow of a commoner could not

Traditional Hawaiian Religion

The essentials of traditional Polynesian culture and religion were brought to Hawai`i by settlers who came over the sea from islands in the southern Pacific Ocean. Because of the great navigational skills of the Polynesians, their culture spread widely.

Before contact with westerners, the Polynesian people of Hawai`i had a well-developed belief system, made of many strands. Their belief system spoke of a primeval darkness (*po*), in the midst of which a separation had occurred, forming the sky and the earth. In the space between the two, all the varied forms of life emerged. (This emergence is beautifully detailed in the *Kumulipo*, the most elaborate of the Hawaiian chants of creation.) The primal deities of sky and earth were Wakea and his female consort Papa. But the Hawaiian religion also spoke of thousands of other deities (*akua*) who were descendants of the earliest gods. Some of these deities may have arisen from the memory of divinized ancestors, and others may have been the personification of specific aspects of nature. Their worship seems to have arisen at different times on different island groups, and systematization took place only slowly, never being static, but growing in layers.

Of the thousands of deities that eventually were said to exist, several dozen were commonly invoked, and the greatest deities had priesthoods dedicated to their worship. Among the most important were Ku and Lono, gods who were in many ways complementary. Ku, with several manifestations, was a god of vigorous action. He was the patron, for example, of digging, bird catching, and fishing. In a darker aspect he was also patron of war.

The second god, Lono, was a god of peace, associated with rain, fertility, love, and the arts. Although a large part of the year was dedicated to Ku, the winter period was a time of truce, under the protection of Lono. During this time the temples dedicated to Ku were temporarily closed. The four-month period dedicated to Lono began when the Pleiades first appeared above the horizon in the night sky—something that happened between late October and late November. This period was called *Makahiki* (literally, "eye movement"), a term which referred to the appearance and movement of the stars. The time was given over to religious services, dance, sports contests, and leisure. During Makahiki, priests of Lono collected offerings in his name. To announce the presence of Lono, his priests bore around each island a white banner made of *kapa* (bark cloth). It was attached to a long pole that had at its top the face of Lono or his birdlike symbol. (The people of Hawai`i thought of Captain James Cook as Lono because the explorer's ship arrived in January during Makahiki, and also because his ship, with its white sails, had a startling resemblance to the banner of Lono.)

Two other gods of importance were Kane and Kanaloa, traveling companions or brothers who came together from their homeland of Kahiki to the Hawaiian islands. The two were said to have introduced and planted all bananas in Hawai`i.[26] Kane was protector of the water but was seen in many other aspects of nature—particularly in thunder and the rainbow. Houses often had a shrine to Kane, the heart of which was a phallic stone, and at it Kane received daily prayer. Kanaloa was associated with the sky and the ocean—particularly with ocean fishponds, marine life, the tides, and sailing.

These major gods (with the possible exception of Kanaloa) had their own temples. In the lunar calendar followed by the Hawaiians, ten days in each lunar month were sacred to one of these four gods and most work was forbidden on those days.[27] Fishing and the planting and harvesting of food plants were regulated by this calendar.

The goddess Pele was also a major subject of devotion. She was worshiped as a goddess of fire, active in volcanoes. Tales about her describe her arrival in Hawai`i at the small island of Ni`ihau, east of Kaua`i; her volcanic activity on Kaua`i, O`ahu, and Maui; and the final movement of her irascible spirit to the Big Island of Hawai`i, where volcanoes are still active. Pele was so important that she also had her own priests and, later, priestesses. Other popular goddesses included Pele's younger sister Hi`iaka, of whom Pele was sometimes jealous; Hina, goddess associated with the moon; and Laka, the patron of hula.

Just as deities had many aspects, they could also manifest themselves in varied shapes (*kinolau*, "multiple selves"). Pele, for example, might show herself as a girl, a white dog, a volcano, fire, or an old woman with long hair. (The ethnobotanist Isabella Abbott recounts a characteristic tale told her by her father. He said that once he gave an old lady a ride in his truck and offered elaborate over time. The heiau generally were outdoor stone platforms, often enclosed by walls. In the heiau, images of the deities (*ki`i*) were set up, food offerings were placed on wooden platforms, and priests performed carefully memorized chants.

A complex system of classification came to exist in all traditional Hawaiian society, and religion provided the taboos (*kapu*). The social divisions seem to have grown stricter and more complex over the centuries, and stern sanctions—often death—reinforced the prohibitions. Society was strongly hierarchical—made of nobles (*ali`i*) of descending grades, common people (*maka`ainana*), and slaves (*kauwa*). Men and women had quite different social roles and ate separately. Women lived apart during their menstrual period. Possibly because of fears about the dangerous power of menstrual blood, prohibitions were imposed on what women could eat, what they could touch, and the kind of work they could perform. They could not eat pork, coconuts, or most kinds of bananas, and they were not allowed to raise or prepare *kalo* (taro), the primary food.

Underpinning the entire social system was a notion of spiritual power, called *mana*. Nobles, who were considered to be representatives of the gods, were believed to have the greatest mana; but their mana had to be protected. Commoners, for example, had to crouch or prostrate themselves when close to nobles.

In 1819, King Kamehameha the Great, who had unified the islands, died. In the same year, his son King Kamehameha II ate with women, an act that represented a clear and public rejection of the old system of prohibitions. (This act was influenced by several decades of Western contact.) Many heiau were destroyed and allowed to fall into ruin, most images of the gods were burned, and the religious priesthoods officially ended. The following year, Protestant Christian missionaries arrived from Boston, and Christianity stepped into the vacuum.

Traditional religion, however, did not entirely die out. Elements of it remain alive even today. Among the clearest are widespread reverence for Pele, veneration of ancestors, and belief in guardian spirits. Blessings and dedications, although performed by modern ministers, are often done in traditional style with sea water and ti leaves (*ki*), and hula and traditional musical instruments are occasionally used during Christian services. Prayerful chants in Hawaiian are performed at the beginning of hula, the goddesses Laka and Hi`iaka

Offerings such as coconuts and fruit are sometimes wrapped in leaves of the ti plant and placed on an offering platform (lele) at a heiau. The platform here is at Pu`u o Mahuka on the island of Oahu.

her a cigarette. Before he had a chance to light her cigarette, however, it had lit by itself and the old lady was smoking it. Then suddenly she disappeared.)

Deceased ancestors were, and are, also thought of as having elements of divinity. Known as *`aumakua,* they act as powerful family guardians. Like the gods, they might appear in varied forms—the best-known shapes being those of animals such as sharks, dogs, owls, turtles, and giant lizards (*mo`o*).

Places of worship varied in size—from enormous stone temples to small wayside shrines, temporary altars, and the site of sacred objects in the home. Many temples and shrines were used for specific purposes, such as treating the sick or requesting good fishing, rain, or an increase of crops. The design of temples, called *heiau,* was derived from that of temples in Tahiti and the Marquesas, and seems to have become more

Although hula is often thought of as entertainment, much of it tells the stories of Hawaiian gods and goddesses.

are often invoked, and the dances frequently retell the stories of the goddesses and gods. Public prayer at dedications is expected, and one frequently hears the prayer leader address both God (Akua) and "our `aumakua." There have also been theoretical attempts at integrating the traditional native polytheism with monotheism, by saying that the many traditional deities are angels or are just aspects of the one God.[28]

The revival in recent decades of hula, Hawaiian language, and traditional arts has brought about a new interest in ceremonies of the traditional religion. A good number of heiau have been repaired and even rebuilt, including several large ones on Maui and the Big Island of Hawai`i. Some traditional religious services have been conducted at the reconstructed heiau, and there may be further attempts to restore traditional religious practices.[29]

Do not kill or injure your neighbor, for it is not him that you injure. Do not wrong or hate your neighbor, for it is not him that you wrong, you wrong yourself. Moneto, the Grandmother, the Supreme Being, loves him also as she loves you.

—Shawnee rules[30]

fall on a member of the nobility. In a strongly hierarchical native culture, such as in many African groups, the health the people and the fertility of the land are believed to depend on the health of the sacred king. To maintain his health, the king is protected by taboos—particularly regarding the people with whom he may associate. Because of these taboos and the fear his role inspires, the sacred king may live a life quite separate from his subjects.

Foods and food sources in many cultures are governed by taboos. Among some African peoples, commoners have been forbidden to touch or eat the food of a king. In traditional Hawai`i, women were forbidden to eat certain foods.

Antisocial actions may also be subject to taboo. In Native American religions, taboos and rules encourage a sense of harmony with other members of one's people. Strong taboos against adultery and stealing within the tribal unit, for example, are enforced by shame, warnings, shunning, and expulsion, often administered by a tribal council. Nevertheless, although harmony is important, warfare against another people has at times been considered justified.

When a taboo has been broken or a spirit must be placated, the person or group must atone for the lapse, often through sacrifice. The usual offering is food and drink. A **libation** (the act of pouring a bit of drink on the ground as an offering) may be made or a portion of a meal set aside for a spirit. An animal may be sacrificed and its blood poured out on the ground or on an altar as an offering of the life force to the deity. Sacrificial animals ordinarily are food animals, such as chickens, pigs, and goats.[31] After the sacrifice, all the participants (including ancestral and nature spirits) may eat the cooked animal—thus pleasing the spirits by feeding them and including them in the meal.

Although it has been rare, human sacrifice (and sometimes cannibalism) has occurred in some native cultures. The sacrifice of human beings was practiced (at least for a time) for specific purposes in Aztec religion, Hawaiian religion, and among tribal peoples of New Guinea; it was much less common among native peoples of North America and Africa.

Before leaving the topic of taboos, it might be good to note that taboos exist plentifully in every society, including our own. Many are associated with sex, marriage, and parenthood. In modern societies, for example, taboos exist against polygamy, incest, and marriage between close relations. Such taboos may seem "natural" to the society that enforces them but "unusual" to outsiders. Taboos are not inherently valid across groups and societies; they are culturally determined.

Shamanism, Trance, and Spiritual Powers

As we have seen, native religions take for granted that a powerful and influential but invisible spirit world exists and that human beings can access it. A **shaman** acts as an intermediary between the visible, ordinary world and the spirit world. The shaman can contact this realm, receive visions of it, and transmit messages from it, often to help or heal others. As one commentator remarks, "The shaman lies at the very heart of some cultures, while living in the shadowy fringes of others. Nevertheless, a common thread seems to connect all shamans across the planet. An awakening to other orders of reality, the experience of ecstasy, and an opening up of visionary realms form the essence of the shamanic mission."[32] Sometimes the spirits speak through the shaman, who knows entry points to their world. The spirits may be reached in dreams or trances by climbing a sacred tree, descending through a cave into the underworld, flying through the air, or following a sacred map.

The shaman understands the primordial unity of things and experiences a shared identity with animals and the rest of nature. Thus the shaman can interpret the language of animals, charm them, and draw on their powers.

I enter the earth. I go in at a place like a place where people drink water. I travel a long way, very far. When I emerge, I am already climbing threads [up into the sky]. I climb one and leave it, then I climb another one. . . . You come in small to God's place. You do what you have to do there. . . . [Then] you enter, enter the earth, and you return to enter the skin of your body.

—Bushman trance dancer[33]

A shaman carries a golden pot during an equinox ceremony in Equador.

The shaman gains the powers of animals and the rest of nature by wearing items taken from important animals, such as deer antlers, lion skins, and eagle feathers.

Part of becoming a shaman involves having one or more encounters with the spirit realm in the form of a psychological death and rebirth. A person may have experienced some great loss—of sight, of a child, or of something equally precious. He or she may have had a mental breakdown, been terribly sick, or suffered a serious accident and come close to dying. Upon recovering from such an extreme experience, this person can have new powers of insight and healing, which can lead to becoming a shaman. Those who have experienced vivid dreams and visions that are thought to be manifestations of the spirit world are also sometimes trained as shamans.

The shaman often blends the roles of priest, oracle, psychologist, and doctor. A common English term for the shaman is *medicine man,* yet it stresses only the therapeutic role and obscures the fact that shamans are both female and male. In Korean and Japanese native religious paths, in fact, shamans are frequently female.

The shamanic trance state that brings visions, both to the shaman and to others, can be induced in several ways: weakening the visual boundaries (for example, by sitting in the darkness of a cave or hut for prolonged periods), fasting, experiencing sensory deprivation, making regular rhythmic sounds (such as drumming, rattling, bell ringing, and chanting), and dancing in a repetitive way, especially in circles. The ingestion of natural substances is also common; peyote cactus, datura, cannabis (marijuana), coca, opium, and the

Isaac Tens Becomes a Shaman

Isaac Tens, a shaman of the Gitksan people of northwest Canada, spoke to an interviewer in 1920 about how he had become a shaman. On a snowy day at dusk, when he was gathering firewood, he heard a loud noise, and an owl appeared to him. "The owl took hold of me, caught my face, and tried to lift me up. I lost consciousness. As soon as I came back to my senses I realized that I had fallen into the snow. My head was coated with ice, and some blood was running out of my mouth."[34] Isaac went home, but he fell into a trance. He woke up to find medicine men working to heal him. One told him that it was now time for him, too, to become a *halaait* (medicine man). Isaac refused. Later, at a fishing hole, he had another fainting spell and fell into a trance again. He was carried home. When he woke up, he was trembling. "My body was quivering. While I remained in this state, I began to sing. A chant was coming out of me without my being able to do anything to stop it. Many things appeared to me presently: huge birds and other animals. They were calling me."[35] Soon Isaac began to treat others.

mushroom *Amanita muscaria* have all been used to induce trance states, both by the shaman alone and sometimes by participants in a ceremony.

Some Native American peoples have used a **calumet**—a long sacred pipe—for smoking a special kind of tobacco that is far stronger than commercial cigarette tobacco; it is so strong, in fact, that it can have a hallucinatory effect. The bowl of the pipe is usually made of clay but sometimes of bone, ivory, wood, or metal, and the stem is made of wood. Many pipes are also made of stone. (A red stone, popular among Plains Indians and Eastern Woodlands Indians for this purpose, was quarried in Pipestone, Minnesota.) The calumet is an object that gives protection to the person who carries it. The pipe is smoked as part of a shared ceremony that establishes strong bonds among all the participants, and oaths sworn at these ceremonies have the greatest solemnity.

Rituals involving the use of peyote have developed primarily within the past two centuries in some native North American tribes.[36] The practice seems to have moved north from Mexico, where peyote grows easily and has long been used for religious purposes. When the fruit of the peyote cactus is eaten, it elicits a psychedelic experience that lasts six or more hours and produces a forgetfulness of the self and a sense of oneness with all of nature. Ceremonies commonly begin in the early evening and last until dawn.

Among North American tribes, the rituals involving peyote are often mixed with Christian elements. For example, a member of the Native American Church described his preparation for the ceremony: "First we set up an altar—a Mexican rug and on it a Lakota Bible in our own language. We use only the revelations of St. John in our meetings. It's . . . full of visions, nature, earth, stars. . . . Across the Bible we put an eagle feather—it stands for the Great Spirit. . . . On the left is a rawhide bag with cedar dust to sprinkle on the fire. That's our incense."[37] The blending of elements, he says, is intentional, because it illustrates that, at their core, all religions are the same. It is interesting to note

The powwow provides opportunities for Indian nations to share their dances and to pass age-old stories to new generations.

that although the ordinary use of peyote is illegal, its religious use by the Native American Church has been legally upheld.

In native African religions and their Caribbean offshoots, powerful but invisible spiritual forces are believed to be able to do either great good or tremendous evil. These powers are directed by diviners and healers through incantations, figurines, and potions in what is sometimes called **sympathetic magic.** Magic in the hands of certain individuals can be used, as one commentator remarks, "for harmful ends, and then people experience it as bad or evil magic. Or they may use it for ends which are helpful to society, and then it is considered as good magic or 'medicine.' These mystical forces of the universe are neither evil nor good in themselves, they are just like other natural things at [our] disposal."[38]

Spiritual powers and trance states are believed to make it possible to look into the past and future, a process called **divination** (from the Latin *divus,* "god," and *divinare,* "to foretell"). Looking into the past is thought to help determine the causes of illness and other misfortune, while looking into the future can guide an individual to act wisely. It is a common belief in African religions that an individual has a predetermined future that can be discovered through divination.

The general worldview common to native religions allows for a number of specialized religious roles. A diviner looks for causes of sickness, depression, death, and other difficulties. A healer works with a person afflicted with physical or mental illness to find a cure. A rainmaker ends drought.

Malevolent sorcerers manipulate objects to cause damage; they may take fingernails, hair, clothes, or other possessions of the victim, then burn or damage them, or bury an object in the victim's path, in order to cause harm. Witches need only use their spiritual powers. "Another belief is that the spirit of the witches leaves them at night and goes to eat away the victim, thus causing him to weaken and eventually die. It is believed, too, that a witch can cause harm by looking at a person, wishing him harm or speaking to him words intended to inflict harm on him."[39] Of course, the powers of these sorcerers and witches are also employed for good ends as well.

Artifacts and Artistic Expression in Indigenous Religions

The masks, drums, statues, rattles, and other objects that are important in native religions were once seen as curiosities to be collected and housed in anthropological museums. Today, however, we view them differently; we realize that we must respect both their importance to the cultures that produced them and their inherent artistic value. The arts of native religions are not created by "artists" as "art" but as functional objects to be used in particular settings and special ways. Navajo sandpaintings, for example, are often photographed and reproduced in books as though they were permanent works of art. In fact, when used by a healer, they are temporary creations that are made and then destroyed as a part of the ritual. And unlike art in most industrialized cultures, sacred objects and images in native religions are not separate endeavors but an essential part of the religious expression itself. Although modern secular culture does not usually think of dance or tattoo or body painting as religious expression, in many native religions these art forms all fulfill that role.

This small section of an early Mayan painting in Guatemala shows the son of the corn god, patron of kings, making a sacrifice. The painting was probably done about 100 B.C.

In religions that do not rely on the written word, artistic expressions take on unique significance because they are filled with meaning and remind practitioners of the specifics of the oral tradition. Statues and paintings, of course, are common in a great many religions, both oral and written. Dance, which takes on particular importance in native religions, incorporates religious objects such as carved and painted masks, headdresses, costumes, ornaments, and musical instruments. In native Hawaiian religion, *hula kahiko* (ancient hula) is danced in conjunction with chanting to honor the gods. Instruments for marking rhythm and *lei* (wreaths of flowers or other plants worn around the head, wrists, and ankles), when used in hula, are considered religious objects.

Chants, too, are essential, for they repeat the sacred words and re-create the stories of the religious traditions. To be used properly in religious ceremonies, they must be memorized carefully. Chanters must not only have prodigious memories and be able to recall thousands of chants, they must also be able to create special variations on traditional chants and oral texts for individual occasions.

Masks play a significant role in native religions, especially when used in dance. When a dancer is wearing a mask and any accompanying costume, the spirit is not merely represented by the masked dancer. The dancer actually becomes the spirit, embodied on earth, with the spirit's powers. Among the BaPunu in Africa, for example, dancers not only wear masks but walk on stilts—the overall effect must be intense. Particularly complex masks have been produced in the Pacific Northwest by such tribes as the Haida, Tsimshian, and Kwakiutl (Kwakwaka`wakw).[40] Some of their masks, especially those depicting animal spirits, have movable parts that make them even more powerful for those who wear and see them.

Besides masks and statues, other forms of wood carving can manifest religious inspiration. Perhaps the most famous of all wood carvings is the carved pole, commonly called a *totem pole,* found in the Pacific Northwest. The totem pole usually depicts several totems, stacked one upon the other. A **totem** is an animal figure—such as the bear, beaver, thunderbird, owl, raven, and eagle— that is revered for both its symbolic meaning and its clan symbolism. The totem animals may be memorials to ancestors or may represent badges of kinship groups, with specialized meaning for the individual or the family responsible for the totem pole.[41] Some totem poles are a part of the structure of a traditional wooden house or lodge. Others—apparently a later development—are raised to stand alone, frequently to mark an important event.

Other important art forms that can have religious meaning are weaving, beading, and basketry. These creations may seem to have less obvious religious significance, but the imagery used is frequently of religious derivation, particularly figures from tribal myths, nature deities, and guardian birds and animals.

Feathers and featherwork also feature prominently in many native religions because of their powerful association with flight and contact with the world above and beyond our own. Richard W. Hill, in an essay on the religious meaning of feathers, remarks that "some cultures associate certain birds with spiritual or protective powers. Birds are believed to have

Sacred images are reinterpreted on this contemporary blanket from the Pacific Northwest coast. The white borders, which originally would have been made of shells, are today made of buttons.

delivered songs, dances, rituals, and sacred messages to humankind. Feathers worn in the hair blow in the wind and evoke birds in flight. For followers of the Ghost Dance religion of the late nineteenth century, birds became important symbols of rebirth."[42] Feathers are worn in the hair, made into headdresses, and attached to clothing. In Native American cultures, they are also attached to horse harnesses, dolls, pipes, and baskets.

The symbols that appear in myths and in dreams are the basic vocabulary of native religious art. Common symbols include a great mountain located at the center of the universe, the tree of life, the sun and moon, fire, rain, lightning, a bird or wings, death's head and skeleton, a cross, and a circle. These images, however, often appear in unusual forms; for example, lightning may be represented by a zigzag, the sun may appear like a swastika, and the tree of life may look like a ladder. Colors are universally used with symbolic meaning, although the exact meaning differs from culture to culture.

PERSONAL EXPERIENCE: GODS IN HAWAI`I

On the southernmost island of the Hawaiian Islands lies Pu`uhonua `o Honaunau ("place of refuge"). It was once a sanctuary for Hawaiians who had done something that was kapu (taboo, forbidden). They could be purified and escape punishment if they could reach this place, or one of its sister sanctuaries, by water or land.

The ki`i at Pu`uhonua `o Honaunau mark this place of refuge as sacred ground.

Seeking refuge from the frenzy of life in Honolulu, I fly to the Kona airport and drive my rental car down the Big Island's southwest coast to Pu`uhonua `o Honaunau, now run by the United States National Park Service. After a short walk toward the shore, I see the tall, long stone wall of the sanctuary. Closer to the ocean are its heiau (temples), made of large, nearly black lava rock. Most dramatic to my outsider's eyes are the tall carved wooden images (in Hawaiian, called ki`i, and in English, commonly called tikis) that once no doubt beckoned to the refugee who sought out this place at the ocean's edge. The offering platform and thatched houses near the ki`i have been restored so that I can see what it might have been like when this was a sacred site within traditional Hawaiian religion. Because the official kapu system was dissolved in 1819 by King Kamehameha II, it is no longer a place for seeking sanctuary—at least officially.

Even on this sunny day, the stone wall, the tall images, and the stark landscape speak not of the "peace and comfort" we may typically associate with a refuge but rather of power, law, and awesome majesty. The ground is hard, black lava rock and white coral, and except for the coconut trees here and there amid the few structures, there is little green vegetation. Ocean waves lap at the shore, but an almost eerie quiet reigns.

Late afternoon: I'm the only person here. It is not hard for me to imagine being a native who has fled from home and now awaits a priestly blessing in order to be made safe for returning home. I sense that the Hawaiian religion drew its power from the land, from this very place. The rocks that make up the heiau are petrifications of fire, water, air, and earth. This is not the tour director's tropical fantasyland. Nor, I realize, is it a place of living religious practice. But that doesn't matter to me today. What I sense in the land is still alive.

As I drive back up the hill toward the main road, I see a small directional sign that says Painted Church. Ready for an experience of contrast, I follow its arrow and soon arrive at Saint Benedict's Catholic Church—a tiny, white wooden structure that has elements of Gothic style. A sign near the door says that its interior was painted a century ago by a Belgian missionary priest. The church sits on a grassy hillside, with a small cemetery spreading out below. I ascend the wooden stairs of the church and walk in.

The interior is "tropical Gothic." Ten small windows have pointed Gothic arches. The wooden pillars look like candy canes, painted with red and white swirls; their tops turn into palm trees, with fronds like painted feathers on the pastel sky of the ceiling. Behind the altar is a mural of Gothic arches, stretching back into an imaginary distance, creating the pretense of a European cathedral. On one side wall, Saint Francis experiences a vision of Jesus on the cross. In another painting, Jesus is being tempted by Satan. The other wall shows a man on his deathbed, his face bathed in heavenly light. A cross of execution, the pains of death—these are not pleasant experiences, but they are softened by the way they are depicted here.

Back outside, from the top of the stairs, I see the shining ocean below and can even see, at the edge of the ocean, the Hawaiian place of refuge that I had visited not long before. This little church, charming as it appears, presents old familiar themes: a High God, a sacrificial victim, an offering of blood, a restoration of justice. The themes may not be obvious, but they are there. This, I reflect, is the religion that replaced the native Hawaiian religion; the cycle of replacement evident here is typical, I think, of what has happened to so many other native religious traditions. Does it make all that much difference how religions die and rise? I am deep in thought as I pass a stone grotto enclosing a statue of Mary and then walk past the resident priest's small house. From inside come the sounds of a baseball game and a roaring crowd. "Strike two!" a voice shouts. Passing a flowerbed of honeysuckle, and preparing to return to big-city life, I get in my car and drive away.

The walls of Saint Benedict's Catholic Church were painted by a missionary to suggest the grandeur (and perhaps superiority) of the missionary's religion.

INDIGENOUS RELIGIONS TODAY

Native religions show many signs of vitality. Some indigenous religions are spreading and even adapting themselves to urban life. For example, religions of the Yoruba tradition are practiced not only in western Africa, their place of origin, but also in Brazil and the Caribbean, and they are growing in cities of North America (see Chapter 11). Awareness of indigenous religions is also becoming widespread, and respect for them is taking many shapes. In some countries (such as Mexico, Ecuador, and Peru) we can see a growth in governmental protection of the rights of

Halloween: "Just Good Fun" or Folk Religion?

Many of us think of native religions as having little connection to our everyday life. Yet elements of them persist in modern culture. Their oral nature is apparent when we see how the manner of practice is taught—not in books of instruction, but by word of mouth and by example. Halloween is an excellent example of this, but other festivals also invite examination.

· *Halloween* means the evening before All Hallows (All Saints) Day, which falls on November 1. Although Halloween gets its name from Christianity, the celebration is, in fact, a continuation of *Samhain* (pronounced *sa´-win*), the new-year festival celebrated in pre-Christian England and Ireland. There is a strong theme of death and rebirth, as winter comes on and the old year disappears. It was believed that spirits of ancestors roamed free at this time and needed to be fed and placated. We see this underlying the practice of children going door to door, receiving food. We also see it in the many Halloween costumes that suggest death (skeletons) and communication with the spirit world (angels, devils, and religious figures).

· Although Christmas has a Christian name and purpose, the origins of this festival, too, are pre-Christian. It began as a festival of the winter solstice, when the days are the coldest and shortest in the northern hemisphere. People compensated by celebrating a holiday of extra light, warmth, and abundance. The lighted Christmas tree and the evergreen wreaths and decorations have nothing to do with the story of Jesus' birth; rather, they are clear symbols of fertility and life, which the celebrants hope will persist through a cold winter. The giving of presents is related to this idea of abundance, and the Christian Saint Nicholas has been transformed over the past two hundred years into the grandfatherly Santa Claus. Like a shaman or wizard, Santa Claus flies through the air, carried by his magical reindeer, dispensing presents from his overflowing bag to children all around the earth.

· Easter's Christian meaning is mixed with elements that derive from the Jewish Passover, but underlying this tradition are symbols of fertility and new life— eggs, flowers, and rabbits. (The name *Easter* comes

The faces of these carved Halloween pumpkins are not unlike those on masks used in indigenous ceremonies across the world.

from an Old English term for a spring festival in honor of Eastre, goddess of the dawn.) Easter has maintained a close tie to nature in that it is always celebrated at the time of a full moon.

We can see in these examples of contemporary folk religion the "universal language" of religious symbols. It is the same language, whether found in folk religion, native religions, or the other religions that we will take up in the chapters ahead.

indigenous peoples. Native peoples themselves are often taking political action to preserve their cultures. In many places (such as Hawai`i, New Zealand, and North America) a renaissance of native cultures is under way. Sometimes this involves primarily cultural elements, but where the indigenous religions are still practiced those religions are increasingly cherished and protected.

In some places, however, indigenous religions appear fragile. There are four principal threats to their existence: the global spread of popular culture, loss of natural environments, loss of traditional languages, and conversion to other religions.

Television, radio, films, airplanes, and the Internet are carrying modern urban culture to all corners of the earth. (American television reruns that are broadcast in Mali are just one example.) Change is also evident in the realm of clothing. Traditional regional clothing began to disappear a century ago, as western styles became the standard. Western business wear is now worn in all the world's cities, and informal clothing—baseball caps and T-shirts—is seen everywhere. Some cultures are trying to hold on to their traditional clothing, especially for formal occasions. (This is common in Korea, the Philippines, and Japan.) Architecture, too, is becoming standardized, as the "international style"—with its plate glass, aluminum, and concrete—takes the place of traditional styles. As modern urban culture spreads across the earth, it tends to dominate everyone's worldview. It would be hard to convince today's young people to undergo the deprivation of a vision quest, when all they need to visit other worlds is a television, a computer, or an airplane ticket. But everywhere we go, we find hamburgers, pizza, rap, rock, and jeans. (Some even believe that popular culture is becoming a religion of its own, displacing all others.)

Another great threat to indigenous religions is their loss of traditional lands and natural environment. Because so much personal and group meaning comes from the natural environment, its degradation or loss can be devastating to a native people's identity. Logging interests are a problem almost universally, but especially in Southeast Asia, Indonesia, Brazil, Alaska, and western Canada. Much of northern Thailand, where many native peoples live, has already been badly deforested, and the logging companies are now beginning the same process in Myanmar, another home of indigenous peoples. Fights are intense over conservation, land ownership, and governmental protection. Luckily, there have been gains (such as in New Zealand and Australia), where aboriginal rights to land have been recognized.

A third threat is the loss of native languages. It has been estimated that of the approximately six thousand languages that are spoken in the world today, in a hundred years only three thousand will remain. A comparison of Native American languages once spoken and still in use illustrates well how many languages and dialects have already been lost. In the United States and Canada, only about 500,000 indigenous people still speak their native languages. A single example of this phenomenon is the Kwakiutl (Kwakwaka`wakw) of

The Green Movement: A New Global Indigenous Religion?

All indigenous religions honor nature in some way. These religions sometimes associate natural forces such as wind, rain, volcanoes, and earthquakes with invisible spirits living beyond the earth. Other traditions see these forces as residing more visibly in mountains, trees, rivers, the moon, and the sun. Whatever form it is conceived as, nature commands respect, and people are expected to show their respect by working harmoniously with their environment.

In contrast with indigenous religions, major religions have traditionally shown limited concern for nature. However, this is changing. Today, many major religions have begun to display a new sensitivity to the earth. The Tibetan religious leader, the Dalai Lama, speaks frequently of the need to show compassion and respect for all living things—not just for human beings. The first Catholic pope elected in this century, Benedict XVI, labeled acts that harm the environment as "sinful." Increasingly, presidents and prime ministers, whatever their religions, as well as ordinary citizens, are making calls to protect the environment, participating in what has become a worldwide Green Movement.

The first phase of the Green Movement in the United States came more than a hundred years ago, when the federal government began to create national parks. People had become aware that the treasures of the scenic natural world needed protection. The second phase began fifty years ago, with the publication of books like Rachel Carson's *Silent Spring*, which warned about the dangers of pesticides. Works like Carson's gave scientific underpinning to growing ecological concern. The third phase is now under way, as environmentalism gains popular support around the world. Individuals, schools, businesses, and governments deliberately "move from gray to green." Part of the world's energy now comes from sunshine, wind, ocean waves, and plants. Construction materials for buildings now include bamboo, reused brick, and recycled wood. A common watchword is *sustainability*, and a well-known mantra is "reduce, recycle, reuse." After decades of being considered a fringe movement of flaky "tree-huggers," environmentalism is entering the mainstream. Industries that were once opposed to environmental needs are beginning to realize the commercial benefits of "going green," and they are at last using their enormous power to make real change.

Indigenous peoples are now also becoming an explicit and vocal part of the Green Movement. For example, in Brazil the Yanomamö (Yanomami) have demonstrated in Brasilia to protect their native lands from roads and mining. In Kenya, Wangari Maathai (b. 1940) is now called "Tree Mother of Africa" because of her work as founder of the Green Belt Movement, which has planted more than 40 million trees. For her efforts, she was awarded the Nobel Peace Prize in 2004.

Those who espouse the Green Movement most likely don't see themselves as embracing a religion, but the movement has many hallmarks of religion. Its statements of political principles form a list of commandments and virtues, which include not only sustainability and biodiversity but also consensus, grass-roots democracy, and non-violence. Its priests are the world's scientists and environmental experts, and its prophets are environmental activists. It promotes a way of life, and it holds promise of rewards and punishments for all inhabitants of this earth.

Whether or not the Green Movement comes to be seen as a world religion makes little difference. If the multinational Green Movement can change human behavior for the good of all, it will be accomplishing as much as many recognized religions. Somewhat ironically, the Green Movement, by leading the world's citizens back to a respect for nature, is also leading people to a new appreciation of the indigenous religions that are built on such respect.

British Columbia. Although their population has been rising, and is now as high as 5,000, only about 250 people speak the native language. Clearly, the loss of a native language endangers the continued transmission of a religion that expresses itself in that language.

A fourth threat is the spread of proselytizing religions, particularly Christianity and Islam. In the Pacific, native cultures are undergoing a revival, but few elements of the native religions of those cultures remain unchanged from their earlier forms. Christianity, brought since the nineteenth century by missionaries (particularly Methodist, Catholic, and, more recently, Mormon), has replaced some beliefs and reshaped others. Christianity has spread widely in sub-Saharan Africa over the past hundred years, creating both mainstream Western denominations and independent African churches. As a result, there are now more black members of the Anglican Church than there are white members. Islam has also gained many converts in Africa.

Despite the threats to their existence, indigenous religions continue to thrive in several forms throughout the world. In their purest form, they live on in those pockets where modern influence has penetrated the least, such as in Borneo and the Amazon River Basin. They may also coexist, sometimes in diluted form, alongside other religions. In Taiwan, Korea, and Japan, for example, shamanism exists side by side with Buddhism, Christianity, and other religions. (Because the shamans there are often female, their native religious practices allow them roles that are not open to them in the adopted religions.) Indigenous religions have also intermixed with mainstream religions. In the Caribbean, the gods of African religions have sometimes been combined with forms of French and Spanish Catholicism in the religions of Voodoo and Santería (see Chapter 11). In Central America, people who are otherwise practicing Catholics also worship deities of earlier native religions. We see similar types of synthesis in Mexico and the southwestern United States.

In North America, in the Pacific, and in Africa, people have continued or are attempting to restore the practices of their ancestral ways. In New Zealand, for example, Maori culture is experiencing a revival in canoe building, tattooing, dance, and wood sculpture. This attempt at revival is complicated by debates over such issues as land ownership and the introduction of Maori language into schools and public life. In Hawai`i, a renaissance of Hawaiian culture, language, and hula necessarily means retelling the stories of the gods and goddesses of Hawaiian mythology. Some schools now teach all their lessons in Hawaiian, and hula schools are flourishing. Citizens of many native nations in North America are instructing their young in traditional dance and other religious practices. Nevertheless, how to deal with a traditional belief in deities in the face of some dominant monotheistic religions presents intriguing questions. One result, as in the Native American Church, is that beliefs and practices now often incorporate both oral and text-based traditions.

Interest in indigenous religions is a potential restorative for cultures that have moved quickly from their traditional rural homes to homes in the city. In native traditions, we see religion before it was compartmentalized. These holistic traditions make us aware of the religious dimensions that can be found in our own everyday life, and they expand our sensitivity to nature. Their remembrance of the sacred past makes holy the present and the future.

READING

BLACK ELK'S VISION

Black Elk (1863–1950) was raised in traditional Oglala Sioux culture before the U.S. government forced the Sioux and the other Native American tribes of the Great Plains to settle on reservations in the late nineteenth century. This autobiographical passage about his childhood shows the traditional Native American respect for visionary experience.

When I was eating, a voice came and said: "It is time; now they are calling you." The voice was so loud and clear that I believed it, and I thought I would just go where it wanted me to go. So I got right up and started. . . .

The next morning the camp moved again, and I was riding with some boys. We stopped to get a drink from a creek, and when I got off my horse, my legs crumpled under me and I could not walk. So the boys helped me up and put me on my horse; and when we camped again that evening, I was sick. The next day . . . I rode in a pony drag, for I was very sick. Both my legs and both my arms were swollen badly and my face was all puffed up.

When we had camped again, I was lying in our tepee and my mother and father were sitting beside me. I could see out through the opening, and there two men were coming from the clouds. . . . They came clear down to the ground . . . and stood a little way off and looked at me and said: "Hurry! Come! Your Grandfathers are calling you."

They turned and left the ground like arrows slanting upward from the bow. When I got up to follow, my legs did not hurt me any more and I was very light. I went outside the tepee, and yonder where the men with flaming spears were going, a little cloud was coming very fast. It came and stooped and took me and turned back to where it came from, flying fast. And when I looked down, I could see my mother and my father, and I felt sorry to be leaving them.

Then there was nothing but the air and the swiftness of the little cloud that bore me and those two men still leading up to where white clouds were piled like mountains on a wide blue plain, and in them thunder beings lived and leaped and flashed.[43]

TEST YOURSELF

1. Although there is no agreement on how to speak of ancient religious ways, they are often inadequately referred to as traditional, aboriginal, indigenous, tribal, _____, primal, native, oral, and basic.
   a. holistic
   b. shamanistic
   c. nonliterate
   d. *wakan*

2. Indigenous religions exist generally within _____ cultures, in which every object and act may have religious meaning.
   a. holistic
   b. sacred
   c. symbolic
   d. sacrificial

3. In many Native American religious traditions, there is little distinction between the human and animal worlds. These native religions see everything in the universe as being alive, a concept known as _____.
   a. taboo
   b. sacredness
   c. origins
   d. animism

4. Sacred time is "the time of _____."
   Among the Koyukon people of the Arctic, it is called "distant time," and it is the holy ancient past in which gods lived and worked. Among Australian aborigines it is often called "dream time," and it is the subject of much of their highly esteemed art.
   a. eternity
   b. ceremonies
   c. life cycles
   d. gods

5. _____ is the doorway through which the "other world" of gods and ancestors can contact us and we can contact them. It is associated with the center of the universe and can be constructed, often in a symbolic shape such as a circle or square.
   a. Dualism
   b. Sacred space
   c. Ceremony
   d. Eternity

6. Most indigenous religions have cosmic tales of their _____. They frequently speak of a High God and make little distinction between a god and an ancestor.
   a. life cycle
   b. ceremonies
   c. taboos
   d. origins

7. In native societies, everyday religious activity and practice are significant, because their primary purpose is often to place individuals, families, and groups in "right _____" with gods, ancestors, other human beings, and nature.
   a. origins
   b. relationships
   c. ceremonies
   d. taboos

8. Special rituals mark a person's entry into adulthood. In Native American religions, a common ritual of early maturity is the "vision quest," or "_____."
   a. dream quest
   b. trance

   c. sacred time
   d. symbolic death

9. A _____ is a rule that forbids specific behavior with regard to certain objects, people, animals, days, or phases of life.
   a. sacrifice
   b. totem
   c. taboo
   d. divination

10. A(n) _____ acts as an intermediary between the visible, ordinary world and the spirit world.
    a. god
    c. artist
    c. totem
    d. shaman

11. Think of a major problem facing twenty-first century Western society. How might a holistic perspective typical of indigenous religions help in dealing with this problem?

12. Imagine you are assigned a research paper on one of the following topics in indigenous religions: life-cycle ceremonies, taboos, or shamanism. Based on what you have read in this chapter, which one would you most want to investigate and why? What challenges do you think you would encounter while researching this topic?

RESOURCES

Books

Abbott, Isabella Aiona. *La`au Hawai`i: Traditional Hawaiian Uses of Plants.* Honolulu: Bishop Museum Press, 1992. A demonstration by a Hawaiian botanist of the holistic nature of traditional religion. Abbott specifically discusses the religious dimensions of Hawaiian agriculture and the use of plants in religious ceremony and hula.

Achebe, Chinua. *Arrow of God.* New York: Anchor, 1989. An exploration of the breakdown of traditional Igbo beliefs under British colonial rule through the framework of a personal struggle between father and son.

Charlot, John. *Chanting the Universe: Hawaiian Religious Culture.* Hong Kong: Emphasis International, 1983. A well-illustrated presentation of the values and ideas of traditional Hawaiian religion and culture.

Cowan, James. *Aborigine Dreaming.* Wellingborough, UK: Thorsons, 2002. An exploration of the spiritual beliefs of the Australian Aborigines.

Deloria, Vine, Jr. *God Is Red.* Golden, CO: Fulcrum, 1994. An updated version of the classic manifesto of Native American religious rights.

Fitzhugh, William, and Chisato Dubreuil, eds. *Ainu: Spirit of a Northern People.* Seattle: University of Washington Press, 2001. A well-illustrated collection of essays on Ainu history, religion, and culture.

Harvey, Graham. *Shamanism: A Reader.* New York: Routledge, 2002. Articles and extracts that examine shamanism, exploring issues of gender, initiation, hallucinogenic consciousness, and political protest.

Johnston, Basil. *Ojibway Ceremonies*. Lincoln: University of Nebraska Press, 1990. An insider's description of the important traditional ceremonies of his people, including the naming ceremony, marriage ceremony, and funeral ritual.

Pijoan, Teresa. *Pueblo Indian Wisdom*. Santa Fe: Sunstone Press, 2000. A collection of the legends of the Pueblo peoples of New Mexico.

Ray, Benjamin. *African Religions*. 2d ed. Englewood Cliffs, NJ: Prentice-Hall, 1999. A presentation of the most important native African religions, with additional information on Christianity and Islam in Africa.

Silko, Leslie Marmon. *Ceremony*. New York: Penguin, 2006. A novel that shows how an emotionally and spiritually wounded Native American veteran, facing a grim future, is healed by a traditional ceremony arranged by the elders of his tribe.

Vitebsky, Piers. *The Shaman: Voyages of the Soul—Trance, Ecstasy and Healing from Siberia to the Amazon*. London: Duncan Baird, 2001. A colorfully illustrated exploration of the history and practice of shamanism around the world.

Film/TV

Dancing in Moccasins: Keeping Native American Traditions Alive. (Films Media Group.) An examination of how contemporary Native Americans keep their traditions alive.

Earl's Canoe: A Traditional Ojibwe Craft. (Smithsonian Institution Center for Folklife and Cultural Heritage.) A documentary of Earl Nyholm, a member of the Ojibwe Nation, as he builds a canoe according to traditional Ojibwe methods and explains his tribe's beliefs concerning the making and using of canoes.

Healers of Ghana. (Films Media Group.) An exploration of the traditional medical practices of the Bono people of central Ghana, which involve the use of herbs and spirit possession.

The Shaman's Apprentice. (Miranda Productions.) A documentary, filmed in the rain forests of Suriname, that shows efforts by Dr. Mark Plotkin to preserve the rain forest and the religious practices of its people.

Walkabout. (Director Nicholas Roeg; Films Inc.) A classic film about two British children abandoned in the Australian outback and rescued by a young Aborigine who is on a walkabout, a sacred initiation intended to convey a boy into manhood.

Whalerider. (Director Niki Caro; Columbia Tristar.) An exploration of the conflict between Maori tribal tradition and one girl's determination to prove herself as a tribal leader.

Music

The Baoule of the Ivory Coast. (Smithsonian Folkways.) Music from the Baoule tribe of Africa.

The Bora of the Pascoe River, Cape York Peninsula, Northeast Australia. (Smithsonian Folkways.) Stories and songs of the Bora aborigines.

Dogon Music of the Masks and the Funeral Rituals. (Inedit.) A collection of traditional ritual music of the Dogon people of Mali.

Sacred Spirit: Chants and Dances of the Native Americans. (Virgin Records.) A compilation of songs that spans the history and tradition of Native American ritual chant and music.

Uwolani. (Mountain Apple Company.) Twenty traditional Hawaiian chants, including creation chants (*ko`ihonua*), name chants (*mele inoa*), chants to honor gods, and chants to recognize the beauty of places, winds, and rains.

Internet

Center for World Indigenous Studies (CWIS): http://www.cwis.org. A Web site devoted to challenges confronting indigenous peoples, research into indigenous topics, conflict resolution, and related conferences.

The Foundation for Shamanic Studies (FSS): http://www.shamanism.org/. Information about a foundation whose goal is to preserve and teach the religious beliefs of indigenous peoples.

Internet Sacred Text Archive: http://www.sacred-texts.com/index.htm. A large electronic archive that contains sections devoted to the tales and folklore of indigenous religions in Africa, Australia, the Americas, and the Pacific Islands.

United Nations Permanent Forum on Indigenous Issues (UNPFII): http://www.un.org/esa/socdev/unpfii/. The official Web site of the U.N. advisory body that addresses indigenous issues, including economic and social development, culture, the environment, education, health and human rights.

KEY TERMS

calumet: A long-stemmed sacred pipe used primarily by many native peoples of North America; it is smoked as a token of peace.

divination: A foretelling of the future or a look into the past; a discovery of the unknown by magical means.

holistic: Organic, integrated; indicating a complete system, greater than the sum of its parts; here, refers to a culture whose various elements (art, music, social behavior) may all have religious meaning.

libation: The act of pouring a liquid on the ground as an offering to a god.

shaman: A human being who contacts and attempts to manipulate the power of spirits for the tribe or group.

sympathetic magic: An attempt to influence the outcome of an event through an action that has an apparent similarity to the desired result—for example, throwing water into the air to produce rain, or burning an enemy's fingernail clippings to bring sickness to that enemy.

taboo: A strong social prohibition (Tongan: *tabu*; Hawaiian: *kapu*).

totem: An animal (or image of an animal) that is considered to be related by blood to a family or clan and is its guardian or symbol.

Visit the Online Learning Center at www.mhhe.com/molloy5e for additional exercises and features, including "Religion beyond the Classroom" and "For Fuller Understanding."

CHAPTER **3**

Hinduism

❋ FIRST ENCOUNTER

The plane that you have taken to Benares circles in preparation for landing at the Varanasi airport. Looking down from your window seat, you can see the blue-white Ganges River, quite wide here. Everything else is a thousand shades of brown. Beyond the coffee-colored city, the beige fields spread out, seemingly forever.

At the small airport, a dignified customs inspector with a turban and a white beard asks, "Why have you come to India?" Before you can think of an appropriate response, he answers his own question. "I know," he says with a smile and a wave of the hand. "You who come to Benares are all the same." He shakes his head from side to side. "You have come for *spirituality*." After pausing briefly, he adds, "Haven't you!" It sounds more like a statement than a question. It takes you a second to understand his quick pronunciation of that unexpected word—*spirituality.* In a way, he is right. You *have* come for that. You nod in agreement. He smiles again, writes something down on his form, and lets you through.

As you take the small black taxi to your hotel, you realize that you have just accepted—willingly or not—the ancient role that the customs inspector has bestowed upon you. You are now just one more pilgrim who has come to Mother India for her most famous product: religious insight. You are now a Seeker.

After unpacking at your hotel, you walk out into the streets. It is dusk. Pedicab drivers ring their bells to ask if you want a ride, but you want to walk, to see the life of the streets. Little shops sell tea, and others sell vegetarian foods made of potatoes, wheat, beans, and curried vegetables. Children play in front of their parents' stores. Down the street you see a "gent's tailor" shop, as a thin cow wanders past, chewing on what looks like a paper bag. Another shop sells books and note-paper, and others sell saris and bolts of cloth. From some-where comes a smell like jasmine. As night falls, the stores are lit by dim bulbs and fluorescent lights, and vendors illuminate their stalls with bright Coleman lanterns. Because you will be rising long before dawn the next day to go down to the Ganges, you soon return to your hotel. You fall asleep quickly.

The telephone rings, waking you out of a dream. The man at the front desk notifies you that it is four A.M. Being somewhat groggy, you have to remind yourself that you are in Benares. You get up and dress quickly.

At the front of the hotel you wake a driver sleeping in his pedicab. You negotiate the fare, climb onto the seat, and head off to the main crossing of town, near the river, as the sky begins to lighten. The pedicab drops you near the *ghats* (the stairs that descend to the river), which are already full of people, many going down to the river to bathe at dawn. Some are having sandalwood paste applied to their foreheads as a sign of devotion, and others are carrying brass jugs to collect Ganges water.

As you descend to the river, boat owners call to you. You decide to join the passengers in the boat of a man resembling a Victorian patriarch, with a white handlebar mustache. Off you go, moving slowly upstream. Laughing children jump up and down in the water as men and women wade waist-deep and face the rising sun to pray. Upstream, professional launderers beat clothes on the rocks and lay them out on the stones of the riverbank to dry.

The boat turns back downstream, passing the stairs where you first descended to the river. In the bright morning light you see large umbrellas, under which teachers sit cross-legged, some with disciples around them. Who, you wonder, are these teachers? The area near the shore is crammed with people and boats. On a nearby boat, people shout, *Ganga Ma ki Jai*—"Victory to Mother Ganges!"

The boat continues downstream. On the shore, smoke rises from small pyres, where bodies wrapped in red and white cloth are being cremated. The boatman warns, "No photos here, please." The boat pulls in to shore downstream of the pyres, and everyone gets off. Walking up the stairs, you see small groups of people quietly watching the cremations. At the pyres, a man tends the fires with a bamboo pole, and a dog wanders nearby.

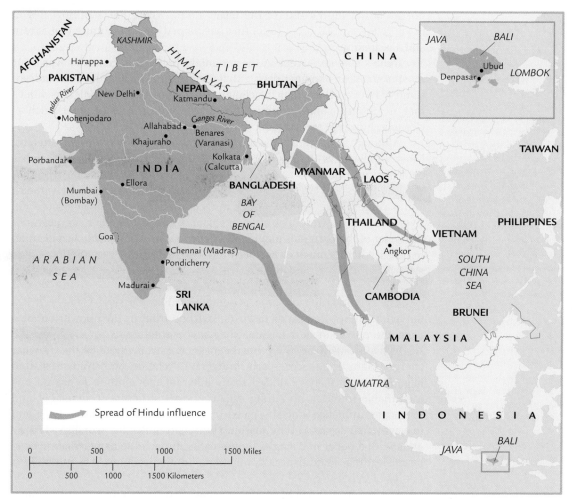

FIGURE 3.1

India, Bali, and the area of Hindu influence.

Later, as you make your way back to the center of town, you notice a pedicab with a covered body tied on the back. It cycles past women sitting beside the road, selling plastic bracelets and colored powders. The pedicab must be on its way to the pyres, you think. The blend of opposites fills your mind: on the banks of the very same river, laundry is washed and bodies are burned; in the streets, life and death appear side by side—yet no one seems to notice the contrasts. Here, the two are one.

THE ORIGINS OF HINDUISM

Looking at a map of India (Figure 3.1) you can see that this subcontinent, shaped like a diamond, is isolated. Two sides face the sea, while the north is bounded by the steep Himalaya Mountains. There are few mountain passes, and the only easy land entry is via the narrow corridor in the northwest, in the vicinity of the Indus River, where Pakistan now lies. It is the relative isolation of India that has helped create a culture that is rare and fascinating.

India's climate, except in the mountain regions, is generally warm for most of the year, allowing people to live outdoors much of the time. Indeed, some may even claim that the climate has helped promote religious values that, at least for some, minimize the importance of material goods such as clothing, housing, and wealth.

Although hot and dry in many parts, India has many rivers and streams. Most important is the Ganges, which flows out of the Himalayas and is enlarged by tributaries as it moves east toward the Bay of Bengal. By the time the Ganges has reached the town of Benares (also known as Varanasi and Kashi), the river is enormous; in fact, after the summer monsoons the river becomes so wide that often one cannot see to the other side. Because the water of the Ganges is regular and dependable, it has enabled civilization to flourish across much of northern India. It has also given Indian culture a sense of security, protection, and even care, which has led to the popular name for the river, *Ganga Ma* ("Mother Ganges").

The religious life of India is something like the river Ganges. It has flowed along for thousands of years, swirling from its own power but also from the power of new streams that have added to its force. Hinduism, the major religion of India, has been an important part of this flowing energy. Many influences—early indigenous religion and influences from later immigrants—have added to its inherent momentum. It has no one identifiable founder, no strong organizational structure to defend it and spread its influence, nor any creed to define and stabilize its beliefs; and in a way that seems to defy reason, Hinduism unites the worship of many gods with a belief in a single divine reality. In fact, the name *Hinduism* can be misleading. Hinduism is not a single, unified religion; it is more like a family of beliefs.

But the limitations of Hinduism may also be its strengths. It is like a palace that began as a two-room cottage. Over the centuries, wings have been built on to it, and now it has countless rooms, stairs, corridors, statues, fountains, and gardens. There is something here to please and astonish—and dismay—almost everyone. In fact, its beliefs are so rich and profound that Hinduism has greatly influenced the larger world, and its influence continues to grow. In this chapter we will explore the various elements of this religion's foundation and the stages in which additions were made to the sprawling house of Hinduism.

The Earliest Stage of Indian Religion

In the early twentieth century, engineers who were building a railroad discovered the ruins of an ancient culture in the Indus River valley. Today, most of the Indus River lies in Pakistan, but it traditionally formed the natural border of northwestern India—in fact, the words *India* and *Hindu*

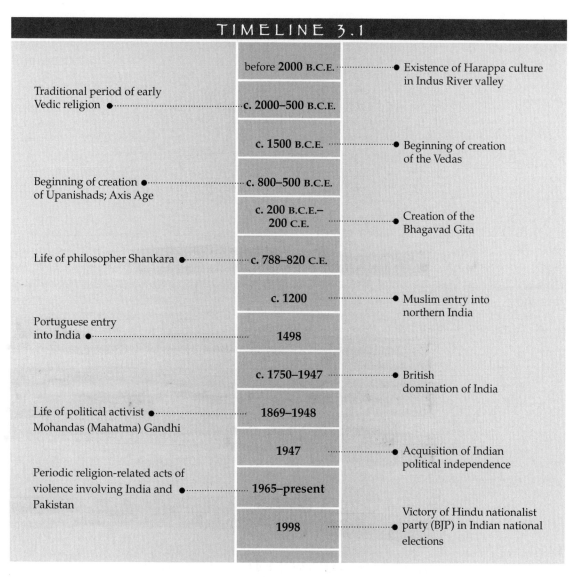

TIMELINE 3.1

	before **2000 B.C.E.** ·········· • Existence of Harappa culture in Indus River valley
Traditional period of early Vedic religion • ·············	**c. 2000–500 B.C.E.**
	c. 1500 B.C.E. ················· • Beginning of creation of the Vedas
Beginning of creation • ············· of Upanishads; Axis Age	**c. 800–500 B.C.E.**
	c. 200 B.C.E.– 200 C.E. ·········· • Creation of the Bhagavad Gita
Life of philosopher Shankara • ·············	**c. 788–820 C.E.**
	c. 1200 ················· • Muslim entry into northern India
Portuguese entry into India • ··············	**1498**
	c. 1750–1947 ·············· • British domination of India
Life of political activist • ············· Mohandas (Mahatma) Gandhi	**1869–1948**
	1947 ················· • Acquisition of Indian political independence
Periodic religion-related acts of violence involving India and • ············· Pakistan	**1965–present**
	1998 ················· • Victory of Hindu nationalist party (BJP) in Indian national elections

Timeline of significant events in the history of Hinduism.

derive from *Indus.* The culture that archeological workers uncovered there flourished before 2000 B.C.E. and is named the Harappa culture, after one of its ancient cities (Timeline 3.1).

Archeologists were amazed by the type of civilization they found. The cities contained regular streets and solid brick houses. Pots and coins were discovered, as well as evidence that running water was used for toilets and baths. As one historian remarks, "no other ancient civilization until that of the Romans had so efficient a system of drains"[1]—a genuine sign of technical development. This complex culture had also invented a writing system, which scholars are still working to decipher.

Property owners marked their belongings with seals bearing the images of animals, such as the bull, tiger, and rhinoceros, as well as images of men and women. Three seals show a male, sitting in a yogic meditation posture, with horns on his head.[2] Small pillars that suggest male sexuality were also found. Because many of these same symbols still appear in contemporary Indian culture, we can assume that some current religious practices have survived from the distant past. For example, the male with the horns on his head may be a deity and an early form of the god Shiva, and the pillars resemble the low columns that some contemporary Indians worship in honor of Shiva. It is also quite possible that the present-day worship of the divine Great Mother and of tree spirits goes back to this early time.

The Religion of the Vedic Period

The ancient scriptures of India are called the **Vedas.** They give a great deal of information about gods and worship during what is often called the Vedic period, generally thought to cover about 2000 to 500 B.C.E. The origin of the Vedas and of the religion they describe, however, is uncertain.

In the late eighteenth century, Western scholars recognized that Sanskrit—the ancient language of India and the language of the Vedas—was related to Greek and Latin. They also realized that many of the gods mentioned in the Vedas were the same gods who had been worshiped in Greece and Rome; they discovered, as well, that gods of similar names were mentioned in Iranian sacred literature. Later scholars theorized that a single people, who called themselves Aryans, moved from present-day southern Russia about 2000 B.C.E. in two directions—westward into Europe and eastward into Iran and India. Entering new lands, these people were thought to have carried their language and religion with them. Scholars initially believed that in India the outsiders imposed their social order quickly and violently on the older culture. According to this theory, called the "Aryan invasion theory," the Vedas were believed to be the religious writings of this invading people.

Next, a variant on the older theory arose: instead of speaking of a single invasion, the newer theory held that there were repeated waves of migrations into Pakistan and northern India, and that from these contacts between foreign and indigenous cultures the religion of the Vedas emerged. More recently, however, this second theory, called the "Aryan migration theory," has been questioned. The migration theory is still commonly held, but some scholars view any theory that assumes influence from outside India to be a continued relic of Western cultural imperialism. Archeological, linguistic, and genetic investigations continue to offer more clues, but their interpretation has not resolved the issue.

No matter what its origins, the religion described by the Vedas seems to have consisted of the worship of mostly male gods, who were believed to control the forces of nature. The father of the gods was Dyaüs Pitr, whose name means "shining father." (He is clearly the same god as the Roman god Jupiter and the Greek god Zeus Pater.) The god Indra, god of storm and war, received great attention because of the strength his worshipers hoped to receive from him. He was possibly the memory of a military ancestor, deified by later generations. The god of fire, Agni (whose name is related to the English word *ignite* and to the Latin word for fire, *ignis*), carried sacrifices up to the world of the gods. Dawn and renewal were the charge of the goddess Ushas, one of the few female deities. The god Rudra brought winds. Varuna was the god of the sky and justice; Vishnu was a god of cosmic order; and Surya was the major sun god. The god Soma was thought to cause altered states of mind and to expand consciousness. He worked through a ritual drink, possibly made from a psychedelic mushroom that had the same name (*soma*) and allowed contact with the realm of the gods. The god Yama ruled the afterlife.

Worship of the gods took place at outdoor fire altars. Priestly specialists set apart a square or rectangular space, purified it with water, and constructed one to three low altars inside the space for sacrifice. The usual offerings were milk, clarified butter (called *ghee*), grains, and sometimes animals. A special horse sacrifice, believed to confer great power on a king, occurred on rare occasions.

Sacred chants, which the priests knew from memory, were an essential part of the ceremonies; and because they believed that the chants had power of their own, the priestly class protected them and handed them down orally from father to son. It is these chants, in written form, that make up the core of the earliest Hindu sacred literature, the Vedas. Although many of the Vedic gods are no longer worshiped, elements of the Aryan religion—such as the use of fire and some of the ancient chants by a priestly class—continue to be of great importance to Hindus today.

The Vedas

The Vedas, which originally were preserved only in oral form but eventually were written down, are the earliest sacred books of Hinduism. The name means "knowledge" or "sacred lore," and related words in English are *vision* and *wisdom*. Although scholars date the earliest versions of the Vedas to about 1500 B.C.E., Hindus consider them to be far more ancient. They say that the Vedas were revealed to *rishis* (holy men of the distant past), who did not create the Vedas but heard them and transmitted them to later generations.

There are four basic sacred text collections that constitute the Vedas. The Rig Veda[3] ("hymn knowledge") is a collection of more than a thousand chants to the Aryan gods; the Yajur Veda ("ceremonial knowledge") contains matter for recitation during sacrifice; the Sama Veda ("chant knowledge") is a handbook of musical elaborations of Vedic chants; and the Atharva Veda ("knowledge from [the teacher] Atharva") consists of practical prayers and charms, such as prayers to protect against snakes and sickness.

The Rig Veda, the most important of the Vedas, has an account of the origin of the universe. The universe is said to have emerged from a division and cosmic sacrifice of a primeval superperson, Purusha. But the account includes an admission of uncertainty: "Who knows it for certain; who can proclaim it here; namely, out of what it was born and wherefrom his creations issued? The gods appeared only later—after the creation of the world. Who knows, then, out of what it has evolved?"[4]

The term *Vedas* sometimes indicates only these four collections. In its more common use, it also refers to some later material as well. Detailed ceremonial rules, called Brahmanas and Aranyakas, were added by later generations to each of the four Vedic collections. The Brahmanas, named for the priests who would use them, give details about the proper time and place for ceremonies, the preparation of the ground, ritual objects, and purification rites. The Aranyakas ("forest books") allowed the rituals to be understood and practiced in nonliteral, symbolic ways by men who had left society and become ascetics in the forests. The four Vedas end with even later works, called the **Upanishads,** which express philosophical and religious ideas that arose in introspective and meditative traditions.

THE UPANISHADS AND THE AXIS AGE

Around 500 B.C.E., Indian civilization experienced such widespread and important changes that the period is known as the Axis Age, meaning that everything turned in a new direction at this time. Interestingly, great changes were also taking place in other religions and cultures as well: it was the time of the Buddha, Confucius, major Hebrew prophets, and early Greek philosophers.

After many centuries, questioning of Vedic religious beliefs and practices began to emerge with strength. It is possible that earlier religious disciplines reasserted themselves, and there may have been resentment against the priestly class. Some critics questioned the value of the Vedic sacrifices, and we know from the Aranyakas that certain people abandoned social life to live alone in the forests, giving themselves much time for thought and religious experimentation. Thinkers questioned the ancient belief in many gods, seeking instead a single divine reality that might be the source of everything.[5] Some went even further and saw all things as being mystically united. And a few rejected religious ritual altogether.

During this period there seems to have been interest in all sorts of techniques for altering consciousness, such as sitting for long periods in meditation, breathing deeply, fasting, avoiding sexual activity, practicing long periods of silence, going without sleep, experimenting with psychedelic plants, and living in the darkness of caves. All of these things could be done by people of any social class—not just by priests. Evidence of this intellectual ferment and the practice of spiritual disciplines is recorded in the Upanishads.

An ascetic carries water
from the Ganges as a cow
pursues its own path.

The Origin of the Upanishads

The Upanishads comprise about a hundred written works that record
insights into external and internal reality. Although several interpretations
of the name *Upanishads* have been proposed, it is commonly thought to
derive from words that mean "sitting near."[6] If the term's derivation is correct, it would suggest disciples sitting near a master, learning techniques
for achieving religious experience. In any case, primary to the Upanishads
is the notion that with spiritual discipline and meditation, both priests and
nonpriests can experience the spiritual reality that underlies all seemingly
separate realities. Unlike much of the earlier Vedic material, which dictates
that only hereditary priests can be religious masters, the Upanishads tell us
that a person who has the necessary experience can be a spiritual master.
The Upanishads thus possibly continue the religious interest of the forest
dwellers of the Aranyakas.

The Upanishads are written primarily in dialogue form, appearing both
as prose and as poetry. Because they were produced over many hundreds

of years, dating them is not easy. It is generally thought that those in prose form (such as the Chandogya, Brihadaranyaka, Taittiriya, and Kena Upanishads) may be earlier works than those in poetic form (such as the Katha and Mandukya Upanishads). About a dozen Upanishads are especially popular.

Important Concepts of the Upanishads

The most important notions in the Upanishads are *Brahman, Atman, maya, karma, samsara,* and *moksha.* These primary concepts, which would become essential notions in much later Hindu spirituality, continue to be taught today.

Brahman and Atman   The term **Brahman** originally stood for the cosmic power present in the Vedic sacrifice and chants, over which the priest had control. (The Sanskrit word *Brahman* is neuter and comes from a stem meaning "to be great.") In the Upanishads the word *Brahman* was expanded to mean a divine reality at the heart of things. One of the most famous dialogues appears in the Chandogya Upanishad. It involves a priestly father and his son in discussion. The young man, Shvetaketu, has been away, studying with a specialist for many years. He has memorized chants and learned priestly rituals. The young man's father questions him about what he has learned, and the son proudly recites the formulas he knows. The father then asks him what he knows about Brahman, the Supreme Spirit; but the young man knows nothing. Trying to assist the son's understanding, the

Brahmins, priests from the highest caste, pray at the beginning of a religious ceremony on the island of Bali.

father asks his son to fill a glass with water, put salt in it, and leave it overnight. The next day he asks his son to find the salt:

"Bring me the salt you put into the water last night."
Shvetaketu looked into the water, but could not find it, for it had dissolved.
His father then said: "Taste the water from this side. How is it?"
"It is salt [salty]."
"Taste it from the middle. How is it?"
"It is salt."
"Taste it from that side. How is it?"
"It is salt."
"Look for the salt again and come again to me."
The son did so, saying: "I cannot see the salt. I only see water."
The father then said: "In the same way, O my son, you cannot see the Spirit. But in truth he is here.
"An invisible and subtle essence is the Spirit of the whole universe. That is Reality. That is Truth. Thou art That."[8]

The Upanishads insist that Brahman is something that can be known—not simply believed in. The Shvetasvatara Upanishad, for example, says "I *know* that Spirit whose infinity is in all, who is ever one beyond time."[9] Brahman, the Divine Spirit, is so real that it may be known directly, and, as the boy Shvetaketu learned, knowledge of it can be as immediate as tasting the flavor of salt.

What is it to know Brahman? The Upanishads insist that it cannot be put fully into words, but they give hints. Brahman is the lived experience that all things are in some way holy because they come from the same sacred source. It is also the experience that all things are in some way ultimately one. This is an experience that seems to defy common sense, since the world appears to be divided into many objects and types of reality. Nevertheless, when we consider reality more deeply, we recognize many unities: a piece of wood can become a boat or a house or fire or ash; water can turn into a cloud or a plant. So, on closer inspection, all apparent separations and divisions blur. To experience Brahman is to know, firsthand, that every apparently individual reality in the world is actually a wave of the same sacred ocean of energy. Brahman, according to the Upanishads, "is the sun, the moon, and the stars. He is the fire, the waters, and the wind."[10] Brahman is "the God who appears in forms infinite."[11]

Brahman is also referred to by three words that help describe its nature as perceived by the knower: Brahman is *sat*, reality itself; *chit*, pure consciousness; and *ananda*, bliss. And although Brahman can be experienced within our everyday world of time and space, those who speak of their experience say that Brahman is ultimately beyond time and beyond space. Thus the Upanishads often add that experiencing the timelessness of Brahman can bring an end to everyday suffering and to the fear of death.

The notion of **Atman** is related to Brahman and is an equally important term in the Upanishads. Although Atman is sometimes translated as "self" or "soul," the notion of Atman in the Upanishads is different from the notion of an individual soul. Perhaps the term *Atman* would be better translated as "deepest self." (Sometimes it is translated as "subtle self.") In Hindu belief, each person has an individual soul (*jiva*), and the individual soul confers uniqueness and personality. But Hinduism asks this question: At the very deepest level, what really am I? I am clearly not just my body—my height and weight and hair color, all of which are subject to alteration. But am I then my tastes, thoughts, and memories? Or is there more? Is there not in me a reality more fundamental than those changing individual characteristics? According to the Upanishads, at the deepest level of what I am is a divine reality, a divine spirit, that everything shares. The Upanishads teach that it is true to say that I am God, because, for the person who understands reality at the deepest level, everything is God. Atman, when experienced fully, is identical with Brahman. Atman, like Brahman, is divine, holy, and timeless. Often the term *Brahman* refers to the experience of the sacred within nature and the external universe, while *Atman* refers to the experience of the sacred within oneself. However, the same divine nature simply has two names, and both terms may be used interchangeably.

Maya   The Upanishads speak of the everyday world as **maya,** which is usually translated as "illusion."[12] This translation, though, needs explanation. Its root suggests illusion and mystery (as in "magic"), but it also has a more positive, objective connotation that suggests the original stuff of which something is made (as in "material"). The word *maya* thus contains both meanings: "magic" and "matter." To say that all reality is "maya" is not to say that the world does not exist or that the world is a totally false perception. The world is real, but not in quite the way most people assume. For one thing, human beings view the world as consisting of individual things and people, all separate. In reality, the world is one basic holy reality that takes on many different forms. The Shvetasvatara Upanishad advises us to "know therefore that nature is Maya, but that God is the ruler of Maya; and that all beings in our universe are parts of his infinite splendour."[13]

People also assume that the world is solid and permanent. In reality, the outside world is more like the inner world of thoughts and dreams—it shifts and changes, just as thoughts and dreams do. People assume that time is real, that it advances at a regular rate, and that past, present, and future are distinct divisions. In reality, time is relative.

The model of reality set forth by the Upanishads is less like a machine made of individual moving parts; it is more like a great consciousness. This view also produces a sense of amazement at the forms and shifts that the universe takes—it is all, ultimately, unexplainable magic.

As I look out at reality from my own individual standpoint, I may see the end of my life as the end of everything. The Upanishads see things differently. First, individuals are not as individual as they suppose. Rather, they are all manifestations of the Divine Spirit, which does not end when the individual dies. They are also the continuation of earlier forms of life that have simply taken new forms. Hinduism, from about 500 B.C.E., generally adopted the belief that everything living has its own life force and that every life force, when it loses one form, is reborn into another. This process is known as reincarnation.

Karma   The general Hindu notion of rebirth assumes that human beings have at one or another time existed as a "lower" form, such as animal, insect, and possibly even plant. Hinduism also recognizes grades of human life, from limited and painful to exceptionally pleasant and free. Human beings are also capable of achieving "higher" forms of life, such as superhuman beings and demigods. Rebirth can move in either direction, and the human stage is a dangerous one because each human being must make dramatic choices about how to live. If a human being does not live properly, he or she may be reborn into a very poor or cruel human family—or possibly in a form of life that may be even more limited and difficult, such as a dog, a pig, or an ant. A human being can also make a spectacular leap upward beyond the human level to a superhuman existence or even beyond, to complete freedom.

What determines the direction of one's rebirth is **karma.** The word comes from a root that means "to do" and implies the notion of moral consequences that are carried along with every act. Karma is the moral law of cause and effect, and belief in karma is a belief that every action has an automatic moral consequence. One well-known saying expresses nicely the nature of karma: What goes around comes around. Karma does not work because it is the will of God or Brahman, but simply because karma is an essential part of the nature of things. It is the way things work. Good karma brings "higher" rebirth; bad karma brings rebirth in "lower," more painful forms. In a certain way, this belief allows for upward mobility, since human beings, by their actions, have influence over their future births. Ultimate freedom comes when karma ceases to operate; rebirth, whether upward or downward on the scale, has entirely ended.

Some teachers say that karma is intrinsically neither good nor bad but only seems so to the person who experiences it. In this conception, karma is like gravity—it works like a force of nature. It is like rain, which can cause a plant to grow just as it can bring a picnic to its end. Karma helps explain why some people are born with great gifts while others are born with no advantages at all.

Samsara   The term **samsara** refers to the wheel of life, the circle of constant rebirth, and it suggests strongly that the everyday world is full of change as well as struggle and suffering. The Hindu view of human life, because of its belief in reincarnation, is rather different from that commonly held in the West. Think of how often you hear someone say, "You only live once." This view of life is not shared by Hindus, who believe an individual is constantly being reborn, having come from different earlier forms and going on to emerge in new forms in the future. Because our present human life is so short, we may think that we would like several lives in the future as well. But how many would each of us really like? Ten might sound reasonable, but a hundred? a thousand? ten thousand? a million? It's tiring just to think about all those lifetimes! And many of those forms would inevitably be unhappy ones. Sooner or later most of us would want to jump off the merry-go-round of life. We would want escape, release, liberation. This leads us to the next important concept of the Upanishads.

Moksha   The term **moksha** means "freedom" or "liberation" and comes from a root that means "to be released." In the Upanishads, moksha is the ultimate human goal. It has various connotations. Moksha certainly includes the notion of getting beyond egotistic responses, such as resentment and anger, which limit the individual. Furthermore, unlike the modern ideal of seeking complete freedom to satisfy one's individual desires, moksha implies liberation even from the limitations of being an individual—from being born a particular person at a specific time to a unique pair of parents—a person with distinct physical characteristics, emotions, desires, and memories. One can take action to overcome these restrictions (for example, by leaving home), which is sometimes a means of attaining moksha, but one can also accept the limitations even while living with them, thereby gaining inner peace and mental freedom.

As one becomes freer, one looks at life less from a selfish and egotistic point of view and more from a perspective that embraces the whole. The unity and sacredness that everything shares become a part of everyday experience. Kindness to all—to animals as well as to people—is one natural result of this insight, and kind actions also generate helpful karma. Detaching oneself from pleasure or pain is another practice that leads to freedom from egotism.

Ultimately, with enough insight and ascetic practice, the individual can go entirely beyond the limited self to know the sacred reality that everything shares. When insight and kindness are perfect, at last the pain of rebirth ends; the limitations of individuality are gone, and only Brahman remains. The Brihadaranyaka Upanishad explains complete freedom: "when all has become Spirit, one's own Self, how and whom could one see?"[14]

The Upanishads, though sometimes obscure, are devoted to promoting an insight into ultimate oneness. But the Upanishads do not give detailed instructions for achieving that kind of insight or for living spiritually in the everyday world. Such guidance would have to be developed by later Hindu commentators and practitioners.

LIVING SPIRITUALLY IN THE EVERYDAY WORLD

The Hinduism that guides people's lives today is a practical mixture of elements. Some of these came from the early stages of religious practice, which we've already discussed, and others developed later. For the ordinary layperson, Hindu practice usually involves devotion to at least one deity. It recommends finding one's proper work and then doing it unselfishly. Hindu practice may also include the study of religious texts, meditation, and other specifically religious disciplines. The following section will deal with the elements of this practical synthesis, much of which can be found in the short classic, the Bhagavad Gita.

The Bhagavad Gita

The **Bhagavad Gita** ("divine song" or "song of the Divine One") is part of a very long epic poem called the Mahabharata. The Mahabharata, written some time between 400 B.C.E. and 400 C.E., tells how the sons of Pandu (Pandavas) conquered their cousins, the Kauravas, with the help of the god Krishna. The Bhagavad Gita was inserted at some time into this poem but has its own identity and is often printed separately from the Mahabharata. The Bhagavad Gita, shaped by the priestly class between 200 B.C.E. and 200 C.E., has become a spiritual classic. It recalls themes from the Upanishads, but it also tries to strike a balance between mysticism and the practical needs of everyday life. Action and adherence to duty are approved and can even be thought of as a spiritual path. As the Bhagavad Gita says, "the wise see knowledge and action as one."[15]

This miniature of Krishna and the *gopis* (milkmaids) dates from the second half of the eighteenth century.

The Bhagavad Gita, like the Upanishads, is written in dialogue form. It occurs almost entirely between two figures: a prince, Arjuna, and his charioteer and advisor, Krishna. Arjuna's royal power is threatened by his hundred cousins, called Kauravas, and he must decide whether to fight with his brothers against them to restore his throne or to accept their rule. He is torn. On the one hand, he knows that his rule is correct, but on the other, he wants to avoid violence. That his enemies are close family members makes the matter even harder. Depressed, Arjuna "[throws] aside his arrows and his bow in the midst of the battlefield. He [sits] down on the seat of the chariot, and his heart [is] overcome with sorrow."[16] In response, Krishna, who later reveals that he is a form of the god Vishnu, explains the need for action. "Now you shall hear how a man may become perfect, if he devotes himself to the work which is natural to him. A man shall reach perfection if he does his duty as an act of worship to the Lord."[17] This means that Arjuna must follow not merely his own desires—neither his fears nor his hope for reward— but he must simply do what is right.

Contrary to the teaching of nonviolence, which was at the time of this epic's creation growing strong in India in such religious traditions as Buddhism and Jainism, Krishna advises Arjuna to fight to protect his throne and the structure of society—to fight is his duty. At a moment of great revelation, Krishna shows Arjuna that a divine reality is at work within everything in the universe—in living and also in dying. Krishna even says that for the warrior "there is nothing nobler than a righteous war.[18]

The recommendation that Arjuna should fight has posed a moral problem for some followers of Hinduism. Mohandas Gandhi (1869–1948) is typical of those who have solved this problem by saying that the Bhagavad Gita is religious allegory. Gandhi held that the call to arms is not about real war but rather a call to fight against dangerous moral and psychological forces, such as ignorance, selfishness, and anger. This interpretation, though it seems to go against the literal intent of the text, has been influential.

The Caste System

When Krishna urges Arjuna to do what his position as a warrior demands, he is reinforcing the **caste** system (a division of society into social classes that are created by birth or occupation). The caste system, the prevalent social system of Hinduism, had already been mentioned in the Rig Veda: "When they divided Purusha [the first person, a superbeing], in how many different portions did they arrange him? What became of his mouth, what of his two arms? What were his two thighs and his two feet called? His mouth became the brahman [priest]; his two arms were made into the rajanya [warrior-noble]; his two thighs the vaishyas [merchants]; from his two feet the shudra [peasant] was born."[19]

The caste system receives further religious approval in the Bhagavad Gita, which recognizes that there are different types of people and that their ways to perfection will differ, depending on their personality types and roles in society.[20] For example, active people will perfect themselves through the unselfishness of their work, and intellectual people will perfect themselves through teaching and study.

Traditionally, the caste system was based on more than one's type of work, and in modern times it does not always indicate the type of work a person does. Castes (as the term is commonly used) are really social classes (*varna*), which are subdivided into hundreds of subcastes.[21] The caste system dissuades members of different castes, and often subcastes, from intermarrying. It remains strongest in the countryside and in more conservative southern India, but it is weakening in the cities, where people regularly eat together in restaurants and travel together in buses and trains. Although an individual cannot change the caste into which she or he is born, it is believed that a good life in one's present caste will guarantee rebirth in a higher caste or better circumstances. Thus, from the perspective of Hinduism, upward social mobility is possible—even if it takes more than one lifetime to accomplish!

Members of society are divided into five main social classes:

1. The priest **(brahmin)**[22] traditionally performs Vedic rituals and acts as a counselor.
2. The warrior-noble (*kshatriya*) has the role of protecting society. This is the traditional caste of the aristocracy.
3. The merchant (*vaishya*) class includes landowners, moneylenders, and sometimes artisans. Males of the three upper castes (brahmin, kshatriya, and vaishya) receive a sacred cord during a ceremony in their youth and afterward are called "twice-born."
4. The peasant (*shudra*) does manual labor and is expected to serve the higher castes. The origin of this caste probably goes back to the Aryan subjection of native people, who were forced to do the work of servants. The peasant is called "once-born."
5. The untouchable (*dalit*) traditionally does the dirtiest work—cleaning toilets, sweeping streets, collecting animal carcasses, and tanning animal hides. Their low status prompted the Indian reformer Mohandas Gandhi to promote another name for the class—*Harijan* ("children of God")—and he urged their inclusion in regular society.[23]

The Stages of Life

Just as the individual's path to "correct action" is suggested by caste and subcaste, traditional Hinduism holds that each stage of life also has its proper way of being lived. Every culture recognizes specific life stages through which each individual passes. In modern secular life the stages seem to be childhood, adolescence, the career years, and retirement (these stages are strongly colored by employment—or the lack of it); but in India the notion of life stages is more religious. The conception was shaped by the ancient ideal of the development of the upper-caste male, particularly of the priestly caste:

1. Student (*brahmacharin*): This first stage is spent laying a religious foundation for life. The young person, between the ages of 8 and 20, studies religious works. Celibacy is a necessary part of the training.
2. Householder (*grihastha*): Marriage (traditionally, arranged by the parents) occurs at about age 20, and the person fulfills the demands of society by raising children.
3. Retiree (*vanaprastha*): When grandchildren arrive, the individual may retire somewhat from ordinary life to spend time once again on religious matters. The ancient ideal was to go into the forest to live, possibly with one's wife, away from society. In reality, retirees often continue to live with their children and with other relatives in an extended-family setting, but they may eat separately from the rest of the family and spend time on religious pursuits with friends.
4. Renunciate **(sannyasin):** To enter this last stage is considered to be appropriate only after retirement. It is not expected of everyone but is

simply an option. If one wishes to live entirely free from society, one is permitted to leave home. For such a person, the entire world is now his home. A man may leave his wife, although he must ensure that she will be supported. Celibacy is expected, and the sign of this devout, celibate state is an orange robe. The sannyasin, considered to be outside the caste system, is free to wander, begging his food along the way, and many temples have endowments to feed such pilgrims. The sannyasin may remain a constant traveler, making pilgrimage to the sacred sites of India, or he may settle in an **ashram** (religious community) or even live in a cave. The purpose of this kind of life is to hasten mystical insight, to free oneself of all attachments, to end rebirth, and to attain moksha.

The Goals of Life

Although the Hindu spiritual ideal—such as the lifestyle of the sannyasin—is generally world-denying, Hinduism also exhibits a respect for more worldly goals. In order of increasing value these goals are pleasure (*kama*), economic security and power (*artha*), and social and religious duty (*dharma*). These life goals, which may be pursued simultaneously, are acceptable and even virtuous, as long as they are tempered by moderation and social regulation. Considered highest of the goals, however, is moksha—complete freedom.

The Yogas

Although the Bhagavad Gita endorses quiet contemplation, it also recommends active spiritual paths. It endorses not only meditation but also the work demanded by one's caste and individual place in society. The various types of **yoga** are methods that can be used to help people live spiritually. The word *yoga* means "union" and is related to the English words *join* and *yoke*. A yoga is a way for people to perfect their union with the divine, and because the yogas suggest roads to perfection, they are also called *margas* ("paths"). There is a tolerant recognition in Hinduism that different sorts of people need different spiritual paths, and an individual's caste and personality type will help determine the appropriate yoga to practice.

Jnana Yoga ("Knowledge Yoga")   This type of yoga brings insight into one's divine nature by studying the Upanishads and the Bhagavad Gita and their commentaries and by learning from teachers who have attained insight. **Jnana yoga** is particularly appropriate for priests and intellectuals.

This yoga was highly refined by a school of philosophy that is still quite vital, the school of Vedanta ("Veda end").[24] The term refers to the Upanishads— which come at the end of the Vedas—and to the fact that the Vedanta school has used the ideas of the Upanishads as its primary inspiration.

The greatest teacher of Vedanta, Shankara (c. 788–820), argued that everything is ultimately one—all is Brahman.[25] According to Shankara, although our ordinary experience leads us to see things as being separate and different, this perception is mistaken. To show that sense perception can be wrong, Shankara used the example of a person who at dusk is frightened by a coil of rope—the observer mistakenly perceives the rope to be a snake. In the same way, Shankara would say, a person who perceives things as being ultimately separate and different from Brahman is mistaken. In his *Crest-Jewel of Discrimination,* the author likened Brahman to gold, which can take many shapes. Brahman "is that one Reality which appears to our ignorance as a manifold universe of names and forms and changes. Like the gold of which many ornaments are made, it remains in itself unchanged. Such is Brahman, and 'That art Thou.' Meditate upon this truth."[26] Similarly, the waves of the ocean and the drops of water in the waves may be considered separate entities; but the larger truth is that they are all just the same ocean in varied, changing forms.

Shankara thought that spiritual liberation was achieved when the individual personally came to understand the unity of all things. Shankara so emphasized **monism**—the oneness of everything—that his branch of the Vedanta school is called *Advaita,* which, literally translated, means "not-two-ness" (*a-dvai-ta*). The significance of the term is very subtle. If I say that all reality is "one," some "other" reality could also exist—something in contrast to the one. But the term *not-two* makes clear that ultimately there is no other reality.

For Shankara, therefore, any devotion to a god or goddess who is thought to be different from the worshiper is also mistaken. This rejection of devotion, however, posed a great problem for those types of Hinduism that emphasized it. As a result, later thinkers of the Vedanta school, such as Ramanuja (d. 1137) and Madhva (active 1240), qualified or denied ultimate monism. They emphasized passages in the Upanishads that seem to speak of Brahman as being separate in some way from the world. They could thereby create systems that made room for religious devotion.

Karma Yoga ("Action Yoga")   This type of yoga proposes that all useful work, if done unselfishly, can be a way to perfection. (The word *karma* here is used in its basic sense of "activity.") Much of what we ordinarily do is motivated by money or pleasure or praise, but deeds performed without a desire for reward are the heart of **karma yoga**. As the Bhagavad Gita says, "Desire for the fruits of work must never be your motive in working."[27]

Bhakti Yoga ("Devotion Yoga")   Most of us have at one time or another fallen in love, and we know that there is something purifying about the experience, because it forces us to look outward, beyond ourselves, to another object of affection. Religions utilize this purifying power when they promote devotion to a god or saint—who is often made visible in a painting or statue. Hinduism, because of its belief in multiple gods, offers rich possibilities for devotion. In the Bhagavad Gita, Krishna tells Arjuna, "Regard me as your dearest loved one. Know me to be your only refuge."[28]

Hindu Meditation: More Than Emptying the Mind

Over the past three decades, meditation has become popular in the Western world. From students in elementary schools to executives in corporate offices, all kinds of people take time out to sit quietly, empty the mind, and let stress float away.

Meditation in Eastern religious traditions, however, is more complex, at least theoretically. The Yoga Sutras, often attributed to the grammarian Patanjali,[29] list eight steps necessary for perfection of meditation:

- Self-control (*yama*) is the fundamental reorientation of the personality away from selfishness. It involves practicing **ahimsa** (not hurting living beings), exhibiting sexual restraint, shunning greed, refusing to steal, and embracing truthfulness.
- Observance (*niyama*) is the regular practice of the five preceding virtuous pursuits.

- Posture (*asana*) is an integral aspect of meditation, particularly the "lotus posture" (*padmasana*), in which the person meditating is seated with the legs crossed, each foot touching the opposite leg.
- Breath control (*pranayama*) involves deep, regular breathing, holding the breath, and breathing in various rhythms.
- Restraint (*pratyahara*) helps the meditator tune out external distractions.
- Steadying of the mind (*dharana*) teaches the meditator to focus on only one object in order to empty the mind of everything else.
- Meditation (**dhyana**) occurs when the mind is focused only on the object of concentration.
- **Samadhi** is the mental state achieved by deep meditation, in which the individual loses the sense of being separate from the rest of the universe.[30]

Bhakti yoga can involve various expressions of devotion—most commonly chants, songs, food offerings, and the anointing of statues. Bhakti yoga can extend also to acts of devotion shown to one's **guru** (spiritual teacher), to one's parents, and to one's spouse. The gods worshiped in bhakti yoga will be described later.

Raja Yoga ("Royal Yoga") This type of yoga promotes meditation. The term **raja yoga** does not appear in the Bhagavad Gita but was introduced later to refer to the steps of meditation described in the box "Hindu Meditation: More Than Emptying the Mind." Nonetheless, chapter 6 of the Bhagavad Gita describes basic meditation—sitting quietly, turning inward, and calming the mind. Done for short periods of time on a regular basis, meditation lowers stress and brings a sense of peace; done for longer periods of time, it can induce new states of consciousness.

There are many types of meditation. Some involve emptying the mind of thought; others involve focusing on some physical or mental object. Meditation can be done with one's eyes closed or open or focused on a point a short distance in front of the face. A word or brief phrase, called a **mantra,** is often recited with each breath to help clear the mind of thought. (The short mantra *Om*—which is sometimes called the sound of creation—is frequently used.) Meditation can be done in silence or to gentle music; it can also be done while gazing at a candle, at the moon, or at moving water. Some advanced types of meditation involve techniques taken from additional yogas. They may have the meditator create symbolic mental images (frequently of a deity), contemplate a sacred diagram (called a *yantra*), or repeat complicated sacred phrases. The many techniques of meditation are called *sadhanas* ("practices").

Hatha Yoga ("Force Yoga")   When most of us in the West think of yoga, we think of the physical exercises of hatha yoga. These exercises, which were originally developed to help make long periods of meditation easier, mostly involve stretching and balancing. Breathing exercises are usually considered a part of hatha yoga.

There are many schools of hatha yoga, often named after their founders. Several have gained great popularity. Among them, Iyengar yoga focuses on correct technique and sequence in doing a large number of traditional breathing exercises and yoga

In recent years, yoga has become a part of daily life for millions of people across the planet.

postures. Bikram yoga involves a series of twenty-six hatha yoga exercises and two breathing exercises in a heated room (the heat is meant to make the muscles limber and to assist circulation). Ashtanga yoga, named after teachings of the Yoga Sutras, is a demanding series of six sequences of highly athletic yogic postures.

Kundalini Yoga   Combining elements of both raja yoga and hatha yoga, **Kundalini yoga** teaches that there are seven psychic centers, called *chakras* ("wheels"), that exist, one above the other, along the spinal column. Meditation and physical exercises (as described below) help the meditator lift spiritual energy—called *kundalini* and envisioned as a coiled serpent—from one center to the next. (Literally *kundalini* means "she who lies coiled.") Each chakra is like a gateway through which the kundalini passes, bringing increased insight and joy. When the kundalini reaches the topmost and seventh center of energy at the crown of the head, the practitioner experiences profound bliss. The topmost center of energy (*sahasrara*) appears in imagery as a lotus flower, and reaching it is compared to the opening of a lotus.

In addition to these six yogas are others. In fact, any systematic set of techniques that leads to greater spirituality can be considered a yoga.

DEVOTIONAL HINDUISM

Indians have been primarily a rural, agricultural people, and even today only about 15 percent of the population lives in cities. The rest live, as they have for centuries, in more than half a million villages. Men in the villages spend most of their waking hours working as merchants, craftsmen, and farmers, while women marry when young and spend most of their time preparing

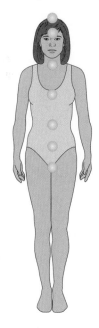

The chakras are centers through which energy rises from the base of the spine to the crown of the head.

food, running their households, and caring for their children. The duties of everyday life leave little time to pursue more philosophical paths.

For the majority of Hindus, then, some of the spiritual disciplines just mentioned—study, meditation, and special physical exercises—have had limited appeal. Instead, the great majority of Hindus have followed the path of devotion **(bhakti)** to a god or gods. Hindus worship their gods in village temples and at home altars. Most worship daily, and there are special days dedicated to individual gods. **Puja,** devotional ritual commonly performed at an altar, involves the offering of flowers, food, fire, and incense to images of a god or gods, as well as the occasional singing of hymns.

The earliest layer of devotional Hinduism, probably traceable to the Harappa culture, seems to have involved the anointing of phallic stones, devotion to female divinities of fertility, and the worship of nature spirits. This type of religious devotion continues in India today.

The Vedic religion introduced its own gods as additional objects of worship. Some of these, such as Indra and Agni, were once highly popular, while others, such as Dyaüs Pitr, lost devotees and moved to the background quite early. In this devotional pattern we can see that a certain fluctuation of interest is natural: throughout history, in all religious devotion, interest in some gods rises and interest in others fades away.

Certain gods and goddesses seem to have emerged separately, not as a part of the Vedic pantheon—of these Krishna is one of the best known. Some animal forms became deified, and all deities were eventually incorporated loosely into what is today a fairly large pantheon.

Although Hinduism is often described as a religion that promotes a belief in many gods, in reality individuals tend to focus their devotion on only one of the gods. Sometimes that god is considered to be the greatest of all divine manifestations. There are also strong tendencies in Hinduism toward both monotheism and even monism, because all gods—and everything else as well—are considered, ultimately, to be expressions of a single divine reality. Devotion to an individual god or goddess is often justified by saying that although the divine is ultimately formless, human beings must worship the divine through its physical manifestations. This belief gives rise to much painting, sculpture, music, and ceremony in honor of many gods, who are described in the following sections.

The Trimurti: Brahma, Vishnu, and Shiva

Three gods have been particularly important in the devotional and artistic life of Hinduism. Although of differing origins, they have sometimes been linked together—particularly in philosophy and art, where they represent the three forces of creation, preservation, and destruction. The three gods are Brahma, Vishnu, and Shiva. When linked together, they are often called the **Trimurti,** which means "triple form."

Brahma represents the creative force that made the universe. He is considered the personal aspect of Brahman and has been thought of as the special patron of the priestly class, the brahmins. Brahma is commonly depicted as an ancient, thoughtful king sitting on a throne. He has four faces, each looking in one of the four directions, and eight arms, each holding symbols of power. His companion animal is a white goose.

In India, worship of Brahma as a separate deity has declined over the past two hundred years, although he is still frequently represented in art, where he is pictured beside Vishnu or Shiva. Perhaps this decline in interest resulted from the popular view of Brahma in India as grandfatherly, distant, and less powerful than either Vishnu or Shiva. (Ironically, however, devotion to Brahma remains quite alive in Thailand, where local Buddhist practice shows many influences from Hinduism. Statues of Brahma appear frequently in outdoor "spirit houses," where food and flowers—and sometimes dance—are offered to him for good luck and protection.)

Vishnu represents the force of preservation in the universe. In the Vedas he is a god associated with the sun, although his role there appears to be small. Thought of as light and warmth that destroys darkness, Vishnu grew in stature until finally becoming a major god of Hinduism. Today Vishnu (in various forms) is the most important object of devotion in India, and about three quarters of all Hindus in India worship him or his manifestations. His followers are called Vaishnavites (or Vaishnavas).

In painting and sculpture, Vishnu is shown in many forms, though usually with a tall crown and a regal manner. Almost always he has four arms,

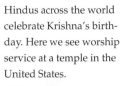

Hindus across the world celebrate Krishna's birthday. Here we see worship service at a temple in the United States.

Stories involving Rama are part of Hindu-influenced cultures throughout Southeast Asia. In this staging of one popular story, Rama heads off to recapture his kidnapped wife, Sita.

which hold symbols of power. His companion animal is a great eaglelike bird, Garuda, on whom he flies through the universe.

Because Vishnu is associated with loving-kindness, it is believed that he can appear on earth at different times and in various physical forms to help those in need. Ten major incarnations (or **avatars**) of Vishnu are commonly listed, of which one is still to appear. Some previous incarnations were in animal form: a fish, a boar, and a tortoise. Another was Siddhartha Gautama, the Buddha—an intriguing inclusion, which helped Hinduism partially reabsorb Indian Buddhism (see Chapter 4). The incarnation yet to come will be a savior figure on horseback who will judge the human race. Two incarnations of Vishnu are wildly popular—Rama and Krishna.

Rama may have been a historical figure who later took on mythic proportions. He appears in the great epic the Ramayana, whose stories have inspired dance as well as art. Rama and his wife, Sita, who are thought of as the ideal couple, are often portrayed together. One of the most commonly told stories concerns the abduction of Sita by Ravan (or Ravana), the demon king of Sri Lanka. Rama, a king, gains the help of Hanuman, leader of the monkeys. Hanuman helps Rama in killing Ravan and in locating and returning Sita. Perhaps because of his image as a helper, Hanuman is today an immensely popular god in his own right. In northern India, Rama is so revered that the term *Ram,* or *Rama,* is really a synonym for "God."

Krishna, another incarnation of Vishnu, may have begun as an object of fertility worship. He is depicted in several forms, which might indicate that he is a coalescence of traditions. In the long epic the Mahabharata, Krishna appears as a mature and solemn god. In later devotional works, the Puranas

The lobby of Bangkok's modern International Airport features this sculpture based on the Mahabharata. It depicts Vishnu helping gods and demons to churn the elixir of immortality from a sea of milk.

("legends"), he is younger; there he is friends with *gopis* (milkmaids who look after herds of cows), and he steals butter and plays the flute, expressing the playful aspect of the divine. In depictions of Krishna, his face and skin are often blue, the color of the sky and of heaven, indicating his true other-worldly nature. His closest milkmaid companion is Radha, with whom he is romantically linked in the Hindu mind.

Shiva, the third of the Trimurti and the god linked with destruction, is the most complicated of the gods, both in origin and in conception. The horned figure, sitting in yogic meditation posture, that is found on seals from the Harappa period may be an early form of Shiva, meaning that some aspects of the present-day god may extend back to pre-Vedic India. Another early form is apparently the Vedic god Rudra, a dangerous god of mountains and winds, whom worshipers probably began to call *shiva* ("lucky") in order to neutralize the fear he inspired. In later times, however, his link with destructiveness is often shown in pictures of Shiva appearing at cremation grounds above a human body that is dissolving in flames.

Shiva's connection with destruction may be hard for many non-Hindus to appreciate. In some religions, destruction is associated with divine punishment for wrongdoing. In Hinduism, however, destruction is considered to be simply another part of the divine energy at work in the world. Destruction is a type of recycling, the necessary loss of form, which occurs so that new forms may appear; and death is always thought of as leading to new life. We know that the seed disappears when the tree grows, and the flower must die to make the fruit. Thus Shiva is also associated with re-creation.

The elephant-headed god Ganesha, son of Shiva, is believed to help devotees overcome obstacles. People often pause before depictions of Ganesha to ask for success.

The destructive side of Shiva is portrayed in the bronze statues called *Shiva Nataraja* ("ruler of the dance"). As he dances, Shiva is surrounded by a ring of fire, which shows his ability to destroy and transform. His long yogi's hair flies in the air. He has four arms, which signify his many powers. In his upper right arm is a drum, symbolizing creation and the beginning of time; and in the upper left arm is a flame, symbolizing destruction. His lower left arm is pointing to his upraised foot, suggesting that everyone should join him in his dance and be as free as he is. His lower right arm is extended in blessing, which in a symbolic way says

"Don't be afraid." He dances on a dwarf-demon, representing the ignorance of all those who do not understand that death is part of the divine
process. The art historian Heinrich Zimmer explains that "conquest of this
demon lies in the attainment of true wisdom. Therein is release from the
bondages of the world."[31]

The aspect of Shiva that brings re-creation is represented by sexually
suggestive forms. (We should note here that in nonindustrial societies the
bearing of children is crucial—both for the economic survival of the family
and for the care of the parents in their old age. Parents pray to have many
healthy children.) A frequent representation of Shiva is a columnar *lingam*—
often black, which adds to its mystery. It usually rests on a *yoni*—a circular
base that is the female complement to the lingam. The lingam may be a large,
natural stone worshiped outdoors; a metal object small enough to be worn
around the neck; or a wooden piece of an appropriate size for worship in
the home. Shaivites (devotees of Shiva) may pour various liquids, such as
milk and rosewater, over the lingam in an act of devotion.

Fertility is further emphasized by Shiva's companion animal Nandi, the
bull, and by Ganesha, the elephant-headed son of Shiva, who has become a
symbol of strength and abundance. Both are frequently found in temples
dedicated to Shiva. Worship of Shiva is most common in Kashmir and southern India. We should note, too, that Shiva is closely linked with destruction
only when he is viewed as part of the Trimurti. Among Shaivites, he is the
sole God and is not exclusively related to destruction.

> Those who have riches
> build temples for Thee;
> what shall I build? I am
> poor. My legs are the
> pillars; this body of
> mine is the temple.
> —Basavaraja, in praise
> of Shiva[32]

Worship of the Divine Feminine: Devi

The three gods of the Trimurti are usually portrayed as masculine. But of all
the great world religions, Hinduism perhaps most strongly recognizes the
female aspects of divinity. This may come from a practical interest in fertility. Worship of female divinities, too, seems to have been a part of pre-Vedic
religion, and elements of that early worship have lived on.

The Great Mother, also called **Devi** ("goddess"), is worshiped throughout India, but particularly in the northeast. She is portrayed in many forms
and can be both loving and cruel. She is especially harsh to those who show
themselves unworthy of her love. Devi is frequently worshiped with extreme
human feeling. The worshiper may take on the emotions and even the clothing
of a child or spouse of the Great Mother. The mystic Ramakrishna (1836–1886),
priest at a temple near Kolkata (Calcutta), spoke of his special devotion to
her. "I practised austerities for a long time. . . . My longing for the Divine
Mother was so great that I would not eat or sleep. I would lie on the bare
ground, placing my head on a lump of earth, and cry out loudly: 'Mother,
Mother, why dost thou not come to me?' I did not know how the days and
nights passed away. . . . When I reached the state of continuous ecstasy, I
gave up all external forms of worship; I could no longer perform them. Then
I prayed to my Divine Mother: 'Mother, who will now take care of me? I
have no power to take care of myself.'"[33]

The goddess Durga overcomes the forces of evil.

The Divine Feminine appears as several goddesses, of which the most popular are Durga and Kali. The goddess **Durga** ("awe-inspiring," "distant") is frequently represented with ten arms, full of implements used to destroy evil. Her face is serene, surrounded by a halo, and she wears a crown. She rides a tiger, which helps her conquer all dangerous obstacles.

Kali ("dark") is more fearsome still. She is often shown wearing a necklace of human skulls, and her fanged teeth drip with blood. Her many arms are full of weapons, which are thought to be dangerous to enemies but protective of her children. Kolkata ("Kali's stairs") is named after her temple in this city.

The important role of the Divine Feminine is also seen in the female consorts who accompany many male deities. They are so much a part of the male god that the god cannot be active without them, and thus they are called *shaktis* ("energies") because they allow the male gods to be effective in the human world.

The goddess Saraswati is the consort of Brahma and is far more popular than he. She is the patron of music, the arts, and culture and is often portrayed with a musical instrument in her hand. The shakti of Vishnu is the goddess Lakshmi, who is commonly dressed as a queen and sits on a lotus. As the consort of Vishnu, she dispenses good luck and protection. Shiva is portrayed with a variety of shaktis, the best known being Parvati and Uma. Sometimes Shiva is himself portrayed as androgynous: half of his body is masculine, while the other side shows a female breast. This androgyny represents the unity that underlies all the apparent opposites of reality—a unity also spoken of in the Upanishads and the Bhagavad Gita.

Divinities of nature are frequently female. The goddess Ganga, who animates the Ganges River, is a good example. Tree spirits, too, are considered female, and frequently it is women who offer them worship.

The Guru as Object of Devotion

Because Hinduism is not organized in a hierarchical fashion, devotion to a guru (spiritual teacher) is a large and ancient component of Hindu spirituality. The etymology of the word *guru* is expressive: "the one who removes darkness." Anyone who seeks spiritual growth—no matter what his or her caste or station in life—may seek a guru, whom the individual can visit regularly to seek advice. Even gurus who have taken vows of silence can offer advice and insight to their disciples by writing on tablets or simply by looking at them with love.

Although the majority of gurus are men, female gurus are not uncommon. The guru need only be recognized as a person of holiness. Because a guru expects to be surrounded by students and devotees, he or she will frequently set up an ashram. Usually an ashram is a commune of people living in a single compound, separate from ordinary society, but it may also be in a town and made up of various buildings owned and used by the devotees. Most gurus stay within their communities, but some travel, even outside India, to set up additional ashrams elsewhere. Frequently an aging guru will designate a successor from among his or her closest disciples and those specially trained.

It is common to touch and even kiss the feet of a guru—an act of reverence that is also performed at times for parents and grandparents. To an outsider, such an act may seem excessive. However, many Hindus believe that the guru is both a saint and a living embodiment of the divine. Behind this conception is the recognition that although divine reality exists within all human beings, most people manifest their divine nature inadequately, because their ignorance and self-centeredness restrict its expression. Such people are compared to glass windows that are so dusty that only a little light shines through. However, some people, over many lifetimes of effort, have reached a stage of such achievement that their ego has disappeared and their charity has grown immense. In these rare people the innate divine light shines brilliantly. This view explains why Hindus believe that simply

As a man may be blindfolded, and led away, and left in a strange place; and as, having been so dealt with, he turns in every direction and cries out for someone to remove his bandages and show him the way home; and as one thus entreated may loose his bandages and give him comfort; and as thereupon he walks from village to village, asking his way as he goes; and as he arrives home at last— just so does a man who meets with an illumined teacher obtain true knowledge.
—Chandogya Upanishad[34]

being in the presence of the guru allows the disciple to benefit—like a plant in the sunshine—from the guru's spirituality.

This belief also explains the intriguing practice of *darshan* ("presence"). Because people of spiritual accomplishment are thought to radiate their divine nature, disciples find opportunities to be in the presence of the holy person. Sometimes also a holy person will sit or stand silently, allowing

While priestly roles are primarily male, females in Hindu families commonly take responsibility for much devotional practice.

devotees to come forward one by one to look into the teacher's eyes and to experience the divine energy that shines out.[35]

Devotion to Animals

Hinduism is distinctive among world religions for its kindness to animals. A devout Hindu does not kill or eat animals. Cows often wander along Indian streets, and cars and taxis take care to drive around them. Furthermore, visitors to some Hindu temples may find monkeys and even mice well fed and running free. Several extremely popular gods, such as Ganesha and Hanuman, have animal features; and gods such as Shiva and Vishnu are regularly portrayed in the company of their animal companions. A Shiva temple would often be thought incomplete without a statue of Nandi, the bull who is Shiva's vehicle.

This devotion to animals in Hinduism has several possible origins: an ancient deification of powerful animals, such as the elephant and tiger; the desire to neutralize dangerous or mischievous animals, such as the snake, rat, and monkey; and even a sense that human beings and animals have the same origin (a belief also common in native religions). Belief in reincarnation has undoubtedly also played a role. When they see animals and insects, many Hindus see prehuman beings who, in their spiritual evolution, will eventually become human themselves. This brings a feeling of closeness to nonhuman forms of animal life.

Among the animals, cows receive special veneration. This tradition may stem from pre-Vedic worship in the Indus River valley of the bull or cow, a symbol of fertility and economic value. In rural India, to have a cow is to have milk and butter, fuel (dried dung), and the warmth and comfort associated with household pets. With a cow, one is never utterly destitute. Affection for the cow may also arise from the strong thread of ancient devotion to the Divine Feminine—hinted at by the commonly used term *gau mata*, "mother cow."

This affection is hard for people outside India to understand. But when one sees an Indian cow, with its gentle face, ambling peacefully along a bustling Indian street, then one experiences clearly why the cow is a powerful symbol in India of all motherliness. (The fact that Muslims butcher cows is a source of terrible friction between the Hindus and Muslims in India.)

Other Forms of Religious Devotion

Indian thought loves multiplicity. "As many as the sands of the Ganges" is a description applied to a variety of subjects. One example of multiplicity is the Hindu recognition of immense numbers of gods. Realizing that each god or goddess may have several forms and may be accompanied by divine consorts and animal companions, we gain a dizzying sense of the limitlessness of devotional possibilities. In everyday life, every person is expected to have a religious practice involving at least one of these deities, but the exact form generally is not dictated, and virtually no form of devotion is rejected.

Hindu Celebrations

Religious festivals are frequent and usually joyous. Some are clearly associated with the seasons, such as a springtime fertility festival and a post-monsoon festival. Others are related to events in a god's life, such as the site of his birth or places he traveled to. Some festivals are regional, and some are national.

Although India is hot during most of the year, winters can be cold, especially in the north. The spring is therefore welcomed with the celebration *Holi*. It is traditional for boys and girls to playfully throw colored water on each other (nowadays some even use squirt guns), thus evoking images of Krishna's exploits with the milkmaids.

After the monsoons of the summer months, the land is green, the air is cool, and there is a sense of peacefulness. The season has the feeling of a second spring and a new beginning. People often spend time repairing any damages the rains may have caused. Holidays at this time reenact the power of goodness to conquer evil forces. For example, *Divali*, recalling the return of Rama and Sita, is a time when people clean their houses and illuminate them outside with candles and lights. Ganesha and Lakshmi, who are both associated with good fortune, are particularly honored at this time.

Durga Puja, held in December and particularly popular in northeast India, celebrates the goddess Durga's ability to overcome dangerous powers. People dance in front of her statues in the street, and in Kolkata the festival ends with the immersion of her statues in the river.

Pilgrimage is a common form of religious expression in Hinduism, as it is in many religions. India is dotted with sites that are held to be sacred to the most popular gods and goddesses, and devotees of a particular deity will often try to visit all the important sites associated with that deity. Pilgrimages can also involve listening to a famous guru's sermons and meditating with the guru's followers.

PERSONAL EXPERIENCE: A CREMATION IN BALI

A stream flows through tall bamboo at one end of the town, and rice paddies stretch out to the west. In the neighboring hills are several fine temples. The splendid setting of Ubud, this town in central Bali, has long attracted artists, and the town has two major museums of Balinese art, which are lovely buildings in their own right. The town is well located for the exploration of the rest of the island.

I was staying in a small hotel down a dirt road, on the outskirts of town. My second-floor room was up a steep outdoor staircase, but it had a large veranda that looked out over the rice paddies, and every day I heard two roosters crow from a house in the middle of the fields. Each morning the woman who lived next door brought out offerings of flowers and rice on green leaves, and she put the offering with incense at a small altar, dedicated to Brahma, in her garden. As soon as she had put out the rice, said her prayer, and left, birds swooped down to take their share.

People associate Hinduism with India, but it is the principal religion in Bali, as well, where it has blended with folk religion in a highly ritualistic form. When I arrived in Ubud, I went down to the main street to find a driver. (You don't want to be your own driver on Bali.) "I'm not interested in shirts or carvings," I said to the first driver who offered his help—"just temples and ceremonies." He laughed, and we came to a rate quickly. Because his name, Nyoman, is so common in Bali, he had given himself a nickname: "Nyoman Blue." He even had business cards with the name. He said he liked the color and the sound of the word. Every morning he and I would meet on the main street, across from the Casa Luna restaurant, to plan our day's excursion.

One morning when we met he said, "We don't have to drive anywhere today. There's going to be a cremation just outside town. We can walk." He took me several blocks away to where the procession would begin. I had brought the sarong that I had to wear when visiting temples, and put it around my waist.

Already people had assembled, and the street was packed. A life-sized red wooden bull, carved from a tree trunk, had been set atop carrying poles. Nearby was a wooden tower, at the base of which was a small "house" that contained the remains of the deceased person, once an important citizen of the town. Men in black-and-white checkered sarongs and gold headbands were chatting cheerfully and smoking Indonesian clove cigarettes. More people came, but no one looked sad. I tried to find shade as we waited, and then, not knowing how long the procession and cremation would last, I went off to buy a bottle of water.

Just as I returned, the men picked up the tower and the red bull on its poles. The procession began, the men weaving left, right, and sometimes in circles, often at a run—they wanted to make sure that the spirit of the dead man could not find its way back and cause difficulties. We started up a hill. The road curved to the left as it rose, then went down into a grove of tall trees beyond the town. At last we reached a grassy clearing. The men set down what they had carried. I stood under a banyan tree, trying to be unobtrusive. A priest dressed in white watched as the shrouded remains were placed within the red bull. The priest then rang a bell and sprinkled water, with a flower in his fingers. Women relatives of the deceased came forward to place offerings within the bull, and a man nearby held a rooster. Suddenly the red bull erupted in flames, which shot up to the leaves of the banyan tree under which I stood. The smoke was intense, and I moved to the other side of the clearing to escape from it. Several men went to burn the wooden tower, which had been set down in the back of the clearing, and they seemed to congratulate each other. People chatted—it reminded me of the social time after a church service—then drifted away slowly. As we went back, I realized at a bend in the road where I was. I could see the veranda of my hotel, which was just barely visible on the ridge across the rice paddy.

A body is cremated in a ritual bull at the end of an elaborate procession and ceremony in Ubud, Bali.

What had struck me was the absence of sadness. Not only was the cremation performed months after the man had died, but any mourning was dissipated by the belief that the deceased had had other lives in the past and would probably have more in the future. The cremation had helped transform a body back to basic elements and would allow the spirit to move onward in the cycle of rebirths and, ultimately, to release.

HINDUISM AND THE ARTS

Given Hinduism's tendency toward multiplicity, it is not surprising that Hindu temples, particularly in southern India, are often covered with statues, many with multiple faces and arms. The concept of multiplicity has a purpose. To appreciate this, think of a wheel that begins to turn. At first, each spoke of the wheel is visible, but as the wheel turns more quickly, the spokes disappear and dissolve into a unity. The profusion of images in Hindu art can be similarly hypnotic, with the experience of multiplicity frequently leading to an overarching sense of unity. Profusion thus fits in well with the mystical orientation common in Hinduism.

Another characteristic of Hindu artistic sensibility is symbolism. One of the clearest examples is the depiction in painting and sculpture of figures with multiple arms and faces, which are not literal but symbolic representations of power and wisdom. Specific symbols are associated with individual deities and allow them to be identified. Krishna, for example, is recognized by his flute.

Hindu painting can sometimes be disappointing, such as the rather garish devotional art sold at temple gates. Many fine paintings of the past have undoubtedly vanished because of the fragility of the paper and cloth on which they were done. The murals that remain, however, demonstrate the heights that Hindu devotional painting has sometimes attained; and some yantras—geometrical paintings used in meditation—are unforgettable.

Hindu sculpture, however, far outshines Hindu painting. Fine pieces of sturdy stone and metal are on display in India and in museums around the world. Metal sculpture advanced quite early. The finest generic example of Hindu sculpture is Shiva in his guise as "ruler of the dance" (Nataraja)—an image that was introduced in southern India more than a thousand years ago but which is still produced today. For many, this sculpture represents the perfection of Hindu art, combining visual beauty with a symbolic meaning that intensifies the visual power.

The power of stone sculpture is often quite sensuous. Given the world-denying aspect of some Hindu thought, one might expect that the great stone sculpture of Hinduism would be ascetic—perhaps elongated and otherworldly. The opposite is true, however. Some of the best-known examples of stone sculpture are the figures of sensuous men and women, enjoying life and each other, on the temples of Khajuraho in central India. This sort of sculpture was influenced by Tantrism, the antipuritanical movement that teaches that everything in the world, including sex, can be used to attain higher states of consciousness.

Popular Hinduism has made use of hymns to many gods as expressions of bhakti yoga. Their regular rhythm and repetition help produce a state of altered consciousness in the worshiper, bringing a sense of selflessness and union with the divine. Instrumental music—especially involving drums and the harmonium, a hand-pumped reed organ—has also been an integral part of religious celebrations for centuries.

Classical Indian instrumental music is less obviously religious, yet much of it has an undeniable mystical quality. It makes use of *ragas,* elements of Indian music that blend features of both scales and melodies. Frequently these ragas are played and musically developed over deep tones that are played as a drone. (The *sitar,* the best-known Indian stringed instrument, has drone strings on its side.) The drone suggests the underlying timeless world of Brahman, against which changing melodies—suggestions of the world of time—move. Musical pieces often begin quite tentatively, then gradually speed up to a very quick pace, and suddenly stop, bringing to the listener (and players) an experience of release and peace.

Indian classical dance is more obviously tied to religion. It interprets stories derived from the tales of the gods, such as Krishna and Rama. Much of it also originated as a part of religious ceremony, performed at religious festivals and in or near temples. Dance is meant to produce delicate states of feeling, some of which are thought to assist contact with particular gods.

HINDUISM: MODERN CHALLENGES

India, as we have seen, is isolated from other lands by mountains and ocean. This has meant that its rural culture and ancient polytheism could develop undisturbed for centuries. But invasions did occur, inevitably bringing new beliefs and values. Many of these new elements were adopted, but others were fought.

One early invasion was only partially successful. Alexander the Great (d. 323 B.C.E.) brought his army from Greece and reached the Indus River, where he talked with sannyasins about religion and philosophy. He had hoped to conquer India and then reach China, too; but his men, sick and discouraged, forced him to turn back, and he died in Babylon on the way home. Had Alexander been able to fulfill his plans, his influence in India would have been immense. Despite his failure to carry them out, though, forms of Greek government and art, brought by the Greek invaders, profoundly influenced northwest India for centuries.

In the past millennium, two additional waves of influence washed across India: Islam and the British. Islam first came into India from Afghanistan, and a sultanate was set up in Delhi in 1206. After invasions from Turkmenistan, the sultanate was supplanted by the Mughal dynasty, beginning in 1398. The Mughal dynasty continued on into the eighteenth century, even as the British were consolidating their control over much of India.

There could hardly be two religions more in contrast than monotheistic Islam and polytheistic Hinduism. The contrast has produced intense conflict, which continues today. The more than five centuries of Islamic rule that began in 1206 were marked by a spectrum of attitudes toward Hinduism,

Behind this Hindu temple roofline in Benares stands the minaret of a mosque. Peaceful coexistence with other religions, especially Islam, is a major challenge for Hinduism today.

moving back and forth between cruel oppression and complete tolerance. The attitude of the state depended on the opinions of the ruler of the time. For example, Akbar (d. 1605) was so tolerant that he invited members of many other religions to speak at court, and he became convinced that India needed a new religion that would blend the best of all older religions. His great-grandson, Aurangzeb (d. 1707), however, was notoriously harsh in his zeal, destroying Hindu temples and sometimes demanding conversion or death.

Of course, not all conversions to Islam were forced. Islam was very attractive to many people. It was appealing to those who appreciated its monotheistic simplicity, its architecture, its literature, and its way of life. (Many beautiful buildings were created by the Mughals; the Taj Mahal, for example, was built by Aurangzeb's father.) Islam was also appealing because it was the religion of the aristocratic ruling classes; and it was greatly attractive to lower-caste Hindus, who felt oppressed by the Hindu caste system. Consequently, by the end of the Mughal period, Islam was the religion of millions in north India. But this fact would later create great problems, particularly when India became an independent state, and it would remain as a major source of religious friction and violence.

European values have also, gradually, posed a major challenge to traditional Hinduism. This process began after 1500 c.e., when European powers took control of parts of India. Goa, on the west coast, became a center of Portuguese culture that lasted until 1960, when Goa was taken over by Indian army forces. Similarly, Pondicherry, on the southeast coast, was at one time a center of French culture. The most significant European influence on India,

Hindu images on secular objects, such as this image of Shiva on a T-shirt, are popular in some Asian markets. However, this use of sacred images can cause controversy.

however, was English. Great Britain controlled most of the subcontinent for about two centuries. Although India became independent of Britain in 1947, British influence is evident in modern India's law, education, architecture, rail transportation, and military life.

Throughout India today one can find former British churches, mostly shuttered and closed, which only hint at both the positive and negative impact of British Christianity on India. The British were not successful in making many converts, but through their schools and colleges British Christian missionaries helped challenge and change some traditional Hindu beliefs and practices. Among those elements that were questioned were untouchability, child marriage, prohibition of remarriage for widows, polytheism, the content of education, and the role of women.

One of the earliest British-inspired Indian reformers was Ram Mohan Roy (1772–1833). He was typical of the many reformers who grew up in Calcutta (now Kolkata), which was for a long time the capital of British India and the center of westernizing thought. While remaining a Hindu and even writing articles in defense of Hinduism, his thinking was influenced by both rationalism and Christianity.[36] He began a movement, the Brahmo Samaj, that adopted Christian-inspired elements: the belief in one God, congregational worship, and an ethical urgency that sought to better the lot of the oppressed. The Brahmo Samaj later split into three branches—all of which are still active.

Possibly as a result of contact with European values, one practice that was made illegal in the early nineteenth century was that of *sati* (or *suttee*, named after the first wife of Shiva). While there is no evidence to suggest that this practice was common, in sati a woman whose husband had died could volunteer, as a sign of her wifely devotion, to be burnt alive on her husband's funeral pyre. Although the British found the notion of sati horrible, they were unwilling to intervene at first. Reform-minded Indians, however, worked with the British to make the practice illegal. Instances of sati still happen today, but they are rare.

Mohandas Gandhi

Mohandas Gandhi (1869–1948) was born in the seaside town of Porbandar in northwestern India, north of Mumbai (Bombay). Because Britain then controlled the country, many Indians advocated violence as a response to British domination. This historic turning point became a defining time in Gandhi's life.

As a young man, Gandhi learned basic ideas of nonviolence from Hinduism and Jainism (see Chapter 5). He was a vegetarian because of his religious upbringing; yet in his day, young Indian boys believed that the British were strong because they ate meat. Young Gandhi tested this theory by eating meat for a year, but he had a dream of a goat crying in his stomach and was compelled to give up his experiment.[37] His marriage at the age of 13 was arranged by his family to a girl named Kasturbai, also 13.

During his late teen years, family members recommended that Gandhi study law in London. Because his pious Hindu mother feared the bad influences he would be exposed to there, he agreed to take a vow that he would not eat meat, drink wine, or touch a woman while abroad. A Jain monk administered the vow, and Gandhi left for London in the fall of 1888 at the age of 19. Kasturbai and their young son, Harilal, remained with Gandhi's parents.

This 1946 photo shows two leaders: a bespectacled Mohandas Gandhi, who eventually led India to its independence; and Jawaharlal Nehru, who was to be the nation's first prime minister.

Feeling rebellious at the time, Gandhi enthusiastically adopted English clothes and manners and even took dancing lessons; but in London he also began serious study. Becoming familiar with the Christian Bible, he was particularly moved by Jesus' call to forgiveness and nonviolence, which he found in the Sermon on the Mount (Matt. 5–7) in the New Testament.

It was in London, too, that he first read the Bhagavad Gita, discovering outside India the wisdom in Hinduism. He took to heart its ideal of the active but selfless human being. Such a person, Gandhi later wrote, is a person who is "without egotism, who is selfless, who treats alike cold and heat, happiness and misery, who is ever forgiving, who is always contented, whose resolutions are firm, who has dedicated mind and soul to God, who causes no dread, who is not afraid of others."[38]

After obtaining his law degree in 1891, Gandhi returned to India; but soon he decided to accept an offer to practice law in South Africa, where there was a large Indian population. There he experienced the inequalities of racial segregation and legal codes that favored Europeans over non-Europeans, and he began to perfect the ideologies that he would later spread in India. His thinking was influenced by writings that advocated simplicity and nonviolence, such as the essay "On Civil Disobedience," by the American author Henry David Thoreau, and the book *The Kingdom of God Is Within You*, by the Russian writer Leo Tolstoy. A farm that Gandhi bought became something of an ashram, while his law office in Johannesburg became a center for nonviolent political action. He began to employ strikes and marches to publicize his goals and to wear Indian clothing (specifically the *dhoti*, a type of loincloth) as a way of identifying with the Indian cause.

Gandhi returned to India in 1915 and dedicated his life to seeking Indian independence from Britain. Although he was repeatedly imprisoned, Gandhi insisted that all his followers remain nonviolent. For him, ahimsa (nonviolence) was fundamental. Gandhi not only believed in nonviolence for its own sake, but he felt that it gave a great moral power to its adherents and that it could sway those who were cruel, thoughtless, and violent. He called this power *satyagraha* ("reality force," or "holding onto truth"). Gandhi made use of every possible nonviolent technique: marches, hunger strikes, talks, demonstrations, and, of course, publicity. He argued that violence only begets further violence and brutalizes those who are violent, whereas nonviolence begets admiration, spiritual greatness, and ultimate freedom.[39]

One brilliant example of Gandhi's nonviolent techniques was the Salt March of 1930. At that time the British taxed all salt eaten in India and made it illegal to possess salt not bought from the government monopoly. Gandhi cleverly led a three-week march on foot from his ashram to the ocean, nearly 250 miles away. Fewer than a hundred people began the march with him, but thousands joined along the way. Reaching the sea, Gandhi collected the natural salt left on the beach by the waves—thus breaking the law. In seashore communities all around India, people came to do the same, and thousands were put into jail along with Gandhi. This march was the turning point. Weakened both by the Indian independence movement and by World War II, the British forces at last agreed to leave India in 1947. Perceiving Gandhi's greatness following the Salt March, the writer Rabindranath Tagore had called him *Mahatma* ("great spirit"). This became his title.

Gandhi believed so much in loving tolerance that he hoped it could keep a newly independent India free of religious battles. Muslim leaders, however, fearful that the Hindu majority would oppress Muslims, worked to create the new separate Muslim state of Pakistan. Some Hindu militants wanted revenge for what they perceived as wrongs done by Muslims to Hindus in the new Pakistan, and one of these Hindu militants assassinated Gandhi early in 1948. Gandhi's last words were *Ram, Ram* ("God, God").

Gandhi's example was so powerful that the idea of satyagraha spread to other countries and was adopted in the 1960s by the Baptist minister Martin Luther King Jr. to help protest racial segregation in the United States. King insisted that activists march peacefully and sit in restaurants quietly, without responding to threats or cruelty. Their gentle persistence, magnified by publicity, brought success.

Contemporary Issues

The issues that moderate Hinduism faces, as it is evolving today, come from three sources: the conservative social teachings of traditional Hinduism, the centuries-old conflict with Islam, and the challenges of the contemporary world.

Some Hindus find religious justification for preserving the rules of untouchability, keeping strictly the divisions of the caste system, and limiting women to traditional roles. The injustices of untouchability have long been recognized, but legal assistance for untouchables came only in the twentieth century. Untouchables, now allowed to enter all temples in India, have made great strides toward some social equality and opportunity. For example, there is a quota system for untouchables to ensure their inclusion in government positions and their admission to universities. The reality, however, is that in the villages untouchables still must live separately from others. They do not feel free to use wells and other water sources that are used by higher-caste persons, and they feel threatened by violence should they attempt to go beyond their traditional limits.

The caste system is weakening, especially in large cities. But a glance at a big-city Sunday newspaper reveals the caste system's continuing hold on contemporary life. It is common, for example, for Indian parents to place ads seeking a spouse for their child, and these ads frequently detail the son or daughter's caste, educational background, and sometimes even complexion.

The role of women has expanded in modern India, but it remains a focus of heated debate. In India's distant, pre-Vedic past, it is possible that women played an important public role. The importance of female deities and the fact that there have been many female gurus may be a continuation of this early tradition. But the dominant Vedic culture was thoroughly patriarchal. Just as it has been canonized in other religions, so male domination in India was canonized by the law code of Manu (second century B.C.E.). This code made the female subservient to the male and the wife subservient to her husband. A good wife was expected to treat her husband as a god, no matter what his character or treatment of her. Women were not trained to read and write, as this was thought to detract from their principal roles as wives and mothers. Nowadays Hindu women commonly learn to read and write, and many go on to higher education and important public roles. Critics, however, point out that women's education is often only basic and that women are largely limited to a few career areas—teaching, secretarial work, nursing, and medicine. Critics also point out that in villages women are sometimes confined to traditional domestic roles under threat of violence from their husbands. A related problem involves the dowry payments made by a bride's family to the bridegroom's family. In instances when the dowry is deemed insufficient, the wives are threatened and sometimes even killed by the husband's family members, thereby freeing the husband to marry again.

Conflict between Hindus and Muslims has been ongoing, particularly since the partition of India and Pakistan in 1947. Gandhi had hoped that India would not have to split into parts along religious lines, but Muslim leaders insisted on separation. Ironically, the partition did not bring peace. Disagreement about the border between India and Pakistan, particularly in Kashmir, has never been resolved. Two wars have already been fought, and a third is a constant threat. Since both countries possess atomic weapons, the potential horrors of such a war are especially great.

Conflicts between the Hindus and Muslims within India itself have also continually flared up. Old wounds were reopened in 1992, when Hindu activists destroyed a mosque at Ayodhya in northern India. They argued that it was the birthplace of Rama and the site of a Hindu temple that had been destroyed by the Muslim ruler Babur and replaced with a mosque. Atrocities on each side have been the result. While India claims to be a secular state, the fact that 85 percent of its people are Hindu gives Hindu causes an undeniable weight, and Muslims argue that the government has not adequately protected them. Similar conflicts have occurred in Kashmir at the site of a Hindu shrine to Shiva. Just as fundamentalism has risen in several other religions, it is now influential in Hinduism.

The third source of conflict comes from the intrusion of contemporary values, particularly individualism, women's rights, sexual freedom, modern fashion, and consumerism. Globalization has made instant some of the conflicts that once arose more slowly. There is now quick communication through e-mail and cell phones, and television brings new values irresistibly into the home. The Western world of banking and financial credit is quickly moving many of its operations to India, where college graduates speak English but salaries are still comparatively low. It is already the case that an American consumer making a routine call for computer help will probably be talking with a computer specialist in Bangalore, Mumbai, or Delhi. These jobs will provide greater economic opportunities for women as well as men, inevitably raising the potential for conflict between traditional values and new freedoms.

Hindu Influence beyond India

Over the centuries, Hinduism has spread to countries near India and afar, often by way of traders and immigrants. In a few places it has remained strong, whereas in others it has surrendered to other religions. Hinduism is the dominant religion of Nepal, where about 80 percent of the population is Hindu. Hinduism was once widespread in Southeast Asia, but today only traces of it remain. In Cambodia is the great ruin Angkor Wat, originally a Hindu complex. In Thailand, vestiges of a Brahmanical priesthood are particularly active in court ceremony, and images of Brahma, Vishnu, and Ganesha are common. Some forms of ritualistic Buddhism in northern and eastern Asia have kept alive a few Hindu gods, such as Indra, in art and ceremony. Hinduism, of course, continues wherever Indians have migrated.

Hinduism was once widespread in Indonesia, where it was introduced by Indian traders. During the Muslim invasions, however, the Hindu court was forced to retreat from the main island of Java and settled to the east on the small island of Bali, where a fascinating example of Hindu culture thrives. Here, Hinduism lives on in a complicated, beautiful form that is mixed with folk religion and Buddhism. Each village has Hindu temples, where dances based on Indian tales (especially about Rama) are performed. Shadow-puppet plays tell Hindu stories, and Balinese wood carvings reproduce images of Hindu gods, goddesses, and heroes. The central temple of Bali, a complex of buildings on the volcanic Mount Agung, is dedicated to the Trimurti. Although the rest of Indonesia is primarily Muslim, some Hindu elements remain in Indonesian dance and puppet plays.

The Hindu Diaspora

The word *diaspora* comes from a Greek word that suggests the sowing of seeds. Like seeds being cast in all directions, Hindus have left India over the last two centuries and settled in many faraway parts of the world, taking their religion with them. The first wave of migration began in the nineteenth century, when the British transported Indians, mostly men, to work as agricultural laborers in their other colonies around the world. Many worked on farms in South Africa, Kenya, Mauritius, Trinidad, and Fiji. One migrant who eventually gained prominence was the political leader Mohandas Gandhi. Though born in India, he began his law career and then his pro-independence work in South Africa. Only later in life did he return to India to become a pacifist leader of the independence movement. Smaller numbers of Indians, in order to pursue trade, moved to many large cities throughout Asia.

The second wave of Indian migration began in the first half of the twentieth century, when Indian soldiers who fought in the British army during the First and Second World Wars settled where they had been stationed. This wave of migration continued after India gained its independence from Britain in 1947 and entered the British Commonwealth. Indians moved to Britain and to Commonwealth countries, particularly to Canada and Australia. The large cities in these countries began to develop important Hindu communities.

The third wave of migration began in the second half of the twentieth century. Indians with academic and business backgrounds moved to the United States and to the European continent to study and to pursue careers in teaching and business. They brought with them not only their vegetarian cuisine, their music, and their love of "Bollywood" films, but also their temples and religious customs. Independent films and novels by writers of Indian background explore the complex experience of diaspora Indians. (Accessible examples are the film *Monsoon Wedding* and the novels of Jhumpa Lahiri.) Such works describe how diaspora Indians are pulled in different directions by their desires to be part of the modern Western world and, at the same time, to fulfill their traditional obligations to their parents, culture, and religion.

Indian communities now exist in more than 150 countries. The result is that Hinduism, the predominant religion of India, is becoming a global religion. Hinduism is not a missionary religion and does not normally seek converts. But Hindu worship is today carried on at thousands of temples outside of India. Those who are interested in learning more about the religion can visit one of the several hundred Hindu temples that exist in the United States and Canada. Most are in metropolitan areas, but some exist in unexpected places, including Mississippi and Nova Scotia. The Internet has detailed lists and further information.

Hinduism has had some influence on the West since the nineteenth century. The earliest impact was intellectual, when translations of the Upanishads and the Bhagavad Gita became available in Latin, French, German, and English. The translations generated great interest among philosophers, scholars, and poets. In the United States, the New England movement called Transcendentalism owes a good deal to its literary contact with Hinduism. Ralph Waldo Emerson (1803–1882), Henry David Thoreau (1817–1862), and Walt Whitman (1819–1892) all spoke in their writings of the sacredness of nature and the ultimate unity of all things, and they sometimes even used terms demonstrating Indian influence, such as *Brahma* and *Oversoul* (another name for Brahman). This literary trend was expressed in another form in England, where composers such as Gustav Holst (1874–1934) and Ralph Vaughan Williams (1872–1958) put selections from the Rig Veda and Whitman's *Leaves of Grass* to music.

Dance retains an important role in traditional Hindu ceremonies. Here, Krishna's birthday is celebrated with music and ecstatic dance.

The next wave of influence occurred when Indian gurus began to travel to the West. The first of these gurus was Swami Vivekananda (1863–1902), who represented Hinduism at the first World Parliament of Religions, held in Chicago in 1893. He was the successor to Ramakrishna (mentioned earlier), the noted mystic and devotee of the Great Mother. Vivekananda began the Ramakrishna Mission and set up Vedanta societies and Ramakrishna centers across Europe, India, and the United States. A Vedantist center has existed in Hollywood since the 1930s, and British writers such as Christopher Isherwood (1904–1986), Aldous Huxley (1894–1963), and Gerald Heard (1889–1971) all practiced meditation there. Isherwood, under the influence of his guru, Swami Prabhavananda, became a Vedantist and translated the Bhagavad Gita into English.

The third wave of Hindu influence in the West occurred in the late 1960s. The American counterculture embraced India as the fount of wisdom. Commercial air travel made it possible for Indian teachers to come to the West and for westerners to travel to India. Some westerners, such as the Beatles, studied in India with the guru Maharishi Mahesh Yogi and became enamored of Hinduism. (George Harrison's song "My Sweet Lord" was written to honor Krishna.) The Maharishi eventually came to the United States and established the Transcendental Meditation movement, which promotes regular daily meditation to achieve health and happiness. (The North American

center of the movement is at Maharishi Vedic City, near Fairfield, Iowa.) Some westerners who went to India became disciples of Sai Baba, a contemporary teacher in south-central India, and still others, such as the psychologist Richard Alpert (who took the name Ram Dass), studied with Indian teachers and returned to write about their experiences. Western visitors to India adopted forms of yoga, Hindu vegetarian cuisine, Indian clothing, and Indian music and then took them back to Europe, Canada, and the United States, where they entered the Western mainstream.

The movement called the International Society for Krishna Consciousness (ISKCON) was founded in New York in 1967 by Swami Bhaktivedanta Prabhupada (1896–1977) to spread a form of devotional practice among westerners. Commonly known as the Hare Krishna movement, ISKCON has succeeded in attracting westerners to live a traditional form of Hindu religious life. Its practitioners worship Krishna as the highest incarnation of the divine, chant daily, eat a vegetarian diet, and, if celibate, wear the traditional orange robe. The impact of this movement in the West has been particularly strong in the area of cuisine, prompting the opening of vegetarian restaurants across Europe, the United States, and Canada.

What we have just discussed—the impact of Hinduism on Western thinkers, musicians, and poets—was in large measure achieved by non-Hindus inspired by Hindu culture. Now Hindus themselves, in and out of India, are producing internationally acclaimed works, especially novels and films. Their particular points of view result from experiences accumulated across centuries in one of the world's richest cultures. Those experiences will in time help global citizens, whatever their origins, to see themselves with an understanding that has been enriched by the Hindu worldview.

Tucked between an international hotel and two elevated Skytrain rails is Bangkok's Erawan Shrine. Although Thailand is officially a Buddhist country, this very popular place of prayer has an image of the Hindu god Brahma at its center. Worshipers offer incense, garlands of marigolds, and prayers for good fortune.

READING

KRISHNA'S ADVICE TO ARJUNA

In the Bhagavad Gita, the god Krishna teaches Arjuna that the wise person rises above pleasure and pain and sees the indestructible Spirit that lies hidden within all the changes of everyday life.

As the Spirit of our mortal body wanders on in childhood and youth and old age, the Spirit wanders on to a new body: of this the sage has no doubts.

From the world of the senses, Arjuna, comes heat and cold, and pleasure and pain. They come and they go; they are transient. Arise above them, strong soul.

The man whom these cannot move, whose soul is one, beyond pleasure and pain, is worthy of life in eternity.

The unreal never is: the Real never is not. This truth indeed has been seen by those who can see the true.

Interwoven in his creation, the Spirit is beyond destruction. No one can bring to an end the Spirit which is everlasting.[40]

TEST YOURSELF

1. The culture that flourished in the Indus River valley before 2000 B.C.E. is named the _____ culture.
   a. Vedas
   b. Harappa
   c. Aryan
   d. Indian

2. The ancient scriptures of India are called the _____. There are four basic text collections: the Rig, the Yajur, the Sama, and the Atharva.
   a. Harappas
   b. Sanskrits
   c. Vedas
   d. "Shining Fathers"

3. Around 500 B.C.E., Indian civilization experienced such widespread and important changes that the period is called the _____ Age.
   a. Philosopher
   b. Prophet
   c. Axis
   d. Ascetic

4. In the Upanishads, the term _____ refers to the experience of the sacred within nature and the external universe; while _____ refers to the experience of the sacred within oneself. Both terms may be used interchangeably.
   a. karma; moksha
   b. Brahman; Atman
   c. samsara; moksha
   d. brahmins; samsara

5. The _____ is part of a very long epic poem called the Mahabharata; it recalls themes from the Upanishads.
   a. Maya
   b. Bhagavad Gita
   c. Pandavas
   d. Jainism

6. Hinduism has a(n) _____ system with five main social classes: *brahmin* (priest), *kshatriya* (warrior-noble), *vaishya* (merchant), *shudra* (peasant), and *dalit* (untouchable).
   a. work
   b. education
   c. ritual
   d. caste

7. The word *yoga* means "_____."
   a. contemplation
   b. enlightenment
   c. practice
   d. union

8. Shankara's belief that spiritual liberation was achieved when the individual personally came to understand the unity of all things is called _____.

    a. devotion
    b. Jnana
    c. monism
    d. meditation

9. When linked together, Brahma, Vishnu, and Shiva are often called the _____.
    a. Trimurti
    b. Shiva
    c. Hindu
    d. sacred text

10. Mohandas Gandhi's use of _____ techniques, including marches, hunger strikes, talks, demonstrations, and publicity, were ad-

opted by Martin Luther King Jr. to help protest racial segregation in the United States.

    a. traditional
    b. nonviolent
    c. disruptive
    d. *Mahatma*

11. Imagine on an exam you are asked to express the most important ideas of the Upanishads in only two sentences. What would you write for your two sentences? How do these sentences capture what is most important in the Upanishads?

12. Choose one of the modern or contemporary challenges facing Hinduism discussed in this chapter. According to Hindu belief, which of the following deities do you think would be especially equipped to assist Hindus in overcoming this challenge: Brahma, Vishnu, Shiva, or Devi? Why?

RESOURCES

Books

Bhagavad-Gita: The Song of God. Trans. Swami Prabhavananda and Christopher Isherwood. New York: Signet, 2002. A justly famous translation, with a valuable introduction by Aldous Huxley.

Gandhi, Mohandas. *The Bhagavad Gita According to Gandhi.* Ed. Strohmeier, John. Berkeley, CA: Berkeley Hills Books, 2000. The first book to include Gandhi's *Gita* text and his commentary in their entirety.

_____. *The Essential Gandhi.* Ed. Louis Fischer. New York: Vintage, 2002. Gandhi's writings on politics, nonviolence, spirituality, and his own life.

Kinsley, David R. *Hindu Goddesses: Visions of the Divine Feminine in the Hindu Religious Tradition.* Berkeley: University of California Press, 1988. A comprehensive survey of Hindu goddesses and the role of the divine feminine within Hinduism.

Lahiri, Jhumpa. *Interpreter of Maladies.* New York: Mariner Books, 1999. An award-winning collection of short stories that chronicle the dislocation experienced by Indian migrants to the United States.

Mittal, S., and G. Thursby, eds. *The Hindu World.* New York: Routledge, 2004. A comprehensive guide to the various literatures, traditions, and practices of Hinduism.

Patel, Sanjay. *The Little Book of Hindu Deities: From the Goddess of Wealth to the Sacred Cow.* New York:

Plume, 2006. An informative and entertaining introduction to the Hindu pantheon, written and colorfully illustrated by an animator at Pixar studios.

Ramana Maharshi, Sri. *The Essential Teachings of Ramana Maharshi: A Visual Journey.* Ed. Matthew Greenblatt. Carlsbad, CA: Inner Directions, 2002. Teachings of a great spiritual teacher, combined with photos of him and his ashram.

The Upanishads. Trans. Swami Prabhavananda and Frederick Manchester. New York: Signet, 2002. A readable translation of twelve basic Upanishads.

Film/TV

Aparajito (English subtitles. Director Satyajit Ray; Merchant-Ivory/Sony.) A depiction of a man's life in Benares and the portayal of the struggles of his father, a poor brahmin priest.

Gandhi. (Director Richard Attenborough; Columbia Tristar.) An epic rendering of the life of Mahatma Gandhi that won several Academy Awards.

Ganges: River to Heaven. (Aerial Productions.) A documentary on a hospice in Benares, where aging Hindus come to die in the hope that death at this site will improve their karma in the next life.

Hinduism: Faith, Festivals, and Rituals. (Films Media Group.) An examination of devotional ceremonies in the southern Indian state of Kerala.

Mahabharata. (Director Peter Brook; Parabola Video.) A modern, English-language production of the great Hindu epic.

Mystic India. (Giant Screen Films.) An epic account of the late-eighteenth-century spiritual awakening of Neelkanth, an 11-year-old yogi who journeys by foot throughout India for seven years and more than seven thousand miles, seeking enlightenment.

Short Cut to Nirvana: Kumbh Mela. (Mela Films LLC.) A documentary exploring the Kumbh Mela, a festival held every twelve years, said to be the largest gathering of human beings in the world.

Music/Audio

The Bhagavad Gita. (Multimedia and Culture.) An unabridged audiobook of the famed discourse between Krishna and Arjuna (translated into English by Juan Mascaró).

Darshana: Vedic Chanting for Daily Practice. (Mother Om Sounds.) A compilation of Vedic chants for daily practice, as performed by Sri Swamini Mayatitananda (Mother Maya).

Hymns from the Vedas and Upanishads, Vedic Chants. (Delos Records.) Traditional hymns and chants from classic religious sources.

Religious Music of Asia. (Smithsonian Folkways.) A recording of Hindu devotional music.

Sounds of India. (Columbia.) Classical devotional music of India, performed by Ravi Shankar.

Internet

HinduNet: http://www.hindunet.org/. A gateway site that allows users to learn about Hindu faith and ritual, visit Hindu temples online, listen to Hindu scriptures, and participate in discussion forums.

Sanatan Society: http://www.sanatansociety.org/. A useful resource for information on Hindu gods, yoga and meditation, Vedic astrology, vegetarianism, and other related topics.

Virtual Religion Index: http://virtualreligion.net/vri/hindu.html. Individual sections devoted to the Vedas, the Upanishads, the epics, theology and devotion, schools and teachers, and yoga.

KEY TERMS

ahimsa (*uh-him'-sa*): "Nonharm," "nonviolence."

ashram (*ash'-ram*): A spiritual community.

Atman (*at'-mun*): The spiritual essence of all individual human beings.

avatar (*ah'-va-tar*): An earthly embodiment of a deity.

Bhagavad Gita (*bhuh'-guh-vud gee'-ta*): A religious literary work about Krishna.

bhakti (*bhuk'-ti*): Devotion to a deity or guru.

bhakti yoga: The spiritual discipline of devotion to a deity or guru.

Brahma (*bruh-mah'*): God of creation.

Brahman (*bruh'-mun*): The spiritual essence of the universe.

brahmin (*bruh'-min*): Member of the priestly caste.

caste (*kaast*): One of the major social classes sanctioned by Hinduism.

Devi (*deh'-vee*): "Goddess"; the Divine Feminine, also called the Great Mother.

dhyana (*dhyah'-nah*): Meditation.

Durga: "Awe-inspiring," "distant"; a mother-goddess, a form of Devi.

guru (*goo'-roo*): A spiritual teacher.

hatha yoga (*hah'-tha yoh'-ga*): The spiritual discipline of postures and bodily exercises.

jnana yoga (*gyah'-nuh yoh'-ga; juh-nah'-nah yoh'-ga*): The spiritual discipline of knowledge and insight.

Kali (*kah'-lee*): "Dark," a form of Devi; a goddess associated with destruction and rebirth.

karma: The moral law of cause and effect that determines the direction of rebirth.

karma yoga: The spiritual discipline of selfless action.

Krishna: A god associated with divine playfulness; a form of Vishnu.

kundalini yoga (*koon-duh-lee'-nee yoh'-ga*): A form of raja yoga that envisions the individual's energy as a force that is capable of being raised from the center of the body to the head, producing a state of joy.

mantra: A short sacred phrase, often chanted or used in meditation.

maya: "Illusion"; what keeps us from seeing reality correctly; the world, viewed inadequately.

moksha (*mohk'-shah*): "Liberation" from personal limitation, egotism, and rebirth.

monism: The philosophical position that all apparently separate realities are ultimately one; the belief that God and the universe are the same, that the universe is divine.

puja (*poo'-jah*): Offerings and ritual in honor of a deity.

raja yoga: The "royal" discipline of meditation.

Rama: A god and mythical king; a form of Vishnu.

samadhi (*suh-mah'-dhee*): A state of complete inner peace resulting from meditation.

samsara (*suhm-sah'-rah*): The everyday world of change and suffering leading to rebirth.

sannyasin (*san-nyas'-in*): A wandering holy man.

Shiva (*shee'-vah*): A god associated with destruction and rebirth.

Trimurti (*tree-mur'-tee*): "Three forms" of the divine—the three gods Brahma, Vishnu, and Shiva.

Upanishads (*oo-pahn'-i-shads*): Written meditations on the spiritual essence of the universe and the self.

Vedas (*vay'-duhs*): Four collections of ancient prayers and rituals.

Vishnu: A god associated with preservation and love.

yoga: A spiritual discipline; a method for perfecting one's union with the divine.

Visit the Online Learning Center at www.mhhe.com/molloy5e for additional exercises and features, including "Religion beyond the Classroom" and "For Fuller Understanding."

4

Buddhism

FIRST ENCOUNTER

You have arrived in Bangkok, the first stop on a study-tour of Southeast Asia that later will also take you to Cambodia and Laos. Your first hours in the city bring you a chaos of sights and sounds. On the bus from the airport, you notice a number of golden temples, but also a monorail and, everywhere, traffic jams. The city's core is a jungle of modern glass skyscrapers, one of which is your hotel. After you check in, you walk outside to see where you are. All around the hotel are vendors with carts cluttering the cracked sidewalks, selling mango slices, chunks of pineapple, little pancakes, orchid plants, sunglasses, watches, keys, false teeth, and toy motorcycles made of soda cans. You're jet-lagged, but you've seen enough to fall asleep, knowing that you are now in the middle of an overwhelming tapestry of humanity.

In the morning, following your hotel's breakfast buffet, your group is bussed to the World Buddhist Federation headquarters, where you listen to a shaven-headed westerner in an orange robe. He says that he is ordinarily a "forest monk" in northeast Thailand but is in the capital for a few days to teach. After explaining that meditation is at the heart of a monk's life, he discusses the principles of meditation, some of which sound familiar. With his guidance, you and your friends then practice different forms of meditation. First you do sitting meditation, simply being aware of your breathing, in and out. After that you do walking meditation. He makes you walk very slowly, telling you to think about nothing other than the experience of each step you take.

After lunch back at the hotel, you have the afternoon to yourself. Just a couple of blocks away, partially visible through an alley, is what looks like a large temple. The monk this morning told you that Thailand's temples are almost always open to the public. So you head up the alley and then walk up a long flight of stairs to the temple's entrance. There are many pairs of shoes outside the door, and you add yours to the collection. You step inside, pause to let your eyes adjust to the dimmer light, and notice the subsiding traffic noise.

Despite all the shoes, you see only one other person, someone sitting very still in the middle of the floor. From her posture, you assume that she is practicing sitting meditation. Not wanting to disturb her, you sit quietly just inside the door. After you cross your legs, you place your hands in your lap and begin to meditate yourself, trying hard to focus only on your breathing.

Eventually you leave, very quietly since the woman sitting on the floor has still not moved. You wonder why people come to a temple to do this. Don't you usually go to temples for services, or to pray? Is meditation a form of praying? How can you pray if you don't use words? You become curious about the life of the Buddha, the founder of this religion, and wonder where all of this began.

THE BEGINNINGS OF BUDDHISM: THE LIFE OF THE BUDDHA

Buddhism is one of the world's oldest and most significant religions. It has spread through almost all of Asia, influencing the many cultures there, and is now gaining followers in the West. But it had its beginnings in India and arose from the experience of one person.

India in the fifth century B.C.E. was in a state of religious ferment. Great enthusiasm for personal religious experience led people to experiment with meditation and deep breathing and to study with gurus. A growing number of schools of philosophy taught new ways of thinking, some of which opposed the growth of the priestly Vedic religion. Into this world came Siddhartha Gautama, who would come to be known as the Buddha, or the Awakened One.

Because so many devout legends have grown up around the story of the Buddha's life and teaching, it is sometimes hard to separate fact from

Siddhartha, a wealthy prince before he attained enlightenment, is here portrayed as the Buddha, with princely crown and raiment. This depiction is frequent in the temples of Myanmar.

fiction.[1] Although there is no single, authoritative biography of the Buddha, his legendary life follows these outlines. Siddhartha was born the son of a prince of the Shakya tribe in what is today Nepal, in the lower Himalaya Mountains. Legend says that his mother, Maya, dreamt that a white elephant entered her side—this was the moment of conception of the future Buddha—and that Siddhartha was born miraculously from her side. Siddhartha's mother died a week after childbirth, and the boy was raised by his aunt.

When a sage inspected the child, he saw special marks on Siddhartha's body, indicating that he would be an illustrious person. At his naming ceremony, priests foretold that his life could go in one of two directions: either he would follow in his father's footsteps, inheriting his position and becoming a great king, a "world ruler"; or, if he were exposed to the sight of suffering, he would become a great spiritual leader, a "world teacher."

Siddhartha, as depicted here, practiced physical deprivation, hoping to achieve insight. This approach proved to be inadequate.

Siddhartha's father, wanting his son to succeed him, took measures to keep the boy from exposure to suffering. Kept in a large walled palace compound, Siddhartha grew up in luxury; married, at an early age, a young woman his father had chosen; and had a son. He was educated and trained as a warrior to prepare for eventually taking over his father's role.

All was going according to his father's plan until Siddhartha disobeyed his father's command not to leave the royal grounds. Visiting a nearby town, he soon witnessed the suffering of ordinary life. He saw—and was moved by—what are called the Four Passing Sights. He came across an old man, crooked and toothless; a sick man, wasted by disease; and a corpse being taken for cremation. Then he saw a sannyasin (a wandering holy man, a renunciate) who had no possessions but seemed to be at peace.

The paintings in Buddhist temples retell dramatically Siddhartha's response to what he saw. At 29, he realized that his life up until then had been a pleasant prison, and he saw the same programmed life stretching forward into his old age. The suffering he had just encountered, however, prompted him to question the meaning of human experience, and it threw him into a depression that kept him from enjoying his luxurious and carefree life any longer.

Siddhartha decided to escape. Legend tells how he took a last look at his sleeping family and attendants and rode to the edge of the palace grounds, where he gave his horse to his servant, removed his jewels, and cut off his long black hair. Putting on simple clothing, he went out into the world with nothing but questions. This event is called the Great Going Forth.

It is common in Indian spirituality to seek a teacher, and Siddhartha did just that. Traveling from teacher to teacher, he learned techniques of meditation and discussed philosophy, but he was ultimately unsatisfied. Begging for food and sleeping outdoors, Siddhartha spent about six years seeking answers to his questions—particularly about the troubling facts of suffering and death. His own mother had died young, a death that was apparently without meaning. Why, he often asked, is there suffering? Why do people have to grow old and die? Is there a God or unchanging divine reality behind the surface of things? Is there a soul and an afterlife? Are we reborn? Can we avoid suffering? How should we live?

Seeking answers to his questions, Siddhartha discovered that his teachers agreed on some issues but not on others. So, in the company of five other nomadic "seekers," he set out to find the answers he needed. To rid himself of distractions and to purify himself spiritually, Siddhartha also practiced great austerity. Living on as little food, drink, and sleep as possible, he hoped that he would find new insight and even gain spiritual powers.

Eventually, Siddhartha collapsed from weakness. He was found resting under a sacred tree by a kind woman, who had come from the nearby town of Gaya to worship the spirit of the great tree. (Siddhartha was so emaciated that she may have thought him to be the tree spirit.) She offered him food, which he accepted gratefully and ate under the shade of the tree, out of the hot sun. Once revived, Siddhartha realized that his austerities had not strengthened him or brought him any closer to the answers he sought. His five companions, having discovered Siddhartha's rejection of asceticism, abandoned him.

Being a practical person, Siddhartha decided to adopt a path of moderation—a middle way between self-indulgence and asceticism. He went to another tree, now called the Bodhi Tree,[2] and sat facing the east, resolving to remain there in meditation until he had the understanding he needed. Various traditions give different details, but every version talks of his struggle with hunger, thirst, doubt, and weakness. Some stories describe the work of an evil spirit, Mara, and his daughters who tempted Siddhartha with sensuality and fear. But Siddhartha resisted all temptation. During one entire night, as he sat meditating under a full moon, Siddhartha entered increasingly profound states of awareness. Legend says that he saw his past lives, fathomed the laws of karma that govern everyone, and finally achieved insight into release from suffering and rebirth.

At last, at dawn, he reached a state of profound understanding, called his Awakening, or Enlightenment (**bodhi**). He saw suffering, aging, and death in a new way, recognizing them as an inevitable part of life, but also seeing the possibility of release. We might wonder about the influence of the tree and the moon on Siddhartha. The tree overhead, with its thousands of leaves and twigs, despite its appearance of permanence, would change, age, and die; and the full moon, with its brilliant light, was a promise of new understanding. Whatever the cause of his enlightenment, Siddhartha arose and said that he was now a person who had woken up. From this came his new name: the Buddha, the Awakened One, taken from a Sanskrit word meaning "to wake up."

The Buddha remained for some time at the site of his enlightenment at Gaya, savoring his new way of looking at life and continuing to meditate. Mythic stories relate that during this time, when a heavy downpour occurred, a cobra raised itself over him to protect him from the rain. (In much of Asia, the snake is not considered a symbol of evil, but rather a protective animal.) At last the Buddha traveled west. He explained his awakening to his five former companions at a deer park at Sarnath, near Benares. Although they had parted with him earlier for abandoning his ascetic habits, they reconciled with him and became his first disciples.

The Buddha spent the rest of his long life traveling from village to village in northeast India, teaching his insights and his way of life. He attracted

A wonder of the world, this huge statue of the Reclining Buddha in Polonnaruwa, Sri Lanka, may be unsurpassed in conveying the serenity that is the core of Buddhist teaching.

many followers, and donors gave land, groves, and buildings to the new movement. The Buddha thus began an order (*sangha*) of monks and later of nuns. The Buddha's way was a path of moderation, a middle path, not only for himself but also for his disciples. It was midway between the worldly life of the householder, which he had lived before leaving home, and the ascetic life of social withdrawal, which he had followed after his departure from home. But the specifics of monastic community life and its relation to the nonmonastic world—on whom the monks relied for food—had to be worked out over time.

Tradition tells of the warm friendship the Buddha shared with his disciples and of their way of life, wandering about begging and teaching. The monks remained in one place only during the monsoon months of summer, when the rains were so heavy that travel was impractical. Looking on the Buddha's lifestyle from a modern vantage point, we can see that it was a healthy one: moderate eating, no alcohol, daily walking, regular meditation, pure air. Probably because of this, the Buddha lived to an old age.

When he was 80, legend says, the Buddha ate food offered by a well-meaning blacksmith named Chunda, but the food was spoiled and the Buddha became terribly sick. Sensing that he was dying, he called his disciples. To those who were crying over his impending death, he reminded them that everything must die—even the Buddha himself. He then offered these final words of advice: "You must be your own lamps, be your own refuges. Take refuge in nothing outside yourselves. Hold firm to the truth as a lamp and a refuge, and do not look for refuge to anything besides yourselves."[3] In other words, the Buddha's final instruction was this: Trust your own insights, and use self-control to reach perfection and inner peace.

Following this pronouncement, the Buddha turned on his right side and died. The many sculptures and paintings of the so-called Reclining Buddha may be images of his serene moment of death.[4] In any case, Buddhists idealize the Buddha's attitude toward death as a model for everyone.

THE BASIC TEACHINGS OF BUDDHISM

It is impossible to know exactly what the Buddha taught. He did not write down his teachings, nor did his early disciples. The only written versions were recorded several hundred years after his death, following centuries of being passed on orally—and of being interpreted in multiple ways. We must rely on the basic trustworthiness of both the oral traditions and the many written texts that pass on his teachings.

The written teachings that have come down to us are in a number of languages, all of which differ from the language (apparently a variation of Magadhi) spoken by the Buddha. One of the most important languages through which Buddhist teachings have been passed down is Pali, a language related to Sanskrit; another is Sanskrit itself—often called the Latin of India because of its widespread use in earlier years for scholarly works.

At the core of what is generally regarded as basic Buddhism are the Three Jewels (Sanskrit: *Triratna*; Pali: *Tiratana*)—that is, the Buddha, the Dharma, and the Sangha. The Buddha is thought of as an ideal human being whom other human beings should imitate; the image of him, seated in meditation, is a constant model of self-control and mindfulness. He is not usually thought of as being dead, but instead as existing in a timeless dimension beyond the world. The **Dharma** (Sanskrit), or Dhamma (Pali), means the sum total of Buddhist teachings about how to view the world and how to live properly. The **Sangha** is the community of monks and nuns.[5]

The Buddha's teachings are like the Buddha himself—practical. Surrounded in the India of his day by every kind of speculation about the afterlife, the nature of the divine, and other difficult questions, the Buddha concentrated on what was useful. He refused to talk about anything

The three jewels of Buddhism are the Buddha, Dharma, and Sangha. In parts of the Buddhist world, all males are expected to join the Sangha, at least for a time. Here, two males are ordained as monks at Wat Bovorn in Bangkok.

else—a benign neglect that has been called his noble silence. He said that a person who speculated about unanswerable questions was like a man who had been wounded by an arrow but refused to pull it out until he knew everything about the arrow and the person who shot it. The wounded man would die before he could get all the information he wanted.

The Buddha wished to concentrate on the two most important questions about existence: How can we minimize suffering—both our own and that of others? And how can we attain inner peace? The Buddha's conclusions are not just intellectual solutions. They are also recommendations for a practical way of living. Buddhist doctrines are not meant to be accepted on blind faith; rather, it is up to each individual to experience them first as truths before accepting them.

The Three Marks of Reality

Common to all forms of Buddhism is a way of looking at the world. Although this view may seem pessimistic at first, it is meant to be a realistic assessment of existence that, when understood, ultimately helps lead a person to inner peace and even joy. According to this view, reality manifests three characteristics: constant change, a lack of permanent identity, and the existence of suffering. This view is the foundation for the Four Noble Truths and the Noble Eightfold Path, which we will discuss shortly.

Change One of the things the Buddha recommended is that we look at life as it really is. When we do, he said, the first thing we notice is life's constant change, or impermanence (Pali: **anichcha;** Sanskrit: *anitya*). We are often surprised by change—and pained by it—because we do not expect it, but the fact is that nothing we experience in life ever remains the same. We get used to things (our own face, family, friends, house, car, neighborhood), and they seem to remain basically the same every time we look at them. But that is an illusion, for they are changing daily, gradually. We usually only notice the changes over time.

Everyone knows the shock of change, such as seeing an old friend after many years apart, or looking at childhood photos. Even old movies on television and old songs on the radio—the performers now aged or even long gone—clearly convey the Buddhist sense of the inevitability of change. A family gathering can have the same effect: the death of a much-loved grandparent may be contrasted by the sight of a great-grandchild playing in a playpen in the corner.

People's viewpoints also change. Think of what the word *love* means to a five-year-old, a teenager, a new parent, or a person who has lost a spouse. Or imagine hearing the news of a divorce between two people you thought were well suited and happily married.

When we truly experience impermanence, we see that all of reality is in motion all the time, that the universe is in flux. As the kaleidoscope of reality slowly turns, its patterns change; and while old patterns disappear, new patterns are born, all of them interesting. As the Buddha taught, the wise person expects change, accepts it, and even savors it. The wise person might also reflect that just as pleasures do not last forever, neither do sorrows.

No Permanent Identity   We know that the Buddha urged people to abandon egotism and a fixation on material objects. Related to this, he denied the existence of the permanent identity of anything. Thus, the second mark of reality is that each person and each thing is not only changing but is made up of parts that are also constantly changing, a concept referred to as "no permanent identity." In the case of people, it is called "no permanent soul" or "no self." The Pali term is **anatta;** in Sanskrit it is *anatman* ("no *Atman*") because of the Buddha's refusal to accept the Hindu notion of timeless, unchanging reality (*Atman*) underlying everything—people, things, essences, and gods.

For the sake of logical convenience, we often talk about each person or thing as if it were a single unified reality. Let us first consider something nonhuman, say, a car. We call it *a car* as if it were one single reality, but actually it is made up of many things—glass, aluminum, rubber, paint, headlights, belts, pistons, wires, and fluids—many of which are either going wrong right now or probably soon will be.

Then think of how each human being, though called by a single name, is actually made up of organs, body parts, instincts, memories, ideas, and hopes—all of which are constantly changing. Consider also one's self-perception. I naively think I am the same person from day to day, even if I get a haircut or lose weight or see a film. But if I recall myself at age 10 and then compare that person with who I am now, I seem now to be someone quite different.

To the Buddha, to believe that a person has some unchanging identity or soul is as mistaken as believing that a car has an unchanging essence. The car is not a car because it has a "car soul"; rather, it is a car because of a social convention that refers to its many related parts by a single word. This tendency is so strong that we sometimes think that a label (*car*) is the reality. Although the Buddhist view may seem strange at first, it is quite rational—and it helps eliminate surprise when my car won't start, when a friend becomes distant, or when a photo reveals the inevitability of aging. All these changes show the same process at work.[6]

Suffering   The third characteristic of reality, known as **dukkha** (Pali), or *duhkha* (Sanskrit), is usually translated as "suffering" or "sorrow," but it also means "dissatisfaction" or "dis-ease." It refers to the fact that life, when lived conventionally, can never be fully satisfying because of its inescapable change. Even in the midst of pleasure, we often recognize that pleasure is fleeting. Even when all the bills are paid, we know that in a few days there will be more. Try as we might to put everything in our lives in order, disorder soon reasserts itself. In the midst of happy experiences, we may worry about the people we love. And there are times when ever-changing life brings misery: the death of a parent or spouse or child, divorce, sickness, fire, flood, earthquake, war, the loss of job or home.

Dukkha encompasses the whole range, from horrible suffering to everyday frustration. Someone once compared the inevitability of dukkha to buying a new car. Your car brings the pleasures of mobility and pride of ownership, but as you go for your first ride you know what lies ahead: insurance premiums, routine maintenance, and costly repairs.

The Buddha concluded that to live means inescapably to experience sorrow and dissatisfaction. But he analyzed the nature and causes of suffering much like a doctor would diagnose an illness—in order to understand and overcome them. Those who say that Buddhism pessimistically focuses on suffering do not see the hopeful purpose behind that focus. Indeed, no one can escape suffering, but each person can decide how to respond to it, as indicated in the Four Noble Truths.

The Four Noble Truths and the Noble Eightfold Path

Perhaps to aid in their memorization, some Buddhist teachings were grouped into fours and eights. The Four Noble Truths are a linked chain of truths about life: (1) suffering exists; (2) it has a cause; (3) it has an end; and (4) there is a way to attain release from suffering—namely, by following the Noble Eightfold Path. Let's look at each concept more closely.

The eight-spoked wheel is an ancient symbol of Buddhist teachings.

The First Noble Truth: To Live Is to Suffer   To say it perhaps more descriptively, "birth is attended with pain, decay is painful, disease is painful, death is painful."[7] Having a body means that we can be tired and sick. Having a mind means that we can be troubled and discouraged. We have so many daily duties that our lives become a long list of things-to-do, and we feel like jugglers trying to keep too many balls spinning in the air. The past cannot be relived, and the future is uncertain. And every day, we have to decide what to do with the rest of our lives. (It has been remarked that adults so frequently ask children "What do you want to be when you grow up?" because the adults themselves are still trying to decide what to do with their own lives.)

To live means to experience anxiety, loss, and sometimes even anguish. In other words, "living means sorrow." Although the message sounds dark, this truth urges us to be realistic, not melancholy; it is also hopeful in the sense that if we recognize why suffering comes about, then we can lessen it.

The Second Noble Truth: Suffering Comes from Desire   When he analyzed suffering, the Buddha saw that it comes from wanting what we cannot have and from never being satisfied with what we do have. The word *trishna* (Sanskrit), or *tanha* (Pali), which is often translated as "desire," might better be translated as "thirst"; it can also be translated as "craving," suggesting both an addiction and a fear of loss. Some of our desires are obvious: food, sleep, clothing, housing, health. Some desires are more subtle: privacy, respect, friendship, quiet, stresslessness, security, variety, beauty. And some desires are simply "wants" that are cultivated by our society: alcohol, designer clothes, tobacco, entertainment, expensive food. We all have desires, and because life around us is always changing, no matter how much we acquire we cannot be permanently satisfied. Desire is insatiable, and the result is discontent, dissatisfaction, and sometimes misery. But is there a way to be free of suffering?

The Third Noble Truth: To End Suffering, End Desire   It is hard to argue with the reasonableness of this truth, yet it goes against modern Western notions. The Western tendency is to strain to achieve every imaginable desire. This tendency seems to thrive in cultures—such as many modern ones—that emphasize individual legal and moral rights, competition between individuals, and individual success in school, in one's job, and in sports. Belief in a distinct and permanent self or an immortal soul may be the origin of such individualism. This tendency is rather different from the sense of self that comes from a worldview that values the individual's membership in the group—a view of self more common, traditionally, in tribal and Asian cultures.

To our modern way of thinking, the Buddha's recommendations may seem rather stark. Nevertheless, he himself left home and family and possessions because he believed—and taught—that *any* kind of attachment will bring inevitable suffering. The shaven head and special clothing of monks and nuns symbolize their radical detachment from worldly concerns.

Buddhists themselves recognize, though, that not everyone can be a monk. Consequently, this third truth is moderated for laypeople. It is commonly interpreted as a recommendation that everyone accept peacefully whatever occurs, aiming less for happiness and more for inner peace. The individual should concentrate on the present moment, not on the past or the future or one's desires for them. Because times of happiness are always paid for by times of unhappiness (the pendulum swings in both directions), a certain emotional neutrality is the best path.

Acceptance is a step to inner peace if I recognize that what I have right now is actually enough. Ultimately, I have to accept my body, my talents, my family, and even my relatives. Of course, some adjustments can be made: I can move, have plastic surgery, change my job, or get a divorce.

Look within.
Be still.
Free from fear and attachment,
Know the sweet joy of the way.
—The Dhammapada[8]

Ultimately, though, much of life simply has to be accepted—and appreciated when possible.

The essence of the Third Noble Truth is this: I cannot change the outside world, but I can change myself and the way I experience the world.

The Fourth Noble Truth: Release from Suffering Is Possible and Can Be Attained by Following the Noble Eightfold Path   The ultimate goal of Buddhism is **nirvana**. (The term is Sanskrit; the equivalent in Pali is *nibbana*.) The term *nirvana* suggests many things: end of suffering, inner peace, and liberation from the limitations of the world. The word *nirvana* seems to mean "blown out," or "cool," suggesting that the fires of desire have been extinguished. Upon attaining nirvana, the individual has self-control and is no longer driven from inside by raging emotional forces or from outside by the unpredictable events of life. It may not necessarily imply the elimination of anger (stories tell of the Buddha's getting angry at disputes within the monastic community), but it does suggest a general inner quiet. Nirvana is also believed to end karma and rebirth after the present life. (More will be said about nirvana later in this chapter.) To reach nirvana, Buddhism recommends following the Noble Eightfold Path.

The Noble Eightfold Path: The Way to Inner Peace   The eight "steps" of the path actually form a program that the Buddha taught will lead us toward liberation from the impermanence and suffering of reality. Together, they describe three main goals: to face life objectively, to live kindly, and to cultivate inner peace. Although they are often called "steps," the eight recommendations are not to be practiced sequentially but rather all together. As it is usually translated, the Noble Eightfold Path sounds so old-fashioned that readers may not immediately perceive its practicality. But keep in mind that the word *right* in the following list is a translation of a word that might better be translated as "correct" or "complete."

1. *Right understanding* I recognize the impermanence of life, the mechanism of desire, and the cause of suffering.
2. *Right intention* My thoughts and motives are pure, not tainted by my emotions and selfish desires.
3. *Right speech* I speak honestly and kindly, in positive ways, avoiding lies, exaggeration, harsh words.
4. *Right action* My actions do not hurt any other being that can feel hurt, including animals; I avoid stealing and sexual conduct that would bring hurt.
5. *Right work* My job does no harm to myself or others.
6. *Right effort* With moderation, I consistently strive to improve.
7. *Right meditation* (*right mindfulness*) I use the disciplines of meditation (**dhyana**) and focused awareness to contemplate the nature of reality more deeply.
8. *Right contemplation* I cultivate states of blissful inner peace (**samadhi**).

THE INFLUENCE OF INDIAN THOUGHT ON EARLY BUDDHIST TEACHINGS

"Right meditation" is practiced not only in monasteries, but also in meditation centers that attract Buddhists and non-Buddhists alike.

It is uncertain whether the Buddha intended to begin an entirely new religion. Early Buddhist literature rejects certain elements of the common Vedic practice of the time, particularly its ritualism, its reliance on priests, its caste system, and its belief in any permanent spiritual reality. Non-Buddhists responded argumentatively when women and slaves entered the Buddhist monastic order. Such evidence leads us to think that early Buddhists saw themselves as outside the mainstream priestly Vedic culture—a fact that may have assisted them in developing their own statements of belief and practice. Nevertheless, we do know that early Buddhist teachings accepted certain elements of Indian thought that are today shared to some extent by Hinduism, Jainism, and Buddhism.

Ahimsa: "Do No Harm"

Foremost among the elements adopted from the Indian worldview of the Buddha's day was the ideal of *ahimsa* ("nonharm"; see Chapter 3). It is not clear how old this ideal is, and it has not always been followed. We do know that Vedic sacrifice at the time of the Buddha sometimes included animal sacrifice (and animal sacrifice in Hindu practice can still be found, particularly in Nepal and Bali). But we also know that the ideal of ahimsa was already prominent in India before the time of the Buddha and may have had ancient and pre-Vedic origins.

For Buddhism, ahimsa is fundamental. The ideal holds that to cause suffering to any being is cruel and unnecessary—life is already hard enough for each of us. Ahimsa discourages causing not only physical pain but also psychological hurt or the exploitation of another. Upon reaching a real understanding that every being that feels can suffer, the individual gains wider sympathy. It is then natural and satisfying for the individual to live with gentleness.

Ahimsa is a high ideal and not always easy to achieve. Furthermore, we must recognize that there will always be a gap between the ideal and actual practice in different Buddhist cultures and among individuals. Nevertheless, however murky the definition of the "best action" may be, the ideal is fairly clear. A compassionate person does everything possible to avoid causing suffering: "ashamed of roughness, and full of mercy, he dwells compassionate and kind to all creatures that have life."[9] This empathetic ideal has been interpreted as recommending, when possible, a vegetarian or semivegetarian diet, and it warns against involvement in any jobs or sports that would hurt others, such as being a butcher, hunter, fisherman, soldier, or weapon maker. The result is a way of life that is harmonious and free of remorse.

The Soul and Karma

The Buddha rejected the notion of a soul (an unchanging spiritual reality), but he accepted some notion of rebirth. How, we might then ask, can an individual be reborn if there is no soul? Buddhism holds that while there is no individual soul, the elements of personality that make up an individual can recombine and thus continue from one lifetime to another. Buddhism offers the examples of a flame passing from one candle to another and the pattern caused by a breeze that passes over many blades of grass. The candles are separate, but only one flame passes between each candle; the blades of grass are rooted to separate places, but the pattern of the breeze travels across them and "unites" them in movement.

Closely related to the notion of rebirth is *karma*. As we discussed in Chapter 3, karma determines how one will be reborn. In Hinduism and Jainism, karma is like something that clings to the soul as it passes from life to life in reincarnation. It works automatically: good actions produce karma that brings good effects, such as intelligence, high birth, and wealth; bad actions produce karma that brings the opposite, including rebirth into animal and insect life-forms. Because the Buddha rejected the existence of a soul, explaining how karma works is more difficult in Buddhism. It is thought to accompany and affect the elements of personality that reappear in later lifetimes. Regardless of their specific manner of functioning, karma and rebirth were already such powerful ideas in the India of the Buddha's time that they continued in early Buddhism and from there have spread well beyond India. They remain highly influential concepts in Buddhist countries today.

Nirvana

In Buddhism, as in Hinduism, the everyday world of change is called **samsara**, a term that suggests decay and pain. Liberation from samsara,

Buddhist images mark these otherwise Hindu structures at Bayon, one of the grandest temples at Angkor.

however, is attained in nirvana. The notion has many similarities with the Hindu goal of *moksha* ("liberation"; discussed in Chapter 3). Nirvana is thought of as existence beyond limitation. Many people in the West associate nirvana with a psychological state, because it is described as evoking joy and peace; but perhaps it is better to see nirvana as being indescribable and beyond all psychological states. Although reaching nirvana occurs rarely, it is theoretically possible to attain during one's lifetime; the Buddha is said to have "entered nirvana" at the time of his enlightenment. Once a person has reached nirvana, rebirth is finished, and in a culture that believes that individuals have already been born many times before this current life, an end to rebirth can be a welcome thought.

THE EARLY DEVELOPMENT OF BUDDHISM

Buddhism might have remained an entirely Indian religion, much as Jainism has, if it were not for an energetic king named Ashoka, who flourished about 250 B.C.E. (Timeline 4.1). Ashoka's plan to expand his rule over a large part of India naturally entailed much fighting. After a particularly bloody battle in eastern India, as Ashoka was inspecting the battlefield, he saw the scene very differently than he had before. The whole experience

	c. 563–483 B.C.E.	Traditional dates of Siddhartha Gautama, the Buddha
Life of Ashoka, Indian king who spread Buddhist values	c. 273–232 B.C.E.	
	c. 50 C.E.	Entry of Buddhism into China
Creation of the Lotus Sutra	c. 100 C.E.	
	c. 300 C.E.	Beginning of the spread of Buddhism in Southeast Asia
Entry of Buddhism into Korea	c. 400 C.E.	
	c. 520 C.E.	Introduction of Bodhidharma's Meditation school of Buddhism to China
Introduction of Buddhism into Japan	c. 552 C.E.	
	c. 630 C.E.	Entry of Buddhism into Tibet
Founding of Tendai and Shingon Buddhism in Japan	c. 820 C.E.	
	c. 845 C.E.	Major persecution of Buddhists in China
Revival of Theravada Buddhism in Sri Lanka and Southeast Asia	c. 1000 C.E.	
	c. 1100–1500	Decline of Buddhism in India
Life of Honen, founder of the Pure Land sect in Japan	1133–1212	
	1158–1210	Life of Chinul, founder of the Korean Chogye order
Beginning of the growth of Zen in Japan	c. 1200	
	1222–1282	Life of Nichiren, founder of Nichiren Buddhism in Japan
Life of Tsong Kha-pa, Tibetan Buddhist reformer	1357–1419	
	1644–1694	Life of poet Matsuo Basho
Beginning of the World Fellowship of Buddhists	c. 1952	
	1989	Award of the Nobel Peace Prize to the Dalai Lama

was so horrifying that Ashoka converted to the ideal of nonviolence. Although it is uncertain whether Ashoka became a Buddhist, he did make political use of Buddhist moral values. A cynic might note that forbidding violence is a practical move for any ruler who wishes to remain on the throne. In any case, the principle of nonviolence is most effective when it is embraced widely; otherwise, the few people who are nonviolent will be preyed upon by the violent.

To bring a large number of the population around to his new nonviolent way of thinking and acting, Ashoka decided to spread the principles of non-violence throughout India and possibly even beyond. To do this, he erected many stone columns inscribed with his principles, placing some at sites important in the Buddha's life. A number of these columns still exist today.

Our historical knowledge of Ashoka is quite limited, but he looms large in Buddhist legend. One story tells us that Ashoka sent as a missionary to Sri Lanka a son or nephew named Mahinda. Whatever the truth of this story, it is a fact that Sri Lanka is largely Buddhist today. Indeed, it may have been Ashoka who gave Buddhism its urge to spread and helped to make it one of the world's great missionary religions.

In the first centuries after the Buddha's death, in response to widespread and long-standing disagreements over the Buddha's teachings, many Buddhist schools and splinter groups arose. Most of these ultimately died out and are only names to us today. A few survived and crystallized into the great branches of Buddhism that we now recognize: Theravada, Mahayana, and Vajrayana.

It was once assumed that each branch emerged after an earlier one, like three waves of thought that came from India in succeeding centuries. But scholars now recognize that essential elements of all three branches frequently existed side by side, possibly even in the earliest days of Buddhism. Sometimes monks of quite different practices lived in the same monasteries, and some still do. In addition, different branches coexisted in or dominated certain regions but then died out. (For example, Mahayana Buddhism, once common in Myanmar, no longer exists there.) Often, too, the boundaries between the branches have been blurred or are even nonexistent.

We should also realize that the three so-called branches are not homogeneous and monolithic. Instead, within them are also divisions and different understandings of belief and practice. (Among Theravada Buddhist orders of monks, for example, some believe they must go barefoot, whereas others wear sandals; some wear orange robes, and others wear brown or burgundy; some believe they must beg for all their food, while others do not; and so on.) The branches are more like families that have many shared elements.

In addition, people who follow a specific Buddhist path are often not aware of other branches. The same is not true of some other religions, in which practitioners are quite aware of the division to which they belong. (For example, Muslims define themselves as Sunni or Shiite, and Christians

Timeline of significant events in Buddhism. ◀

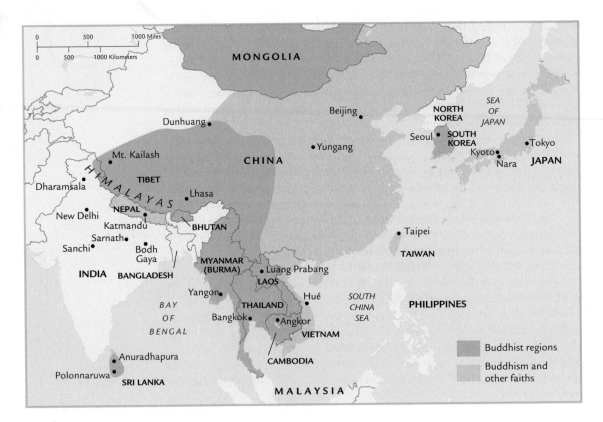

FIGURE 4.1

The birthplace and traditional home of Buddhism: India, China, Japan, and Southeast Asia.

as Protestant, Catholic, or Orthodox.) But Buddhist believers of one branch, even if they know of other forms, generally do not define themselves in contrast to those other branches. Instead, they define themselves more according to Buddhist "lineages," tracing their beliefs and practices back to the great teachers of the past who, in a long chain of masters and disciples, handed on the traditions that they follow.

Thus, before we divide Buddhism into these so-called branches, we must realize that to talk of three "branches" is to greatly oversimplify the complex reality of Buddhism. This approach is only meant to enhance the understanding of the richness of Buddhist history, belief, and practice.

THERAVADA BUDDHISM: THE WAY OF THE ELDERS

In the early centuries of Buddhism, several schools claimed to adhere to the original, unchanged teachings of the Buddha. All of them shared the Buddha's opposition to Vedic ritual and the brahmin priesthood, as well as his appreciation for simplicity, meditation, and detachment. They took a conservative approach, hoping to protect the Buddha's rather stark teachings and simple practice from being altered. Of all the conservative schools, one has survived to the present day: Theravada. Its name is often used today to refer to the entire conservative movement.

The Theravada school takes its name from its goal of passing on the Buddha's teachings unchanged. It means "the way (*vada*) of the elders (*thera*)." Theravada monks originally passed on the teachings in oral form, but they eventually wrote them down. Although the school's claim to have kept its teachings relatively unchanged over time is doubtful, it is true that Theravada has a deliberately conservative orientation. Since the nineteenth century, the name *Theravada* has been commonly used to refer to the forms of Buddhism that are found mostly in Sri Lanka and Southeast Asia.

The heart of Theravada Buddhism is its community of monks. As a school, it has always stressed the ideal of reaching nirvana through detachment and desirelessness achieved through meditation. (This, of course, is an ideal that some would point out has been contradicted by the Sangha's having courted wealth and temporal power.) Although Thera-

Buddhists typically visit their local temple at the New Year. They leave offerings and receive blessings from the temple's monks.

vada does accept that laypeople can attain nirvana, the life of the monk offers a surer path. The notion is enshrined in the ideal of the **arhat** (Sanskrit; Pali: *arahat,* meaning "perfect being," "worthy"), a person who has reached nirvana.*

The Theravada monastic community had its distant origins in the wandering sannyasins and in the groups of Hindu ascetics who lived in the forests. (A sign of this connection is the orange robe; it is used by Hindu ascetics and is also worn by many orders of Theravada Buddhist monks.) But even during the Buddha's lifetime, his monks began to live a settled life during the summertime monsoon season, giving their time to discussion and inhabiting caves or groves and parks donated by lay followers.

Theravada spread very early from India to Sri Lanka, where it has gone through several phases of growth and decline. By the fourth century, it had

---

*In the discussion of Theravada Buddhism, it would be more accurate to use the Pali terms *nibbana, arahat,* and *sutta,* as opposed to the Sanskrit terms *nirvana, arhat,* and *sutra;* however, for the sake of consistency, the text throughout this chapter will reflect the terminology (whether Pali or Sanskrit) that is most familiar in the West.

These Myanmar nuns with trays on their heads go into the community every morning to receive food offerings.

been carried—along with other elements of Indian culture—to Myanmar (Burma) and to Thailand. Theravada did not become predominant in Myanmar until the mid-eleventh century, when Bagan began to flourish as a great Buddhist city and center of Theravada under King Anawratha. Fourteenth-century Thailand, having freed itself of Khmer domination, also adopted Theravada Buddhism. The conservatism of Theravada was politically appealing to rulers for its moral rigor. Today it is the dominant religion in Sri Lanka, Myanmar, Thailand, Laos, and Cambodia.

Theravada monks must beg daily for their food, which has meant that they, like the Buddha's early followers, have to live close to laypeople. In fact, Theravada monasteries are often in the middle of towns. Many monasteries run schools, meditation centers, and medical clinics, as well as care for stray animals (which sometimes overrun the grounds). In return, monks are the beneficiaries of regular donations. When Theravada monks go out on their begging rounds in the early morning, people who wish to donate food freely offer them rice and vegetables. Donors believe they are receiving beneficial karma from their acts of generosity, and people support

Buddhism in Thailand

Theravada Buddhism is the state religion of Thailand, and more than 90 percent of Thais are Buddhists. Thai Buddhists, however, practice a religion that blends elements from Buddhism, Hinduism, and folk belief. Perhaps because Buddhism so emphasizes tolerance, Buddhism as it is actually practiced is rich with elements from many sources.

Buddhism's prevalence in Thailand is evident in everyday life. Thais frequently act publicly on the assumption that doing good deeds will "make merit"—bring good karma for this life and for future lives. To make merit, Thais offer coins to the needy on the street, give food and robes to monks, attend Buddhist services, and help animals. And Buddhist monks can be seen everywhere—walking in the streets and riding in the back of buses (which they ride free), in *tuk-tuks* (three-wheeled cabs), and on riverboats.

Yet equally visible are "spirit houses." These look like miniature temples, and they are erected on high posts at the corner of a piece of land, on high-rise rooftops, or under large, old trees. Spirit houses are dedicated to the guardian spirits of the property and to the spirits of former owners. Worshipers offer food and flowers to them daily.

Frequently the Hindu god Brahma is the figure inside the spirit houses, and small images of dancing girls—derived from Hindu temple worship—are left as permanent offerings. In shops a visitor might see a statue of Ganesha, the elephant-headed Hindu god associated with success. Another influence of Hinduism is readily apparent in Thai art and dance, which tell the stories of Rama, Sita, and Hanuman, whose tales are retold in the Ramakien, the Thai version of the Ramayana.

A strong magical dimension is part of Thai Buddhism as well. Thai males often wear a necklace of Buddhist amulets to defend themselves against sickness and injury (the owners will describe in happy detail the origin and power of each of the amulets). Tattoos, often with images of the Buddha, Rama, and Hanuman, are thought to have a similar effect. And taxi drivers—not to mention their often anxious passengers—hope that the multiple Buddhist images on their dashboards will offer needed protection in traffic.

---

the monasteries much like other societies give to libraries and other social agencies. At Buddhist festivals monks are given new robes and pails of essential items, such as soap, toothpaste, razors, and canned goods. Donations are especially given at the New Year festival and at the beginning and end of the rainy season. (This period, often called "Buddhist Lent," begins in late summer and lasts for three months. During this time monks stay in their monasteries for study.)

Most weddings, funerals, and other family events are considered incomplete without the presence of monks, who are expected to chant from the *sutras* (sayings of the Buddha, which we will discuss shortly) to provide merit for the family members. Monks are also an important part of festivals, many of which are organized by monasteries themselves. (It is not unusual to see monks under a small pavilion that has been set up specially at a festival for the exhibition of puppet shows, acrobatics, and even kickboxing.) Older monks are consulted for advice on business and marriage, and some are firmly believed to have special powers (such monks are consulted for picking winning lottery ticket numbers). Statues of old and wizened monks— monks who are believed to be wonderworkers—may even be found for sale in markets. They are bought and placed on a high shelf in people's homes,

where the statues receive signs of hopeful veneration in the form of flowers, water, and incense.

In Theravada Buddhism, not only is ordination performed for men who are planning to become monks for life, but "temporary ordination" is also commonly performed. Frequently, temporary ordination lasts for an entire rainy season, but it may also be done for shorter periods. Temporary ordination is considered an effective way to "make merit" for oneself and one's family. It is thought to positively influence the formation of young men's characters, and it is sometimes undertaken by whole groups, such as policemen, for whom it is viewed as a sign of sincerity and goodwill.

Monasticism, as we see, permeates society and everyday life in Theravada Buddhist cultures. As mentioned earlier, monasteries exist even in the centers of cities, where monks can be seen everywhere. There is a fluidity to monastic life, too, since Theravada monks often choose to leave monastic life, even after many years. But during the time that men are monks, they are considered role models and are expected to live up to strict moral standards.

The earliest Western translators and scholars of Theravada Buddhism saw Buddhism through the lens of their own culture. Key to their conception of what makes a religion was a body of written scriptures; the scholars assumed that written scriptures played a central role in believers' lives. More recent scholarship points out that Buddhist teachings have been largely passed on orally. Because the vast majority of Buddhists have been unable to read, they have learned their religious beliefs and practices not from books, but from hearing sermons, seeing temple paintings, and listening to older family members. And long before written material existed, certain monks were known as specialists in chanting the words of the Buddha, the rules of their order, and the precepts of right living. Eventually this oral material was indeed written down and codified. But, as we learn about the written scriptures, we must understand the primary role that oral transmission has played.

In addition to the so-called canonical scriptures, folktales have been influential. The most famous are the hundreds of Jataka Tales. They are similar to Aesop's Fables, and early forms of them may have influenced those tales and similar collections in other countries. The tales are about human beings and animals, and each tale teaches a moral lesson about a particular virtue, such as friendship, truthfulness, generosity, or moderation. In Theravada Buddhism the tales are often put within a Buddhist context. Typically, the tale begins with the Buddha telling the tale. The tale then ends with the Buddha saying that in a past life he was one of the animal or human figures in the story. The Jataka Tales are frequently the subject of art, plays, and dance in Southeast Asia.

Theravada Teachings and Literature

The Theravada collection of the Buddha's teachings is called the Pali Canon. As a whole, this mass of material is called *Tipitaka* (Pali), or **Tripitaka** (Sanskrit), which means "three baskets." The name comes from the fact that the writings were divided according to their subject matter into three groups.

The first collection (called *vinaya*—Pali and Sanskrit) outlines the procedural rules for monastic life. These include rules on begging, eating, relations with monks and nonmonks, and other disciplines.[10] The second collection comprises sayings of the Buddha in the form of sermons or dialogues. This type of material is called *sutta* (Pali), or **sutra** (Sanskrit). A third collection, developed later, is called *abhidhamma* (Pali), or *abhidharma* (Sanskrit), meaning "the works that go beyond the elementary teachings." It systematized the doctrine presented more or less randomly in the sutras.

Theravada Art and Architecture

Images of the Buddha did not appear in the earliest centuries of Buddhism; instead, artists used symbols to represent him and his teachings. One symbol was the eight-spoked wheel, which derived from the Noble Eightfold Path and represented all the basic Buddhist teachings, the Dharma. (The wheel may have been suggested either by the disk of the sun, symbolizing light and health, or by the wheel of a king's chariot, a symbol of royal rulership.) The umbrella, often carried to protect an important person from the hot sun, symbolized the Buddha's authority. Other common symbols included a set of footprints, a lotus flower, and an empty throne. Many types of **stupas,** which began as a large mounds, arose over the remains of Buddhist monks and at important Buddhist sites. Symbols may have been used at first simply because artists were struggling with the basic challenge of depicting simultaneously the humanity of the Buddha and his great spiritual attainment, his enlightenment. By the first century of the common era, however, images of the Buddha

The Reclining Buddha at Wat Po in Bangkok, which fills an entire temple, is one of the most revered images in Thailand. If you look closely at the bottom of the image, you will see worshipers standing in front of the altar.

began to appear. (Scholars debate the possible influence of Greek sculptural traditions.[11]) In Theravada countries we now frequently see statues of the Buddha meditating, standing (with hand outstretched in blessing), walking, or reclining. Some of the most beautiful sculptures are the Reclining Buddhas of Sri Lanka and Thailand.

MAHAYANA BUDDHISM: THE "BIG VEHICLE"

The second great branch of Buddhism is called Mahayana, a word that is usually translated as "big vehicle." It suggests a large ferryboat in which all types of people can be carried across a river, and it hints at the broad scope of the Mahayana vision, which can accommodate a wide variety of people seeking enlightenment. Mahayana emphasizes that nirvana is not only attainable by monks but is a possibility for everyone. Mahayana also stresses that enlightenment is a call to compassion, for "the Mahayana tradition maintains that a person must save himself by saving others."[12]

Some critics of Mahayana Buddhism claim that it has allowed ritual and speculation—which had been deemphasized by the Buddha—to creep back in. It is possible that the Indian love of ritual and imagery remains alive in a new form in Mahayana. For example, the fire ceremony of some Mahayana sects certainly derives from Vedic practice. But this is really to say that Mahayana initially was thoroughly Indian and sought to express its truths in very Indian ways.[13]

It is possible that some practices or attitudes of early Buddhism did not always fulfill the religious needs of the many laypeople who appreciated ritual. Mahayana Buddhism, however, has abundantly met almost every religious and philosophical need.[14] It is the source of some of the most extraordinary creations of the human mind—in its art, architecture, philosophy, psychology, and ceremony.

New Ideals: Compassion and the Bodhisattva

In Mahayana Buddhism, the religious ideal broadened: from the exemplar of the monastic person, fairly detached from family life, it expanded to include nonmonks, women, and the married. Mahayana began to explore the possibilities of following a religious path that was active in the world. This difference signaled a shift in the notion of what is virtuous. It might have represented a reaction against Indian asceticism and the cult of the sannyasin, or it might have indicated a new form of devotionalism and love of ritual. It might also have come from a widening of the concept of nirvana. Nirvana was now thought to be found within samsara, the everyday world of change. This devotional shift began in India and in central Asia, but it grew in strength when Mahayana entered China, a culture that has long valued nature and the physical world in general. In Mahayana, the human body and the material realm are viewed positively, and there is a great openness toward art and music. Mahayana grew as the senses and emotions were increasingly viewed as means of spiritual transformation.

The Hindu ritual of anointing sacred objects became a part of Mahayana devotional practice, as seen here in the anointed dome of Boudhanath in Nepal.

In Mahayana, wisdom remained an important goal, but the pairing of wisdom and compassion was central to its teachings. Compassion became an essential virtue and the preeminent expression of wisdom. The term for this compassion is **karuna**, which may also be translated as "empathy," "sympathy," or "kindness." Karuna is somewhat different from the Western notion of kindness, in which one separate human being, out of an abundance of individual generosity, gives to another separate human being. Rather, karuna implies that we all are part of the same ever-changing universe. Deep down, the individual is not really different from anyone or anything else. To be kind to others is actually to be kind to oneself. Karuna in action simply means living out this awareness of the unity of the universe. With this perception of the interrelatedness of all beings, including animals, compassion comes naturally: if I am kind, my kindness must be shown toward anything that can feel pain. The great prayer of Buddhist compassion is this: May all creatures be well and happy. It is a common Mahayana practice to mentally project this wish to the world every day.

The esteem for karuna influences the human ideal in Mahayana. Instead of the Theravada ideal of the arhat, who is esteemed for detached wisdom and unworldly living, the ideal in Mahayana Buddhism is the person of deep compassion, the **bodhisattva** ("enlightenment being"). Because a bodhisattva embodies compassion, it is often said that a bodhisattva will refuse to fully enter nirvana, in order to be reborn on earth to help others. A person may even take the "bodhisattva vow" to be constantly reborn until all are enlightened.

The same kind of openness to a variety of religious paths that we saw in Hinduism is also typical of Mahayana Buddhism. Mahayana recognizes that people differ greatly and find themselves at different stages of spiritual development. For example, a person who would not benefit from study or meditation might be able to achieve a new level of understanding through the use of ritual, imagery, and religious objects. It is possible to find the influence of bhakti yoga (see Chapter 3) in Mahayana, because Mahayana even endorses devotion to deities. Some critics may label such practices as superstition. Regardless, Mahayana is open to anything that can lead to greater spiritual awareness, a concept known as "skillful means" (Sanskrit: *upaya*).

Mahayana Thought and Worldview

Mahayana has encouraged a vision of reality that is imaginative, wide, and often profound. A legendary story tells of a Chinese emperor who began reading certain Mahayana sutras; he then said in astonishment that the experience was like looking out over the ocean. He sensed the vastness of the Mahayana vision, as he experienced both the quantity and the quality of the sutras that he was attempting to understand.

Several key notions must be introduced here. They show a worldview of a universe populated by holy personalities and full of the divine. These notions may seem dry when they are only read about, but they will become very meaningful when a person is experiencing Mahayana art in temples and museums. These ideas underlie Mahayana sculpture, painting, and belief.

The Three-Body Doctrine (Trikaya Doctrine)   In Mahayana, the Buddha nature can express itself in three ways. This is called the **trikaya** ("three-body") doctrine. The historical Buddha who lived in India came to be considered the manifestation of a divine reality, "the cosmic Buddha nature." The Sanskrit term for this is *Dharmakaya* (often translated as "law body," "form body," or "body of reality"). According to Mahayana Buddhism, the cosmic Buddha nature, although invisible, permeates all things. (It is sometimes compared to the Hindu notion of Brahman, which may have influenced it.) In people, the cosmic Buddha nature frequently presents itself as potential. In fact, it is our true nature that we need to recognize and realize. Dharmakaya also exists in the natural world, for all things are a sacred manifestation of the cosmic Buddha nature. When we experience the mystery of the natural world, we experience the Dharmakaya.

At Boudhanath in Katmandu, Nepal, these eyes represent the omnipresent Buddha nature.

Siddhartha Gautama's physical body, because it is considered an incarnation of this divine reality, is called Nirmanakaya ("transformation body"). The notion that the historical Buddha was a divine manifestation reminds us of the Hindu notion of the multiple incarnations of Vishnu, and this Mahayana notion may have been influenced by that Hindu belief.

In keeping with the notion of many incarnations, many Mahayana schools believe in more than one transformation body of the Buddha. We might recall that both Theravada and Mahayana schools describe the Buddha's knowledge of his past lives. Both branches of Buddhism also believe that another historical Buddha, **Maitreya** (Sanskrit; Pali: Metteya), will appear on earth in the future to inaugurate a golden age. In several Mahayana cultures, this belief has taken on great importance. In China and Vietnam, the Buddha who will come is called Mi-lo-fo and is often shown as an overweight, joyful, "laughing Buddha." In Korea, the notion of Miruk (as Maitreya is known there) has been especially influential in generating belief in a messianic future, which has prompted the creation of many beautiful statues in his honor. He is often shown seated on a stool or raised platform in the so-called Western style, with one leg down on the floor and the other crossed over it, his head resting thoughtfully on one hand as he contemplates the future.

In Mahayana philosophy, the cosmic Buddha nature has also taken bodily shape in supernatural Buddhas who live in the heavens beyond our earth. These Buddhas have radiant, invulnerable bodies and live in constant happiness. In Sanskrit, they are called Sambhogakaya Buddhas ("perfect-bliss-body" Buddhas). Mahayana Buddhism envisions many Buddhas existing simultaneously, each with his own sphere of influence (called a "Buddha Land"). Particularly important is the bliss-body Buddha who created a Buddha Land in the western direction of the setting sun. There he receives the dying who wish enlightenment after death. His name in India was **Amitabha Buddha** (Chinese: Amito-fo; Japanese: Amida Butsu). Many devout Buddhists hope to be reborn in his paradise. After attaining enlightenment there, they can return to the world to save other beings. Their devotion to Amitabha Buddha has inspired a great body of fine painting and sculpture that depicts a large Buddha seated on a lotus flower, surrounded by peaceful disciples in pavilions set in gardens full of flowers.

In Mahayana, the bodhisattva Guanyin is venerated as a manifestation of compassion.

Heavenly Bodhisattvas We have already discussed the focus of Mahayana on the earthly bodhisattva, a saintly person of great compassion. But Mahayana Buddhism also holds that many bodhisattvas who are eager to help human beings also exist in other dimensions beyond the earth. They, too, are beings of great compassion. Some once lived on earth and have been reborn beyond this world, but they retain an interest in it. They may appear miraculously on earth when needed or possibly may even be reborn to help others.

The most significant of the heavenly bodhisattvas has been Avalokiteshvara, who looks down from a location above in order to give help. In India, Avalokiteshvara was portrayed as male, but in China this bodhisattva was conceived as feminine because of her association with compassion and mercy. Her name in Chinese is **Guanyin** (Kuan-yin,* "hears cries"). She first appeared in early depictions as having both male and female characteristics, but eventually she became entirely feminine. (As an object of devotion, she plays a role in Asia similar to that of Mary in Europe.) East Asian paintings and sculpture frequently show her with a very sweet face, dressed all in white, holding the jewel of wisdom or a vase of nectar, and with the moon under her feet or in the sky behind her. Other artistic renderings of her,

---

Note: Two systems are currently used for transcribing Chinese words into English: the *pinyin* and Wade-Giles systems. Because the Chinese government and the United Nations have adopted pinyin, it has become the most commonly used system. The older Wade-Giles was the standard transcription system until pinyin was adopted, and it is still frequently encountered (as in the spelling of *Kuan-yin*). For major Chinese terms in this book (both here and in Chapter 6), the pinyin spelling is given first and the Wade-Giles spelling second.

particularly in temple sculpture, show her with a halo of many arms (she is said to have a thousand), representing her many powers to help. In the palm of each hand is an eye, symbolizing her ability to see everyone in need. In China and Japan (where this bodhisattva became popularly known as Kannon), many temples were dedicated to her.

Shunyata   One Mahayana doctrine asserts that all reality is *shunya* ("empty"; that is, empty of permanent essence). Literally, **shunyata** may be translated as "emptiness" or "zero-ness." But what does this mean? The notion is an out-growth of the basic Buddhist view of reality that everything is constantly shift-ing, changing, taking new form. If we consider an individual person, we can say the "individual" is a pattern, made of parts in continuous change. If we broaden our scope, larger patterns appear, such as the patterns of a family, a city, or a society. Similarly, nature is a combination of smaller patterns making larger patterns, like wheels within wheels. And even the parts themselves ulti-mately disintegrate as new parts are born. To better understand this concept, think of clouds, which look large and substantial but are forever appearing and disappearing, moving past each other and changing shape and size. Because everything is in constant change, each apparently individual person and thing is actually "empty" of any permanent individual identity. The notion of shun-yata also suggests the experience that everything is a part of everything else, that all people and things exist together.

Tathata   Literally translated, the word **tathata** means "thatness," "thus-ness," or "suchness." This is a rich notion that invites each person's experi-ence and interpretation. Tathata represents a view of experience that says that reality is revealed in each moment, as we savor patterns, relationships, and change. Because no moment is exactly the same, and no object is exactly the same, each can be observed and appreciated as it passes. Thus, simple, everyday events reveal the nature of reality. We may experience "thatness" when two elements come together in an unexpected way—for example, when a small child says something childlike but wise. Sometimes it comes when we notice a moment of change, such as when, after a long string of muggy summer days, we get up to add a blanket to the bed on the first crisp autumn night. Or it might be when we notice elements coming together somewhat unexpectedly—for example, when a bird drinks from a water fountain or a dog joyously sticks its nose out of the window of a passing car. It might be when we recognize the uniqueness of a simple object or event, such as the beauty of a particular apple in the supermarket, or the special way that the shadow of a tree falls on a nearby building at this particular moment. The experience can also come from something funny or sad. Although tathata involves the mundane, it is also a poetic moment that will never return in exactly the same way.

The wonder that can be seen in everyday life is what the term *tathata* suggests. We know we are experiencing the "thatness" of reality when we experience something and say to ourselves, "Yes, that's it; that is the way things are." In the moment, we recognize that reality is wondrously beautiful but also that its patterns are fragile and passing.

Mahayana Literature

Mahayana Buddhism in India developed versions of the Tripitaka in Sanskrit. A host of additional written works also became canonical. Many of the new Mahayana works were called sutras because they purported to be the words of the Buddha, but in reality they were imaginative, colorful creations written at least several centuries after the Buddha lived, from about 100 B.C.E. to about 600 C.E. The teachings of these sutras, however, may be seen as a natural development of basic Buddhist insights.

Primary among these texts are the Prajnaparamita Sutras ("sutras on the perfection of wisdom"), the earliest of which may have been written about 100 B.C.E. These sutras attempt to contrast ordinary understanding with the enlightened understanding that everything in the universe is interdependent.

The influential Vimalakirti Sutra teaches that it is possible to live a devout Buddhist life without necessarily becoming a monk. The hero of the sutra is the man Vimalakirti, who was, as one historian describes him, "a layman rich and powerful, a brilliant conversationalist, a respected householder who surrounded himself with the pleasures of life, but was also a faithful and wise disciple of the Buddha, a man full of wisdom and thoroughly disciplined in his conduct."[15] Because the main figure is not a monk but more like a devout gentleman, we can see why this sutra became popular with laypeople. Its purpose, though, was serious. It showed that individuals can work successfully amidst the dangers of worldly life, can avoid causing harm, and can actually help themselves and others.

Two works that would have great influence on East Asian Buddhism were the Pure Land Sutras (two versions of the Sukhavati Vyuha Sutra, "sutra of the vision of the happy land"). The sutras speak of a heavenly realm, the Pure Land, established by the merciful Amitabha Buddha, where human beings can be reborn. All that is necessary for rebirth in the Pure Land is devotion to this Buddha, as shown by repetition of his name as a sign of total trust in him. These sutras would eventually give birth to a wildly successful movement, the Pure Land movement, which is still popular today. (We will discuss the Pure Land school of Mahayana a little later in this chapter.)

One of the most widely loved works of Mahayana was the Saddharma Pundarika Sutra ("lotus sutra of the good law"), known simply as the Lotus Sutra. In this sutra, the Buddha shows his transcendent, cosmic nature. As he preaches to thousands of his disciples, his light and wisdom extend out into the universe. Using parables, the sutra insists rather democratically that all people have the Buddha nature and that all, therefore, can become Buddhas. Many of its parables talk of the "skillful means" that can lead people of differing types and mentalities to enlightenment.

Worshipers are dwarfed by the Buddha image in this Mahayana temple of southern China.

The Spread of Mahayana in East Asia

Mahayana Buddhism spread out of India to central Asia and to China, which it entered in the first century of the common era. As Buddhism spread to China and its neighboring regions, Sanskrit writings were translated bit by bit into at least thirteen central Asian languages. In China, several Chinese versions were made of most of the major works. By the eighth century, an enormous number of Buddhist works had been translated into Chinese.[16]

The appeal of Mahayana Buddhism in ancient China is worth considering. In some ways, the Buddhist ideal of monastic celibacy went against the grain of the Chinese Confucian culture, which (1) saw moral demands existing within family relationships, (2) venerated ancestors, and (3) valued continuity of the family line (see Chapter 6). Yet Mahayana Buddhism had virtues that appealed to a wide spectrum of the population. It accepted local cults and continued their practice of using rituals that promised magic, healing, and fertility for the masses of ordinary people. It created great temples with beautiful art and ceremony. It promoted peace and family harmony. It answered questions about the afterlife and performed funeral and memorial services for the dead. It provided a secure way of community life for people not interested in having children or creating their own families. It offered philosophical insights not already present in Chinese culture. And it provided many rulers with prayers and rituals that would help protect the nation and the rulers themselves.

How many individual schools and lineages existed is still being debated. Some forms of Mahayana may have been entirely separate schools, and others merely different interpretations of rules and teachings that existed within the same monasteries. Despite occasional persecution as a dangerous, foreign import, Mahayana spread throughout China. In particular, two forms of Mahayana flourished. The school of meditation (Chan, Ch'an) became highly influential among monks, poets, and artists. The Pure Land movement, with its devotion to Amitabha Buddha, became the primary form of devotion for laypeople. Ultimately, Buddhism was linked with Daoism and Confucianism as one of the officially sanctioned "Three Doctrines," and it became an essential part of Chinese culture.

Buddhism and its literature were carried into Korea from central Asia and China as early as 372 c.e.[17] Buddhism was adopted widely for its supposed powers to protect the three kingdoms then ruling the peninsula. Monasteries were thought of as powerhouses, sending monks' prayers to powerful Buddhas and bodhisattvas and receiving their celestial care in return. Korea was unified by the Silla kingdom, producing the Unified Silla dynasty (668–918 c.e.), and this unification led to a blending of religious elements from Daoism, Confucianism, shamanism, and Buddhism. Buddhism became the state religion and primary practitioner of official ritual.

At a Korean temple, people sit or kneel before images such as these. Congregants typically either meditate or study Buddhist scriptures.

Buddhist Festivals

The most important Buddhist festivals focus on the birth of the Buddha, his enlightenment, his death, the celebration of the New Year, and sometimes the commemoration of the dead. The exact dates for these celebrations and memorials differ from culture to culture.

In Theravada Buddhist countries, one great celebration (Vesak) recalls the birth, the enlightenment, and the death of the Buddha. It is celebrated at the time of the full moon in May.

In Mahayana Buddhism, the three festivals of the Buddha's life are separate. His birth is celebrated on the eighth day of the fourth month; his enlightenment is commemorated in winter on Bodhi Day, the eighth day of the twelfth month; and his death is recalled in early spring on the fifteenth day of the second month.

(Chinese and Korean Buddhists follow the lunar calendar, while Japanese Buddhists use the Western calendar.)

Celebration of the New Year often includes a visit to a temple to end the old year and the sharing of a vegetarian meal to welcome the new year. (The Japanese keep the Western New Year, while the Chinese celebrate their lunar New Year in February.)

In Japan the dead are remembered in a midsummer festival called O-Bon, derived from older Chinese practice. It has blended with Shinto elements and a belief in the Mahayana bodhisattva Jizo, who guides the dead back to the spirit world. If possible, the spirits' return is lighted with candles that drift down a stream or out into the ocean.

During summer, O-Bon is celebrated across the world at Buddhist temples that have origins in Japan. At every temple, there is special dancing. At temples near bodies of water, lanterns with the names of dead ancestors may be set afloat.

Buddhism in Korea reached its height during the Koryo dynasty (918–1392 C.E.). During this time, 80,000 wooden blocks were carved for the printing of all Korean and Chinese Buddhist texts of the Korean Tripitaka. After the first set of blocks was burned during a Mongol invasion, another set, which still exists, was finished in 1251. One of the greatest exponents of Korean Buddhism at this time was the monk Chinul (1158–1210). Given to a monastery as a young boy, he began meditation and textual study early. He had three great experiences of insight, all prompted by his reading of Mahayana materials. He founded the Chogye order, which combines textual study with regular meditation. It is still influential today.

Buddhism was supplanted by Confucianism as the state religion during the Yi dynasty (1392–1910). Nevertheless, although the aristocracy identified with Confucianism, the common people remained Buddhist.

Buddhism entered Japan in the sixth century C.E., where it began to grow after some initial resistance. It became so powerful in the early capital of Nara that in 794 the new capital city of Kyoto (then called Heian-kyo) was founded partly in order to be free from the influence of Buddhist clergy. The new capital was designed on a grid pattern, after Chinese models, and Japanese culture imported many elements of the Chinese culture of the time. Because the founding of the new capital coincided with a vibrant period of Mahayana Buddhism in China, Japanese Buddhism also imported Chinese Buddhist practices and teachings.

The history of Buddhism in Japan shows a movement toward increasing the power of laypeople. The first period, when the capital was at Nara, was dominated by essentially monastic Buddhist schools. In the second period, after the capital moved, the dominant schools (Shingon and Tendai; Figure 4.2) were ritualistic and appealed to the aristocracy. Their prominence lasted for about four hundred years. In the thirteenth century, however, two schools (Pure Land and Zen) particularly appealed to commoners and the military. Because Zen was adopted by many in the military, which controlled Japan until 1868, it became enormously influential in Japanese culture in general. (The separate schools are described in the following section.)

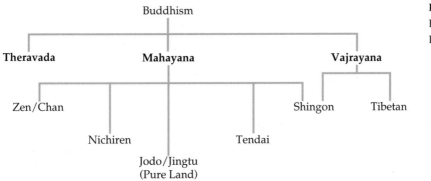

FIGURE 4.2
Branches and schools of Buddhism

At this Vietnamese Buddhist temple in Honolulu, congregants celebrate the lunar New Year.

Some Major Schools of Mahayana

The many ideals of Mahayana Buddhism contain the seeds for a variety of schools of intellectual interpretation and practice. One such ideal—the notion that kindness is the supreme sign of enlightened awareness—has allowed many pre-Buddhist beliefs and practices to continue within Mahayana Buddhism: old gods receive new names, making them into heavenly Buddhas and bodhisattvas; old beliefs are absorbed; and old practices persist with new meanings. As we discussed earlier, Mahayana Buddhism also recognizes that people find themselves at different stages of spiritual evolution. Thus, whatever helps a person move to the next stage of awareness may be religiously acceptable. This is the notion of "skillful means": some people need images to look at and gods to pray to; other people need a community of devout friends; and a very few need only silence and emptiness. Finally, the multiplicity of Mahayana texts invites many philosophical and practical approaches, as one Buddhist group focuses on one text and another Buddhist group focuses on another. The sects of Mahayana Buddhism thus show a wide variety of attitudes toward the use of art and ritual, toward the acceptance of pleasure, and toward worldly success.

These interesting differences are exhibited in the major sects of Japan, as described in the following pages. It was traditionally thought that these

An image of the bodhisattva Jizo is backed by a painting of the Shingon Kongo-kai mandala.

individual sects (except for one) began in China and were then introduced to Japan. Exactly how separate the sects originally were in China, however, is a matter of current debate. In Japan and Hawai'i, the sects have remained rather separate, and their differences may be easily experienced by interested travelers.

Shingon   The name of this school is Shingon (Chinese: Zhen-yan, Chen-yen) and means "true word" or "word of truth." The title refers to the use of sacred chants, called mantras. We might recall that the spread of Mahayana Buddhism in China was due in part to the magical effects that were thought to come from Buddhist ritual. People believed that Buddhist ritual, if carefully performed, would provide security for rulers, children for married couples, and more favorable agricultural conditions for farmers.

Behind Shingon ritual is a focus on experiencing union with the cosmic Buddha nature. This can be accomplished through the chanting of mantras, accompanied by a multitude of rituals and ritual objects. Foremost among these rituals is a fire ceremony, the *goma*, a continuation of the Vedic fire ceremony. In this ceremony, the priest builds a fire within a square sacred space bounded by colored cords. The priest throws wood and leaves slowly into the fire, symbolically destroying all egotistic hindrances to mystical union.

Shingon uses two **mandalas,** which are geometrical designs, usually painted on cloth, that present reality in symbolic form. One mandala, the Kongo-kai ("diamond-world") mandala, shows the universe from the point of view of the wise person, who sees the universe as whole and perfect. It represents the universe seen as nirvana. The other mandala, the Tai-zo ("womb") mandala, shows the universe from the point of view of the compassionate person. It sees the universe as samsara, a place of suffering and growth that needs our help.

Shingon developed from a type of magically oriented Buddhism that originated in India and was introduced to China. It was established in Japan by Kukai (774–835 C.E.), a Japanese monk who studied in China and returned to Japan with new knowledge of ritual and with books, mandalas, and altar implements. After his death, he received the name Kobo Daishi ("the Great Master who spreads the Dharma"), and under that name he has become a venerated cultural hero in Japan. Shingon, because of its love of ritual, has inspired many arts, particularly sculpture and painting. It has similarities with Tibetan Buddhism, and it thus contains some elements of Vajrayana Buddhism (discussed later in this chapter).

Tendai   The Tendai (Chinese: Tiantai, T'ien-t'ai) sect is named for the great Chinese monastic institution at Mount Tiantai ("heavenly terrace"), where the sect is thought to have begun in eastern China. A large complex of monasteries arose there.[18]

By the eighth century C.E., there were many varied Buddhist texts, some written up to a thousand years after the time of the Buddha. When they had been translated into Chinese, the result was great confusion. How could the Buddha have uttered so many sermons, some with apparently contradictory ideas? The solution was to organize the teachings according to levels of complexity. It was taught that the Buddha had revealed his most basic insights to everybody, but that he had revealed his most difficult thoughts only to those disciples who could understand them. The Tiantai (Tendai) sect attempted to categorize all the teachings and present them in a meaningful way, as a kind of ladder of steps leading to full enlightenment. Naturally, its own special teachings were at the top.

In Japan, this sect was favored by the emperor and his court for the expected benefits and protection it would bring to the country. The Japanese monk who went to China and returned with skills in Tendai Buddhism was Saicho (767–822 C.E.), who later received the honorary title Dengyo Daishi ("the Great Master who transmits the teachings"). Tendai's center, Enryaku-ji, is located on Mount Hiei, north of Kyoto.

Jodo, or Pure Land   The Pure Land (Chinese: Jingtu, Ching-t'-u) school created a devotional form of Buddhism that could be practiced by laypeople as well as monks. The cult of bodhisattvas already existed in India and central Asia, but it had great appeal in China too. Pure Land Buddhism in China can be traced back to the monk Tan Luan (T'an Luan, c. 476–542). Legend says that he instituted the devotion to Amitabha Buddha as the result of a vision. Complete devotion to this Buddha, the monk thought, would result in the believer's rebirth in Amitabha's Pure Land, the Western Paradise. Devotees regularly repeated a short phrase, derived from Mahayana scriptures and praising Amitabha Buddha. At first the repetition of the Buddha's name was a monastic practice, but it then spread to the laity. In Chinese, the phrase is *Namo Amito-fo;* in Japanese, *Namu Amida Butsu*. Both mean "Praise to Amitabha Buddha." Daily repetition and recitation at the moment of death were thought to ensure the believer's rebirth in the Western Paradise.

In Japan, the Pure Land movement was spread by the monk Honen (1133–1212), who was originally a Tendai monk at Mount Hiei. His movement became a separate sect called Jodo Shu ("Pure Land sect"). Shinran (1173–1262), a disciple of Honen, continued the laicization of the *nembutsu,* as the chant is called in Japanese. He taught that human actions to attain salvation were unimportant in comparison to the saving power of the Buddha. Convinced that monastic practice was unnecessary, Shinran married. (He has often been compared with Martin Luther, who also married and emphasized simple trust as the way to salvation.) The movement that Shinran began eventually grew into the Jodo Shin Shu ("True Pure Land sect"). Pure Land sects have been extremely popular in China and Japan, and this popularity has made them the largest form of Mahayana Buddhism.

It was once common to think of the Pure Land as a real location somewhere beyond the earth. Today, however, it is often considered a metaphor for a compassionate and joyful way of living in the everyday world.

Pure Land Buddhism has inspired—and continues to inspire—the arts. In sculpture and painting, Amida (Amitabha) is often shown at the center of a triad. At his left and right are two bodhisattvas. Amida is also seen alone, surrounded by beams of light, descending from the sky to offer help and receive the departed. The same images, sometimes drawn in gold on indigo paper, often appear in manuscripts of the Lotus Sutra.

Nichiren Unlike the other sects discussed thus far, Nichiren Buddhism began in Japan. Its founder was a Tendai monk, Nichiren (1222–1282). After being trained at Mount Hiei, Nichiren sought a simpler path than Tendai, which used many sutras and practices in the search for enlightenment. Out of the thousands of Mahayana texts, Nichiren wanted to find one that contained all the essential teachings of Buddhism. Following the lead of the Tendai tradition, which had already given much attention to the Lotus Sutra, Nichiren asserted that the Lotus Sutra was indeed the embodiment of all essential religious teaching. He thought of himself as a reincarnation of a minor Buddha in the Lotus Sutra (his monastic name Nichiren means "sun lotus"). His sect uses a chant that honors this sutra: *Namu Myoho Renge Kyo,* meaning "Praise to the mystic law of the Lotus Sutra." Devout followers repeat the mantra many times a day, especially in the morning and evening. They believe that doing so will connect them with the divine power of the universe.

Nichiren Buddhism has produced several branches. Among the most important are Nichiren Shu ("Nichiren sect"), Nichiren Sho-Shu ("True Nichiren sect"), and Soka Gakkai ("Value Creation Educational Society"). The Nichiren Shu treats its founder as a bodhisattva, or Buddhist saint. The Nichiren Sho-Shu elevates Nichiren to the role of a reincarnation of the Buddha, "the Buddha of the present age." The Soka Gakkai branch was formerly a lay arm of Nichiren Sho-Shu. However, an angry split occurred in 1991–1992, and Soka Gakkai became fully independent. There is in all of these branches an acceptance of the material world and an attempt to improve it. Soka Gakkai particularly works to reform society through political means, seeking peace through inter-cultural understanding.

Nichiren Buddhism was little known outside Japan until after World War II. It has now established itself all around the world. The goal-oriented chanting of some Nichiren groups has been very attractive to some westerners, and several celebrities (such as Tina Turner) practice a form of this faith.

Zen Zen Buddhism, a school of Mahayana Buddhism, began in China and was carried to Japan. Its influence has been so significant that it merits discussion in some detail.

Zen takes its name from the seventh step of the Noble Eightfold Path—*dhyana* ("meditation"). In Chinese the word is *chan* (*ch' an*), and in Japanese it is *zen*. (In the discussion here, Chan refers to the sect in China, and Zen refers to the sect as it developed in Japan.) The complexity that had overtaken Chinese Buddhism helped create a counterbalancing movement toward simplification. For the Chan sect in China, simplification came from looking directly to the enlightenment experience of Siddhartha

Buddhists are faithful in remembering the dead, honoring their spirits at home altars or temple columbaria (vaults containing ashes of the dead). Some temples even encourage relatives to "make merit" as a way of speeding relatives' progress toward nirvana.

Gautama. Siddhartha had become the Buddha, the Enlightened One, through his practice of meditation. Although he did not deny the value of ritual, the Buddha did not think that it led to enlightenment. Taking after the Buddha, the members of the Chan movement, in their desire for enlightenment, favored the technique of seated meditation, just as Siddhartha Gautama had.

Chan Buddhism traditionally traces itself back to a Buddhist monk named Bodhidharma, who is said to have come to China (about 500 C.E.) from India or central Asia and in China began his Meditation school. Bodhidharma is often shown sitting in meditation, with Western facial features, swarthy skin, a light beard, and an earring. In paintings, he faces a wall to indicate his strong desire to block out anything that would distract him from his meditation. It has been said that he meditated for so long that his legs became withered. He is the embodiment of patience and persistence.

The native Chinese religious and philosophical movement called Daoism (see Chapter 6) undoubtedly paved the way for Chan Buddhism and influenced it. Daoism had similar ideals: silence, detachment, acceptance, distrust of symbolization, and union with the universe. Daoism also practiced meditation. Daoism may have added to Buddhism its own esteem for the natural world and its appreciation for humor, although exactly how Daoism influenced Chan is debated. There are also Confucian elements in Chan and Zen, such as the communal nature of monastery life and the transmission of realization from master to disciple.

In the long history of Buddhism, some teachers have emphasized the importance of regular meditation and the effectiveness of meditative techniques, saying that they produce enlightenment gradually but inevitably, like the coming of dawn. Others have stressed that enlightenment can occur as a sudden awakening to one's true nature, like a flash of lightning, anywhere and at any time. The enlightenment experience (called **satori,** or *kensho*) brings an awareness of the unity of oneself with the rest of the universe. The enlightened person knows that human distinctions and separations—mine, yours; this, that; one, many—are distinctions that societies and individuals' minds create and then project onto other people and things. Such distinctions are not ultimate, though, for all human beings consist of the same basic energy of the universe, appearing in many varied shapes. This experience of ultimate unity brings new insights and emotions to the art of living: less anxiety over attaining goals, less concern about death, and an appreciation for the preciousness of everyday life.

The most fundamental Zen technique for reaching enlightenment is regular "sitting meditation," called *zazen.* In Zen monasteries, zazen is normally done for several hours in the morning and evening. It involves sitting in silence with one's back straight and centered, keeping the body still, and taking deep and regular breaths. These are just simple techniques for quieting the mind and focusing on the moment. The mind becomes more peaceful, and ideally, with long practice, a state of simple awareness takes over as one's "true nature" is revealed.[19]

The **koan** is another technique for attaining awareness. Its origin is uncertain, but the name derives from the Chinese *gong-an* (*kung-an*), translated as "public discussion." The koan is a question that cannot be easily answered using logic. It demands pondering. Consider, for example, the question, Why did the monk Bodhidharma come from the West? An appropriate answer could be, "the bush in the garden"—or any response that mentions an ordinary object. The meaning of this apparently odd answer is that Bodhidharma's whole purpose was to make people wake up to the wondrous nature of even simple objects in everyday life. Sometimes a good answer to a koan need not be a verbal response but rather an appropriate action, such as lifting up a hand, taking off a shoe, holding up a flower, or even raising an eyebrow.[20]

As teachers, monks pass on the traditions they received from their own teachers, including knowledge of the arts. Here a monk in Vietnam teaches calligraphy. ▶

Manual labor is also essential to Zen training. In a Zen monastery, work in the garden and kitchen and the repair and cleaning of the monastery are techniques to combat the inadequacy of words to describe reality. Zen, influenced here by Daoism, maintains that words are often barriers that keep us from immediate contact with the true nature of things. Silent meditation blended with direct experience of the physical world can take us beyond words and thoughts to experience reality itself.

Buddhism and Japanese Arts

Many people assume that Buddhism has had a role in shaping the arts of Japan. As a matter of fact, what we think of as "Japanese style" is a mixture of Shinto (see Chapter 7), Buddhist influences (especially Zen), and traditional Japanese attitudes toward nature. Over the past three hundred years, these arts have taken on a life of their own, carried on by laypeople and practitioners of several branches of Mahayana Buddhism.

HAIKU

A *haiku* is an extremely short poem. In Japan, longer Chinese poetic forms were telescoped and refined. The model haiku is a short poem written in three lines. The ideal traditional haiku should mention or suggest the season, and, like a good photograph, it should capture the essence of a moment before it passes.

Matsuo Basho (1644–1694) is considered the greatest of Japan's haiku writers. The following poem is widely quoted and considered to be his masterpiece:

> Old pond:
> A frog jumps in.
> Sound of water.

Why, we may wonder, is this poem held in such esteem? On first reading, it seems simple, insignificant. But on closer inspection, it reveals intriguing balance and contrast. There are many possible interpretations. The old pond suggests timelessness, but the splash is momentary, representing every daily event when seen against the backdrop of eternity. Or the frog could represent a human being; the pond, the mind; and the splash, the sudden breakthrough to enlightenment. Perhaps the frog signifies the Buddhist monk in meditation, while the pond suggests all of Buddhist teaching. Or maybe the frog symbolizes the poet himself and the splash the poet's insight. Thus, the imagery can be taken both literally and in several equally valid symbolic ways.

TEA CEREMONY

The making, drinking, and offering of tea to guests has developed into a fine art in Japan, called *chado* (or *sado*, "the way of tea"). Bringing guests together for a ritual tea ceremony in Japanese is called *cha no yu* ("hot water for tea"). The drinking of tea was first used in Chinese monasteries for medicinal purposes and as an aid for staying awake during meditation. There, tea drinking also developed some ritual elements. Tea drinking was then carried to Japan and was practiced assiduously by both Zen monks and lay disciples. Under the tea master Sen no Rikyu (1522–1591), the tea ceremony took on its current highly stylized form.[21]

The essence of the Japanese tea ceremony is the gathering of a few guests, the preparation of green tea, and the offering of tea and sweets. The tea ceremony normally takes place in a tea pavilion, whose design is inspired by a rustic country hut, often mentioned in Chinese poetry. The purpose of the ceremony is to create and enjoy together an atmosphere of harmony and beauty, where each object, action, and word contributes to the tranquil experience.

CERAMICS

Bowls used in the tea ceremony look deliberately natural, almost as if they were dug up out of the ground. They often look rough and unfinished, with earth-colored glazes dripping down their sides. The rims sometimes are not quite even, and the colors are not always uniform. Sometimes there are even bubbles and cracks in the ceramic. All this is deliberate. The accidents of firing the bowls in the kiln are appreciated, as are the subtle shades of earth tones that are produced. The aim is, paradoxically, to create pieces that exhibit deliberate naturalness and a calculated spontaneity.

IKEBANA

The word for Japanese-style flower arrangement— *ikebana*—means "living flower." Flower arrangement can be traced back to the offerings of flowers placed on altars in the temples of China and Japan. But ikebana grew into a unique art form of its own, and examples of ikebana now are found in restaurants, offices, and homes.

Ikebana is quite different from Western flower arrangement, which tends to be dense, symmetrical, and colorful. Ikebana is the opposite. The arrangements are airy, asymmetrical, and generally of no more than two

A famous example is the rock garden at Ryoan-ji, in northwest Kyoto. Ryoan-ji garden, enclosed on two sides by a low earthen wall, consists of five clusters of large boulders set in raked white gravel. The rocks and gravel suggest mountain peaks rising through clouds or islands in a river. The fascination of the garden is the relation between the clusters of boulders. Viewed this way, the boulders seem more like ideas in a great mind. The only vegetation in the garden is the moss at the base of the stones and the trees beyond the wall. Really more like an X-ray of an ideal garden, Ryoan-ji would seem to be unchanging because of its stony nature; but it changes a great deal, depending on the season, the weather, the light, and the time of day.

CALLIGRAPHY AND PAINTING

Calligraphy (Greek: "beautiful writing") is a highly prized art form in China and Japan. Because the characters used in Japanese and Chinese writing are closer to pictures and to drawing than they are to alphabet letters, they have a great range of vitality and beauty. The Zen ideal is to produce what is spontaneous but also profound, and because writing is done with an inkbrush, great expressiveness in darkness, weight, movement, and style of characters is possible. Furthermore, the ink cannot be erased, and the result is thought to be the immediate expression of the writer's personality and level of awareness. When fine calligraphic talent is employed to write a striking phrase or poem, the result is doubly powerful. The supreme example of Zen simplicity in art is the *enso*, a black circle, almost always done in a single, quick stroke on paper or a piece of wood. The empty circle represents the emptiness of all reality.

Elements that are typical of Zen design include simple elegance, asymmetry, the use of stone and wood in their natural state, and the near emptiness that is characteristic of the rock garden. Over the past one hundred years, Zen has had global impact as well—in architecture, art, interior design, and fashion. It is apparent, for example, in the domestic architecture of Frank Lloyd Wright and his followers, which popularized the use of large windows and natural stone. It seems even to have influenced retail chains such as The Gap and Banana Republic, where we see natural wood floors, uncluttered space, and clothing in muted earth tones.

Ikebana suggests a bit of nature brought into a home, tearoom, or temple. It reminds viewers of Buddhist teaching on the impermanence of all things.

colors. Effective ikebana is temporary art, lasting but a few days and changing every day. Thus, some see ikebana as a manifestation of Buddhist insight into impermanence. Ikebana is Buddhist sculpture.

GARDEN DESIGN

In China and Japan, gardens have long been an essential part of architecture, planned along with the buildings they complement. Garden designers are ranked as highly as poets and artists. Some gardens are created for strolling, others for seated contemplation from under an eave. They are not essentially Buddhist, of course, and not all monasteries have a garden. But they are found frequently enough in Buddhist environs for us to say that gardens have been used to present Buddhist ideals.

VAJRAYANA BUDDHISM: THE "DIAMOND VEHICLE"

Mahayana Buddhism in India developed practices and beliefs that have sometimes been called esoteric (hidden, not openly taught), such as the use of special chants and rituals to gain supranormal powers. When some of these traditions entered Tibet, Indian Mahayana Buddhism blended with Tibetan shamanism to create Tibetan Buddhism, a complex system of belief, art, and ritual. Although Vajrayana actually includes other forms of esoteric Buddhism, Tibetan Buddhism is its most prominent expression.

The name *Vajrayana* means the "vehicle of the diamond" or "vehicle of the lightning bolt." The name suggests strength, clarity, wisdom, and flashes of light, all of which are associated with the enlightened awareness that this vehicle seeks to transmit. Vajrayana is considered by some to be simply a special form of Mahayana. But most consider Vajrayana to be a third branch of Buddhism, because of its complexity and unique elements.

Origins, Practice, and Literature of Tibetan Buddhism

The pre-Buddhist Tibetan religion worshiped the powers of nature. As was the case with many native religions, these powers were often envisioned as

The most prominent missionary of Vajrayana was Padmasambhava, known in some areas as Guru Rimpoche ("precious jewel"). Here, the abbot of Kurjey Lhakhang in central Bhutan dresses as Guru Rimpoche and parades among the faithful as part of the celebration of the Guru's birthday.

Long trumpets, bells, and drums often accompany chanting in Vajrayana ceremonies.

demons that had to be appeased. Shamanistic rituals involving animal sacrifice and the use of bones, dance, and magical incantations were intended to control the demonic powers.

This Tibetan religion was challenged by a new religion, a special type of Buddhism practiced in northeast India, named Tantric Buddhism for its scriptures, the Tantras ("spread out"). Tantric Buddhism opposed the original Buddhist detachment from the world and its negative attitude toward bodily pleasure. The Tantras taught that the body and all its energies could be used to reach enlightenment. For Tantric Buddhism, enlightenment is an experience of ultimate oneness that occurs when a practitioner unites all opposites. Sexual union is a powerful experience of unity, and Tantric Buddhism uses the imagery and (rarely) the practice of sexual union to help attain enlightenment. In its imagery and belief system, Tantric Buddhism shows influence from Hinduism—particularly its tendency to pair a male and a female deity and its love of multiple deities. Vajrayana believes the divine Buddha nature expresses itself in a multitude of male and female deities.

A form of Tantric Buddhism first entered Tibet in the seventh century and was spread by Indian missionaries. Tradition holds that a king named Song-tsen-gam-po (active c. 630) became its patron and made it the national religion. In the beginning, native priests fought against this new religion, but a legendary Buddhist monk named Padmasambhava, who came from India in the late eighth century, reconciled the two religions and turned the native demonic gods of Tibet into guardian deities of Buddhism.

The resulting religion blended shamanistic interests, the sexual imagery of Tantric Buddhism, and traditional Buddhist elements such as the chanting of sutras, meditation, the ideal of nonviolence, and the search for enlightenment.

Monks thus were called upon not only as teachers but also as doctors and shamans; they were expected to bring health, control weather, and magically protect worshipers from death. A Tibetan spiritual teacher is often called **lama** (a Tibetan translation of the word *guru*), and this title is thus frequently used as a title of honor for all monks.

Although the Indian ideals of the wandering holy man and cave-dwelling solitary did not die out in Tibetan Buddhism, they were not well suited for a climate as severe as that of the cold and barren Tibetan plateau. More compatible, it seemed, were the large monastic complexes that had grown up in late Indian Buddhism. The Tibetan version of such a complex often looked like a fortified hilltop castle and was in effect a complete city for sometimes thousands of monks, containing libraries, prayer halls, kitchens, storage areas, and large courtyards used for public performances. A written form of the Tibetan language was created for the translation of Buddhist scriptures from India. It also made possible the writing of scriptural commentaries and other treatises.

Over time, the practice of celibacy declined, and the heads of Tibetan monasteries frequently passed on their control to their sons. The consumption of meat and alcohol became common as well. A reform movement, however, emerged under the monk Tsong Kha-pa (1357–1419), demanding that monks be unmarried and that strict monastic practice be reinstituted. His sect, as a result, came to be known as Gelug-pa, meaning "party of virtue." (It is also commonly called the Yellow Hat sect because of the tall, crested yellow hats that the monks wear during religious services.) This sect grew powerful. It helped create many of the greatest monasteries, full of art and complete sets of Buddhist scriptures, and it provided Tibet with its political leadership for several centuries. The executive head of the Gelug-pa is called the Dalai Lama ("ocean superior one").

It became a common belief in Tibetan Buddhism that certain major lamas are reincarnations of earlier lamas, who in turn are considered emanations of Buddhas and bodhisattvas. (A belief in reincarnation thus solved the problem of transmission of leadership, which in a celibate monastic order cannot pass to a son.) The lineage of the Dalai Lama, for example, traces itself back to a nephew of Tsong Kha-pa, the first of the line of succession. Each Dalai Lama is considered to be an emanation of Avalokiteshvara, the heavenly bodhisattva of compassion. When a major lama dies, his reincarnation is sought, found, and trained. The current Dalai Lama, for example, was found in eastern Tibet. A delegation of monks, after consulting a state oracle about the place of rebirth, took objects (such as prayer beads) that had been used by the previous Dalai Lama and mixed them with similar objects. The boy who was recognized as the current Dalai Lama selected only those objects used by the previous Dalai Lama, helping to prove his identity. (The movies *Kundun, Seven Years in Tibet,* and *Little Buddha* vividly portray the selection of the Dalai Lama and other Vajrayana practices.) The current Dalai Lama fled from Tibet in 1959 and lives in northern India.

The literature of Tibetan Buddhism consists of two large collections of writings. The Kanjur is the core, made up of works from the Tripitaka (mostly Mahayana sutras and the vinaya, with Tantric texts). The second part, the Tenjur, comprises commentaries on scripture and treatises on a wide variety of disciplines, such as medicine, logic, and grammar. The collection exceeds four thousand works.

Ritual and the Arts

Vajrayana Buddhism is interested in the acquisition of both internal and external powers and holds that such powers may be attained through proper ritual. The ritual allows the individual to become identified with a particular Buddha or heavenly bodhisattva, thus giving the individual the power and protection of that heavenly being.

Because correctly performed ceremony brings identification with a powerful deity, ceremonial objects play significant roles. We noted earlier that some devices, such as the mantra and mandala, were used in Mahayana practice. These devices were subsequently adopted by Vajrayana. But in Vajrayana these objects and techniques take on special importance. Among the significant ritual objects is the **vajra,** a metal object somewhat like a divining rod or scepter that represents a stylized bolt of lightning. The vajra is associated with diamond-hardness, power, and insight. It is held in the right hand and suggests kind action. A bell is held in the left hand and symbolizes wisdom. When used together, one in each hand, they represent the union of wisdom and compassion. The vajra and bell are essential to Tibetan Vajrayana ritual in a way that other religious objects (mentioned in the following paragraphs) are not.

Another important Tibetan Buddhist object is the prayer wheel, which comes in all sizes—from very tiny to as tall as a two-story building. A prayer wheel is a cylinder that revolves around a central pole. Inside the cylinder are pieces of paper inscribed with sacred phrases. It is believed that the turning of the written prayers creates as much good karma as if one were to recite them. Believers often carry small prayer wheels and turn them as they walk, while the devout push or pull large prayer wheels at temples and in public places. Some prayer wheels are placed in streams, where the flowing water turns them. The same principle applies to the wind blowing through prayer flags, which consist of square or triangular pieces of cloth containing inscriptions.

Certain ritual objects evoke awe at first because of their connection with death. They are meant to inoculate the believer against the fear of dying by forcing the individual to accept death long before it comes. For example, human thighbones are used to make small trumpets, and half of a human skull, decorated with gold or silver, might be used as a ceremonial bowl. Paintings and statues of fierce deities often have a similar function.

Music and dance, used by shamans to protect against demons, also play an important role in Tibetan Vajrayana. Drums, long trumpets, bells, and

Costumed monks dance before a huge *thondrol* (Buddhist tapestry), here portraying Guru Rimpoche in his many manifestations. The tapestry is unfurled for a few hours once a year at Bhutan temple ceremonies. Viewing the thondrol is said to liberate one from the cycle of rebirths.

cymbals are used to accompany a deep, slow droning chant. The effect is hypnotic and evokes the sacredness that underlies reality.

In Vajrayana as well as Mahayana, a mantra is chanted or written to bring power and wisdom through repetition. The most highly revered mantra in Tibetan Vajrayana is *Om mani padme hum!* (literally translated, "Om—the jewel—oh lotus—ah!"). One translation employs Tantric sexual symbolism: "The jewel is in the lotus." The jewel and lotus represent sexual opposites, and the mantra represents sexual union—symbolic of enlightenment. In yet another symbolic translation—"The jewel *is* the lotus"—the jewel represents the divine Buddha nature, and the lotus represents the everyday world of birth and death. Hence, the mantra means that this world of suffering is the same as the Buddha nature and that the enlightened person sees that they are the same. However, it is also possible to interpret the mantra as merely a prayer to the bodhisattva Avalokiteshvara, who may be pictured holding each of the two objects. The mantra then would be "Hail to the jewel-lotus one!" No matter what the origin and meaning of the mantra, the ordinary believer simply thinks of it as a powerful prayer. In addition to this mantra, there are many others, each of which is believed to be sacred to a particular Buddha or bodhisattva or is believed to be valuable for obtaining a certain result.

Symbolic hand gestures (**mudras**) on stat-ues of the Buddha are common throughout all forms of Buddhism. For example, the right hand extended with the palm outward and the fingers pointing up is a mudra of blessing; if the palm is open but the hand is turned downward, the mudra symbolizes generosity. In Vajrayana, a large number of mudras have evolved to convey more esoteric meanings, such as the unity of opposites. Mudras also help distinguish indi-vidual Buddhas and bodhisattvas within the large pantheon of deities. Moreover, mudras can be performed to a chant, with the two hands simultaneously forming mudra after mudra to create a harmonious balance of opposites.

The Vajrayana tradition encourages monks to create and meditate upon elaborate paintings of Buddhist teachings, including the intricate form known as the mandala. Here, a twenty-first-century Vajrayana monk silently works on a mandala in a shopping mall.

The mandala that is used in some forms of Mahayana takes on great variety and complexity in Tibetan Buddhism. We might recall that a mandala is a sacred cosmic diagram, often used in med-itation. It may represent in symbolic form the entire universe, the palace of a deity, or even the self. A common design is a circle within or enclosing a square, or a series of circles and squares that grow smaller and smaller as they come closer to the center of the design; another form looks like a check-erboard of many squares. A mandala usually appears as a painting on cloth, but it may take many forms. For some ceremonies, monks create a mandala in sand and then destroy it at the end of the ritual, expressing vividly the Buddhist teaching that everything must change.

Any painting on cloth is called a *thangka* (pronounced *tan'-ka*). In addition to mandala designs, a wide variety of subjects can appear on thangkas. Com-mon images are Buddhas, bodhisattvas, and guardian deities, painted in both benevolent and terrifying forms (the terrifying forms both frighten away demons and chasten the believer). The female deity Tara, who represents mercy, appears in two major forms (white and green) and in several minor forms. We also find frequent representations of the monk Padmasambhava and other noted teachers. The existence of so many celestial beings and saints—with their attendants and symbolic objects—provides artists with a multitude of subjects to paint and sculpt.

PERSONAL EXPERIENCE: THE MONKS AND THE POND

On a recent trip to Southeast Asia I heard of an old and beautiful temple, entirely made of teakwood and known for its wonderful carvings. Tourists rarely visited it, I was told, because it was far off in the countryside. I would have to cross a river and then walk a good distance to the temple. It was suggested that I go with a guide.

All began according to plan. My guide was a woman who was also a teacher. We took a small bus to the river, where we waited for a ferryboat. People around us carried baskets of produce, and many had bicycles. It was a humid, brilliantly sunny day. We stood patiently under the black umbrellas we had brought for protection from the sun. At last a wooden ferryboat arrived, people wheeled their bicycles aboard, and the boat crossed.

Luckily for my guide and me, an enclosed horsecart was standing under a tree at the other side of the river. Its driver was pleased to see us. We negotiated a fare and jumped in back. The horse ambled pleasantly along the dirt road, moving in and out of the shadows of the trees at each side; but because of all the potholes, the cart bounced wildly, and we had to hold on to the sides of the cart to avoid being thrown out.

Soon I began to hear the sound of chanting over loudspeakers. (One cannot escape electronically amplified sounds these days, even in the countryside.) Coming around a bend in the road, I could see a white pagoda and white stucco temple at the base of a hill. It must be a temple fair, I thought. But as we drove closer, I saw that the temple was deserted. Instead, people were crowded together on the nearby hillside. Could it be a special ceremony?

"May we stop and look?" I asked.

The driver came to a halt near the temple. We jumped out of the cart and started walking quickly up the hill. As we came close to the top, we were astonished to see a woman lying on the ground, the people surrounding her closely. Her long black hair was in disarray, and she was in a state of great emotion. Her eyes were unseeing. She seemed to be in a trance. It was then that we saw, in the crowd behind her, four men holding a very thick and powerful-looking snake. We advanced no farther. The woman on the ground was talking excitedly. The people stood motionless but attentive, listening to her. Everyone seemed calm and unafraid. After a few minutes, monks began walking among the people.

Protected by the arms of another, this entranced woman is believed to be speaking the words of the snake.

"What's happening?" I asked my guide.

"It's a miracle," she said. "A miracle!"

"And what is the woman saying?"

"The snake is speaking through her. He is saying, 'Do not harm me. I only need for you to dig a pond for me here at the temple. I will live in the pond and protect you.'"

"And what are the monks doing?"

"They are taking up a collection to make the pond."

I was silent. We returned to the horsecart and continued on our way to the teakwood temple. Along the way I thought of the decorative snakes that adorn the handrails of so many temples in Southeast Asia. I recalled the story in the Jataka Tales of a snake whose heroic willingness to die had actually saved its life. And I recalled the story of the snake Muchalinda, king of the cobras, who had protected the Buddha at the time of his enlightenment. Even more, I thought of how varied the expressions of Buddhism are, ranging from complex philosophies to unexpected forms of popular practice. One has to be ready for everything.

At last we arrived at the famous wooden temple. After all the excitement at the first temple, this was an oasis of peace. On one side of the building, an old monk sat comfortably beside an open window, reading a local newspaper. Near him five children recited the alphabet out loud together. Passing several large statues of the Buddha, I walked to the other end of the temple. There, four monks sat on the wide wooden floor, studying scriptures in a pool of sunlight.

Three young monks study scripture with their teacher on the porch of an old teak temple not far from Mandalay.

Buddhist Meditation

Because meditation is a core practice of Buddhism, many kinds of meditation have developed. Some of them have made their way to the West, where they have occasionally been modified.

In the Theravada tradition, one approach to meditation is especially significant. It is called *Vipassana* ("insight"), because it emphasizes being fully attentive to the present moment. This attentiveness, sometimes called *mindfulness,* is primarily accomplished by sitting quietly and paying attention to one's exhalation and inhalation. The same type of meditation may also be done while walking. The meditator walks extremely slowly on flat ground, being aware at each moment of the motion of the right, then left, foot. (In Sri Lanka and elsewhere, some monasteries have special walking tracks for this type of meditation.)

Seated meditation, particularly cultivated by Chan and Zen, is the most significant form of Mahayana meditation. Like Vipassana, it begins with a focus on breathing. It may then include reflections on a question given by a master or on the meaning of a line of poetry. It may also involve the silent repetition of a single meaningful word or phrase.

The Vajrayana tradition, with its love of art and ritual, has developed many complex meditations. Vajrayana meditation tends to make use of ritual objects (bells, candles, butter lamps), images, mandalas, Sanskrit words (mantras), hand gestures (mudras), and visualization exercises. Frequently the meditation involves reconstructing in one's imagination the image of a favorite deity. The meditator then takes on the identity of that deity for the duration of the meditation. Other meditations involve contemplating the moon, clouds, or water. Some meditations make use of imaginative techniques; the meditator mentally creates a lotus, a moon disc, a written Sanskrit syllable, an altar of deities, colors, or rays of light, often imagining these in a certain order.

All three traditions also have some form of what can be called a meditation of compassion. The meditator reflects on the many different kinds of sentient beings—human, animal, and insect. The next step of the meditation is to recognize that all of these beings are struggling to survive, that all are trying to avoid pain, and that many are suffering. The meditation ends when the meditator projects outward the wish that all sentient beings may be well and happy. This wish is sometimes accompanied by a mental image of light and warmth radiating outward.

Beginners who are interested in Buddhist meditation can try simple seated meditation. A quiet spot is best, and the meditator should sit on a cushion or sofa, with legs drawn up. (If that is not possible, then one may sit on a chair, with the feet flat on the ground.) Some people like to face outside, looking into a garden. The back should be straight, the position comfortable, and the breathing deep, slow, and regular. The eyes may be either open or closed. The meditator should remain as still as possible and focus on each breath as it goes in and out. Thoughts need not be banished, but should simply be "watched," like seeing clouds passing. One can start by meditating a short amount of time—even as little as five . minutes per day. Soon it will be possible to meditate for longer periods once or twice a day. Many report that the exercise leaves them with a greater sense of inner peace and often even oneness with their surroundings.

BUDDHISM AND THE MODERN WORLD

Although Buddhism originated in India and then spread primarily through Asia, it has now become a worldwide religion. Buddhist temples and meditation centers can be found in many countries, particularly in the industrialized countries of Europe and the Americas. Part of the attraction of Buddhism is that many of its essential teachings seem to agree with modern values. Some people appreciate what they see as its emphasis on awareness, self-reliance, and insight. Others think that Buddhism fits in well with the

views of modern science. Still others are attracted to the Buddhist ideal of nonviolence as a standard for civilized behavior in a multicultural world—an attraction that was magnified by the Dalai Lama's selection in 1989 for the Nobel Peace Prize.

Critics point out that the modern world has adopted what it likes from Buddhism and ignored the rest. The modern world, for example, has not been quick to embrace the celibacy of the Buddha or of Buddhist monks and nuns—who traditionally represent the core of the religion. The modern world believes in recycling, but not in reincarnation. And the modern world turns a blind eye to the actual practice of many Buddhist believers, whose real-life Buddhist activity is performed in order to "make merit," gain health or wealth, and have good luck. Critics scorn the modern "cafeteria approach" to Buddhism. The contemporary world, they explain, has adopted only the elements it likes—meditation, Zen design, and the exoticism of Tibet—and with these it is now creating a new kind of Buddhism in its own image. Buddhism, they say, is becoming a yuppie supermarket of meditation cushions, gongs, and Dalai Lama posters.

All of these complaints have some truth. And yet . . . Buddhism is forever changing. In its long history, as the ship of its teachings has sailed from one cultural port to the next, some of its goods have been tied to the mast

Is a new form of Buddhism being born among European and American converts to the religion? The Dalai Lama's sermons in New York City's Central Park attracted audiences in the tens of thousands.

while others have been tossed overboard. This fact is even truer today, and it makes studying the interrelation of Buddhism and the modern world all the more fascinating.

Buddhism's first contact with the West occurred in the late eighteenth century, when translations of primarily Theravada material were carried to Europe from Sri Lanka and Myanmar by English colonials. Because so many of these colonials were missionaries, they were especially impressed by Buddhist moral teachings. Thus, the view of Buddhism that they spread emphasized the religion's admirable ethical system.

The opening of Japan to foreigners in the second half of the nineteenth century created a second wave of interest in Buddhism. French, English, and American people began to read about Japanese culture and to see photographs of early Buddhist temples and examples of Buddhist-inspired art. Foreign interest dovetailed with anti-Buddhist government actions in Japan after 1868, which forced many Buddhist temples to sell some of their art. Japanese art was then collected widely in Europe and America, both by private collectors and by museums.

Just as many see Buddhism's influence on Japanese art, so Buddhism has influenced Western art via Japan. There is no doubt that the Japanese influence on Western art has been extraordinary since Japan opened to the West. French art of the late nineteenth century was invigorated by the discovery of Japanese prints and scrolls, which flooded into France after 1880. Asymmetry, a love of nature, and an appreciation for the passing moment—features of much Japanese art—began to appear in the work of the Impressionists and Postimpressionists, particularly Vincent van Gogh (1853–1890), Henri de Toulouse-Lautrec (1864–1901), and Claude Monet (1840–1926). (One of van Gogh's self-portraits was almost certainly influenced by pictures of Buddhist monks that he had seen.) Monet's Japanese-style water garden, with its pond of water lilies at Giverny, near Paris, is a good example of the influence Japan had at the turn of the century in France.

Haiku and other forms of Japanese poetry began to influence Western poetry at the same time. We see this particularly in the Imagist school, which produced short poems that depended on a few strong images presented in simple language. Poets who exemplified this style include Ezra Pound (1885–1972), e. e. cummings (1894–1962), H. D. (Hilda Doolittle, 1886–1961), and William Carlos Williams (1883–1963).

A third wave of Buddhist influence came in the decades just after World War II, when U.S. soldiers returned from the American occupation of Japan. The great interest of the time was Zen (perhaps only loosely understood), which influenced the poetry of the Beat movement and the lifestyle of the counterculture. The novels of Jack Kerouac (1922–1969) show a Zenlike love of the spontaneous. His book *On the Road,* about a cross-country trip with friends, inspired readers to make similar explorations. Zen love of the moment is also evident in the jazzlike poetry of Allen Ginsberg (1926–1997) and the ironic poetry of Lawrence Ferlinghetti

Women and Buddhism

In Southeast Asia, it is quite common to see a sign in English reading "No ladies beyond here" in front of the sanctuary area inside Buddhist temples. At the famous Golden Rock Shrine in Myanmar, only men may "earn merit" by applying gold leaf to the large boulder that is believed to hold a hair of the Buddha. And while women may shave their heads and become nuns, their status is generally lower than that of male monks, and they are not allowed to be fully ordained. These examples and others reveal that women have second-class citizenship in several Buddhist traditions.

Yet anyone who travels in Buddhist countries sees that women play a large role in the religion. Typically, most worshipers are female. Women are in frequent attendance at temples, except in monks' quarters. They typically clean the shrines and tend to the offerings, such as flowers and candles, and they help prepare meals for the monks. It is primarily women who get up long before dawn to cook the extra rice and vegetables that their family will donate to the monks each morning in order to "earn merit." All in all, Buddhism as an institution could not exist without women.

Ambivalence about women has existed in Buddhism from the very beginning. Initially, the Buddha did not allow women to join the Sangha; because monks must be chaste, he taught that the presence of women within their community would encourage temptation, even scandal. But the Buddha's aunt, who was also his step-mother, petitioned him several times to allow her to enter the Sangha. Finally, the Buddha relented, allowing her and other women to enter the order. However, after his death, debate over allowing women into the Sangha reemerged. Some monks even argued that women had to be reborn as men in order to become monks.

Some Buddhist traditions, particularly the Mahayana traditions in Taiwan, Korea, and Vietnam, have always ordained women. In contrast, the Theravada traditions in Sri Lanka and Southeast Asia once ordained women, but the practice eventually died out. Traditional Tibetan Buddhism did not ordain women. Change, however, is occurring. Although women are not yet fully ordained in the Theravada tradition of Thailand, they are being ordained in Sri Lanka. Recently, the Dalai Lama has promoted full ordination of women in Tibetan Buddhism.

Women have also begun to play a major role in institutional Buddhism. A Taiwanese female monastic, Master Cheng Yen, began the influential Tzu Chi Foundation to help the needy. It has grown to become a worldwide social welfare agency. Western women who have become Buddhist nuns—among them, the teachers and writers Pema Chodron, Tenzin Palmo, and Karma Lekshe Tsomo—have been particularly outspoken in demanding major roles for women in Buddhism. With few exceptions, men still remain the actual leaders in Buddhism. But theoretical acceptance of equality is widespread, and real equality is coming.

(b. 1919). San Francisco, where many of the Beat writers were based, became an early headquarters of Zen thought and practice in America, as it still is today.

Zen centers, often under lay leadership, were established at this time in major cities in North and South America and Europe. These centers have allowed westerners to learn directly about Zen through both instruction and meditation. Some centers have also opened bookstores, vegetarian restaurants, and retreat centers.

A fourth wave of Buddhist influence is more recent and involves several types of Buddhism. Tibetan Buddhism has established communities of immigrant Tibetans and converts in many places in the United States (California, Colorado, New York, Hawai`i) and in Europe (Switzerland, France, Great

Britain), and Tibetan Buddhist art is now regularly acquired and exhibited by museums. Forms of Pure Land and Nichiren Buddhism have made many converts, particularly in large cities of North America. And Asian immigrants from Taiwan, Hong Kong, and Southeast Asia have all begun their own temples and celebrations where they have settled.

From the middle of the nineteenth century to the middle of the twentieth century, Buddhism outside Asia was primarily made up of ethnic Buddhists (mostly immigrants) and so-called elite Buddhists (non-Asian intellectuals and academics). These two groups have interacted and been joined by a large middle-class following. A new type of Buddhism is emerging from the interaction of the three groups: "engaged Buddhism." This movement comprises a wide variety of people who, as Buddhists, work for social betterment. A broadly based Western Buddhism, in Europe, North America, and Australia, is taking on such a life of its own that it is beginning to be called the "fourth vehicle" (*yana*) of Buddhism.

Ironically, even as it gains followers in the West, Buddhism has been weakened in many countries and regions that have been its traditional home. When Communist governments took over Mongolia (1921) and China (1949), Buddhism was severely repressed, and many temples and monasteries were destroyed. This pattern continued when Tibet was taken over by the Chinese government (1959). The Dalai Lama went into exile and at least a million Tibetans are thought to have died in the ensuing persecution. In China, several thousand monasteries were destroyed, particularly during the Cultural Revolution (1966–1976), causing both human suffering and an incalculable loss to the world of art. In recent years a modest amount of rebuilding has occurred in all these regions, with the financial support of Buddhists from abroad. On the one hand, governments fear that monasteries can become centers of antigovernment activity; but governments also recognize the importance of Buddhist sites both to the inhabitants and to tourists, whose goodwill (and foreign exchange) they wish to encourage. In Sri Lanka, the separatist movement in the north leads Hindus and Buddhists to fight against each other, straining the tradition of nonviolence in both religions. In Myanmar (Burma), the government officially supports Buddhism, yet Buddhist human rights activists have been jailed.

On the other hand, relations with the non-Buddhist world have brought new vigor to Buddhism in its traditional areas. For example, we now see emerging what has been called "Green Buddhism." Although early Buddhism does not mention explicit environmental ideals, it does include principles that fit in well with environmentalism. Among these are harmony, frugality, compassion, reverence, and respect. Trees, in particular, play an important role in Buddhism. The Buddha was born, meditated, was enlightened, and died under trees. For centuries, monks in Southeast Asia have regularly set up meditation huts and small temples in wilderness forests. In Thailand, monks have played leadership roles in protecting forests. Monks use their moral authority to encourage villagers to plant new trees and to limit tree

Following his shadow, this lone monk with his eating bowl slowly places one foot in front of the other as he engages in walking meditation.

burning. Temples receive small trees from the Royal Forest Department and donations from town-bound supporters who want to earn merit by improving the natural environment. Monks have even temporarily "ordained" trees by tying orange robes around those that they hope to save from loggers.

Buddhism is clearly entering a new phase in its long journey. In part, Buddhism can predict what that phase will bring: the one constant, as always, is change.

READING

THE DHAMMAPADA: "WE ARE WHAT WE THINK"

The Dhammapada is a devotional text that explains the Buddha's teachings in ways that are easy for people to understand. It is particularly popular among Theravada Buddhists. This section deals with the first step on the Noble Eightfold Path, "right understanding."

We are what we think,
All that we are arises with our thoughts.
With our thoughts we make the world.
Speak or act with an impure mind
And trouble will follow you
As the wheel follows the ox that draws the cart.

We are what we think.
All that we are arises with our thoughts.
With our thoughts we make the world.
Speak or act with a pure mind
And happiness will follow you
As your shadow, unshakable.

"Look how he abused me and beat me,
How he threw me down and robbed me."
Live with such thoughts and you live in hate.

"Look how he abused me and beat me,
How he threw me down and robbed me."
Abandon such thoughts and you live in love.

In this world
Hate never yet dispelled hate.
Only love dispels hate.
This is the law,
Ancient and inexhaustible. (Chap. 1)[22]

TEST YOURSELF

1. Siddhartha's encounters with an old man, a sick man, a corpse, and a wandering holy man, which prompted him to leave his luxurious and carefree life, are called the _____.
   a. temptations
   b. Four Passing Sights
   c. Enlightenment
   d. Awakening

2. After Siddhartha spent and entire night meditating under a full moon, he finally achieved insight into release from suffering and rebirth. Buddhists believe that he reached a profound understanding, called his _____.
   a. *Dharma*
   b. *stupa*
   c. asceticism
   d. *enlightenment*

3. At the core of what is generally regarded as basic _____ are the Three Jewels: the Buddha, the Dharma, and the Sangha.
   a. suffering
   b. Enlightenment
   c. Buddhism
   d. existence

4. According to Buddhism, reality manifests three characteristics: constant change, lack of permanent identity, and the existence of _____.
   a. truth
   b. suffering
   c. death
   d. deprivation

5. According to a view common to all forms of Buddhism, reality manifests three characteristics: constant change, a lack of permanent identity, and the existence of suffering. This view is the foundation for the _____ and the _____.
   a. Four Noble Truths, Noble Eightfold Path
   b. Tripitaka, Maitreya
   c. Vehicle of the Diamond, Dharmakaya
   d. Tendai, Jodo

6. In Buddhism, as in Hinduism, _____ suggest(s) decay and pain.
   a. change
   b. Four Noble Truths
   c. *samsara*
   d. reality

7. Liberation from decay and pain is called _____.
   a. *nirvana*
   b. *samsara*
   c. *moksha*
   d. Awakening

8. The key notions of _____ Buddhism are *trikaya* (the "three-body doctrine"), *shunyata* ("emptiness"), and *tathata* ("thatness").
   a. Ahimsa
   b. Theravada
   c. Mahayana
   d. Vedic

9. In _____ Buddhist countries, one great celebration (Vesak) recalls the birth, the enlightenment, and the death of Buddha. It is celebrated at the time of the full moon in May.
   a. Western
   b. O-Bon
   c. Mahayana
   d. Theravada

10. In Tibetan Buddhism, the executive head of the Gelug-pa is called the Dalai Lama, which means "_____."
   a. the Awakened
   b. ocean superior one
   c. heavenly bodhisattva
   d. compassion

11. Think of a social group you are a part of, such as a family, business, or student organization. How do you think the group dynamic would change if its members lived in accordance with the ideas of anichcha and anatta? Why?

12. Consider the following statement: "Buddhism has no real deity." Using what you learned in this chapter, why might you agree or disagree with this statement? Address the different branches of Buddhism in your response.

RESOURCES

Books

Dalai Lama. *The Universe in a Single Atom: The Convergence of Science and Spirituality.* New York: Broadway, 2005. An argument for a constructive dialogue between religion and science.

Faure, Bernard. *The Power of Denial: Buddhism, Purity, and Gender.* Princeton, NJ: Princeton University Press, 2003. An exploration of the role of gender in Buddhism and the extent to which the religion liberates or limits women.

Friedman, Lenore. *Meetings with Remarkable Women: Buddhist Teachers in America.* New York: Random House, 2000. Portraits of the author's encounters with seventeen women teachers, giving insight into the growth of roles for women in modern Buddhism.

Gross, Rita. *A Garland of Feminist Reflections.* Berkeley: University of California Press, 2009. A collection of essays by a foremost expert in both Buddhism and feminist thought.

Gunaratana, Bhante H. *Mindfulness in Plain English.* Boston: Wisdom Publications, 2002. A good guide for the practice of Vipassana meditation, presented by a monk of Sri Lanka.

Kabat-Zinn, Jon. *Wherever You Go, There You Are.* New York: Hyperion, 1995. Short meditative chapters about topics such as patience, doing chores, and breathing—meant to help bring mindfulness to everyday life.

Lopez, Donald, Jr. *Buddhism and Science.* Chicago: University of Chicago Press, 2008. A critical analysis of claims that Buddhism and science are compatible.

Nanayon, Upasika. *Pure and Simple: The Buddhist Teachings of a Thai Laywoman.* Boston: Wisdom Publications, 2005. A collection of the writings by the late Thai teacher of Buddhism.

Thich Nhat Hanh. *The Heart of the Buddha's Teaching.* New York: Broadway, 1999. A compelling introduction to Buddhism by a renowned Vietnamese Buddhist teacher.

Williams, Paul. *Buddhist Thought: A Complete Introduction to the Indian Tradition.* New York, Routledge, 2000. An exploration of the history, practice, and philosophy of Indian Buddhist tradition.

Music/Audio

Chants and Music from Buddhist Temples. (Arc Music.) A diverse compilation of recordings, including Buddhist chants from temples in China, India, Sri Lanka, Taiwan, and Thailand.

Japanese Traditional Music: Gagaku and Buddhist Chant. (World Arbiter.) A remastered release of an original 1941 recording Japanese court music and Buddhist chant performed for the Imperial Household.

Nirvana Symphony. (Composer Toshiro Mayuzumi; Denon Records.) Modern classical music inspired by Buddhism.

Tibetan Master Chants. (Spirit Music.) A recording of the deep-voice chanting of one of the world's foremost Tibetan chant masters, including the mantra "Om Mani Padme Hum."

Film/TV

Buddha Wild: Monk in a Hut. (Carpe Diem Films.) A group of Thai and Sri Lankan monks discuss their commitment to Buddhism and its way of life.

Kundun. (Director Martin Scorsese; Buena Vista.) A colorful biography of the current Dalai Lama, focusing on his escape from Tibet.

Little Buddha. (Director Bernardo Bertolucci; Miramax.) A film that interweaves two stories: the historical life of the Buddha and the modern search in Seattle for the reincarnation of a lama.

10 Questions for the Dalai Lama. (Rick Ray Films). A documentary that examines some of the fundamental questions of our time, filmed with the Dalai Lama at his monastery in Dharamsala, India.

Internet

BuddhaNet: http://www.buddhanet.net/. A large variety of Buddhist information and resources, including a worldwide directory, e-library, online magazine, and notice board.

Virtual Religion Index: http://virtualreligion.net/vri/buddha.html. The "Buddhist Studies" page at the Virtual Religion Index site, containing individual sections devoted to general resources, the life of the Buddha, and Theravada and Mahayana Buddhism.

Wikipedia's Buddhism Portal: http://en.wikipedia.org/wiki/Portal:Buddhism. The "Buddhism Portal" page at Wikipedia, offering links to subcategories such as culture, branches of Buddhism, deities, festivals, history, philosophical concepts, practices, temples, terms, and texts.

KEY TERMS

(Buddhist terms are often anglicized in English pronunciation. For the following terms with two pronunciations, the second is the anglicized version.)

Amitabha Buddha (*ah-mee-tah'-buh*): The Buddha of the Western Paradise, a bliss-body Buddha in Mahayana.

anatta (*un-nah'-tuh*): "No self"; the doctrine that there is no soul or permanent essence in people and things.

anichcha (*uh-nee'-chuh*): Impermanence, constant change.

arhat (*ahr'-hut, ahr'-haht*): In Theravada, a person who has practiced monastic disciplines and reached nirvana, the ideal.

bodhi (*boh'-dee*): Enlightenment.

bodhisattva (*boh'-dee-suh'-tvah, boh-dee-saht'-vuh*): "Enlightenment being"; in Mahayana, a person of deep compassion, especially one who does not enter nirvana but is constantly reborn to help others; a heavenly being of compassion.

Dharma (*dhur'-mah, dar'-muh*): The totality of Buddhist teaching.

dhyana (*dee-yah'-nuh*): "Meditation"; focusing of the mind; sometimes, stages of trance.

dukkha (*doo'-kuh*): Sorrow, misery.

Guanyin: A popular bodhisattva of compassion in Mahayana.

karuna (*kuh-roo'-nuh*): Compassion, empathy.

koan (*koh'-ahn*): In Chan and Zen Buddhism, a question that cannot be answered logically; a technique used to test consciousness and bring awakening.

lama: A Tibetan Buddhist teacher; a title of honor often given to all Tibetan monks.

Maitreya (*mai-tray'-yuh*): A Buddha (or bodhisattva) expected to appear on earth in the future.

mandala (*mun'-duh-luh, mahn-dah'-luh*): A circular design containing deities, geometrical forms, symbols, and so on that represent totality, the self, or the universe.

mudra (*moo'-druh*): A symbolic hand gesture.

nirvana (*nir-vah'-nuh*): The release from suffering and rebirth that brings inner peace.

samadhi (*suh-mah'-dee*): A state of deep awareness, the result of intensive meditation.

samsara (*suhm-sah'-ruh, sahm-sah'-ruh*): Constant rebirth and the attendant suffering; the everyday world of change.

Sangha (*suhng'-huh*): The community of monks and nuns; lowercased, *sangha* refers to an individual monastic community.

satori (*sah-toh'-ree*): In Zen, the enlightened awareness.

shunyata (*shoon'-ya-tah*): The Mahayana notion of emptiness, meaning that the universe is empty of permanent reality.

stupa (*stoo'-puh*): A shrine, usually in the shape of a dome, used to mark Buddhist relics or sacred sites.

sutra (*soo'-truh*): A sacred text, especially one said to record the words of the Buddha.

tathata (*taht-ha-tah'*): "Thatness," "thusness," "suchness"; the uniqueness of each changing moment of reality.

trikaya (*trih-kah'-yuh*): The three "bodies" of the Buddha—the Dharmakaya (cosmic Buddha nature), the Nirmanakaya (historical Buddhas), and the Sambhogakaya (celestial Buddhas).

Tripitaka (*trih-pih'-tuh-kuh*): The three "baskets," or collections, of Buddhist texts.

vajra (*vuhj'-ruh, vahj'-ruh*): The "diamond" scepter used in Tibetan and other types of Buddhist ritual, symbolizing compassion.

Visit the Online Learning Center at www.mhhe.com/molloy5e for additional exercises and features, including "Religion beyond the Classroom" and "For Fuller Understanding."

CHAPTER **5**

Jainism and Sikhism

FIRST ENCOUNTER

On a street in Southeast Asia, you ask a policeman for directions. This leads to further conversation, since your accent gives you away and he has relatives in the United States. "Maybe you know them?" he asks. "Do you live close to Tennessee?"

Even though you don't know his relatives, you are soon learning all about his family. He has two sons, already married, and a willful daughter who is of marriageable age. He is frightened that she might fall in love with a person of a different religion, and then what will he do? Soon he is taking you into his nearby *gurdwara*—the religious center for Sikhs—where he will be doing volunteer work this afternoon and having something to eat.

At the entrance, your new friend takes a piece of orange cloth and makes a turban to cover the top of your head. He does the same for himself. "We do this for respect, he says. Upstairs, you meet the resident priest, a bright-eyed man in blue, who wears an orange cap. "Our congregation brought him from India to be our priest,"

189

your Sikh friend explains as you walk to the altar area. Soon the priest is showing you copies of the Adi Granth, the sacred book of the Sikhs. They are housed in a special air-conditioned sanctuary beside the altar. Then you see the sword collection at the side of the room and discuss the *kirpan* (ritual knife) that the priest wears. "Sikhs had to learn to defend themselves," your friend explains. "These are symbols of our strength."

Afterwards, you are invited downstairs to an enormous kitchen and dining room. Large vats gleam. You and your friend sit at a long table, drinking tea with milk and eating a late-afternoon snack with the kitchen workers.

At the entrance, before leaving, you give back your turban to the Sikh policeman and thank him for his kindness. You commiserate about his daughter and take the names and addresses of his relatives in the United States, whom you plan to contact on your very next visit to their state. He helps you find a taxi and, as it stops, invites you to a service three days from now. "There will be wonderful Sikh music. You must come." As you are climbing into the taxi, he adds, "There will be much good food, too."

Turbans, you decide as your taxi snakes through the traffic, are fine. But swords? And priests who wear knives? Are these suitable symbols for any religion? How can religions hold such differing attitudes about violence?

SHARED ORIGINS

India is now home to two religions that are not well known in the West: Jainism and Sikhism. The first is ancient, and the other is relatively young. Adherents of the two religions can be found in limited numbers around the world, but the majority live in India.

Both religions have some connection with Hinduism, sharing with it certain characteristics, such as a belief in karma and rebirth. Furthermore, both of them, having developed in opposition to Hindu polytheism and ritualism, strive toward greater religious simplicity. In spite of their similarities, however, Jainism and Sikhism differ in their views of reality and in their emotional tones. It is therefore interesting to look at them side by side. Jainism rejects belief in a Creator and sees the universe simply as natural forces in motion, yet it also recognizes the spiritual potential of each person. Like early Buddhism, Jainism emphasizes the ideals of extreme nonattachment and nonharm (ahimsa). Sikhism, to the contrary, embraces a devout monotheism and accepts meat eating and military self-defense. Regardless of their differences, both religions stress the importance of the individual's struggle to purify the self, to act morally, and to do good to others.

JAINISM

BACKGROUND

As the Vedic religion expanded eastward into the Ganges River valley, it created opposition. As we saw in Chapter 4, some people rebelled against the growing strength of the caste system, and nonbrahmins, especially the aristocrats, felt threatened by the power of the priests. Moved by compassion, some people opposed the animal sacrifices that were often a part of the Vedic ritual. Two great religious movements grew out of this opposition. One—Buddhism—is well known because it spread beyond India. The other movement—Jainism—has remained less well known because, until recently, it has not sought converts in other lands. When they arose, both Buddhism and Jainism were influenced by some early Hindu ideas, but they may have also practiced much older ascetic traditions.

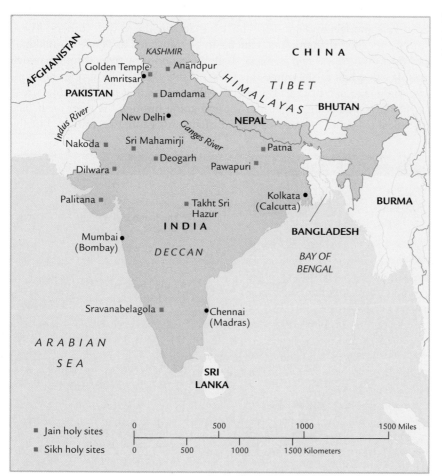

FIGURE 5.1

Jain and Sikh holy sites in India.

It is possible that Jainism has not spread widely because it is uncompromising: in it we find an extremist quality that is fascinating, thought provoking, and often noble. Tendencies toward nonviolence and austerity apparent in Hinduism and Buddhism are carried to their logical endpoint in Jainism, and the skepticism of early Buddhism is practiced rigorously. The study of Jainism, in fact, gives greater clarity to our understanding of those two other Indian religions.

Although Jainism did not spread widely, its strong ideal of nonviolence has attracted interest throughout the world. We see its influence directly in the thought and work of Mahatma Gandhi and, indirectly, in the thought and work of Martin Luther King Jr.

MAHAVIRA AND THE ORIGINS OF JAINISM

Jains date the origins of their religion to the distant past. They believe that in the present cycle of the universe, twenty-four great people have reached perfection; and though living in quite different centuries, these saints have been role models and guides who have shown the way to others. These saints are called **tirthankaras,** which can be translated as "crossing makers" or "ford finders"—a *ford* being a shallow section of a river through which people can wade to the other side. It is notable that the term does not convey the image of a bridge. The point of the term is that people cannot cross to the other side without getting wet and going through the river itself. The historical existence of most of these tirthankaras cannot be proven, but the

Timeline of significant events in the history of Jainism and Sikhism.

TIMELINE 5.1

	c. 850–800 B.C.E.	● Life of Parshva, the legendary twenty-third tirthankara
Life of Mahavira, the ● twenty-fourth and most recent tirthankara	c. 599–527 B.C.E.	
	c. 350 B.C.E.	● Split between Digambara and Shvetambara sects
Life of Nanak ●	1469–1539 C.E.	
	1563–1606	● Life of Arjan
Life of Gobind Singh ●	1666–1708	
	1984	● Indian troops retake the Golden Temple from Sikh separatists

twenty-third one, Parshva, may have been a real person who lived in India, possibly between 850 and 800 B.C.E. (Timeline 5.1).

The most recent tirthankara is considered to be the greatest of them all and is often thought of by outsiders to be the founder of Jainism. His name was Nataputta Vardhamana, but he is usually referred to by an honorary title: Mahavira, meaning "great man" or "hero." When he lived is not entirely certain. An older dating, accepted by Jains, puts his life entirely in the sixth century B.C.E. (c. 599–527 B.C.E.), but some scholars believe he lived a bit later (540–468 B.C.E.), possibly as a contemporary of the Buddha.

Mahavira's life story is surrounded by legend, although the basic outline—which somewhat resembles the story of the Buddha—seems clear. He was born into an aristocratic family of a noble clan. Luckily, he was the second son and thus had fewer responsibilities to care for his parents than did his older brother. One branch of Jains holds that he never married; another says that he married and had a child. But all agree that he left home at about age 30 to live the life of a wandering holy man.

After leaving home, Mahavira embraced extreme asceticism, and legend tells of his harshness toward himself and of the harshness received from others. He is said to have pulled out his hair when he renounced the world, and villagers taunted him during his meditations

Women pray at India's Ranakpur Jain Temple, said to contain 1,444 columns, each carved with a different design.

by hurting him with fire and with pins that they pushed into his skin. Dogs attacked him, but he did not resist. In order to avoid all attachments to people and places, he moved to a new place every day; and after losing his loincloth, he went entirely naked for the rest of his life. He lived as a wandering holy man, begging for his food along the way. He was so gentle that to avoid causing injury to any living thing, he strained whatever he drank to keep from swallowing any insect that might have fallen into his cup, and he stepped carefully as he walked down a road to avoid crushing even an ant.

After twelve years of meditation, wandering, and extreme mortification, Mahavira, at the age of 42, had an experience of great liberation. He felt completely free of all bondage to the ordinary world—no longer being troubled by pain, suffering, shame, or loss. He now felt fully in control of himself, sensing that he had won out over all the forces that bind a person to the world. As a result of his liberating experience, Mahavira is called a **jina** ("conqueror"). It is from this title that the religion Jainism takes its name.

Mahavira spent the next thirty years of his life teaching his doctrines and organizing an order of naked monks. He died at about 72 at the village of Pava, near present-day Patna, in northeastern India.

WORLDVIEW

Jainism, like Buddhism, rather starkly rejects belief in a Creator God. The Mahapurana, a long Jain poem of the ninth century C.E., states that "foolish men declare that Creator made the world. The doctrine that the world was created is ill-advised and should be rejected."[1] Jainism offers the following philosophical arguments: If God is perfect, why did God create a universe that is imperfect? If God made the universe because of love, why is the world so full of suffering beings? If the universe had to be created, did not God also need to be created? And where did God come from in the beginning?

Jains respond to these questions by denying any beginning and asserting instead that the universe is eternal. Although the universe has always existed, it must continually change, and in the process of eternal change, structure arises on its own. Jainism (like Hinduism) teaches that the universe goes through regular great cycles of rise and fall. During the periods when human beings exist, there first is moral integrity, followed by inevitable moral decay; luckily, however, in each human age, tirthankaras appear to point the way to freedom.

According to Jainism, everything is full of life and is capable of suffering. This view of reality, called **hylozoism** (Greek: "matter-alive"), may be quite ancient. In addition, Jain philosophy is dualistic, for Jains teach that all parts of the universe are composed of two types of reality, which are intermixed. There is spirit, which senses and feels, and there is matter, which is not alive and has no consciousness. Jainism calls these two principles **jiva** ("soul," "spirit," "life") and **ajiva** ("nonsoul," "nonlife"). Jains, however, see life and consciousness where others do not—even in fire, rocks, and water. Thus they extend the notion of spirit and feeling beyond human beings, animals, and insects. They are also aware of the minuscule life-forms that live in earth, water, and wood. Their way of looking at reality makes Jains cautious about injuring anything—even that which does not at first appear to have the capacity to suffer.

Jainism sees the human being as composed of two opposing parts. The material side of the human being seeks pleasure, escape from pain, and self-interest, while the spiritual side seeks freedom and escape from all bondage to the material world and from the limitation of ego. Because other forms of reality are not aware of their two opposing aspects, they can do nothing about the essential incompatibility of the two parts. Human beings, however, have the ability to understand their dual nature and to overcome their limitations. With discipline, human beings can overcome the bondage of the material world and the body, liberating their spirits through insight, austerity, and kindness.

Enriching this vision of the human situation are the Jain beliefs in karma and reincarnation. Like Hindus, Jains believe that spirits are constantly being reborn in various forms. A spirit can move up or down the scale of rebirth, as well as free itself entirely from the chain of rebirths.

What controls the direction of rebirth is karma, which is produced by every action. As discussed earlier, karma is an important notion in Hinduism and Buddhism, but for Jains, karma has a quite physical quality: it is like a powder or grime that settles on and clings to the spirit. The level of rebirth is determined automatically, according to one's state of karma at the time of the death of one's current body.

Jains traditionally have believed that superhuman beings exist in realms of the universe above the earth. Often these beings are called gods or deities, but such terms can be misleading. We must recall that Jains believe that these superhuman beings are also subject to karma and change. When the karma that has brought them rebirth as gods has run out, they will be reborn in lower parts of the universe. Some Jains, however, do believe that when in their superhuman form, these celestial beings can be of help to people on earth who pray to them. Jains also believe that some beings exist in painful realms below the earth, and Jains hope to avoid being reborn there.

The Jain goal is to reach a state of total freedom. Liberated spirits, at last freed of their imprisoning material bodies, live on in the highest realm, which is thought to be at the very top of the universe. Mahavira and other tirthankaras dwell there, and although they cannot assist human beings (as deities might), they are role models whom human beings devoutly recall in order to gain strength and courage.

JAIN ETHICS

Jainism has five ethical recommendations, which monks and nuns are expected to keep quite strictly. Laypeople, however, have the flexibility to adjust their practice to their particular life situations. (We must also recall that these are ideals that are not always lived out perfectly by individuals.)

Nonviolence (ahimsa) A more accurate English translation of *ahimsa* might be "gentleness" or "harmlessness." Ahimsa is the foundation of Jain ethics, and Jains are best known for their extreme measures in this regard. Believing that Mahavira swept the ground in front of him as he walked and before he sat down, Jain monks and nuns sometimes use a small, soft brush to move ants and other insects out of the way so that no life-form—even the tiniest—will be crushed. Feeling a kinship with the animal world as well, Jains have established hospitals to care for sick animals. They have been known to buy caged animals and set them free. Jains are also strict vegetarians, and some reject the use of animal products such as leather, feathers, and fur.

The saint, with true vision, conceives compassion for all the world. . . . The great sage becomes a refuge for injured creatures, like an island which the waters cannot overwhelm.
—Acaranga Sutra 1:6, 5[2]

Jains and a Holy Death

Because it so values nonattachment, Jainism defends a person's right to end his or her own life. (This is also true of Hinduism but not so for many other religions—although most religions are indeed concerned with a good and holy death.) Jain scriptures even teach that Mahavira and his parents died by self-starvation. We must be cautious here, however, in using the word *suicide.* Jains do accept ending one's own life, but we must understand the practice from the Jain point of view and within that context. Jains see all life as a preparation for the liberation of the spirit (jiva) from the body, and when a person is sufficiently evolved spiritually, that person can make the final choice to no longer create more karma.

The Jain ideal thus allows and esteems ending one's life only after a long life of virtue and detachment, and it must be done with consideration for others. Gentle methods of ending one's life are the best, such as walking into an ocean or lake. The most highly esteemed method, however, is self-starvation, called **sallekhana,** "holy death." Jains prepare for sallekhana over the years by practicing fasting. When a person is old and growing weak, eating less and less is seen as an appropriate way to hasten the end. Self-starvation, or "the final fast," involves giving up food but continuing to drink liquids; death comes in about a month. This kind of death by self-starvation is considered an ultimate, noble expression of non-attachment and freedom.

Because Jain laypeople avoid occupations that would harm insects or animals, hunting and fishing are forbidden, as are slaughtering or selling animal flesh. And although some Jains are farmers, farming is often avoided because the necessary plowing could hurt small animals and insects living in the fields. Jains, instead, have gravitated to careers that ideally cause no hurt, such as medicine, education, law, and business. As an indirect result, the Jains in India make up a powerful business class whose reputation for virtue earns them the trust of others.

Nonlying Jainism discourages the telling of any falsehood and avoids exaggeration, even when meant humorously. Lying and exaggeration are dangerous, Jains think, because they often cause hurt. Although these ideals are not always followed, Jains' general mindfulness of their speech and their reputation for honesty in their contractual agreements have earned them great respect.

At the same time, Jainism teaches that "absolute truth" is impossible to find or express, because everyone sees a situation from a unique point of view. A famous story illustrates the relativity of truth. In this story, several blind men touch the same elephant but experience it quite differently. The first man touches the ear and says it is a fan; the second man touches the leg and says it is a tree trunk; the third man touches the tail and says it is a rope; and so on. (Although this story is popular among Jains, it is doubtless older than Jainism itself.)

Nonstealing Jains may not take from others that which is not given. Stealing arises from improper desire and causes pain to others.

Chastity For the monk or nun, this means complete celibacy, and for the married individual, this means sexual fidelity to one's spouse.

A devotee anoints the feet of a Jain statue. The vines on each side (showing at the top corners of the photograph) hint at the immobility and perseverance of the tirthankara.

Mahavira saw sex as a danger, because it strongly binds a person to the physical world, strengthens desires, and can create passions that harm others. For those who are sexually active, improper sex is that which hurts others.

Nonattachment Human beings form attachments easily—to family, to home, to familiar territory, to clothes, to money, and to possessions. Jainism asserts that all attachments bring a certain bondage and that some attachments, especially to money and to possessions, can take complete control of a person. For laypeople, the ethical requirement of nonattachment suggests cultivating a spirit of generosity and detachment and limiting one's possessions to what is truly necessary. For monks and nuns, this requirement is interpreted more severely. Jainism teaches that Mahavira abandoned all attachments—family, possessions, even his clothing—and that monks and nuns must imitate him to the best of their capacity.

THE DEVELOPMENT OF JAINISM AND ITS BRANCHES

Jainism first developed in northeastern India, in the same area that gave rise to Buddhism. Both Mahavira and the Buddha rebelled against aspects of Vedic religion: they refused to accept the authority of the Vedas, the Vedic gods, or the importance of a priestly class, and they placed emphasis, instead, on meditation and self-purification.

Although Buddhism followed a deliberate path of moderation—a "middle way"—Jainism gloried in austerity. While the Buddha rejected both nakedness and suicide as well as all extreme austerity, Mahavira's breakthrough experience of liberation, most Jains believe, was due to his extreme harshness toward himself. He was successful precisely because he accepted—and even sought—cold, heat, poverty, nakedness, and humiliation.

The way of extreme austerity, however, is for rare individuals only. For most people, even for monks and nuns, the harshness must be softened according to life's circumstances. Because Jainism spread to different parts of India, with their differences in culture and climate, several branches of Jainism arose, which interpret the basic principles and teachings with some variations.

FIGURE 5.2

Branches of Jainism.

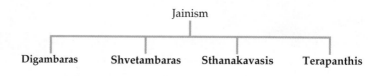

Digambaras

The name of this sect is beautiful and means "clothed in sky" or "atmosphere-clad." It is a pleasant way of referring to the monks' ideal of going completely naked, even in public. The **Digambara** branch holds that everything must be renounced, including the last scrap of clothing and the consequent shame of nakedness.

Most members of this branch live in southern India today. As tradition explains, a famine that occurred in the north drove many Jains southward. Divergences developed between those who had remained in the north and those who had moved south. Thinking that northern followers had lost an essential seriousness, the southern branch became conservative, continuing to insist on renunciation of the most literal type. Its conservatism shows itself in many ways. For example, Digambara Jainism does not accept women into monastic life, holding that they may become monks only when they have been reborn as men. Possibly because of its high regard for celibacy, it also rejects the tradition that Mahavira was ever married.

Shvetambaras

The name of this sect means "clothed in white" and comes from the fact that its monks dress in white robes. The **Shvetambara** branch allows women to enter monastic life as nuns and to dress in white as well. (Being clothed was allowed not only in deference to modesty but also because it was demanded by the colder climate of northern India.) Shvetambara Jainism teaches that Mahavira was indeed married at one time but that he left home to find liberation. Nowadays this branch has members not only in the northeast but also in western and northwestern India.

Sthanakavasis

By the standards of India, the **Sthanakavasi** branch is fairly young, having grown up within the past few hundred years. It is a reform movement that emerged from the Shvetambara branch in the early eighteenth century. Popular Jainism had increasingly developed the practice of venerating statues of Mahavira and other tirthankaras, influenced by the Hindu practice of **puja** (devotional ritual performed in front of statues and at altars). Some Jain reformers opposed this practice because it seemed to turn the tirthankaras into deities to be prayed to for help. The Sthanakavasis, therefore, do not make use of either temples or images. (Their name comes from the simple buildings—*sthanakas*—in which they meet.) Rather than concentrate on temple ceremony, Sthanakavasis focus on meditation and individual austerities.

Terapanthis

An even newer reformist movement is the **Terapanthi** branch. It was founded in 1817 by Acharya Bhikshu (1788–1860), also called Swami Bhikkanji Maharaj. The origin of the name Terapanthi, which means "thirteen," is debated. It may come from the thirteen moral principles outlined by the founder or from the number of persons comprising the earliest disciples. Like the Sthanakavasis, the Terapanthis reject the use of images. To ensure discipline, the founder instituted a hierarchical structure with a supreme guru, the *Acharya*, at the top, who oversees all operations. The Terapanthis, while being strict in their practice, have been at the forefront in spreading Jainism outside of India and in spreading basic Jain principles among non-Jains, both within India and beyond.

JAIN PRACTICES

Because they emphasize the ability of individuals to purify themselves and to perfect their own characters, Jains do not stress that devotional acts—directed toward gods or deceased leaders—bring help. Nonetheless, the practice of puja—offered to both the tirthankaras and to deities—has been adopted by most Jains. (Exceptions are the Sthanakavasis and Terapanthis.) There is a general feeling that the devotional acts have a good effect on one's state of karma and that they focus the mind on saintly behavior. Jain temples, therefore, contain statues of the tirthankaras, especially Rishaba (the first tirthankara), Nemi (the twenty-second), Parshva, and Mahavira. The temple statues often look the same. In Digambara temples, the statues are unclothed and simple; in Shvetambara temples, they may be clothed and more ornate. Puja is performed before statues regularly, both by Jains and (in some places) by brahmin Hindus employed for the task. Puja ordinarily involves the offering of food, incense, the flames of oil lamps, and flowers, and sometimes the statues are bathed and devotees circumambulate (walk around) the statues. In some areas, large outdoor statues are bathed in milk and other liquids on special occasions. Many Jains also maintain home altars where they perform puja.

Fasting is regularly practiced by monks and nuns, particularly at the times of full and new moons. Laypeople join the monks in fasting on the last days of the Jain year in late summer, before the celebration of the New Year begins (in August or September). This period of fasting (*paryusana*) lasts fifteen days for the Digambaras and eight days for the Shvetambaras. The religious year ends with a confession of wrongdoing and a plea for pardon from anyone the devotee might have offended.

Pilgrimage is an important part of Jain spirituality, and the village near Patna, where Mahavira died, is a great pilgrimage center. Jains also visit the great temple complexes (some of which are on mountaintops in western India) and attend the bathing of large statues. Jains celebrate the birthday of Mahavira in the spring and his experience of liberation in the autumn.

JAIN SCRIPTURES

Jains speak of ancient scriptures, the Purvas, that exist no longer in their entirety but only as limited quotations in later scripture. Disagreement exists among the sects over what is to be accepted as canonical (authoritative). The literature preserved by the Shvetambara sect consists of forty-five works, divided into the canonical scriptures and later noncanonical works. At the heart of the canonical material are the eleven Angas ("limbs"). (A twelfth is said to have existed at one time.) Jainism holds the Angas to be the teachings of Mahavira, although they were not given final form until two centuries after his death. There are also twelve Upangas ("lesser limbs"), a collection of laws, rituals (particularly associated with assistance in dying), and other miscellaneous texts. Later noncanonical works include biographies of holy persons, commentaries on canonical works, and books of philosophy and science.[3] The Digambara sect does not fully accept the authenticity of the Angas, maintaining that the words of Mahavira were remembered and transmitted imperfectly after the first division of the Jains had taken place. The Sthanakavasis do not recognize any literature as scripture.

JAIN ART AND ARCHITECTURE

The most striking examples of Jain art are the statues of Mahavira and other tirthankaras. Although the seated statues resemble Buddhist sculpture, other sculptural forms contrast greatly with their Buddhist counterparts. Buddha

figures are often gentle looking, with a preternatural sweetness in the faces; Jain figures, however, tend to be bold, powerful, and imposing. This is particularly true of statues of tirthankaras shown naked and standing: their nakedness somehow adds to their strength, and the standing figures are often presented with their legs and arms surrounded by vines, their immobility suggesting persistence and strength of character. The tirthankara seems to dare the viewer to be equally as strong.

Jain temple architecture does not echo the simplicity of the sculpture. Some Jain temples show as much love for richness and decoration as some Hindu temples do. (The Jain temples on Mount Abu, in western India, are famous for their intricately carved marble ceilings.) Sometimes, as in Kolkata (Calcutta), the temples also feature exuberant elements borrowed from European architecture, such as Corinthian columns and stained glass.

The Jain temple at Jaisalmer seems to be a mirage emerging from the desert.

SIKHISM

BACKGROUND

Sikhism grew up in an area called the Punjab, which today is part of northwestern India and eastern Pakistan. Although the region has a long history of religious conflict between Hindus and Muslims, it is also an area in which significant attempts have been made to bridge division and misunderstanding. It is not surprising, then, that Sikhism, nurtured in the midst of conflict and resolution, exhibits elements reminiscent of both groups.

It is hard to imagine two religions more divergent than Hinduism and Islam. Hinduism recognizes many gods, while Islam recognizes only one; Hinduism cherishes religious images, whereas Islam prohibits them; and Hinduism promotes vegetarianism, but Islam, although it has dietary restrictions, allows the killing and eating of many animals, including cows.

Both religions, though, share an appreciation for religious devotion and value the attainment of mystical consciousness. In Hinduism, these traditions have been cultivated by the devotees of bhakti yoga, and in Islam they have been cultivated by Sufis (see Chapter 10). (Some scholars maintain that Sufism in fact derived much early inspiration from Hinduism.) Both religions also recognize the important role of a spiritual master—a *guru* or a *shaykh.* And while Islam is known for its rejection of images, some Hindus have also spoken against an exaggerated love of images.

Before Sikhism began, there were already people, called *sants*, who practiced a spirituality that drew from both religions and that sought to overcome religious divisions. The greatest exponent of the sant tradition was the mystic Kabir (1440–1518), whose poetry has had enormous influence in India. It is from this interest in a mystical spirituality beyond the restrictions of any one religion that Sikhism emerged, and it was in the Punjab, where two often-opposing religions collided, that the founder of a new religion was born.

NANAK AND THE ORIGINS OF SIKHISM

The founder of Sikhism, Nanak, was born in 1469 in what is today Pakistan. He grew up in a Hindu family, married, had two children, and held several jobs—first as a herder and then as a clerical assistant to a sultan. Because Nanak's life as a householder was accompanied by a strong religious interest, he and a Muslim friend named Mardana created a devotional association and met in the evenings to sing hymns and to discuss religious ideas.

One day Nanak had an experience so powerful that he saw it as a revelation. After bathing and performing religious ablutions in a nearby river, Nanak went into the adjacent forest and did not reemerge for three days. During that time he felt himself taken into the divine presence. He would later say that he had experienced God directly. This shattering experience revealed to him that there is but one God, beyond all human names and conceptions.

Nanak referred to the fundamental divine reality as the True Name—signifying that all names and terms that are applied to God are limited, because the divine is beyond all human conception. Nanak now understood that Hindus and Muslims worshiped the same God and that a distinction between the two religions was mistaken. Nanak became famous for insisting that when the True Name of God is experienced, rather than just talked about, there is no "Hindu" and there is no "Muslim."

Nanak's revelation is similar to stories of the life-changing prophetic calls of Isaiah, Zarathustra, and Muhammad (as we will see in later chapters). His revelatory experience resolved his earlier doubts and was the great turning point of his life. Having decided to spread his new understanding, Nanak left his family and home, accompanied by his friend Mardana. As homeless wanderers, they visited holy sites throughout northern India. Wherever they went, Nanak preached and sought disciples, which is the meaning of the word **Sikh** (disciple). As a part of his preaching, Nanak sang devotional songs while Mardana, who was from a social class of musicians, played musical accompaniment.

Particularly startling was Nanak's style of clothing, which deliberately blended Hindu and Muslim elements. He wore the Hindu *dhoti* (a cloth drawn up between the legs to form pants), along with an orange Muslim coat and Muslim cap. He adorned his forehead with Hindu religious markings. The combination of elements was an important prophetic statement, predictably causing consternation among both Hindus and Muslims.

Nanak and Mardana continued their devotional teaching together until Mardana's death in his late 60s. Not long after, when Nanak sensed his own end approaching, he passed on his authority and work to a chosen disciple. He died in 1539 at age 70. Nanak is commonly called Guru Nanak and is recognized as the first of a line of ten Sikh gurus ("spiritual teachers").

THE WORLDVIEW AND TEACHINGS OF NANAK

Just as Nanak's clothing combined elements of Hinduism and Islam, so too did his worldview, at least on the surface. Earlier commentators spoke of Sikhism merely as a combination of Hindu and Muslim elements, yet Sikhs themselves—and more recent scholars—see Sikhism as an entirely unique religion. They speak of Nanak as having rejected both Islam and Hinduism, and they hold that Sikhism comes from a totally new revelation.

Nanak accepted—as does Hinduism—a belief in reincarnation and karma. His view of the human being was similar to that of the Sankhya school of philosophy, which views the human being as a composite of body and spirit. Because the body and physical world by nature bind and limit the spirit, the spirit must overcome physicality as it seeks freedom and absorption in the divine. This process may take many lifetimes to accomplish.

In spite of Nanak's acceptance of reincarnation and karma, there were other elements of Hinduism that he rejected. From a very early age, for example, he resisted Hindu love of ritual, criticizing it for taking human attention away from God. Similarly, he disdained Hindu polytheism, particularly Hindu devotion to images of various gods and goddesses. It is possible that Nanak's views in this regard were influenced by Islam. Islamic practice also supported Nanak's acceptance of meat eating. (Nanak believed that the animal world was created for the use of human beings.)

According to Nanak's view of God, although God is ultimately beyond personhood, God does have personal qualities, such as knowledge, love, a sense of justice, and compassion. Because of these qualities, God can be approached personally by the individual. In Nanak's view, God is the primary guru. Although Nanak saw himself as God's mouthpiece, he preached that God dwells within each individual and can be contacted within the human heart.

Despite his emphasis on finding the divine within the individual, Nanak believed that true religion has a strong social responsibility. He criticized both Islam and Hinduism for their deficiencies in helping the poor and the oppressed. In response to his convictions, Nanak organized religious groups, called *sangats,* which were to offer both worship to God and assistance to fellow human beings.

THE DEVELOPMENT OF SIKHISM

Sikhism has gone through several stages of development. In its earliest stage, Sikhism was not defined as a distinct religion. It was simply a religious movement that sought to coexist peacefully with other religions. In the next stage, Sikhism was forced to adopt a militant, self-protective stance toward the world, and it took on some of the elements of a more formalized religion—a sacred book, a sacred city, and clearly defined religious practices. After that period of self-definition and consolidation, Sikhism, in its third and final stage, was able to move beyond its land of origin and to make converts elsewhere.

The earliest stage was that of the first four gurus—Nanak, Angad, Amar Das, and Ram Das. During this period, hymns were written, numerous communities were organized, and a village headquarters was created at Amritsar, in northern India.

The next stage—of consolidation and religious definition—began with Guru Arjan (1563–1606), a son of Ram Das. In his role as fifth guru, Arjan built the Golden Temple and its surrounding pond at Amritsar. Collecting about three thousand hymns—written by himself and earlier gurus and saints—Arjan created the sacred book of the Sikhs, the **Adi Granth** ("original collection"). Because he resolutely resisted attempts by the Muslim emperor Jahangir to make him adopt Islamic practice, Arjan died of torture.

Arjan's son, Har Gobind, steered Sikhism in a more self-defensive direction. In response to his father's persecution, Har Gobind enlisted a bodyguard and an army to protect him and his followers. He adopted the practice of wearing a sword, thus abandoning the Hindu ideal of ahimsa. The growing militancy of evolving Sikhism was successful in averting persecution during the tenure of the next gurus, Har Rai and Harkishan.

The ninth guru, Tegh Bahadur, however, was imprisoned and decapitated by the Muslim emperor Aurangzeb, who saw Sikhism as a serious

Devotees receive food as part of a festival celebration at Anandpur Sahib shrine, near Chandigarh, India.

threat to his control. In response, the tenth guru, Gobind Rai (1666–1708) idealized the sword. Because of his military power, Gobind Rai came to be known as Gobind Singh ("Gobind the lion"). He inaugurated a special military order for men, called the Khalsa, and devised a ceremony of initiation, called the baptism of the sword, which involved sprinkling initiates with water that had been stirred with a sword. The Khalsa was open to all castes, for Gobind Singh had ended all caste distinctions among Sikhs. Every male within the Khalsa took the name Singh ("lion").

Over time, Gobind Singh suffered the deaths of his four sons and was left without a successor. Possibly foreseeing his own assassination, he declared that the Adi Granth was to be considered both his successor and

The "Five K's" of the Sikh Khalsa

In India and in big cities of the West, Sikhs today are often associated with turbans. In fact, their characteristic dress reflects not one but five practices. These practices are not observed by all Sikhs, however, but only by those who have entered the Khalsa, the special Sikh military order. The five practices were originally adopted by members of the Khalsa to promote strength and self-identity. Because the names of the practices each begin with the letter *k*, they are called the Five K's:

· *Kesh:* uncut hair and beard—in association with the lion and its power; the hair on the head is usually worn in a topknot and covered with a turban or cloth.
· *Khanga:* hair comb—to hold the long hair in place.
· *Kach:* special underwear—to indicate alertness and readiness to fight.
· *Kirpan:* sword—for defense.
· *Kara:* bracelet of steel—to symbolize strength.

In addition, members of the Khalsa are required to avoid all intoxicants. For a long time, the Khalsa was open only to men, but eventually it was opened also to women.

---

the final, permanent Guru. The sacred book, both in Amritsar and in Sikh temples (**gurdwaras**), is therefore treated with the same reverence that would be shown a living guru. As such, it is called Guru Granth Sahib. At the death of Gobind Singh, Sikhism was now clearly defined as a religion, with the means to spread beyond its place of origin.

SIKH SCRIPTURES

The primary book of Sikh scripture, the Adi Granth, is divided into three parts. The first and most important part is the **Japji,** a moderately long poem by Guru Nanak that summarizes the religion. It speaks of the indescribability of God and the joy of union with him. Its opening words declare, "There is only one God whose name is true, the Creator, devoid of fear and enmity, immortal, unborn, self-existent."[4] The second part consists of thirty-nine *rags* ("tunes") by Guru Nanak and later gurus. The third part is a collection of varied works, including poems and hymns from Hindu, Muslim, and Sikh gurus and saints.

Because the Adi Granth is believed to contain the living spirit of Nanak and his successors, it is treated with utmost reverence and given personal honors as the embodiment of the gurus. At the Golden Temple in Amritsar, it is brought out in the early morning by a gloved attendant, set on a cushion under a canopy, read from aloud by professional readers, fanned throughout the day, and then "put to bed" at night. In gurdwaras, copies of the Adi Granth are enshrined and read. It is consulted for solutions to problems by opening it freely and reading from the top of the left-hand page. (Even children are named by this method, being given names corresponding to the first letter read at the top of the left-hand page when the Adi Granth is opened randomly.) Sikh

homes may have a room to enshrine the Adi
Granth, and devout Sikhs daily read or recite
its passages from memory.

An example of the poetic nature of the
Adi Granth is the following canticle by Nanak
in praise of God:

> Wonderful Your word, wonderful Your
>   knowledge;
> Wonderful Your creatures, wonderful
>   their species;
> Wonderful their forms, wonderful their
>   colors;
> Wonderful the animals which wander
>   naked;
> Wonderful Your wind; wonderful Your
>   water;
> Wonderful Your fire which sports won-
>   drously;
> Wonderful the earth . . . ;
> Wonderful the desert, wonderful the
>   road;
> Wonderful Your nearness, wonderful
>   Your remoteness;
> Wonderful to behold You present.[5]

SIKHISM AND THE MODERN WORLD

Because of their military training, Sikhs were
employed by the British as soldiers. After the
British left the Indian subcontinent in 1947,
however, the Sikhs experienced painful dislo-
cation. More than two million left Pakistan to avoid conflict with the Muslim
majority, and most settled in northwestern India, where today some Sikhs hope
to create an independent state. Antagonism has flared up between the Sikhs
and the Indian government over this matter, and although Sikh separatists
have taken over the Golden Temple at Amritsar, Indian government forces have
repeatedly taken it back. In retaliation for her support of Indian government
troops during the first of these takeovers, Prime Minister Indira Gandhi was
assassinated in 1984 by Sikhs who were among her bodyguards.

Sikhs have begun to settle widely outside India, particularly in countries
open to Indian immigration, such as England and former British territories.
(There is a considerable community, for example, in Vancouver, British
Columbia.) They have established gurdwaras, which serve as daily prayer
centers as well as charitable kitchens and social meeting places. Although

A temple assistant explains
the significance of the
repository that houses
the Adi Granth and other
books sacred to Sikhs.

Sikhs do not have a tradition of making converts, their simple and self-reliant lifestyle has attracted many new members. Their success and continued growth is likely.

PERSONAL EXPERIENCE: A VISIT TO THE GOLDEN TEMPLE

The Golden Temple of Amritsar sits in the midst of a busy Indian city on an island in an artificial lake. On the day that I visited, however, the water of the lake had been drained, and about thirty workers were moving about and chatting down below as they cleaned and made repairs. While I surveyed the scene, I overheard what sounded like American English being spoken nearby. A man with black hair and a short black beard, his blond wife, and his young daughter were taking photos and discussing the restoration work. I offered to photograph them against the backdrop of the Golden Temple, and then we fell into conversation. The man introduced himself and his family. Mr. Singh and his wife Marianne were not American, he said, but Canadian.

"I was born in Vancouver just after my parents immigrated to Canada from India. We've come here to visit my grandparents and to see the Golden Temple," he explained. "And I'm from Alberta, originally," added Mrs. Singh. "I'm not a Sikh—at least not yet. I was raised Catholic. My parents immigrated to Canada from Poland and have a farm north of Calgary. My husband and I met in college at the University of British Columbia." She turned to the girl, "This is our daughter, June." After shaking hands, we went across the walkway together into the Golden Temple.

The interior was hot and muggy, but a feeling of devotion overcame my discomfort. A venerable-looking man with a long white beard was reading from the Adi Granth while an attendant waved a feather fan overhead. People moved very slowly in line, but our time inside was actually short, because the crowds kept us from staying too long. Outside, we decided to have lunch together. We found a restaurant not far away where we ate and talked.

Mr. Singh pointed to his short hair and neatly clipped beard. "As you can see, I do not practice all the traditions of my religion. I am proud of my religion, though, and particularly proud of the emphasis it puts on strength and endurance."

Mrs. Singh nodded. "Being in a mixed marriage, we've certainly needed strength at times, and we've found elements in both our religions that help us. I think, though, that we are typical of many Canadian couples, and our mixed marriage has been a rich experience for both of us."

"For our parents, too," Mr. Singh added, and both laughed and shook their heads knowingly. "My name means 'lion,'" he continued. "I want to use my strength to be a strong individual, not just a representative of a single religious path. Where I live, there's a large Sikh community, and it would be easy to deal exclusively with people of my own religion and ethnic background. But I want to be more universal, while keeping my religion in my heart."

Workers regularly clean and restore the Golden Temple and its pond.

As we got up to leave and were saying our good-byes, Mr. Singh lifted his arm. "Though I cut my hair and beard, I always wear this." He pulled back the cuff of his long-sleeved shirt and proudly showed me his kara—his steel Sikh bracelet.

READING

THE ADI GRANTH ON WOMEN

The Adi Granth is the sacred scripture of Sikhism. Although Sikh males are expected to play leadership roles in their families and religious ceremonies, and early leaders were exclusively male, women nonetheless have high status. Following is a passage on the dignity of women:

We are born of woman,
we are conceived in the womb of woman,
we are engaged and married to woman.
We make friendship with woman
and the lineage continued because of woman.
When one woman dies,
we take another one,
we are bound with the world through woman.

We grow up stronger and wiser having drunk
  milk from the breast of woman.
Why should we talk ill of her,
who gives birth to Kings?
The woman is born from woman;
there is none without her.
Only the One True Lord is without woman.[6]

209

TEST YOURSELF

1. In Jainism, the greatest of all _____ was Nataputta Vardhamana, who is usually referred to by the honorary title Mahavira.
   a. buddhas   c. tirthankaras
   b. mahatmas   d. priests

2. As a result of his liberating experience, following twelve years of meditation, wandering, and mortification, the Mahavira is called a _____. It is the title from which Jainism takes its name.
   a. *jiva*   c. *singh*
   b. *devi*   d. *jina*

3. The Jain goal is to reach a state of _____.
   a. total freedom   c. physical perfection
   b. reincarnation   d. intellectual greatness

4. One of the five ethical recommendations of Jainism is _____.
   a. ahimsa   c. nakedness
   b. dukkha   d. yoga

5. Although Buddhism followed a deliberate path of moderation, Jainism gloried in _____.
   a. the Vedic religion   c. the middle way
   b. austerity   d. the priestly class

6. The founder of Sikhism, Guru _____, is recognized as the first in a line of ten Sikh gurus ("spiritual teachers").
   a. Gautama   c. Bahkti
   b. Singh   d. Nanak

7. Sikhism was mostly influenced by Hinduism and _____.
   a. Islam   c. Buddhism
   b. Jainism   d. Taoism

8. Nanak accepted, as does Hinduism, a belief in reincarnation and _____.
   a. polytheism   c. karma
   b. atheism   d. Trimurti

9. Sikhs wear a bracelet of steel, called _____, that symbolizes strength.
   a. *kesh*   c. *kirpan*
   b. *kach*   d. *kara*

10. The primary book of Sikh scripture is the _____, which is believed to contain the living spirit of the ten gurus.
    a. Koran   c. Adi Granth
    b. Vedas   d. Purvas

11. Consider the following statement: "Sallekhana ('holy death') violates the Jain principle of ahimsa because it is an act of violence against oneself." Using examples from the chapter, what points might a follower of Jainism make to argue against this statement?

12. Discuss the similarities and differences between Jainism and Sikhism. What do you think is the most important similarity? What is the most important difference? Use specifics to support your answers.

RESOURCES

Books

Cort, John E. *Jains in the World: Religious Values and Ideology in India*. New York: Oxford University Press, 2001. A portrait of Jainism as practiced today.

Grewal, J. S. *The Sikhs of the Punjab*. Cambridge: Cambridge University Press, 2008. Possibly the most comprehensive and informative single-volume survey of Sikh history and religion currently available.

Mann, Gurinder Singh. *The Making of Sikh Scripture*. New York: Oxford University Press, 2001. A detailed study of the creation of the Sikh canon.

Parikh, Vastupal. *Jainism and the New Spirituality*. Toronto: Peace Publications, 2002. An exploration of Jainism and its connection to peace movements and ecology.

Rankin, Aidan. *The Jain Path: Ancient Wisdom for the West*. Delhi: Saujanya Books, 2007. A book that uses traditional Jain belief and philosophy to call for a new global movement of compassion and interdependence.

Singh, Patwant. *The Sikhs*. New York: Knopf, 2000. An examination of Sikh history.

Tobias, Michael. *Life Force: The World of Jainism*. Fremont, CA: Jain Publishing, 2000. An introduction to Jainism, as experienced by a Western practitioner interested in ecology.

Film/TV

Around the World in 80 Faiths. (BBC). An eight-part series that documents eighty sacred rituals across six continents in the space of a single year. Episode six includes a segment on a Sikh ritual honoring the three-hundredth anniversary of the guru Gobind Singh and another segment on Jain ritual in South India.

Gandhi. (Director Richard Attenborough; Columbia Tristar.) The life of Mahatma Gandhi, who was strongly influenced by Jainism.

Sikhs in America. (Sikh Art and Film Foundation.) An Emmy Award–winning documentary profiling the Sikh community in the United States.

Music/Audio

Ho Shankheswarwasi. (RajAudio Music.) A compilation of ten Jain devotional chants.

Music of Asia. (Smithsonian Folkways.) A recording of Asian religious music, including a Jain puja and a Sikh Adi Granth recitation.

SikhNet Gurbani Collection—Volume 1. (SikhNet.com.) A collection of Sikh devotional recordings from around the world.

Internet

Jainism: http://www.cs.colostate.edu/~malaiya/jainhlinks.html. A resource that contains links organized by categories, such as "Songs and Prayers," "Vegetarianism and Ahimsa," "Jain Texts," "Jain Pilgrimage," "Jain Images," and "Regional Organizations."

JainWorld: http://www.jainworld.com/. Information on Jain philosophy, societies, education, literature, and temples.

All About Sikhs: http://allaboutsikhs.com/. A comprehensive resource portal for Sikhism, including an encyclopedia, list of books, and general information on Sikh gurus, history, way of life, temples, and scriptures.

KEY TERMS

Adi Granth (*ah'-dee grahnt*): "Original collection"; the primary scripture of the Sikhs.

ajiva (*uh-jee'-va*): Matter without soul or life.

Digambara (*di-gam'-ba-ra*): "Clothed in sky"; a member of the Jain sect in which monks ideally do not wear clothing.

gurdwara (*gur-dwa'-rah*): A Sikh temple.

hylozoism: The belief that all physical matter has life and feeling.

Japji (*jahp'-jee*): A poem by Guru Nanak that begins the Adi Granth; the poem is recited daily by pious Sikhs.

jina (*jee'-na*): "Conquerer"; the Jain term for a perfected person who will not be reborn.

jiva (*jee'-va*): Spirit, soul, which enlivens matter.

puja (*poo'-ja*): Ritual in honor of a tirthankara or deity.

sallekhana (*sahl-lek-hah'-nuh*): "Holy death"; death by self-starvation, valued in Jainism as a noble end to a long life of virtue and detachment.

Shvetambara (*shvet-am'-ba-ra*): "Clothed in white"; a member of the Jain sect in which monks and nuns wear white clothing.

Sikh (*seek*): "Disciple"; a follower of the Sikh religion.

Sthanakavasi (*stun-uk-uh-vuh'-see*): "Building person"; a member of a Jain sect that rejects the use of statues and temples.

Terapanthi (*teh-ra-pahn'-tee*): "Thirteen"; a member of the newest Jain sect.

tirthankara (*tihr-tahn'-kah-ruh*): "Crossing maker"; in Jainism, one of the twenty-four ideal human beings of the past, Mahavira being the most recent.

Visit the Online Learning Center at www.mhhe.com/molloy5e for additional exercises and features, including "Religion beyond the Classroom" and "For Fuller Understanding."

6

Daoism and Confucianism

﷯ FIRST ENCOUNTER

You have gone to Taipei to see one of the world's greatest collections of Chinese art at the National Palace Museum and to experience the color and complexity of Chinese culture. City life is indeed as colorful as you hoped it would be. Taipei is a jumble of sights and sounds. Half the city's population seems to be riding motorbikes. More than once you've seen a whole family—father in front, mother and child in the middle, grandmother at the rear—balanced on a single scooter.

Wandering alternately along bustling boulevards and back streets, you come upon a large temple, seeing first its walls and then behind them its tall, sloping tile roofs with ceramic dragons and other figures at the corners. You know you are approaching the entrance when you reach sidewalk stalls selling temple offerings: oranges, grapefruit, red candles, flowers, and long sticks of incense bunched in red-and-gold paper packets. You decide to buy some incense.

Inside the gates, you feel as if you have just walked into a fair. People cluster to talk and then break off, walking in random directions. Near you someone is taking a plate with fruit to a large table, one of several in the center of the big open courtyard. Standing next to the table, a man with a boat-shaped red hat blows on an animal horn. Around a great central brazier, smoke rises in clouds. The smell of incense is so overpowering you have to move away to breathe some fresh air.

At each side of the central courtyard are two lines of people who seem to be waiting for some sort of medical treatment. A woman in a blue smock stands at the front of each line and pats and rubs people on the shoulders and arms and back as they come forward. You stop to watch. A friendly gentleman nearby, happy to practice his English with you, turns and explains, "These women are healing. They used to suffer themselves but were healed, and now they pass on the healing to others."

You notice a young couple putting a few sticks of incense in each of several braziers that front different altars. The gentleman, who is now walking along with you, explains, "They are going to get married and are seeking help from all the gods here in the temple."

You stop at a painting of a young woman in flowing robes. Below her are high ocean waves. Your new friend tells you that this is Mazu (Matsu), a Chinese girl who died young but became a goddess. She is especially powerful as a protector of fishermen. The gentleman calls her Heavenly Mother.

A group of elderly people, each carrying incense sticks and fruit, follows a shirtless young man who appears to be in some kind of trance. He leads the group around to the rear of the temple. "They are here from the south to ask advice," the gentleman says. "The young man has special gifts. He can speak with the main god of this place."

You and your companion continue walking around together, talking about the images and placing your lighted incense sticks at several altars. In front of a small altar, a bent old woman throws what look like two large, wooden, crescent-shaped beans on the floor in front of her. "She is seeking help with her future," says your friend. Behind the scenes, along side corridors, you notice men stretched out asleep, some propped against bright red pillars. Near the exit, you pause to watch a woman fold yellow, red, and gold squares—"spirit money" that she will leave or burn as an offering.

At the exit, you say good-bye and offer thanks to your kind guide. He bows and shakes your hand at the same time. When you reach the large outside gate, the vendor from whom you bought your incense smiles and nods, and you smile back as you turn to walk down another crowded, noisy street.

BASIC ELEMENTS OF TRADITIONAL CHINESE BELIEFS

Confucianism, Daoism (Taoism*), and Buddhism have been collectively called the Three Doctrines, and together they have had a profound influence on Chinese culture and history. Buddhism, as we saw in Chapter 4, was an import to China, with roots in Indian belief. Confucianism and Daoism, on the other hand, sprouted and grew up, side by side, in the soil of indigenous Chinese belief. We thus begin our study of these two Chinese religious systems by considering some of the features of traditional Chinese belief and practice.

Early Chinese belief was a blend of several elements. Some of them, such as a belief in spirits, can be traced back more than three thousand years. The following elements provided a basis for later developments in Chinese religion and were especially important to the development of Confucianism and Daoism.

> *Spirits* Early Chinese belief thought of spirits as active in every aspect of nature and the human world. Good spirits brought health, wealth, long life, and fertility. Bad spirits caused accidents and disease. Disturbances of nature, such as droughts and earthquakes, were punishments from spirits for human failings, but harmony could be restored through rituals and sacrifice.

> *Tian* During the Shang dynasty (c. 1500?–c. 1100 B.C.E.) the omnipotent power that was believed to rule the world was called Shang Di (Shang Ti) and was thought of as a personal god, capable of being contacted by diviners. Perhaps Shang Di was the memory of an ancestor, and the veneration of Shang Di was part of the ancient practice of honoring ancestors. In the Zhou (Chou) dynasty (c. 1100–256 B.C.E.), a new political regime—the Zhou kings—ignored the Shang belief and began explaining life in terms of a different conception, Tian (T'ien), which is usually translated as "Heaven." It appears that Tian was envisioned both as an impersonal divine force that controls events on earth and as a cosmic moral principle that determines right and wrong.

> *Veneration of ancestors* The same cautious reverence that was shown to spirits was also naturally felt for ancestors. Ancestors at death became

---

*Note: As mentioned earlier, the pinyin system of romanizing Chinese words will be used in this book, with the older Wade-Giles spelling of important names given in parentheses afterwards. (Pinyin pronunciation is generally similar to English usage, except that the pronunciation of *c* is *ts*, *q* is *ch*, and *x* is *sh*.) The pinyin spelling of all Chinese words is used by the United Nations and is becoming standard in the world of scholarship and art. The older Wade-Giles spelling of *Taoism, Tao,* and *Tao Te Ching* are still common, but they are now being supplanted by *Daoism, Dao,* and *Daodejing* (also spelled *Daode jing, Daode Jing,* and *Dao De Jing*).

At the Temple of Heaven, in Beijing, the emperor performed ceremonies to honor Tian ("Heaven").

spirits who needed to be placated to ensure their positive influence on living family members. Veneration of ancestors provided the soil for the growth of Confucianism.

Seeing patterns in nature China's long and mighty rivers, high mountain chains, distinct seasons, and frequent floods, droughts, and earthquakes all influenced the Chinese view of the natural world. To survive, the Chinese people had to learn that while they could not often control nature, they could learn to work with it when they understood its underlying patterns. Some of the patterns were quite easy to discern, such as the progression of the seasons, the paths of the sun and moon, and the cycle of birth and death. Others were more subtle, like the motion of waves and the ripple of mountain ranges, as well as the rhythm of the Dao (which we will discuss shortly) and the alternations of yang and yin.

Daoism may be traced back to this concern for finding—and working within—natural patterns.

Yang and yin After about 1000 B.C.E. the Chinese commonly thought that the universe expressed itself in opposite but complementary principles: light and dark, day and night, hot and cold, sky and earth, summer and winter. The list was virtually infinite: male and female, right and left, front and back, up and down, out and in, sound and silence, birth and death, "strong" foods (meat and ginger) and "weak" foods (fish and rice), and "dynamic" (odd) numbers and "stable" (even) numbers. The names for the two complementary principles are **yang** and **yin.**

These principles are not the same as good and evil. Yang is not expected to win over the force of yin, or vice versa; rather, the ideal is a dynamic balance between the forces. In fact, the emblem of balance is the yin-yang circle, divided into what look like two intertwined commas. One half is light, representing yang; the other is dark, representing yin. Inside each division is a small dot of the contrasting color that represents the seed of the opposite. The dot suggests that everything contains its opposite and will eventually become its opposite. Both forces are dynamic and in perfect balance as they change, just as day and night are in balance as they progress. We can think of yang and yin as pulsations or waves of energy, like a heartbeat or like breathing in and out.

Divination Divination (a system of methods for knowing more about the future) was an integral part of early Chinese tradition. The oldest technique involved the reading of lines in bones and tortoise shells. Later, an elaborate practice was developed that involves the **Yijing (I Ching),** the Book of Changes. It is an ancient book that interprets life through an analysis of hexagrams. A hexagram is a figure of six horizontal lines. There are two kinds of lines: divided (yin) and undivided (yang). A hexagram is made of two trigrams (figures consisting of three lines each) and is "constructed" by tossing sticks or coins and writing down the result, beginning with the bottom line. Thus sixty-four different hexagrams are possible. The hexagrams are thought to represent patterns that can develop in one's life, and the Yijing gives an interpretation of each hexagram. With the help of the Yijing, a person can interpret a hexagram as an aid in making decisions about the future.

We now turn to two great systems of Chinese religious thought, Daoism and Confucianism, which many consider to be complementary traditions. Daoism is often thought to emphasize the yin aspects of reality and Confucianism the yang. Together they form a unity of opposites. Although we'll discuss these systems separately, one before the other, separate treatment is something of a fiction. The two systems grew up together and actually, as they developed, helped generate each other. We must keep this in mind as we study them.

Yang and yin, symbolized by a circle of light and dark, represent the complementary but opposing forces of the universe that generate all forms of reality.

This hexagram for "contemplation" is made from two trigrams. The lower trigram means "earth," and the upper trigram means "wind."

DAOISM

Because it incorporated some of the previously mentioned elements and many others from traditional Chinese belief and practice, Daoism is really like a shopping cart filled with a variety of items: observations about nature, philosophical insights, guidelines for living, exercises for health, rituals of protection, and practices for attaining longevity and inner purity. We should note, however, that Daoism and Chinese folk religion are not exactly the same thing, although the terms are often used interchangeably, and in some cases the border between the two is not clear.

Daoism includes ideas and practices from the earliest phases, represented in the Daodejing and Zhuangzi (Daoist scriptures, which we'll discuss shortly), as well as innumerable later developments. It was once common to make a distinction between the earliest phase, which was praised for its philosophy, and later ritualistic and religious development, which was less appreciated. But scholars in recent decades have given great attention to a host of Daoist topics: liturgy, lineages of masters, religious communities, monasticism, deities, prayers, art, clothing, and even dance. Scholars see these developments as a part of the organic growth of the early insights. While continuing to value the ideas espoused in the early documents, scholars today point out that the "real" Daoism is the entire spectrum of development, from the earliest ideas to contemporary practices.

THE ORIGINS OF DAOISM

The origins of Daoism, quite appropriately, are mysterious. Its earliest documents contain many threads—shamanism, appreciation for the hermit's life, desire for unity with nature, and a fascination with health, long life, breathing, meditation, and trance. These many threads point to a multiplicity of possible sources, which seem to have coalesced to produce the movement.

Laozi (Lao Tzu)

Every movement needs a founder, and Daoists trace themselves back to a legendary figure named **Laozi (Lao Tzu),** whose name means "old master" or "old child." Whether Laozi ever existed is unknown. He may have been a real person or the blending of historical information about several figures or a mythic creation.

In the traditional story, Laozi's birth (c. 600 B.C.E.; Timeline 6.1) resulted from a virginal conception. According to legend, the child was born old—hence the name "old child." Laozi became a state archivist, or librarian, in the royal city of Loyang for many years. (Legendary stories also relate how Confucius came to discuss philosophy with the old man.) Eventually tiring of his job, Laozi left his post and, carried by an ox, traveled to the far west of China.

TIMELINE 6.1

Period of legendary Laozi (Lao Tzu)	c. 600–500 B.C.E.	
	c. 551–479 B.C.E.	Life of Confucius
Life of Mozi (Mo Tzu)	c. 470–391 B.C.E.	
	c. 371–289 B.C.E.	Life of Mencius
Life of Zhuangzi (Chuang Tzu)	c. 369–286 B.C.E.	
	c. 350 B.C.E.	Creation of the Daodejing (Tao Te Ching)
Life of Xunzi (Hsün Tzu)	c. 298–238 B.C.E.	
	c. 630 C.E.	The ordering of all provinces of China to conduct regular services in honor of Confucius
Life of Zhu Xi (Chu Hsi)	1130–1200	
	1445	Publication of the Daoist canon
Life of Wang Yangming	1473–1529	
	1949	Communist takeover of mainland China, repression of religion
Discovery at Mawangdui of two ancient versions of the Daodejing and one version of the Yijing	1972–1974	
	c. 1982	Revival of Daoism in mainland China
Discovery at Guodian of the oldest-known version of the Daodejing, written on bamboo and dated about 300 B.C.E.	1993	
	2004	Founding of the First Confucius Institute

Timeline of significant events in the history of Daoism and Confucianism.

At the western border, Laozi was recognized as an esteemed scholar and prohibited from crossing until he had written down his teachings. The result was the Daodejing, a short book of about five thousand Chinese characters. After Laozi was finished, he left China, traveling westward. Later stories about Laozi continued to elaborate his myth. He was said to have taken his teachings to India, later returned to China, and ascended into the sky. He was soon treated as a deity, the human incarnation of the Dao. In this capacity he came to be called Lord Lao. Many stories were told of his apparitions. He continues to be worshiped as divine by many Daoists.

The Daodejing

The **Daodejing** (**Tao Te Ching**) is generally seen as one of the world's greatest books. It is also the great classic of Daoism, accepted by most Daoists as a central scripture. Its title can be translated as "the classical book about the Way and its power." Sometimes the book is also called the Laozi (Lao Tzu), after its legendary author. Possibly because of its brevity and succinctness, it has had an enormous influence on Chinese culture.

The book has been linguistically dated to about 350 B.C.E., but it seems to have circulated in several earlier forms. In 1972, at the tombs of Mawangdui, archeologists discovered two ancient copies of the text that differ from the arrangement commonly used. Another shorter ancient version was found in a tomb at Guodian in 1993. It contains about one-third of the standard text.[1] The version that is commonly known and used is from the third century C.E.

In the eighty-one chapters of the Daodejing, we recognize passages that seem to involve early shamanistic elements, such as reaching trance states and attaining invulnerability (see chapters 1, 16, 50, and 55). The book shows some repetition, has no clear order, and exhibits a deliberate lack of clarity. In form, each chapter is more poetry than prose. This combination of elements suggests that the book is not the work of a single author but is rather the assembled work of many people, gathered over time. It may be a collection of what were once oral proverbs and sayings.

What was the original purpose of the book? One theory holds that its overall purpose was political, that it was meant as a handbook for rulers; another sees it primarily as a religious guidebook, meant to lead adherents to spiritual insight; and still another views it as a practical guide for living in harmony with the universe. It is possible that the Daodejing fulfilled all these purposes and that its passages can have several meanings at the same time. Part of the genius of the book is its brevity and use of paradox: its meaning depends on who is interpreting it.

Throughout the Daodejing are references to the **Dao.** The book speaks of its nature and operation; it describes the manner in which people will live if they are in harmony with the Dao; and it gives suggestions for experiencing the Dao. The book also provides images to help describe all of these things. What, though, is "the Dao"?

The Daodejing begins famously by saying that the Dao is beyond any description. It states that the Dao that can be spoken of is not the eternal Dao. In other words, we cannot really put into words exactly what the Dao is—a fact that is ironic since the book itself uses words. Yet the book goes on to tell us that the Dao is "nameless"; that is, it is not any individual thing that has

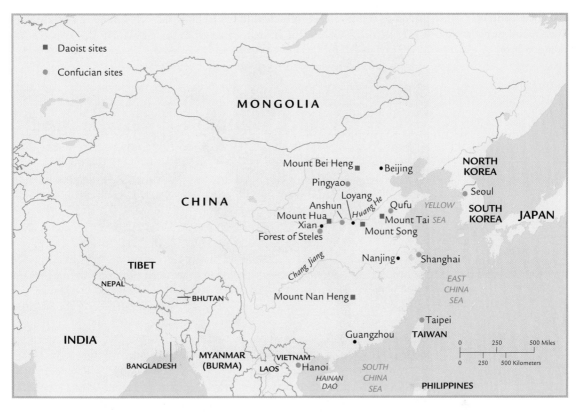

FIGURE 6.1
Daoist and Confucian
religious sites.

a name—such as a *door,* a *tree,* a *bird,* a *person.* The Dao cannot be named because it has no form. But the Dao *can* be experienced and followed by every individual thing that has a name. The Daodejing says the Dao is the origin of everything and that all individual things are "manifestations" of the Dao.

Although the Dao is the origin of nature, it is not "God," because it does not have personality. It neither cares about human beings nor dislikes them—it only produces them, along with the rest of nature. Because the Dao makes nature move the way it does, it can be called the way or the rhythm of nature.

To experience the Dao, we must leave behind our desires for individual things, a concept that runs counter to everyday concerns—how much something costs, what time it is now, whether something is big or small. In fact, the Daoist way of seeing things is so odd to some people that at first it seems like trying to see in the dark, as the end of the first chapter of the Daodejing describes:

Darkness within darkness.
The gate to all mystery.

The Daoist sees things differently. To illustrate, there is an intriguing example in the twentieth chapter of the Daodejing: A Daoist is observing a

Laozi, the "father of Daoism," is here portrayed riding on an ox.

group of people who are in a park, celebrating a holiday. They all seem happy as they climb up to the top of a terrace where a ceremony will occur. They appear to know what they are doing and where they are going. Not the Daoist, though, who feels "formless" and "like the ocean"—adrift.[2] The Daoist is troubled by the contrast. The others seem happy and sure of themselves, but the Daoist can only watch, and feels strangely like an outsider. Then the chapter ends with a sudden, extraordinary affirmation. The Daoist recognizes something intensely personal and difficult, but willingly accepts the sense of separateness from the others and from their conventional way of seeing things. The Daoist accepts, and concludes,

> I am different.
> I am nourished by the great mother.

Thus, the Dao cannot be "known" in the same way that we see a car or hear a sound, for example. It cannot be perceived directly but rather by intuition. Perhaps it is like the difference between hearing only musical sounds and recognizing a song.

The Daodejing presents several powerful images wherein the Dao seems most active and visible. Contemplating them can help us experience the Dao, and by taking on some of the qualities of these images, we begin to live in harmony with the Dao that inhabits them. Several common images follow:

> *Water* Water is gentle, ordinary, and lowly, but strong and necessary. It flows around every obstacle. Chapter eight of the Daodejing praises it: "The highest good is like water."[3] It assists all things "and does not compete with them."[4]
>
> *Woman* The female is sensitive, receptive, yet effective and powerful.
>
> *Child* The child is full of energy, wonder, and naturalness.
>
> *Valley* The valley is yin, and it is mystery.
>
> *Darkness* Darkness can be safe, full of silence and possibility.

Zhuangzi (Chuang Tzu)

Daoism was enriched by the work of **Zhuangzi (Chuang Tzu)**, who was active about 300 B.C.E. What we know of him comes from the writings he left behind. His personality seems playful, independent, and in love with the fantastic. The book of his writings, called the Zhuangzi (Chuang Tzu), is composed of seven "inner chapters," which are thought to be by the author himself, and twenty-six "outer chapters," whose authorship is less certain.

The Zhuangzi, unlike the poetry of the Daodejing, contains many whimsical stories. It continues the themes of early Daoist thought, such as the need for harmony with nature, the movement of the Dao in all that happens, and the pleasure that we can gain from simplicity. It underscores the inevitability of change and the relativity of all human judgments. It also adds to Daoism an appreciation for humor—something that is quite rare in the scriptures of the world.

Perhaps the most famous of all the stories in the book tells of Zhuangzi's dream of being a butterfly. In his dream he was flying around and enjoying life, but he did not know that he was Zhuangzi. When he woke up he was struck by a question: Am I a person dreaming that I am a butterfly, or am I a butterfly dreaming that I am a person? This story hints that the boundary between reality and the imaginary is not really as clear as we might think.

Another story makes fun of people's judgments and the arbitrariness of their joy and anger. A trainer gave his monkeys three acorns in the morning and four at night. When the monkeys conveyed their dissatisfaction with receiving too few acorns in the morning, the trainer obliged, giving them four acorns in the morning and three at night. As a result, "the monkeys were all delighted."[5]

The Zhuangzi rejects every barrier, including that between the ordinary and the fantastic, between the normal and the paranormal, as hinted by the story of the butterfly dream. But the love of the marvelous really shows itself best in some stories that talk of the supernatural powers that a wise person can attain. The Zhuangzi tells of an exceptional person who could

The Seasons of Life

A famous story illustrates what it means to live in harmony with nature: Upon hearing of the death of Zhuangzi's wife, a friend, Huizi (Hui Tzu), goes to offer sympathy. Although he expects to find Zhuangzi crying and in ritual mourning, Huizi finds Zhuangzi instead singing and drumming on a bowl. Huizi is shocked—and says so. Responding in a thoughtful way, Zhuangzi says that at first his wife's death saddened him terribly, but then he reflected on the whole cycle of her existence. Before his wife was a human being, she was without shape or life, and her original self was a part of the formless substance of the universe. Then she became a human being. "Now there's been another change, and she's dead. It's just like the progression of the four seasons, spring, summer, fall, winter."[6] When winter comes, we do not mourn. That would be ungrateful. Similarly, a human being goes through seasons. Zhuangzi describes his wife as now being like someone asleep in a vast room. "If I were to follow after her

bawling and sobbing, it would show that I don't know anything about fate. So I stopped."[7]

In this story, note that Zhuangzi is singing and playing on a bowl. Rather than mourn passively, he does something to counteract his sorrow. His singing is a profound human response, quite believable. And Zhuangzi does not say that as a result of his insight he no longer feels sad. Rather, he says that as far as mourning is concerned, "I stopped." In other words, despite his feelings, he deliberately behaves in a way that seems more grateful to the universe and therefore more appropriate than mourning.

This tale suggests that to live in harmony with nature means to accept all its transformations. The great Dao produces both yang and yin, which alternate perpetually. The story says that yin and yang are our parents and we must obey them. If we cannot embrace the changes, we should at least observe them with an accepting heart.

tell everything about one's past and future, another who could ride on the wind, and another who was invulnerable to heat or pain. The Zhuangzi thus elaborates the potential results of being one with the Dao.

BASIC EARLY TEACHINGS

The main teachings of the Daodejing and the Zhuangzi can be summarized as follows:

Dao This is the name for whatever mysterious reality makes nature to be what it is and to act the way it does. The Chinese character for *Dao* is commonly translated as "way," but it has also been translated as "existence," "pattern," and "process." Primarily, the Dao is the way that nature expresses itself—the natural way. Human beings can unite themselves with the Dao in the way they live.

Wu wei: The ideal of effortlessness To have stern commandments would go against the nature of Daoism; but it does offer recommendations about how to live—recommendations that do not come from a divine voice but from nature, the model of balance and harmony. The recommendation most often mentioned in the Daodejing is **wu wei,** which literally means "no action." Perhaps a better translation is "no strain"

The boatman who goes with the river's flow is an example of wu wei in practice.

or "effortlessness." The ideal implies the avoidance of unnecessary action or action that is not spontaneous. If we look at nature, we notice that many things happen quietly, effortlessly: plants grow, birds and animals are born, and nature repairs itself after a storm. Nature works to accomplish only what is necessary, but no more. Consider the plain strength of the ordinary bird nest. Birds build homes according to their needs, and what they make is simple and beautiful; they don't require circular driveways, pillars, or marbled entryways. The ideal of "no strain" is the antithesis of all those sweat-loving mottoes such as "No pain, no gain" and "Onward and upward."

Simplicity Daoism has often urged its followers to eliminate whatever is unnecessary and artificial and to appreciate the simple and the apparently ordinary. In this regard, Daoists have tended to distrust any highly formal education, owing to its inherent complexity and artificiality. (This was one of their major complaints against the Confucians, who put so much trust in education.) In a passage that has delighted students for centuries, the Daodejing in the twentieth chapter states its opinion: "Give up learning, and put an end to your troubles."

Gentleness Because Daoists pursue the gentle way, they hate weapons and war. The wise person loves peace and restraint and avoids all unnecessary violence. The wise person "does not regard weapons as lovely things. For to think them lovely means to delight in them, and to delight in them means to delight in the slaughter of men."[8]

Relativity People see things from a limited point of view that is based on their own concerns. They see things in terms of divisions: I-you, good-bad, expensive-cheap, valuable-worthless, beautiful-ugly, and so forth. Daoists believe that it is necessary to attain a vision of things that goes beyond these apparent opposites.

DAOISM AND THE QUEST FOR LONGEVITY

Daoism has absorbed many practices that are thought to bring a person into union with the Dao. These practices help the person feel the flow of nature, attain spiritual purity, and live a long life.

To use the word *yoga* to describe Daoist exercises could be misleading, because *yoga* is a Sanskrit word. But this word is useful for conveying to nonspecialists the physical aspect of Daoism. The canon of Daoist literature includes recommendations for many types of arm and body movements, breathing regulation, diet, and massage. Today, several popular physical disciplines continue this interest. Most influential is *taiji* (*t'ai-chi*), a series of slow arm and leg motions thought to aid balance and circulation. An astounding sight to see in the early morning in China are hundreds of people doing taiji exercises in the parks. The spectacle looks like ballet in graceful slow motion.

One "yogic" practice is called *internal alchemy.* It aims at transforming and spiritualizing the life force (**qi, ch'i**) of the practitioner. Some later forms of internal alchemy teach exercises that move the life force from its origin at the base of the spine upward to the head. From there it circles back, via the heart, to its origin. This movement is accomplished through certain postures, muscular exercises, and practices of mental imagery. Some Daoists have held that these techniques of internal alchemy can create an entity—the "immortal embryo"—that can survive the death of the body.

In ancient China, some people experimented with physical alchemy, hoping to create an elixir that could extend life and even make a person immortal. Because gold did not rust, individuals attempted to make gold either into a drinkable liquid or into a vessel from which an elixir could be drunk. Jade, pearl, mother-of-pearl, and compounds of mercury were also utilized. Some people undoubtedly died as a result of these experiments. When there seemed to be little success in this direction, the alchemical search became a metaphor for the development of the type of internal alchemy just described. In Chinese culture there remains, however, a great interest in pills, foods, and medicines that are believed to prolong life. Some of these (such as ginseng, garlic, and ginger) seem to have genuine medical benefits.

THE DEVELOPMENT OF DAOISM

Early Daoism was not an "organized religion." Many of its earliest practitioners lived alone, as some still do today. The reclusive lifestyle of the hermit dates back to ancient China, and some chapters of the Daodejing may have emerged from that way of life.

As time went on, however, the movement took on many organized forms. Elements of Daoism appealed to individuals and groups interested in achieving a variety of goals. Among their aims were longevity, supernatural abilities, control over disease, social reform, political control, and spiritual insight. Because of the wide variety of interests and capacity within Daoism to easily form new groups, there emerged over centuries a multitude of sects, branches, and religious communities. Their power waxed and waned, depending on their ability to maintain themselves and on the interest of current rulers. (For example, Daoism reached perhaps its lowest point of influence in 1281, when the emperor commanded that Daoist books be burned.) Among the many organizations that developed, two proved to be particularly long-lived and influential. Both still exist today.

One is an ancient organization called the Way of the Heavenly Masters (or Celestial Masters; Tianshi, T'ien-shih). The organization traces itself back to a second-century teacher, Zhang Daoling (Chang Tao-ling), who was believed to have had visions of Laozi. Zhang Daoling is thought to have developed an organization that helped Daoism survive into the present. Control of the organization is based on a hereditary model, with power usually passing from father to son to grandson. The heads of the organization have the title of Heavenly Masters. The organization set up a system of parishes. It is strong in Taiwan and has come to life again, after severe repression by the Communist government, on the mainland.

The second persistent form of Daoist life involved monasteries and related groups of celibate monks. Although this form of Daoism was also suppressed in the early days of the Communist government, it has resumed in mainland China, though under careful governmental control. This monastic order is known as the Way of Complete Perfection (Quanshen, Ch'üan-chen). It deliberately has blended elements of Daoism, Buddhism, and Confucianism. Its principal prayer book was reprinted in 2000. Morning and evening

Daoist priests lead an extended family in its annual ceremony to honor its ancestors. The family temple is located on a quiet street in Penang, Malaysia.

services that make use of the prayer book may be attended at many of its monasteries—most notably at the White Cloud Monastery (Baiyunguan) in Beijing.

One of the stimuli that influenced Daoism to take an organizational path was Buddhism, which entered China in the first century C.E. Buddhism was brought by a monastic clergy who set up monasteries and temples that had impressive rites. Daoism followed these models in its own development. By the fifth century C.E., Daoism had grown into an organization with significant political influence.

Daoism also imitated Buddhism in its production of a vast number of sacred books. The range of topics was wide: guidebooks on meditation, breathing exercises, and sexual yoga; stories of wonderworkers and of ecstatic excursions made to the stars; recipes for longevity and magical powers; manuals of alchemy; and descriptions of ritual. A small sample of titles conveys the flavor of Daoism: Scripture of Wondrous Beginning, Scripture of Great Simplicity, Like unto a Dragon, Wondrous Scripture of Inner Daily Practice, Pillowbook Scripture, Biographies of Spirit Immortals, The Yellow Court Scripture, and Scripture on Going Beyond the World. A collection of more than a thousand authoritative books was gathered and makes up the Daoist canon (Daozang, Tao Tsang). A major edition of the canon was published in 1445, but supplements continued to be added later.

Daoism developed a pantheon of hundreds of deities. Some are powers of the universe; others are people who became immortal; others are ancestral spirits. The deities include Laozi, spirits of nature, protective household gods, deified historical figures, and many others. Most important are the Three Purities (Sanjing, San Ching). These constitute a Daoist trinity (probably modeled on the Buddhist notion of the three bodies of the Buddha). The first of the Three Purities is the primordial Dao; the second, a deity responsible for transmission of Daoist insight, is called the Heavenly Worthy of Numinous Treasure; and the third is the deified Laozi, whose image may be recognized by its white hair. Several female deities are important. Among them are Mother Li, the mother of Lord Lao; Mazu (mentioned earlier), a deified girl who has become the patroness of fishermen; Doumu, a star deity called Mother of the Big Dipper; and the Queen Mother of the West, who is a mother figure responsible for all the immortals. The Jade Emperor, an ancient legendary figure, is thought of as an emperor who rules heaven and earth and who judges people's deeds at the end of each year.

Other commonly worshiped gods are household gods, such as the gods of the hearth and the doorway, and gods of the sky, earth, water, and town. Worship is also given to regional deities and to the spirits of ancestors. Daoist temples represent many of these gods with statues and paintings, and offerings of food, water, and incense are regularly placed in front of the images.

Daoism is strong in Taiwan, Hong Kong, and in overseas Chinese communities, such as in Malaysia and Singapore. After initially being repressed by the Communist Party, Daoism is experiencing a resurgence on the mainland. A large statue of Laozi was erected in 1999 in southeastern China, and pilgrims from Taiwan and elsewhere routinely travel to the mainland to honor the goddess Mazu at her pilgrimage site, Meizhou Island in southeast China.

Because of government support on the mainland for Complete Perfection Daoism, many of its temples and monasteries are being rebuilt, particularly in traditional mountain locations. Heavenly Master Daoism is also growing on the mainland. It was never suppressed in Taiwan, and is the major form of ritualized village Daoism. Its clergy do ministerial work, attending to the needs of the public. Exorcists, who are often identified by their red hats or

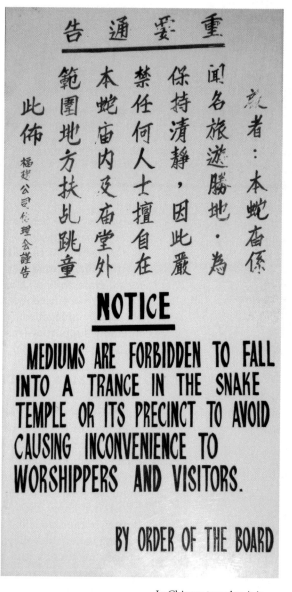

重雲通告

歲者：本蛇奮係
聞名旅遊勝地。為
保持清靜，因此嚴
禁任何人士擅自在
本蛇廟內及廟堂外
範圍地方扶乩跳童
此佈

福建公司總理會謹告

NOTICE

MEDIUMS ARE FORBIDDEN TO FALL INTO A TRANCE IN THE SNAKE TEMPLE OR ITS PRECINCT TO AVOID CAUSING INCONVENIENCE TO WORSHIPPERS AND VISITORS.

BY ORDER OF THE BOARD

In Chinese temples, it is not unusual to encounter entranced shamans and their followers. Some temples try to keep shamans away with signs.

The Chinese Garden—Bridge to the Infinite

The philosopher Wing-Tsit Chan has written of the semireligious role that a Chinese garden can play:

Nature is never looked upon by the Chinese as chaotic or disorganized. Heaven and earth co-exist in harmony, and the four seasons run their course regularly. . . . This harmony of man and nature in the flow of the great stream of rhythm makes the Chinese garden more than something merely secular. It is true that no one would look upon the Chinese garden as a religious structure. . . . But in spite of all this, we cannot deny the fact that the garden is regarded as an ideal place for meditation. Meditation may be purely moral, an effort at self-introspection. Intense and sincere meditation, however, inevitably leads to the absorption in the Infinite.[9]

---

scarves, work to heal and restore harmony. Priests, identified by their black caps, primarily perform blessings, funerals, and other rites.

Daoist practices and beliefs are kept alive not only by Daoists, but also by the Chinese tendency to blend beliefs of several systems. It is common, for example, to find Daoist images in Buddhist temples. In the mind of most Chinese, there need be no argument. In ordinary practice, elements from Daoism, Confucianism, and Buddhism are combined. The three religions are mutually supportive—as their members have generally agreed.

DAOISM AND THE ARTS

It is possible to see Daoist influences in many Chinese art forms, although the extent of the influence is impossible to determine with precision. Paintings of Laozi riding on an ox are clear examples of Daoist influence, as are references to Zhuangzi in poetry, but beyond that it is perhaps more accurate to say that poetry and the arts share many of the same concerns of Daoist thought—just as they do of Chinese Buddhist and Confucian thought.

As we know, the immensity, flow, and mystery of nature are common themes in the Daodejing, and some of the book's most important images are flowing water, the valley, and the uncarved block of stone. These themes and images are abundant in Chinese painting.

In Chinese nature painting, perspective is important. Images drawn from nature are often presented either very close up or at a great distance. Paintings of a bird or a stalk of bamboo seen close-up help the viewer see the mysterious energy at work in these nonhuman forms of life: a bird perches in a certain way on a branch, and a stalk of bamboo emerges in its own special way into the sunshine. These paintings make us look more closely at the humbler elements of nature—cats, rabbits, birds, deer—and recognize that they, too, have their own interests and patterns of living and that our human patterns are only a small part of the much wider repertory of nature.

The great genius of Chinese nature painting is particularly evident in the paintings of landscapes seen at a distance. These paintings often depict

The garden is more than the supplement to the house. It fulfills a higher function of life, the function that only art can fulfill.

— Wing-Tsit Chan[10]

This painting captures a
bird perched atop a branch
of plum blossoms. It
was painted by Chen
Hongshou (Ch'en Hung-
shou, 1599–1652) toward
the end of the Ming
Dynasty.

Chinese gardens unite natural and constructed elements to produce a sense of harmony between human beings and nature.

hints of mountains far away and, beyond them, infinite space. Some portray a person gazing far into the distance, even beyond the painting itself. What we most notice in these works is the fascinating use of empty space. Some of the paintings are almost half empty, but they do not feel unfinished, as if something were missing. Ma Yuan (c. 1160–c. 1225) was a master of this effect. In his painting entitled *A Scholar and His Servant on a Terrace*, a gentleman looks out past pine branches into the distance; the upper left half of the painting, in the direction of the man's gaze, is entirely empty. In his painting *Walking on a Mountain Path in Spring*, a man strolls into an emptiness—virtually the entire right side of the painting—inhabited only by one small bird. The space of the paintings is the positive emptiness to which the Daodejing draws our attention.

Chinese poetry frequently praises themes also found in the Daodejing and the Zhuangzi: the joy of life in the countryside, away from the complications of the city; the change of seasons; simplicity; and harmony with nature. The poet who is often praised for his fine expression of Daoist ideals was Li Bai (also spelled Li Bo and Li Po). He lived during the Tang

dynasty and died about 762 C.E. Little is known about his life, but his death is famous. According to tradition, he died as the result of a poetic accident. Sitting drunk in a boat one night, Li Bai reached out to embrace the moon's reflection on the water, but he fell in and disappeared beneath the surface. One of his poems is about Zhuangzi's dream of being a butterfly. Another is about Li Bai's being so absorbed in nature that he did not notice dusk coming on; when he stood up at last, flower petals fell off his clothes. His poems are so highly regarded that they have been memorized and recited by the Chinese for centuries to express their own deepest feelings.

Chinese garden design is an art form that complements and completes Chinese architecture. The house is yang, the realm of the square and the straight line; the garden is yin, the realm of the circle and the curve. Inside is family harmony; outside is harmony with nature. One realm supports the other. Chinese garden design differs from that of common Western design. Instead of straight lines and symmetry, walkways meander, and bridges may zigzag. Gates, in imitation of the moon, may be round. And water moves in its natural manner—that is, not upward, as in a fountain, but only gently down.

The serpentine form pictured here is a classical Chinese "poetry stream." Wine-sipping gentlemen challenged one another to compose a complete poem in the time it took a wine cup to float from the beginning of the stream to its end.

The dragons and other figures along the rooflines of this temple in Vietnam show its Chinese roots.

DAOISM AND THE MODERN WORLD

Daoism may be expected to regain much of its earlier standing. Because it has never been suppressed in Taiwan, Hong Kong, or overseas communities of Chinese, it will remain strong there, and its only challenge will come from the secularizing forces of the contemporary world. On the Chinese mainland, as we have seen, there are many indications of a revival. In mainland China, Daoist temples are being rebuilt, often with financial aid from abroad, and Daoist temples may now be found at many traditional mountain sites, in urban locations, and in villages. Daoist pilgrimage seems to be reviving—particularly in southeastern China, probably because of its geographical proximity to travelers from Taiwan.

In world culture, Daoist ideas such as those found in the Daodejing and Zuangzi continue to spread their influence. (After the Bible, the Daodejing is the world's most frequently translated book.) Daoist art and ritual are gaining increased attention as the result of recent museum exhibitions, particularly through the work of the Art Institute of Chicago and the Asian Art Museum of San Francisco. And contemporary scholars of Daoism, by shedding light on actual Daoist practice, are introducing Daoism to a wider public.

CONFUCIANISM

Daoism, as we just saw, seeks to bring human beings into union with the Dao, particularly through imitating certain qualities in nature—its harmony, lack of strain, and flowing mystery. The complex of ideals and beliefs that helped give shape to Laozi's teachings also influenced Confucius, the major teacher of the second great Chinese school of thought. Thus, it is not surprising to find Confucianism as concerned with the Dao as Daoism is; as one Confucian classic says, "He is the sage who naturally and easily embodies the right *way*."[11] This "way" is the cosmic Dao that permeates the entire universe—the Dao that we see in the everyday life of the noble person also "in its utmost reaches, . . . shines brightly through heaven and earth."[12]

THE DAO IN CONFUCIANISM

There is a difference, however, between Daoist and Confucian notions of the Dao. For Confucians, the Dao of primary interest is the Dao within the *human* world, manifested in "right" relationships and in a harmonious society. It was social harmony that Confucius described when he listed his particular wishes: "[In] regard to the aged, to give them rest; in regard to friends, to show them sincerity; in regard to the young, to treat them tenderly."[13]

In Daoism, everything is a part of the rhythm of nature—the Dao. In Confucianism, however, although birds and clouds and trees are what they should be, human beings do not automatically become what they should be. The sweet, spontaneous infant can quickly turn into the selfish child. The Confucian would say that training in virtue is necessary in order to enable the Dao to manifest itself clearly in the human being.

The Doctrine of the Mean, an important Confucian text (discussed later in this chapter), recommends several types of training, including training in the cultivation of personal equilibrium and harmony. We should recall that the Daoist ideal of the Daodejing warns against such "training," feeling that formal education has a potential for distorting one's originally pure state. Confucians, however, hold that the best training does not contaminate character but, by cultivating virtues, gives it definition and clarity.

THE LIFE OF CONFUCIUS

Confucius was born in 551 B.C.E., at a time when China was not a single empire but a group of small kingdoms. His name was Kong Qiu (K'ung Ch'iu). He later became known by the title of Kong Fuzi (K'ung Fu Tzu), meaning "Master Kong," but he is known in the West by the Latin version of his name, which was created and spread by European Catholic missionaries.

Tradition relates that Confucius was from a once-noble family that had fled at a time of political danger to the state of Lu (south of present-day Beijing). His father died when Confucius was a child, and despite their poverty, his mother raised him as an educated gentleman. He enjoyed chariot riding, archery, and playing the lute. In his teens, he became seriously interested in pursuing scholarship. He is said to have held a minor government post as tax collector, probably to support his mother and his studies. His

The Master said, "At fifteen, I had my mind bent on learning. At thirty, I stood firm. At forty, I had no doubts. At fifty, I knew the decrees of Heaven. At sixty, my ear was an obedient organ for the reception of truth. At seventy, I could follow what my heart desired, without transgressing what was right."
—from the Confucian Analects[14]

This image of Confucius, which presides over the Temple of Learning in Hanoi, expresses the ideal of human nobility.

mother died when he was in his late teens, and he entered into a state of mourning. When the period of mourning was over, he began his public life as a teacher.

Despite his eventual success as a teacher, Confucius had always wanted to play an influential part in government, and it is possible that for a time (c. 500–496 B.C.E.) he became a government minister. Confucius married and is believed to have had a son and a daughter. He lived for about fifteen years outside of his home state but eventually returned to Lu to take a somewhat ceremonial post as senior advisor. He died about 479 B.C.E.

LIVING ACCORDING TO CONFUCIAN VALUES

The period in which Confucius was born was a time of social turmoil because of the disintegration of the feudal system. Seeing families and individuals suffering from the social disorder, Confucius concluded that society would function properly only if virtues were taught and lived.

The ideals of Confucius were two: he wanted to produce "excellent" individuals who could be social leaders, and he wanted to create a harmonious society. He believed that these ideals were complementary: excellent individuals would keep society harmonious, and a harmonious society would nurture excellent individuals.

Confucius believed that each human being is capable of being good, refined, and even great; but he differed from the Daoists because he was convinced that a human being cannot achieve those qualities in isolation. In

Today, as in past centuries, the Chinese devote themselves to study—here in a study hall of the former Confucian Imperial Academy in Beijing.

his view, a human being becomes a full person only through the contributions of other people and through fulfilling one's obligations to them. These other people include parents, teachers, friends, aunts and uncles, grandparents, ancestors, and even government ministers.

Confucius also believed that more than social interaction (which even animals have) is needed to achieve personal excellence. For Confucius, that "more" is what makes *ordinary* human beings into *excellent* human beings, "superior persons." What constitutes that "more"? What are the sources of human excellence?

According to Confucius, excellence comes partly from the cultivation of an individual's virtues and intellect. Thus, education is essential. We should recognize, though, that for Confucius education meant more than knowledge; it also involved the development of skills in poetry, music, artistic appreciation, manners, and religious ritual. Confucius valued education because it transmitted the lessons of the past into the present. He believed that much of the wisdom required to produce excellent human beings is already expressed in the teachings of the great leaders of the past. Convinced that the past provides fine models for the present, Confucius thought that education could show the way to wise and happy living.

Moreover, Confucius saw civilization as a complicated and fragile creation; because of this, he believed that civilized human beings must be full of respect and care. Care must be given to the young, who will continue human life on earth, and to the elders, who teach and pass on the traditions. There should be reverence for everything valuable that has been brought from earlier generations.

Confucius's idea of a perfect society was one in which every member of society would be cared for and protected, and no one would feel abandoned. (Contrast this with modern industrial society; in a city full of people an individual can feel utterly alone.) Confucius believed that a perfect society

The Ideal Human Being

Confucianism is often thought of as a system for the regulation of social groups. Yet Confucianism is also a system for the transformation of the individual. Undergirding Confucianism is not just the ideal of an orderly society but also the ideal of a perfect human being.

This perfect person is the **junzi (chün tzu)**—a term usually translated as "superior person," although a better translation may be "noble person." The following quotations give a sense of the virtue that guides the junzi—the person who shows humanity at its best. In such a noble human being the Confucian ideals have been inculcated since childhood, and the virtues have been practiced for so long that the whole Confucian manner of relating to the world has become completely natural. The "noble person," as Alfred Bloom nicely describes, is

> distinguished by his faithfulness, diligence, and modesty. He neither overpowers with his knowledge, nor is afraid to admit error. He looks at all sides of any issue, is cautious and not concerned for personal recognition. Carrying himself with dignity, he appears imperturbable, resolute, and simple. He is exemplary in filial piety and generous with his kin. In his relations with others he looks for good points, though he is not uncritical. As a leader, he knows how to delegate responsibility

and when to pardon or promote. He is sensitive to the feelings and expressions of others.[15]

A subtle portrait of such a person is given by George Kates, who describes the man who became his personal tutor in China. Kates writes about the civilized manner that manifested itself in all his tutor's actions, even in the cultivated way the tutor entered a room and sat in a chair. The tutor, Mr. Wang,

> had contrived to make his humdrum life, composed of a daily routine of monotonous teaching and domestic privation, symmetrical and reasonable indeed. . . . His eyes were kind; and his glance could at times glow when some new thought would catch and hold him. His side-face made you like him. . . . He . . . remained closed and therefore secure, if only because he knew so well by indirection how to turn aside effectively any indiscreet remark or lolloping conduct on the part of some new and immature pupil. . . . When Mr. Wang became assured that we thus had the same sense of decorum, barriers fell. Yet I remained more unwilling than ever now to press in upon his carefully guarded privacies; and upon this base we built a tranquil relation, partial it is true, but one that lasted us peaceably through many years. He became my formal teacher.[16]

could come about if people played their social roles properly. His sense of social responsibility was codified in the five great relationships.

The Five Great Relationships

In Confucianism, relationships are just as real as any visible object. Human beings are not merely individuals. They are also interwoven threads of relationships with many people. To a great extent, in Confucian thinking human beings *are* their relationships.

All relationships, however, are not equal. The level of a relationship may be determined by personal factors, such as friendship or family connection, or by more formal social factors, such as age or social status. Confucianism recognizes this inequality and actually lists relationships according to a hierarchy, beginning with the most important:

1. *Father-son* Family is the foundation of society for Confucians, with the relationship between father and son at its core. This relationship also represents all parent-child relationships. Parents must be responsible

for the education and moral formation of their children. The children must be respectful and obedient to their parents, and they must care for them in their old age. Confucianism has extended this parental role in ways that some people in more individualistic societies today might not appreciate; for example, the parents are expected to help in the selection of a career and a marriage partner for each child. But the relationship of obligation is mutual: parents and children must show care for each other. The obligation of mutual care does not end upon death; even after their parents' death, children are expected to honor their parents' memory, especially by venerating photos of them at a home altar and by maintaining their graves. The parent-child relationship is considered so fundamental that it often functions as the model for all similar relationships, such as those between boss and employee and between teacher and student.

The hierarchy of relationships governs the responsibilities between and among individuals. The responsibilities of eldest males in a family line are among the most significant. Here, a grandfather proudly displays his first grandson.

2. *Elder brother–younger brother* Languages such as English, French, and Spanish do not distinguish between an elder brother and a younger brother. But the Chinese, Korean, Vietnamese, and Japanese languages—which all have been strongly influenced by Confucian thought—have different words for the two kinds of brothers. In their cultures, the distinction is important. An elder brother must assume responsibility for raising the younger siblings, and the younger siblings must be compliant. The practicality of this arrangement becomes clear when we appreciate the possibility of an elderly father dying before all his children have been raised. The paternal responsibility then would shift to the eldest son, who has a unique status in the family.

3. *Husband-wife* Each person in this relationship is responsible for the other's care. In Confucian thought, the relationship is hierarchical. The husband is an authoritative protector, and the wife is a protected homemaker and mother. The Confucian notion of marriage also implies much less romantic expectation than does the modern Western notion; in Confucian societies wives, over time, can even become quite motherly toward their husbands.

4. *Elder-younger* All older people have responsibility for younger people, because younger people need care, support, and character formation.

This means, as well, that younger people must show respect to those older than themselves and be open to their advice.

Important to this relationship is the role of the mentor, which is taken very seriously in Confucian cultures. The elder-younger relationship exists between a teacher and a student, between a boss and an employee, between older and younger workers, and between an expert and an apprentice. (The traditional characters for *teacher* in Chinese and Japanese literally mean "earlier-born." The term suggests the relationship of master-disciple, and it has overtones of strong mutual obligation.)

In some versions of the Five Great Relationships, the friend-friend relationship is listed fourth. The relationship between elder and younger and that between friend and friend are actually quite close, however. In friendship there is often a certain hierarchy: the friends may differ in rank, health, wealth, or knowledge. And if the difference is not evident at first, time will bring it about. In this relationship, the more powerful friend has a responsibility to assist the other friend, who is in need. The relationship between friends, especially male friends, has meant to China what romantic love has meant to post-Renaissance Europe and to the West in general. In Confucian culture, a friendship entails serious commitment, and a friendship made in youth is expected to last a lifetime.

5. *Ruler-subject* It might seem that this relationship should be listed first, and sometimes it is.[17] However, more often it appears last in the lists, reflecting the Confucian perspective on the role of the ruler: above all, a ruler must act like a father, assuming responsibility and care for the subjects who are like his children. Thus, the father-son relationship is primary in that it is the model for most other relationships. Confucianism holds that social order begins in a harmonious home and then extends outward—to town, province, and country. This last relationship, then, brings the list full circle, back to the smallest unit of society—the family.

The Five Great Relationships signify that each person must live up to his or her social role and social status. This has been called the *rectification of names.* I have only to consult my social role and title to know my duty. For example, a father must be a caring father, a manager must be a responsible manager, and a friend must be a good friend.

In Confucian societies, people see each other quite strongly in terms of their relationships and social roles. This means that proper ways of creating and maintaining relationships are crucial. Good manners are essential. The civilized person is expected to be respectful in vocabulary, tone, volume of voice, action, manner of dress, and even posture. Etiquette must especially be followed in all formal interactions—for example, between social superiors and their inferiors, between people meeting each other for the first time, and between people participating in an important social event. To follow the rules of etiquette is to show respect.

Gift-giving plays an important role in Confucian cultures. Gifts soften the anxiety of meeting new people and strengthen existing relationships. But gifts must be carefully chosen and appropriate to the situation; they must not be too personal or too impersonal, nor lavish or stingy. (When in doubt, gift boxes of food are often a safe choice). Gift wrapping is also important; when money is given—such as in the case of a funeral offering—it must be presented in a proper envelope. At formal ceremonies, certificates and other objects are given and received carefully, with both hands extended and with a bow of the head.

The bow itself is an art form that varies according to the occasion. A small inclination of the head is used for greeting an equal; a bow from the shoulders is given to a social superior; and a deep bow is used to show profound respect, make a serious request, or offer an apology. Confucian etiquette such as this may seem artificial to an outsider, but this respectful behavior is inculcated from childhood in Confucian societies and seems perfectly natural to the participants. All of these elements are important because they are relationships made visible.

Because the family is the primary model for all groups, age determines position. We see interesting implications of the Five Great Relationships in Confucian countries today. For example, modern Japanese and Korean companies often act like large families, and management plays a fatherly role. (Bosses have a prominent place at weddings—and sometimes even oversee the matchmaking.) Similarly, an employee's identity comes largely from his or her place in the company, and job titles are significant. The exchange of business cards—on which the person's title is prominently featured—is a careful ritual. Seniors have responsibility for juniors, and one's pay and role are largely based on seniority. Privacy and individual rights are not highly emphasized, and there is far more togetherness. Harmony is all-important.

The Confucian Virtues

Just as social harmony comes from the living out of the Five Great Relationships, so personal excellence comes from the manifestation of five virtues. Although they emphasize harmony between people, the Confucian virtues do not lead to antlike conformity. Some Confucian virtues, such as love of education and the arts, help individuals develop their unique talents. But the virtues most prized by Confucianism are indeed largely social virtues. Individual uniqueness, although valued by Confucianism, is expected to be muted, subtle, and considerate of others.

Ren (jen) The Chinese character for **ren (jen)** illustrates the word's meaning by blending two simpler pictographs—for "person" and "two." When we look at the Chinese ideogram for the virtue of ren, we understand its meaning: to think of the other. It is translated in many ways: "sympathy," "empathy," "benevolence," "humaneness," "kindness," "consideration," "thoughtfulness," and "human-heartedness."

The words of Confucius, often literally carved in stone, are teachings for those who live today. Rubbings made from inscribed surfaces are convenient reminders of his wisdom.

Some people, though, do not know how to be kind, or they have difficulty in certain situations being kind spontaneously. In Confucian thinking, to follow social conventions is an important way for such people to show ren. After all, underlying all worthy social conventions is considerateness. A motto that reflects the essence of ren is, "If you want to be kind, be polite."

Li This word is often translated as "propriety," which means "doing what is appropriate" or "doing what is proper to the situation." Originally, **li** referred to carrying out rites correctly. More generally, it means knowing and using the proper words and actions for social life. For each situation, there are appropriate words to say, proper ways to dress, and correct things to do. Sometimes propriety entails the control of one's own desires. The **Analects,** which are thought to record the sayings of Confucius and his followers, assert, "To subdue one's self and return to propriety, is perfect virtue."[18] In Western culture, which values what is different and individualistic, the notion of li may seem oppressive and suggest personal weakness. Confucianism, on the contrary, sees self-control as a sign of strength—and practicality. We all recognize that every social situation has its hidden structure. Chew gum at a job interview and you will not get the job; wear shorts to a funeral and you will probably cause hurt to the mourners. Li means good manners. It is putting ren into practice.

Shu The usual translation of **shu** is "reciprocity," but its essence addresses the question, How will my action affect the other person? It is also another version of the Golden Rule: Do unto others as you would have them do unto you. The Confucian version, interestingly, is stated in negative terms: "Do not do unto others what you would not wish done to yourself."[19] It is therefore often called the Silver Rule. The Silver Rule helps me consider my actions from the other person's viewpoint. This virtue also implies that obligations entailed by relationships are mutually binding.

Xiao (hsiao) The word **xiao (hsiao)** is usually translated as "filial piety" (devotion of a son or daughter to a parent). It also means the devotion that all members have to their entire family's welfare. It encompasses several notions: remembrance of ancestors, respect for parents and elders, and care for children in the family. Ideally, it means valuing the entire extended family—of past, present, and future. It is possible that later generations of Confucians emphasized this virtue more than did Confucius himself. This virtue was especially spread by the Classic of Filial Piety (Xiaojing), written at least a century or two after the time of Confucius.

Wen The term **wen** means "culture" and includes all the arts that are associated with civilization. Confucianism has a special love for poetry and literature, as well as a fondness for calligraphy, painting, and music. The educated person is expected not only to have a knowledge of these arts but to have an amateur skill in them as well. Wen can also entail the general notion of art appreciation, or connoisseurship. A connoisseur has a highly developed aesthetic sense and is able to know and appreciate beauty in its many forms.

This shop window displays writing brushes and, to the left, stones that are to be incised with owners' personal seals. Proper use of these materials exhibits personal cultivation.

Confucianism stresses other virtues, too—particularly loyalty, consensus, hard work, thrift, honesty, uprightness, and emotional control. One virtue frequently mentioned is sincerity. The Confucian notion of sincerity, however, is not the same as the Western notion; in fact, it is virtually the opposite. The Western notion of sincerity concerns something that an individual says or does that is personal and "from the heart," free of social control. The Confucian notion of sincerity, however, means to choose naturally and automatically to do what is correct for society. It teaches that the individual should restrain selfish desires in order to fulfill job duties and social obligations properly. Through this kind of unselfish sincerity, the noble person becomes united with the force of the universe, which is already—according to Confucian thought— sincere. "Sincerity is the way of Heaven. . . . He who possesses sincerity is he who, without an effort, hits what is right. . . . He who attains to sincerity is he who chooses what is good, and firmly holds it fast."[20]

CONFUCIAN LITERATURE

Confucius considered himself primarily a transmitter of wisdom. Consequently, much of what is called the literature of Confucianism actually preceded him and was subsequently edited and added to by Confucian scholars. It is now recognized that many of the great Chinese classics, even those attributed to one person, were actually produced in layers and over many years. Books could circulate in many forms, with several generations adding their insights until a final form eventually became authoritative. We have already seen this in the case of ancient Daoist literature. Thus, it is not always possible to separate with certainty the teachings of Confucius, his predecessors, and his followers.

The most authoritative Confucian literature is made up of the **Five Classics** and the **Four Books.** It includes pre-Confucian works of poetry, history, and divination; the sayings of Confucius and his disciples; and the sayings of Mencius, a later Confucian teacher.

The Five Classics and the Four Books

THE FIVE CLASSICS (WUJING, WU-CHING)

The Book of History (Shujing, Shu Ching) is an anthology of supposedly historical material about kings from earliest times up until the early Zhou (Chou) period (c. 1100–256 B.C.E.).

The Book of Poetry (Shijing, Shih Ching) is a collection of three hundred poems of the Zhou period, once believed to have been selected by Confucius.

The Book of Changes (Yijing, I Ching) speaks of the basic patterns of the universe. It is used to understand future events and to work with them properly. It is also an important Confucian document because it tells how the noble person will act in the face of life's events.

The Book of Rites (Liji, Li Chi) lists ancient ceremonies and their meaning. Another classical book, the Book of Music, is said to have once been a part of the classics but no longer exists separately. Part of it may perhaps survive, embedded in the Book of Rites.

The Spring and Autumn Annals (Chunqiu, Ch'un Ch'iu) allegedly comprises historical records of the state of Lu, where Confucius lived, and ends with a later commentary.

THE FOUR BOOKS (SISHU, SSU-SHU)

The Analects (Lunyu, Lun Yü) are presented as the sayings of Confucius and his followers. Tradition holds that his disciples collected his sayings and wrote them down, but this work may better be attributed to many later generations of followers. It is now thought that the Analects were written over a period of at least two hundred years, being created in layers and subject to regular rearrangement. The twenty sections of the Analects contain little stories and short sayings—sometimes only a sentence or two long—that often begin with the phrase "The Master said." They cover a wide variety of topics but often discuss the character of the noble person. Here are two typical sayings: "The Master said, a gentleman takes as much trouble to discover what is right as lesser men take to discover what will pay";[21] and "A gentleman covets the reputation of being slow in word but prompt in deed."[22]

The Great Learning (Daxue, Ta Hsüeh) is a short discussion of the character and influence of the noble person. It is actually a chapter from the Book of Rites that has been printed separately since the thirteenth century C.E. It was the very first book to be memorized and studied by Chinese students. This book stresses that one must begin with self-cultivation and personal virtue if one wishes to produce order in the family and state. "From the Son of Heaven [the emperor] down to the mass of the people, all must consider the cultivation of the person the root of everything besides."[23]

The Doctrine of the Mean (Zhongyong, Chung Yung), another work taken from the Book of Rites, speaks in praise of "the mean," or equilibrium. Its beginning—with its references to "heaven" and the "way"—hints at the mystical side of Confucianism. "What Heaven has conferred is called the nature [of humanity]; an accordance with this nature is called the path of duty; the regulation of this path is called instruction. The path may not be left for an instant."[24] A human being who follows "the way of Heaven" avoids extremes and remains in harmony. This balance unites the individual with the balance of the universe. "Let the states of equilibrium and harmony exist in perfection, and a happy order will prevail throughout heaven and earth, and all things will be nourished and flourish."[25]

The Mencius (Mengzi, Meng Tzu) is a long collection of the teachings of Mencius, a Confucian who lived several centuries after Confucius. Like the Analects, the sayings of the Mencius frequently begin with the phrase "Mencius said." Sometimes the tone seems quite gentle, such as in this saying: "Mencius said, The great man is he who does not lose his child's-heart."[26]

Early on, Confucian literature became the "core curriculum" of Chinese education. China was the first country in the world to use regular examinations as the gateway for entering the civil service, but these came to be based on the Confucian books and their commentaries. Any male could take the examinations, and success in them often guaranteed a post with the government.

Because the Confucian books were part of the established educational system, the sayings of Confucius and Mencius came to pervade Chinese culture. They have been quoted as authoritatively in China as the Bible is quoted in the West or the Qur'an is quoted in Muslim societies. They also have put a heavy stamp on the neighboring cultures of Korea, Japan, Singapore, and Vietnam, as well as overseas Chinese communities everywhere. Although the literature is no longer an essential part of the educational curriculum in Asia, Confucian values continue to be taught both formally in school and less formally in the family and surrounding culture.

THE DEVELOPMENT OF CONFUCIANISM

Schools of Philosophy

The basic nature of human beings has been one of the great topics of discussion throughout the history of China. Is human nature good or bad or somewhere in between? This is not a theoretical question at all, because how one answers this question has crucial practical results. If human nature is basically good, it should be left on its own and trusted, and moral training, laws, and punishments are of little importance. If human nature is basically evil, human beings need strict moral education, stern laws, harsh punishments, and a strong ruler. A middle position is also possible: if human nature is neutral, human beings need education that is not coercive and a ruler who governs primarily through example.

Before Confucianism was adopted as official state policy during the Han dynasty (206 B.C.E.–220 C.E.), major schools of thought on this topic already had emerged, reflecting a full spectrum of opinion. The Confucian schools took a middle course between extremes, recognizing both the great abilities of human beings and the need for their formation.

The most liberal of the thinkers were the early Daoists, who were so optimistic about the natural goodness of human beings that they resisted formal education. The Daodejing shows clearly the Daoist rejection of artificial formation.[27] The entire book presents instead a vision of people living simple lives in small villages, governing themselves with natural good sense.[28] Laws should be few, because if life is lived simply, order will arise spontaneously. (Of course, as Daoism evolved, it became more positive about human culture and the rules needed to sustain it. Monastic Daoism, in particular, offered many regulations about correct behavior.)

Closer to the center, but still to the left, was the teaching of Mencius, a Confucian who flourished about 300 B.C.E. (His name is the Latin version of his Chinese name—Mengzi, Meng Tzu.) The teachings of Mencius were ultimately so acceptable to many that the book of sayings attributed to him became one of the Four Books.

Mencius did not merely repeat the thoughts and values of Confucius; it seems he was a bit more optimistic about human nature, perhaps because of his contact with Daoism. There are innumerable Daoist-sounding passages among his sayings. One of them, for example, uses an image loved by Daoists: "The people turn to a benevolent rule as water flows downward."[29]

Mencius was struck by the many virtues that could be found in ordinary people: mercy, kindness, conscience. "The feeling of commiseration belongs to all men; so does that of shame and dislike; and that of reverence and respect. . . ."[30] In human beings, he thought, there is an "innate goodness," and virtues exist in everyone, at least in seedling form. The sprouts need only the proper nurturing, which education can provide by helping naturally good tendencies in a child to grow properly and to flower. Education does not radically redirect human nature but helps it to become what it already potentially is.

Mencius was aware of the ideal of universal love but thought that such an ideal was impossible and unwise. According to Mencius, in society there is a hierarchy of love and responsibility: we must love our families first, then our friends and neighbors, and then the rest of society; and to reject that structure would bring about social disorder. Education is valuable in making the natural order clear and in helping individuals live with it dutifully.

Confucius's position on human nature seems to have been fairly close to the center. We have already seen this in his view on the importance of education. Confucius was also optimistic; he believed that human beings respond to kindness and good example.

A darker view of human nature was held by Xunzi (Hsün Tzu), who was active about 250 B.C.E. He is also considered a Confucian, but because of his pessimism about human nature his thought did not ultimately receive the official support that was eventually given to Mencius. Mencius and Confucius tended to view Heaven, the power that rules the universe, as ultimately benevolent. But for Xunzi (as for the Daoists), the universe is totally uncaring; it works according to its own nature and patterns.

Xunzi viewed human nature and human beings as functioning in a similarly mechanistic way. Human beings will veer toward self-interest unless they are taught differently. Consequently, education is not social refinement of an already good person; instead, it must be a radical moral and social reformation of human tendencies that are primarily selfish and individualistic. Education must inculcate proper ceremonies, manners, laws, and customs, for these artificial rules help transcend selfish individual interest and make civilization possible. "All propriety and righteousness are the artificial production of the sages, and are not to be considered as growing out of the nature of man. It is just as when a potter makes a vessel from the clay . . . or when another workman cuts and hews a vessel out of wood. . . ."[31]

Holding a view of human nature similar to Xunzi's was the **Mohist** school, although its exact position is not easy to categorize. Mozi (Mo Tzu,

c. 470–391 B.C.E.) was known as a self-disciplined, idealistic person who lived simply and worked actively against war and for the betterment of common people. He thought that without laws, people are predatory, and that with laws, although there is order, society is inequitable. He held that social problems arise because people's love is graded and partial. The answer, he thought, is to practice equal love for everybody. "Who is the most wise? Heaven is the most wise. And so righteousness assuredly issues from Heaven. Then the gentlemen of the world who desire to do righteousness cannot but obey the will of Heaven. What is the will of Heaven that we should all obey? It is to love all men universally."[32]

The **Legalists**, who were influential from about 400 to 200 B.C.E., also had a view of human nature like Xunzi's and Mozi's but possibly even starker. For the Legalists, human beings are fundamentally selfish and lazy. They will lie, cheat, steal, and kill whenever it is in their interest. "Civilization" is just a very thin veneer, easily shattered; and without stern laws and punishments, people will destroy one another. According to the Legalists, the education of children should consist mainly of warning and punishment, and society must continue these sanctions with adults, because adults are really just children in disguise.

For several centuries after the time of Confucius, the various philosophical schools strove for influence. Legalism triumphed for a time in the third century B.C.E. The foundation of the Han dynasty, however, provided an opportunity to find a school of thought that could make the greatest contribution to social order. Around 135 B.C.E., a scholar proposed to the emperor that Confucianism would help unite the country. This scholar, Dong Zhongshu (Tung Chung-shu), also recommended that the emperor set up a Confucian school for the education of government officials. The emperor followed his advice, and Confucian thought began to gain recognition as an important political philosophy.

The Development of Confucianism as a Religious System

Confucianism grew in response to many needs and interests. In its first phase, as we have just seen, it was challenged by rival philosophies. Next, it was challenged by religion.

When Buddhism entered China in the first century C.E., it brought new ideas and practices (as we saw in Chapter 4). One radical idea was a general deemphasis of worldly human concerns and duties, as exemplified by unmarried Buddhist monks. Monks did not have children to continue the family line, nor could they take care of their parents in old age—another deficiency that seemed counter to the virtue of filial piety (xiao). Buddhism appeared to focus on the topics of death, karma, nirvana, past lives, and future lives, and it built expensive temples and practiced elaborate ceremonies. It is important not to overstate the case, but to some Confucians these tendencies were socially deficient.

Of course, the aspects of Buddhism that some Confucians discounted were what made it so appealing to many people. Buddhism was colorful,

Laozi, the Buddha, and Confucius are frequently pictured together in harmony. This Qing dynasty image shows Confucius presenting the young Gautama Buddha to Laozi.

imaginative, and ritualistic, and it gave people hope that there were super-natural beings who could help them. Chinese who became monks and nuns also benefited because they had a fairly secure life and paid no taxes.

Partially in response to Buddhism's success, Confucianism entered a second phase and took on explicitly religious characteristics. Members of Confucius's family had made sacrifices to the spirit of Confucius at his tomb long before Buddhism entered China. Several Han emperors did likewise. But in succeeding centuries, Confucius received posthumous titles, and in the seventh century, every province of China was expected to establish a Confucian temple and to support regular ceremonies. Statues of Confucius were set up, along with pictures of his disciples; and elaborate ceremonies, with sacrifice, music, and dance, were conducted in spring and autumn. Authorities began to place Confucianism on a par with Buddhism and Daoism, and the three traditions were viewed as a religious triad. The three systems (which, many agreed, complemented each other) were compared to the sun, the moon, and the planets, each one a necessary part of a complete religious cosmos. Pictures and statues of the three founders—Laozi, Confucius, and the Buddha—began to appear, with the three figures side by side in friendly poses. This practice continues today.

In its third phase, after 1000 C.E., Confucianism was enriched by scholar-ship and philosophy. The movement, called Neo-Confucianism, clarified texts and codified the elements of Confucian thought. It attempted to deter-mine which Confucian schools taught doctrine that was consistent with the views of Confucius. It also sought to provide a metaphysical vision of all reality for Confucianism, akin to that found in Daoism and Buddhism.

The greatest exponent of Neo-Confucianism was Zhu Xi (Chu Hsi, 1130–1200 C.E.), a scholar who gave Confucianism its mature shape as a complete system of thought and action. The prestige of Zhu Xi's commentaries on the Four Books helped the Four Books, along with his commentaries, become the basis for the civil service examinations.

Zhu Xi attempted to formulate a general vision of reality by using notions found in the teachings of Confucius and Mencius. He rejected the Mahayana Buddhist notion of ultimate emptiness and instead adopted a view of reality that was closer to the Daoist notion of the constant generation of reality. His view, though not scientific in the modern sense, was positiv-istic and stressed the natural order of things.[33]

Another Neo-Confucian of importance was Wang Yangming (1472–1529). Unlike Zhu Xi, he did not stress the need to look outward. Rather, he believed that truth could be discovered through intuition. Wang Yangming compared the mind to a mirror, which had the native ability to reflect but needed pol-ishing and cleaning to keep it working properly. He saw a close connection between knowledge and virtue, holding that innate insight gives a person not only an understanding of fact but also an appreciation for virtue. Those who know about goodness, he said, will practice it.

An attempt to purify Confucian ceremony came during the Ming dynasty (1368–1644), when an imperial command dictated a simplification of Confucian temples and their ritual. Statues of Confucius and his disciples were replaced by tablets inscribed with their names and titles. Ritual became simpler in order to conform to what were considered ancient patterns, and the Confucian temples took on an archaic spareness that seemed truer to the spirit of Confucius. This spareness is still quite moving today.

If we look back at the 2,500-year history of Confucianism, we can see general patterns and turning points. In the first 500 years after Confucius, Confucianism began to emerge as an officially endorsed philosophy. Over the next 1,000 years, state temples and ritual were organized. In the succeeding millennium, Confucianism absorbed philosophical elements from Daoism and Buddhism but moved toward greater simplicity in its ceremonial life. About a century ago, formal Confucian education and ritual lost its governmental support in China. However, as we shall see later, official support did not entirely die out, especially beyond mainland China; and even on the mainland it is experiencing a revival. More importantly, many Confucian values live on in family, corporate, and government life.

CONFUCIANISM AND THE ARTS

Confucianism has been a great patron of the Chinese arts. The ideal human being, the junzi, does not need to be rich, but he or she must be a well-rounded lover of history, art, poetry, and music. Because of Confucianism's high esteem for education and books, the noble person must cultivate, in particular, all aspects of writing—the premier art form of Confucianism.

Confucianism so values the written word that calligraphy has been the greatest influence of Confucianism on the arts. In the West, calligraphy is not valued in the same way that it is in China and the countries China has influenced. The importance of artistic writing is easily apparent to any visitor of a country in east Asia.

(Calligraphy can appear in unexpected places. I remember a bus driver in China who was deeply pleased with a purchase he had made. We had stopped for lunch in a small, dusty town in western China. After lunch, as the passengers climbed back on board, the bus driver held a rolled-up scroll he had just bought at a tiny shop. With just the faintest urging, he unrolled the scroll carefully. The Chinese passengers were hot, tired, and ready to sleep, but everyone at the front of the bus strained to look over each other's shoulders at the scroll. The Chinese characters were solid but lively, with fine balance between the heavy black ink of the characters and the white paper. On the narrow scroll the vertical Chinese message was this: "To see the view, climb higher." I could easily envision the same scene playing out a thousand years earlier, only in an ox cart.)

The tendency to place Chinese calligraphy on the walls of homes, restaurants, and hotels is still strong wherever Chinese culture has penetrated, both in and out of China. It is sometimes even done where ordinary laypeople (such as in Korea) can no longer read many of the Chinese ideograms.

Ancestors' names are frequently inscribed on small tablets that are displayed on an altar, in keeping with Confucian values. Here we see such a memorial altar in Malaysia.

Calligraphy came to be considered one of the greatest of the Chinese arts because it combines so many elements of value. A work of calligraphy can show physical beauty, as well as intellectual and moral beauty. It manifests the cultivated nature of the person who wrote it, shows respect for poets and thinkers of the past, and inspires the viewer to scholarship and virtue.

Just as Daoism has considerably influenced Chinese art—particularly in nature painting—so too has Confucianism, most notably in its portraiture of ancestors. It was common in the past for Chinese families to commission paintings of parents and immediate ancestors and to keep these in the home to represent the presence of the deceased person. (Nowadays a photo is used, and sometimes a wooden plaque with the ancestor's name is a suitable substitute.)

Not only did Confucianism influence the arts; it seems the sensual nature of the arts may have softened the sharp edges of Confucianism. One cannot love the arts and hate the physical world, because the arts celebrate its beauty. But Confucianism has recognized that all artworks have a moral aspect. At the lowest level, the morality of an artwork can be judged in a way that depends on the obvious. A simple person, for example, may think that an art object is automatically moral if it has a proverb written on it. At a more sophisticated level, however, we recognize that an artwork conveys morality by its quality. Thus we say that there is "bad art" and "good art." It is interesting that we use the terms *bad* and *good* to describe both art and human behavior. Confucians would say that this usage is quite correct and that good art makes good people.

PERSONAL EXPERIENCE: QING MING, A CEREMONY IN SPRING

Manoa Valley is lush and beautiful, surrounded by green mountains and thick with large, old trees. But bring your umbrella. Since the valley reaches so far back into the mountains, sunshine is often mixed with mist and rain—especially now, in early spring. Each year on April 5, the Chinese community of Honolulu gathers at the tomb of the Grand Ancestor in the hillside cemetery at the back of the valley. Here the community celebrates the spring festival of Qing Ming (Ch'ing Ming, "Clear-Bright"). This is a time for clean-

A representative of the Chinese community makes an offering to the ancestors as part of the Qing Ming celebration in Honolulu's Manoa Valley.

ing tombs, for remembering ancestors, and for sharing a picnic. Today, the grass in the Chinese Cemetery is newly trimmed. Under the large banyan tree at the top of the hill, a pavilion has been set up. As we gather, a small orchestra plays traditional Chinese music.

I make my way up the steep road to the pavilion, the sun shining through the mist and lighting up the red ti leaves around the graves. The red contrasts with the new green of the grass, making it seem especially bright. I see little offerings on many tombstones—oranges, soda, even cans of beer. At one grave, people are burning silver and gold paper money; at others, families are lighting incense and arranging ceramic cups.

Under the red-and-white tent that is set up near the hilltop, I receive a program and find a seat. At the offering table, two women are putting the last touches on plates of rice, fish, chicken, and a whole roast pig. Two other women sit down at my left, and we talk. "We are sisters," one tells me, "and our grandmother used to bring us here every year when we were little."

"We wanted to come here again, to remember our parents and grandparents," the other sister adds. "It's been too long since our last visit here."

Resplendent in a black-and-gold coat, the master of ceremonies taps the microphone and begins the program. He thanks each of the dignitaries in the front row. In true Confucian order, he names each one according to social rank. First he thanks the mayor, then the organizers of the event, the heads of the

With smoke from his firecrackers still lingering behind him, a cemetery assistant, perhaps proud to have driven away evil spirits, turns back toward the main Qing Ming ceremony.

Chinese societies, officials at the Chinese Cultural Plaza, the Narcissus Queen and her four princesses (who are in silver tiaras and blue sashes), and, finally, members of the orchestra.

The master of ceremonies reads aloud letters of congratulation from our two senators, our members of the House of Representatives, and our governor, who all wanted to be here today but could not, owing to other commitments. The master of ceremonies recalls the long history of the event and the labors of ancestors who constructed the cemetery. He thanks those involved over the past year in the building of the new red entry gate.

The mayor is called on to speak. Dressed in a dark blue suit and black tie, he says how precious these old traditions are. "Since the time I was little, I have loved the ceremonies of the many groups who have lived around my family. All the different traditions enrich our communities. The ceremonies also allow us to show gratitude for the work of the people who have gone before us, who loved us and made our lives possible."

The master of ceremonies then calls on the heads of Chinese societies to come forward. All of the representatives, I notice, are male and dressed in black suits and ties. They go up to light candles and sticks of incense close to the tomb of the Grand Ancestor. Next, they hold up the offering bowls of various foods—rice, pork, fruit, tea. They bow formally with each offering. There is music from the orchestra. I wonder about the memories in the minds of the silent people in the chairs around me.

It is time to drive away all evil spirits. An assistant in a yellow raincoat, who has been standing on the edge of the crowd, goes to the grass beside the terrace and lights a long string of firecrackers. Many of us rush over to the side to watch. Other people plug their ears with their fingers as the fireworks go off. Beyond all the smoke, I see marines and veterans marching up the hillside. When the fireworks are finished, the marines halt and give a 21-gun salute.

I look around and wonder, What will happen next? How will it all end? A few years ago, the ceremony closed with rosebuds and carnations dropping from a helicopter high in the air. But this year the final event begins closer to the ground. Several cages are opened, and out fly scores of doves. These are not ordinary doves; each one has been dyed pink, blue, red, or yellow. But quickly the rainbow doves are out of sight. One of the two sisters leans over and whispers, "Don't worry. They're trained to come back."

Just as we begin to sit down again, the master of ceremonies offers a welcome invitation: "There's lots of good food. Please come up and take a plate."

CONFUCIANISM AND THE MODERN WORLD

The modern world has been hard on government-sponsored Confucianism. In 1911 the Qing (Ch'ing) dynasty collapsed and with it also collapsed the public system of Confucian ceremony and education. When faced with the new scientific knowledge introduced to China from Europe, Confucianism as a total educational curriculum seemed desperately inadequate. As young Chinese sought a whole new form of education, traditional Confucianism could not compete. Confucian temple ritual also came to an end in China, having always relied on support from the state.

Early attacks on Confucianism were made by the New Culture movement, beginning in 1916. While some members wished to hold on to basic Confucian ethics, others thought that all vestiges of Confucianism should be destroyed. Some of the movement's leaders had studied in the West. Among these was Hu Shih (1891–1962), who studied at Columbia University under the philosopher John Dewey (1859–1952) and returned to China to teach and write. The New Culture movement embraced the views of pragmatic thinkers, such as William James (1842–1910), John Dewey, and Bertrand Russell (1872–1970), and criticized Confucianism on many counts. Confucianism was accused of enslaving women to their fathers and husbands, of subjugating sons to tyrannical fathers, and of keeping alive a culture and literature that only looked to the past.

The Communist takeover of mainland China in 1949 further weakened Confucianism as a belief system. Continuing the earlier anti-Confucian themes, Communism has been highly critical of Confucianism for several reasons. First, Confucianism preaches elitism rather than egalitarianism. Although Confucianism maintains that anyone can become a junzi (noble person) through training, in fact Confucian education has often been limited to only those whose parents could afford it. Communism, in contrast, proposed to educate all equally.

Second, the Communists accused Confucianism of valuing males over females, reserving education and power for males, and providing no official power to wives and daughters. With only one exception in all of Chinese history (the empress Wu, who ruled from 683 to 705 c.e.), the official role of emperor has been confined to males. Women's roles have been traditionally concerned with childbearing, and women have derived much of their social identity from men. Communism has preached (at least in theory) that Confucianism's sexist tendencies have created oppression and a loss of talent for society.

Third, the Communists criticized Confucianism for focusing on the old rather than the new and on the humanities rather than the sciences. To

The Confucius Institute

During the second half of the twentieth century, the Chinese Communist government typically vilified Confucius as a backward thinker whose philosophy had kept China from modernization. Confucian thinking, government authorities believed, would keep the "masses" forever in servitude to privileged and powerful landowners because of its praise for social hierarchy. But in recent years, perhaps as a sign of the Chinese government's growing confidence and broadening ideological orientation, Confucius has been "rehabilitated." Confucian rites are once again carried on in his home town of Qufu, and his teachings are again becoming a part of the Chinese educational curriculum.

An interesting manifestation of this cultural change is the Confucius Institute. Headquartered in Beijing, the institute is run by the Chinese Ministry of Education. As part of a large-scale government plan to support international training in Chinese language and culture, this organization has helped universities throughout the world to set up their own satellite Confucius Institutes,

of which there are now more than 100 operating in over forty countries.

Although the institutes bear Confucius's name, they are not focused on the study of his philosophy and its history but instead promote Chinese language study and contemporary cultural understanding, assisting academic and business exchanges between China and other countries. Unlike the Goethe Institutes, which promote German culture, and the British Council, which promotes British cultural contacts, all Confucius Institutes are affiliated with and exist only within foreign universities.

Because Confucius Institutes are under control of universities rather than national governments, critics see the institutes as ways that the Chinese government promotes its own interests abroad. But supporters appreciate the assistance that host universities receive in offering courses in Chinese culture. No one, of course, knows how the institutes might be viewed by Confucius himself.

Communism, this focus on the past reflects a backward vision, like driving a car by looking through the rearview mirror.

Many Communists thought that only when Confucianism was destroyed could China move forward. On the mainland, these views led to either the destruction of Confucian temples or their use for other purposes, and to the development of a Western-based curriculum for education and government jobs. Mao Zedong (Mao Tse-Tung; 1893–1976), the leader of the Communist Revolution, hated the rigidity and old-fashioned thinking that he saw in Confucianism. Mao's anti-Confucian ideals were particularly destructive during the Cultural Revolution (1966–1976), when students reviled their teachers and destroyed much that was considered to be antiquated. On the other hand, Mao also cultivated the image of himself as a benevolent Confucian ruler and father figure. He was a poet and writer; and many of the virtues he encouraged in his people are reminiscent of Confucian ideals—particularly duty, sacrifice, and self-cultivation.

The system of Confucianism has fared better in neighboring Asian countries and regions, such as South Korea and the island of Taiwan. There, Confucian temples and ritual are maintained, although in diminished form, by the government or private families. But in every country influenced by China, such as Japan and Singapore, we find the Confucian system of virtues and behaviors still very much alive. Although these countries have adopted Western science into their curriculums, their cultures maintain an ethic that is Confucian. They highly value the extended family, education, personal discipline, and public order.

Ironically, according to many scholars, Confucian virtues may have helped lead many Confucian countries to modern economic development. This fact has not been lost on the government of mainland China, which has begun to soften its earlier anti-Confucian stance. Early Communists would be astonished to see the grand birthday ceremonies held yearly, with government support, in Qufu, the hometown of Confucius. Taiwan celebrates annually the birthday of Confucius as Teacher's Day on September 28, when early-morning ceremonies are held at all the Confucian temples on the island. Confucius's birthday is also celebrated in Singapore, South Korea, and places around the world where there is a significant Chinese population. (Its traditional date is the twenty-seventh day of the eighth lunar month.) Confucian ceremonies are held in spring and autumn at several places in South Korea, and a spectacular Confucian ceremony, widely televised, is held in Seoul on the first Sunday of May.

A growing public respect for Confucius and his thought has brought about a restoration of some Confucian materials to the curriculum and

The birthday of Confucius is once again celebrated every year in Qufu, his birthplace.

a teaching of Confucian virtues, blended with science, mathematics, and computer technology. The leaders of Confucian countries are horrified by what they have seen of the chaotic individualism and violence in some Western countries. They see the Confucian ethic as an antidote to social ills and therefore continue to view education as character building, not merely as intellectual formation. Singapore has already developed a national educational curriculum that explicitly teaches Confucian virtues, and this may become a model elsewhere. Confucian virtues continue to be promulgated in schools, companies, and government work in many East Asian countries. It is also intriguing to see how much Confucian instruction appears on television in East Asian countries. There, behavior expressing the values of harmony, loyalty, and filial piety is visible both in historical dramas and in many stories of modern life. (Such behavior is extremely apparent, for example, in the Korean television dramas that have become popular in many countries.)

Confucian teaching is, in practice, being modified for modern life. The lesser status of the female is being abandoned widely as women are beginning to demand equal opportunity. Confucian societies everywhere now offer curriculums that blend science and a focus on the future with studies of the past.

257

Greater latitude is gradually being given to individual needs and personalities. With these modifications, Confucianism is gaining a renewed attractiveness.

Rather than dying, Confucianism is possibly beginning a new stage in its long life. The core of Confucianism is unassailable. It is primarily ethical, because it focuses on correct behavior. Yet it is more, because it rests on a vision of human unity and a connection with the harmony of the universe.

READING

SAYINGS OF CONFUCIUS, FROM THE ANALECTS

The sayings of Confucius are effective because of their succinctness and moral authority. They speak in many ways of nobility of heart, largeness of vision, courtesy, virtue, and devotion to the right path.

"Don't worry that other people don't know you. Worry that you do not know other people." (1:16)

"Ideal people are universal and not clannish. Small-minded people are clannish and not universal." (2:14)

"Hear the Way in the morning, and it would be all right to die that evening." (4:8)

"Exemplary people are even-tempered and clear-minded. Petty people are always fretting." (7:36)

A disciple asked Confucius about humaneness. Confucius said, "To master oneself and return to courtesy is humaneness. . . . Do not regard what is not courteous. Do not listen to what is not courteous. Do not say what is not courteous. Do not do what is not courteous." (12:1)

"Cultivated people reach upward. Petty people reach downward." (14:24)

"If you make a mistake and do not correct it, this is called a mistake." (15:30)

"Cultivated people have nine thoughts. When they look, they think of how to see clearly. When they listen, they think of how to hear keenly. In regard to their appearance, they think of how to be warm [welcoming]. In their demeanor, they think of how to be respectful. In their speech, they think of how to be truthful. In their work, they think of how to be serious. When in doubt, they think of how to pose questions. When angry, they think of trouble. When they see gain to be had, they think of justice." (16:10) [34]

TEST YOURSELF

1. Confucianism, Daoism, and Buddhism have been collectively called the Three _____.
   a. Jewels
   b. Doctrines
   c. Schools
   d. Institutions
2. The legendary founder of Daoism, which means "old master" or "old child," is _____.
   a. Mencius
   b. Confucius
   c. Laozi
   d. Mozi
3. The great classic of Daoism, accepted by most Daoists as a central scripture, is the _____.
   a. Daodejing
   b. Tripitaka
   c. Three Baskets
   d. Doctrines

4. According to Daoism, the _____ is the origin of everything and all individual things are "manifestations" of it.
   a. Yin
   b. Dao
   c. Jiva
   d. Qi

5. One of the stimuli that influenced Daoism to take an organizational path was _____.
   a. Hinduism
   b. Buddhism
   c. Jainism
   d. Christianity

6. For Confucians, the Dao of primary interest is the Dao within the human world, manifested in _____.
   a. right relationships and in a harmonious society
   b. traditional mountain sites and in heavenly constellations
   c. natural signs and in symbols
   d. complex meditation and in universal love.

7. The Five Great Relationships signify that each person must live up to his or her social status. This has been called the _____.
   a. rectification of names
   b. path of righteousness
   c. way of the gods
   d. enlightenment

8. The devotion that all members have to their entire family's welfare is _____.
   a. *shu*
   b. *wen*
   c. *junzi*
   d. *xiao*

9. The most authoritative Confucian literature is made up of the Five Classics (Wujing) and the _____ Books (Sishu).
   a. Three
   b. Four
   c. Five
   d. Two

10. The Neo-Confucianist _____ attempted to formulate a general vision of reality by using notions found in the teachings of Confucius and Mencius.
    a. Zhu Xi
    b. Laozi
    c. Mao Zedong
    d. Wang Yangming

11. Explain a situation in which following the Daoist principle of wu wei might be beneficial to yourself or to others. In what situation might following the principle of wu wei be harmful in some way?

12. Based on what you have read about schools of philosophy in the development of Confucianism, who do you think had a more accurate view of human nature—Mencius or the Legalists? Use examples from the reading to support your answer.

RESOURCES

Books

Confucius. *The Analects.* Trans. D. C. Lau. New York: Penguin, 1979. A clear translation of the sayings of Confucius.

Kidd, David. *Peking Story.* New York: Clarkson Potter, 1988. A description by a unique individual of life in an aristocratic family at the time of the Communist Revolution.

Kingston, Maxine Hong. *The Woman Warrior: Memoirs of a Girlhood Among Ghosts.* New York: Vintage, 1989. A now-classic memoir, based on the author's youth, which explores the clash between traditional Chinese beliefs and modern Western values.

Kohn, Livia. *Daoism and Chinese Culture.* Cambridge, MA: Three Pines Press, 2001. A summary of the history and essentials of the religion, with attention to new interpretations that have emerged in the past thirty years.

Lopez, Donald, Jr., ed. *Religions of China in Practice.* Princeton, NJ: Princeton University Press, 1996. An anthology of unusual selections from Chinese religions, including poetry, folktales, chants, and visions.

Oldstone-Moore, Jennifer. *Confucianism: Origins, Beliefs, Practices, Holy Texts, Sacred Places.* New York: Oxford University Press, 2002. A clear overview of Confucianism.

Porter, Bill. *Road to Heaven: Encounters with Chinese Hermits.* San Francisco: Mercury House, 1993. The journal of a search for and conversations with Daoist and Buddhist hermits in modern China.

Wong, Eva. *Seven Taoist Masters: A Folk Novel of China.* Boston: Shambhala, 2004. A work of historical fiction that relates the stories of seven Daoist masters—six men and one woman—who overcome hardships on the journey to self-mastery.

Xinzhong Yao. *An Introduction to Confucianism.* Cambridge University Press, 2000. A comprehensive introduction to Confucianism.

Film/TV

Around the World in 80 Faiths. (BBC.) An eight-part series that documents eighty sacred rituals across six continents in the space of a single year. Episode two includes a segment on the rituals at a Chinese Confucian temple and another segment profiling Daoist devotion.

Crouching Tiger, Hidden Dragon. (Director Ang Lee; Sony.) A popular martial arts film that illustrates both Daoist and Confucian values.

The Joy Luck Club. (Director Wayne Wang; Buena Vista.) A film in which a young Chinese American woman takes her mother's place in a social club after her mother's death. There she discovers secrets her mother kept from her. Its depiction of traditional Chinese family values reflects the values of Confucianism.

Mulan. (Disney). An animated film—based on the tale of a Chinese girl who disguises herself as a man—that depicts filial piety, gender roles, and ancestor worship consonant with traditional Confucian values.

Pushing Hands. (Director Ang Lee; Cinepix Film Properties.) A film in which a taiji master and widower moves from Beijing to New York to live with his son; the father uses a particular taiji technique called "pushing hands" to deal with the many challenges he faces.

Raise the Red Lantern. (Director Yimou Zhang; Miramax.) The story of Songlian, the fourth wife of the wealthy Chen, and the intrigues and humiliations she shares with his other three wives in a traditional Chinese household. (English subtitles.)

Star Wars. (Director George Lucas; Lucasfilms.) A film that borrows heavily from Daoism in its conception of the Force, which corresponds very closely to the Dao, and of the guiding philosophy of the Jedi Knights, as articulated by characters such as Obi Wan Kenobi and Yoda.

Music/Audio

Chinese Taoist Music. (Arc Music.) A collection of traditional Daoist music as performed by the Taoist Music Orchestra of the Shanghai City God Temple.

Classical Chinese Folk Music. (Arc Music.) A 24-track, two-disc compilation of the traditional folk music of China.

Dao De Jing: A Philosophical Translation. (Narrator Ralph Lowenstein; Simply Audiobooks.) An audio version of a primary Daoist text, translated by Roger T. Ames and David L. Hall

Ellie Mao: An Anthology of Chinese Folk Songs. (Smithsonian Folkways.) Traditional Chinese folk songs, some of which embody Daoist or Confucian values.

Internet

Confucian Traditions: http://www.religiousworlds.com/confucian.html. An online resource listing for the Confucian tradition at ReligiousWorlds.com, which includes categories on Confucius, the Confucian classics, and issues related to the interpretation of Confucius.

Tao Te Ching: http://www.taoteching.org/. A complete public-domain English translation of Daoism's foundational text.

Virtual Religion Index: http://virtualreligion.net/vri/china.html. The "East Asian Studies" page at the Virtual Religion Index site, containing a list of online resources on Chinese culture and philosophy, Daoist sources, and Confucian classics.

Wikipedia's Daoism Portal: http://en.wikipedia.org/wiki/Portal:Taoism. A comprehensive reference that includes entries on scripture, deities, religious figures, texts, temples, and religious practice.

KEY TERMS

Analects: The book of the sayings of Confucius.

Dao (Tao; *dau*): The mysterious origin of the universe, which is present and visible in everything.

Daodejing (Tao Te Ching; *dau duh jing*): The classic scripture of Daoism.

Five Classics: The classical literature of the time preceding Confucius, including poetry, history, and divination.

Four Books: The major Confucian books, which include the sayings of Confucius and Mencius.

junzi (chün-tzu; *joon'-dzuh*): "Noble person," the refined human ideal of Confucianism.

Laozi (Lao Tzu; *lau'-dzuh*): The legendary founder of Daoism.

Legalists: The strictest of the Chinese philosophical schools, which advocated strong laws and punishments.

li (*lee*): Appropriate action, ritual, propriety, etiquette.

Mohists: A Chinese school of philosophy that taught universal love.

qi (ch'i; *chee*): The life force.

ren (jen; *ren*): Empathy, consideration for others, humaneness; a Confucian virtue.

shu (*shoo*): Reciprocity; a Confucian virtue.

wen: Cultural refinement; a Confucian virtue.

wu wei (*woo'-way'*): "No action," "no strain"; doing only what comes spontaneously and naturally; effortlessness.

xiao (hsiao; *shyau*): Family devotion, filial piety; a Confucian virtue.

yang (*yahng*): The active aspect of reality that expresses itself in speech, light, and heat.

Yijing (I Ching; *ee jing*): An ancient Confucian book of divination, one of the Five Classics, still in use today.

yin: The receptive aspect of the universe that expresses itself in silence, darkness, coolness, and rest.

Zhuangzi (Chuang Tzu; *jwang'-dzuh*): Author of the Zhuangzi, a book of whimsical stories that express themes of early Daoist thought.

Visit the Online Learning Center at www.mhhe.com/molloy5e for additional exercises and features, including "Religion beyond the Classroom" and "For Fuller Understanding."

CHAPTER **7**

Shinto

FIRST ENCOUNTER

In a lush park of Tokyo stands Meiji Shrine, a Shinto shrine created in the early twentieth century to honor the spirit of the emperor who, with other leaders, helped Japan open to the modern world. After the emperor died in 1912, schoolchildren all over Japan contributed trees for the grounds. The trees, which have since grown very tall, surround spacious beds of purple and white Japanese iris that bloom thickly in the summer.

You enter the shrine by walking through a **torii,** a simple, tall wooden portal. As you move toward the compound of shrine buildings, you see large stone basins of flowing water. You watch visitors dip bamboo ladles into the basins, pour a bit of water over their hands, touch their faces, and then dry their hands with white handkerchiefs before proceeding. The worshipers walk quietly along the gravel path toward the main buildings. They climb the steep stone stairs, stand reverently on the landing before the entrance to the shrine hall, and clap their hands several times. They bow their heads silently before descending the stairs. Off to the side, two women attach small pieces of white paper to a tree, while other visitors crowd in front of booths that sell amulets, mementoes, and poetry that was written by the emperor. Meanwhile, five men in white robes, wearing stiff black hats and large, oddly shaped black shoes, stride silently across the courtyard single file.

You wander slowly to the iris garden. It is so full of people admiring the flowers that you must inch your way along the gravel and stone paths that wind between the gardens and ponds. Several people, to your amazement, have set up easels in front of the irises and are actually painting, despite the crush of people trying to take photos behind them.

You take a vacant seat on a stone bench and pause to look at the flowers and the people. What was meant by the clapping of hands? Why did people pour water over their hands at the entrance to the courtyard? Who were the men in the white robes, and what does all this have to do with the spirit of an emperor? Why does the complex look more like a park than a church or temple?

THE ORIGINS OF SHINTO

Like many ancient religious traditions, Shinto has no known person or group as its founder. In fact, its mysterious origins date back to the ancient people of Japan and their stories of how the world came into being. Like many people long ago, the people of the Japanese islands (Figure 7.1) lived close to nature, and Shinto as a religion reflects that reality in its worship of the spirits who are believed to inhabit the natural world. Shinto seems to have arisen from a human awareness of the power of nature and the need to be in harmony with it. Shinto retains elements of shamanism, contact with nature spirits, and mysterious healing. While most of the world's old religions of nature have disappeared, Shinto still exists in modern Japan, a fact that is sometimes marked by a shrine tucked between concrete skyscrapers.

Shinto is more, however, than a nature religion. It also has ethnic and family dimensions. The spirits that are worshiped include the spirits of departed family members, distant ancestors of one's clan, and great leaders—such as the emperor for whom the Meiji period is named, who did so much to modernize Japan.

The name *Shinto* presents a problem. It is not a Japanese term, but emerged when Buddhism came from China to Japan. Before that time, there was no need to name the religion that was already present—it was simply what everyone did. In fact, the Japanese name for Buddhism, *Butsu-do* ("the way of the Buddha"), helped give a name to the religion that Buddhism encountered. The religion that was already practiced in Japan came to be called the *shen-dao* ("the way of the gods") in Chinese, pronounced *shin'-to* in Japanese. ("The way of the gods" is also expressed in the Japanese language by the phrase *kami-no-michi*.)

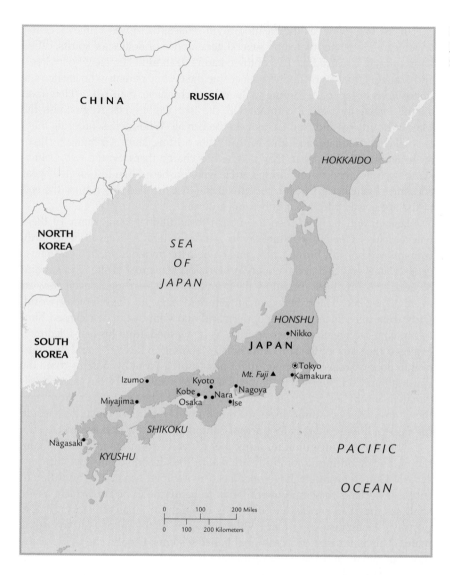

FIGURE 7.1
Japanese cities with major
Shinto shrines or festivals.

Like the origin of Shinto, the origin of the Japanese people is also mysterious. Although Japanese often think of themselves as a single "race," they apparently descended from several immigrant groups that came from the northwest, possibly Siberia and Korea, and from the south, possibly from the Malay Peninsula. (We should be aware that even older peoples already lived in Japan. The Ainu, an early people who live in the north of Japan, may be their descendants.) Although the immigrant groups may have focused their primary worship on different natural forces (such as the sun and the moon), it seems their traditions eventually mixed, ultimately blending a large number of gods into a pantheon and yielding a single creation myth.

In the beginning, as the creation myth relates, there was primeval chaos, which came to be populated by several generations of deities, or spirits, called **kami** (possibly, "sacred").[1] Two of these kami—**Izanami** ("female who invites") and **Izanagi** ("male who invites")—became the cosmic parents who created the first islands of Japan. According to an ancient chronicle, the Kojiki, "Hereupon all the Heavenly Deities commanded the two Deities His Augustness the Male-Who-Invites and Her Augustness the Female-Who-Invites, ordering them to 'make, consolidate, and give birth to this drifting land.' Granting to them an heavenly jeweled spear, they deigned to charge them. So the two Deities, standing upon the Floating Bridge of Heaven, pushed down the jeweled spear and stirred [the ocean] with it . . . ; the brine that dripped down from the end of the spear was piled up and became an island."[2]

Izanagi and Izanami then gave birth to additional kami, many of them nature deities. One of the nature deities was a fire god. As a result of his birth, Izanami was horribly burned, died, and went to the underworld. In his immense grief, Izanagi traveled to the underworld to find Izanami, but she rebuffed him because of her ugliness caused by the burn and decay—maggots even crawled through her body. Horrified, Izanagi returned alone to the everyday world. Dirty from his contact with the underworld and with death, he cleansed himself in water to regain a state of purity. As he washed, from his tear-filled eyes emerged the spirit of the sun, **Amaterasu** ("shining in heaven"), and the spirit of the moon, Tsukiyomi ("moon night possessor"). From his nostrils came the spirit of the wind, Susanowo ("impetuous male").[3] Eventually, the sun goddess Amaterasu sent her grandson to bring order to the islands of Japan. From him, the myth continues, came Jimmu, the first human emperor of Japan. As a result, the imperial house mythically traces its origin back to the goddess of the sun.

This story is intriguing for a number of reasons. It puts the kami of sun, moon, and wind into a family relationship, thus harmonizing the stories of several kami who might have once been worshiped separately by different tribes. It declares the emperors of Japan to be divine in origin (which, as we shall see, has had serious ramifications throughout Japan's history). It also portrays Amaterasu as female, while the kami of the moon, Tsukiyomi, is male. (This is unusual in traditional belief systems; usually the deity of the moon is female and the deity of the sun is male.)

This story also expresses a concern with purity—a major focus of Shinto. Pollution (*tsumi*) comes especially from contact with death, but purity can be restored by washing and ritual expiation (*harai*).

Another significant aspect of this creation story is that the islands of Japan are believed to be the creation and the home of divine spirits. Japan is thus a sort of "this-worldly" heaven, which human beings share with divine beings. (Traditional Japanese belief maintains that the spirits live in an "upper world" but that their realm is not separate from this world and thus they can exist and appear in this world.) Such a view differs significantly from those religions that see this world not as a paradise but as a place of suffering—a prelude to a heaven that can be reached only after death. In the more optimistic Japanese view, the task of human beings is to live up to the heavenlike world into which they have been born.

THE HISTORICAL DEVELOPMENT OF SHINTO

As we have already mentioned, the entry of Buddhism into Japan in the sixth century (Timeline 7.1) forced Shinto to define itself. It was a process that was complicated by the tendency of Mahayana Buddhism not only to tolerate but also to absorb native religious elements. Buddhist monks viewed Shinto kami simply as different forms of Mahayana buddhas, bodhisattvas, and other heavenly beings, and they preached that the Buddhist deities were already being worshiped in Japan under Shinto names. This approach made the introduction of Buddhism fairly easy. At first there was some resistance, and the new religion was viewed as dangerous and foreign. But

Timeline of significant events in the history of Shinto.

TIMELINE 7.1

Left events	Date	Right events
	c. 660 B.C.E.	Period of the legendary Emperor Jimmu
Worship of sun and fertility	PRE-c. 350 B.C.E.	
	c. 350–550 C.E.	Unification of clans and of kami worship
Introduction of Buddhism to Japan	552 C.E.	
	712 C.E.	Writing of the Kojiki
Writing of the Nihongi	720 C.E.	
	c. 1650–1850	Shinto scholarly revival
Life of Nakayama Miki	1798–1887	
	1836–1918	Life of Deguchi Nao
Beginning of the Meiji Restoration and modernization of Japan	1868	
	1882	Beginning of State Shinto
End of State Shinto	1945	
	1946	Emperor Hirohito rejects title of divinity
Death of Emperor Hirohito and ascension of Emperor Akihito	1989	

over time, elements from both religions were drawn upon, and a certain blending of religious practice occurred.

Along with Buddhism came a torrent of cultural elements from China. Before contact with the mainland, Japan already had a culture of its own, but it was fairly simple in comparison to that of China. Contact with China introduced a system of writing, which the Japanese began to adapt for their own use. It also introduced Chinese architecture, poetry, ceramics, art, and all sorts of new ideas—from philosophy to cuisine, from clothing design to city planning. The Japanese were fascinated by all these novelties, and the importation of Chinese culture continued, with some interruptions, for a thousand years.

Accommodation with Buddhism and Confucianism

Despite the enthusiasm for Buddhism and the accompanying aspects of Chinese culture, Shinto did not disappear. Instead, the two religions reached an accommodation. Although there were many exceptions, several patterns emerged: Shinto was often associated with agriculture, fertility, and birth, while Buddhism was called on for philosophy, help with serious illnesses, funerals, and the afterlife.

The accommodation was signaled in various ways. Shinto shrines frequently contained a Buddhist place of worship or had some Buddhist rites for the kami, while Buddhist temples often had a Shinto shrine on their grounds. Shinto also adopted the Buddhist practices of preaching sermons, venerating statues, and using incense. Furthermore, Shinto shrines featured Chinese architectural details, such as tile roofs and red paint. Often the mixture was so thorough that a place of worship was neither exclusively Shinto nor Buddhist. In the late nineteenth century, however, the two religions were forced to disentangle themselves. At that time, the Meiji government began to emphasize the belief that the emperor was a descendant of the founding deities, and Shinto was appropriated by the government for instilling patriotism. Nonetheless, one can still see many examples of their mutual influence today.

Confucianism was also introduced to Japan along with Chinese culture. It meshed nicely with Japanese practices such as the veneration of ancestors, who were thought of as kami, and the loyalty given to family and clan. As it had in China, Confucianism in Japan began to play the role of an ethical system that supported education, family, and government. The whole nation began to view itself as being joined in a family relationship, with the emperor as father and the government ministers as elder brothers. Family and school instilled the Confucian virtues of respect for the emperor, reverence for ancestors and elders, care for juniors, loyalty, discipline, and love of learning. Many of these values were subsequently reinforced by Shinto.

Shinto and Japanese National Identity

Japan tends to swing back and forth between a great enthusiasm for outside cultures and a strong desire to assert Japanese uniqueness. Chinese cultural

Early in the typical Shinto ceremony, priests and people bow to be cleansed by a purification wand.

imports, which were strong in the seventh and eighth centuries, weakened but then returned again in another wave in the thirteenth century. Western influence, which arrived with the Portuguese in the sixteenth century, was considered so dangerous that Japan largely sealed itself off from the outside world until the mid-1800s. After that came a great wave of Western influence that strengthened over the rest of the nineteenth century. Except for the years just before and during World War II, direct Western influence has continued through to the present.

When the West challenged Japan to modernize in the late nineteenth century, Shinto was enlisted as a cultural counterweight that would preserve the "Japanese spirit." In 1868 a young man, Mutsuhito, came to the throne and assumed real, rather than merely symbolic, power. Known to history as the Emperor Meiji, he began a deliberate process of bringing Japan into the modern world. He imported European and American experts to build up the governmental, military, and educational systems according to Western models. It was a turning point in Japanese history, known as the Meiji Restoration. Shinto was forced to separate from Buddhism, and places of worship had to decide whether to declare themselves Shinto or Buddhist. For a short time Buddhism even suffered persecution, as Japan's leaders emphasized the divine origins of the emperor and began to tie Shinto to a growing spirit of nationalism.

Kamikaze Pilots and Shinto

During World War II, Japanese pilots who made suicidal crash attacks achieved such notoriety in the West that a new word entered the English language: **kamikaze.** Containing the word *kami,* it means "spirit wind." Does it have a connection to Shinto?

We know that Shinto priests blessed the planes and the kamikaze pilots. The blessings were part of the larger governmental use of Shinto to further the military effort. But we might also see elements of Buddhism and Confucianism in the creation of the kamikaze pilot. Buddhism teaches the need to accept bravely the transience of life. Confucianism stresses loyalty to government leaders and superiors.

Both concepts helped generate the warrior code of loyalty, duty, and honor, called **bushido** ("warrior way"). Although bushido developed after the twelfth century as the code of the fairly small **samurai** class, it had immense influence throughout the Japanese military.

During certain periods, Shinto has been utilized to promote war, and it is possible to argue that Shinto has sometimes lent itself to nationalistic use. (The veneration of the spirits of deceased military at Yasukuni Shrine in Tokyo is a current source of debate.) In fairness, we should note that most Buddhist sects in Japan also supported Japan's role in the war effort.

Shinto was now a tool in the national buildup, and in 1882 a national religion called State Shinto was established. Thousands of shrines received a special national status, with government financial support and control by the Home Ministry. Priests at these shrines were official government employees, and in return for financial support, they were supposed to represent the imperial household and maintain traditional values. All other nongovernmental Shinto shrines and organizations were treated as independent, self-supporting institutions and together were called Sect Shinto.[4]

Unfortunately, these developments set the stage for the exploitation of Shinto during the militaristic expansion that occurred after Japan's victory (1905) in the Russo-Japanese War. The government increasingly used State Shinto to generate patriotism, both during the military buildup of the 1930s and then during World War II. The divinity of the emperor—the descendant of Amaterasu—was officially taught in schools, and schoolchildren memorized and recited daily a special statement endorsing this view, the Imperial Rescript on Education.

When World War II ended, the Occupation forces demanded that Japan become a secular country. State Shinto was abolished by the government; the emperor renounced his divine status; Shinto shrines were returned to private religious practice; and all religions were placed on an equal footing. In theory Shinto became a strictly private religion, but in reality Shinto retains a special place in national life.

ESSENTIALS OF SHINTO BELIEF

The heart of Shinto is a sensitivity to the mysterious powers of nature. Kami are not thought of so much as beings living in another, distant realm, but rather as powers in or near this world whose presence might be felt, for example, when we are standing in a grove of trees or looking at a waterfall or contemplating a distant mountain. The kami can also cause dread, such as what one might feel in the midst of a terrible storm or being lost on an ocean. The kami are the energies that animate nature: they cause rice to grow and wind to blow; they cause volcanoes to spew lava and earthquakes to split the land. The kami of nature are especially seen in places of natural power and beauty.

Kami are treated as persons and are given names—a fact that enables human beings to approach them and feel closely related to them. We have already learned the names of the major kami: Izanagi, Izanami, Amaterasu, Tsukiyomi, and Susanowo. In addition there are lesser kami. Among them are the spirit of fire, the deity of grain, ocean spirits, mountain spirits (among whom the kami of Mount Fuji is preeminent), and spirits of great trees, rivers, and waterfalls. There are also animal spirits, particularly of animals thought to have mysterious cunning, such as the badger, the fox, and the snake.

Ancestors—who have also become kami—live close by, ready to return to see how their descendants are faring.[5] Shinto is thus a way of maintaining a connection with family and clan members.

After Buddhism entered Japan, influential members of the court sought to record the early myths, both to preserve them and to defend the religious foundation of aristocratic claims. In the early eighth century, at imperial request, the myths were written down, using the new script that had come from China. The ancient myths appear in the beginnings of two core works, the **Kojiki** ("chronicle of ancient events," 712 C.E.) and the **Nihongi** ("chronicle of Japan," 720 C.E.).[6] These works also contain genuinely historical material. Ancient Shinto ritual and prayers (*norito*) were recorded in the tenth century.

Although Shinto has no clearly defined code of ethics, a type of morality does flow from the Shinto system of values and its way of looking at life. The Western notion of internal guilt is not found in Shinto. There is no moralistic God who gives commands or judges a person, nor is there a sense of original sin or of any basic sinful tendency. Instead, human beings are fundamentally good, the body is good, and this earthly life is good. Shinto worships fertility and new life, and sex is viewed positively, without guilt. Sexual imagery—particularly phallic rocks and wood carvings—can be seen at many shrines.[7]

Unlike many other religions, Shinto tends to turn its focus away from death, which is thought of as the opposite of life and growth.[8] Because Shinto worships the life force, it works to counteract whatever brings sickness or death. Just as dirt is removable, so too are all other pollutants. According to Shinto, we must keep our bodies, houses, and clothes clean and bright; and when they become dirty or contaminated, we must wash them, get rid of the dirt, and purify them with blessings. In Japan, washing, sweeping, and cleaning—seen everywhere daily—have religious implications.

The head priest, here in red, officially greets the kami by chanting prayers handwritten on a scroll.

One's character must be unstained, too, and human relations must be kept healthy. Similarly, the human character must have "sincerity" (*makoto*)—it must be pure, without egotism, committed. (Many of Emperor Meiji's poems, available for sale at Meiji Shrine, are about the importance of sincerity.) Human beings conserve and restore their purity by fulfilling all obligations, repaying debts, and apologizing for misdeeds.

Because kami are everywhere, living with them demands that we show them reverence. One way is to visit them at their shrines, which are their homes. Another way is to show respect for nature, which is one reason for Japan's high esteem for farming and carpentry and for the architectural use of elements such as wood and stone in their natural state. Respect for nature also means maintaining a harmony with nature and all its processes.

SHINTO RELIGIOUS PRACTICE

Shinto practice occurs at several levels. It encompasses formal worship and blessings by priests at shrines; blessings by priests away from the shrine; Shinto observances of holidays, the seasons, and nature; everyday practice by individuals in their homes; and the ceremonial practice of Shinto by the emperor and other authorities. Active shrines have a priest—a job that is frequently hereditary.

Worship at Shrines

People visit shrines to pray for health, for success in school and career, and for the well-being of those they love. A visit begins by passing under the torii, which looks like a ceremonial entrance or gateway and is sometimes tall and magnificent.[9] Worshipers wash their hands and mouths at a water basin just inside the entrance. They proceed through an open courtyard to the building—the *haiden*—where the kami is worshiped. Behind the haiden (and often visible from it) is a small hall or cabinet where the kami is enshrined. In smaller shrines, there may be no front worship hall but only a small place where the kami is enshrined. (It is possible that the earliest shrines had no buildings at all.[10])

Worshipers ascend the stairs to the haiden or to the space in front of the room where the kami is enshrined. They bow, donate a coin, then often ring a bell and clap several times to gain the kami's attention. They bow again and pray, either silently or by chanting. Then they bow again and leave. Sometimes they tie small wooden plaques (*ema*) or pieces of paper, with their requests written on them, to fences or to the branches of a nearby sacred tree.

When worshipers visit a shrine for a blessing, a priest says a prayer and waves over them a branch or wand adorned with paper streamers. This implement is used to purify the devotees and the surrounding area.

Each shrine has its special festival days (*matsuri*). These may be celebrated with grand processions and various types of entertainment. Sometimes, to honor the kami, celebrants parade the kami in a hand-carried litter, an *omikoshi*. On festival days, temporary booths are set up to sell foods and religious souvenirs. (Large shrines, such as Meiji Shrine, have permanent booths.) Among the souvenirs are amulets of various kinds, some in brocade bags, which are thought to bring good luck. Some amulets are kept in the home, and small ones are kept in a car for protection.

People visit shrines for blessings at important times in their lives. Babies are brought for a blessing a month after birth. Children are brought for additional blessings when they are young, when special protection is thought to be valuable. This practice is known as "7-5-3"; girls are brought at ages 3 and 7, and boys are brought at age 5.

Shinto priests also perform ceremonies, such as weddings, away from the shrine. Once held in homes, weddings nowadays often occur in large hotels or reception rooms, because they are usually followed by a banquet. Priests also bless construction sites, houses, and cars, as well as perform exorcisms at locations that have come to be associated with misfortune, in order to make people feel comfortable there again.

Shinto priests wear long robes (often white, symbolizing cleanliness and purity), which are based on old Chinese aristocratic design that became popular in the court of the Heian period. Priests' shoes are made of carved wood (like Dutch wooden shoes) and covered with black lacquer, and they wear high caps of black lacquered horsehair. The hats of dignitaries have a long flexible extension, which is attached at the top or back of the hat. The extension, created in China, is believed to represent the tail of the horse. (A

Shown here is a typical local shrine, with offerings of fruit, sake, and mochi. The mirror behind the jars of sake represents the kami of the sun. Words on the two large lanterns seek protection of the home and success in business.

symbol of energy and strength, the horse came to be considered a sacred animal. A few Shinto shrines have even kept stables of horses.)

Some shrines also have female attendants (*miko*), who wear bright red skirts. They assist in ritual, play short metal musical instruments covered with bells, and represent a vestige of early shamanism.

A Shinto priest uses a purification wand to symbolically drive out spirits during the blessing of a new car.

Celebration of the New Year

New Year's is a very special time in Shinto practice. In preparation for the holiday, the home must be thoroughly cleaned in order to make it attractive to the spirits, who are invited to visit. The main gate or door is decorated with a special arrangement called the *kadomatsu* ("entry pine"), which is made up of three pieces of cut green bamboo, a small branch of pine, and, if possible, a sprig of plum. The bamboo signifies persistence; the pine, freshness and life throughout the winter; and the plum, the first sign of life in early spring. Together, the branches of greenery in the kadomatsu symbolize human virtue.

During New Year's, rice is pounded into a soft dough called *mochi,* then made into round shapes that are piled on top of each other and topped with a tangerine. Rice signifies wealth and fertility, and the mochi anticipates the planting of rice in the spring. On New Year's eve, the family gathers to eat a special soup made of vegetables and mochi, called *ozoni,* which is thought to promote health. On New Year's day, men and women dress in kimono, take offerings to Shinto shrines, and pray there for success in the coming year. Over the following days, they make formal visits to relatives and friends and renew relationships. The themes of the whole holiday season are cleansing and the renewal of life.

Observances of the Seasons and Nature

Traditionally, Shinto has marked the seasons with special practices, particularly for planting and harvesting rice. In the industrial nation of Japan today, however, these rituals are becoming less important.

Men carry shrine of offerings during a cherry-blossom festival in San Francisco. While Shinto shrine ceremonies are typically formal and sedate, some nature celebrations can be raucous.

Because respect for nature is at the heart of Shinto, reverential objects and small shrines are sometimes placed in the midst of forests, in fields, or on mountains. Among these are torii (which can even be found in the ocean), a pile of stones (possibly phallic in origin), or a sacred rope. Respect for the spirits of ancestors is shown by pouring water or tea over gravestones and by leaving offerings of food and flowers.

One noteworthy Shinto practice is purification with water, a practice that must be very ancient because it appears in several myths about the kami. As we have already mentioned, devotees always wash their hands with water at the entrance to a shrine. A related ritual, called **misogi,** involves standing under a waterfall as a ritual act of purification. Before entering the water, the devotee does calisthenics and deep-breathing exercises. The practitioner is then cleansed with a bit of salt. Backing into the water, the person stands for some time as the water falls full-force on his or her shoulders. The practitioner may shout and cut the air with a hand to enhance the experience of purification. The ritual ends with a drink of *sake* (rice wine) and possibly a meal, if it is performed with others. Misogi combines the ritual of cleansing with the ideal of self-discipline and probably began in the practices of ascetics who lived in the mountains.

Another Shinto practice is the climbing of a sacred mountain to gain union with the spirit of that mountain. The climb up Mount Fuji, for example, is something that many Japanese hope to accomplish at least once in their lifetime, and several Shinto sects specifically worship the kami of Mount Fuji.

Other Practices

Daily worship occurs in the home, where a small Shinto shrine called the **kamidana** is maintained, often on a high shelf. It may contain a mirror, and offerings are made there, especially of rice and water. It is common to offer prayers at the kamidana at the beginning of each day. Some homes also maintain an outdoor shrine in the garden.

A semiofficial form of Shinto that is practiced by the emperor and his household is also still part of the religion. The emperor has traditionally been considered the high priest of Shinto, and his reign is inaugurated with Shinto rites. In order to guarantee the fertility of the rice harvest for the entire nation, he participates every spring in a ceremonial rice-planting on the palace grounds. He and his family also visit the shrine of **Ise** annually to pray for the country. And when he dies, every emperor is buried with Shinto rites—something quite rare, because among ordinary Japanese people, funeral services are conducted by Buddhist priests.

PERSONAL EXPERIENCE: A TEMPLE HIGH ABOVE KYOTO

On my first trip to Kyoto, I had planned to spend a full day walking in its beautiful eastern hills. My ambitious plan was to begin at the north end, to continue south through the eastern part of the city, and to end finally at the Buddhist "mother temple" of Kyoto, Kiyomizu-dera ("clear water temple"). I had heard that it was a wonderful spot for watching the sun disappear and the night begin.

As sunset grew near, I arrived at the stairs that lead up to the temple. To call the place a single "temple" is misleading. It is really a large complex of wooden buildings scattered across a wooded hill. The main part of the temple is built on top of an enormous deck that extends far out over the hillside, supported by wooden pillars that rise high above the treetops.

Standing on the deck, I could see across all Kyoto. Other people were there, too, standing patiently at the railing waiting for the sunset. All of us watched reverently as the sun slipped beneath the horizon; then the clouds turned pink, and the city was engulfed in an orange haze. As daylight faded and the gray city turned blue, nighttime Kyoto was being born. It was easy to imagine, down below, the dinner restaurants, noodle shops, and tiny bars all coming to life. Up here, however, the antique atmosphere of Kiyomizu-dera embraced us with its distance from the world.

Visitors to Kiyomizu-dera
catch and drink water
from a sacred stream.

On the way out was a triple stream—the "clear water" that gave the temple its name. As I walked down the high temple stairs, I could see, far below, the three thin streams of water that cascaded into a pool. Coming closer, I noticed in the twilight the bamboo ladles that lay there for visitors to use to take a drink. As I reached the bottom of the stairs, I looked again. There, at the base of the three waterfalls, obscure in the dimness and plunging water, a man in a white robe stood motionless, knee-deep in the water. I saw that his palms were held together in a gesture of prayer. I took a drink from the waterfall, then retreated toward the path that leads out into the valley below the temple. I looked back one last time at the falling water. The man had not moved.

I'd gone to Kiyomizu-dera expecting a beautiful sunset, the scent of incense, and perhaps the sound of a Buddhist chant. What I hadn't expected to find, near the temple's base, was the practice of the Shinto ritual misogi.[11] Yet how fitting, I thought, that a religion in Japan that grew up in close contact with the native religion should today have, as the basis for its name and at the base of this grand temple's frame, waters sacred to a Shinto kami.

SHINTO AND THE ARTS

Shinto worships beauty, but the influence of Shinto on art is not immediately clear. There is no strong Shinto tradition of figurative art, in which gods are portrayed in paintings and sculpture. There are some exceptions, but kami are thought of almost universally as invisible presences, not to be portrayed. Instead, the defining features of Shinto art are openness, a use of natural elements, and a deliberate simplicity.

It can be argued that Shinto's high esteem for nature has had a profound influence on Japanese art and architecture. The Japanese screens and scrolls that portray nature that are often said to be the product of Daoism or Zen are equally the product of Shinto. This can also be said of all the fine and decorative art forms, such as ceramics and kimono design, in which elements of nature are a primary inspiration. Traditional Japanese architecture, with its floor of rice matting and its unpainted wooden walls, also shows Shinto influence.

Perhaps because Shinto places almost no emphasis on doctrines and ethical demands, it has focused instead on the beauty of ritual, giving Shinto an important relationship with the arts. Its love of ceremony has demanded that attention be paid to all objects and clothing used in its sacred ritual, to the places where the ritual takes place, and to the exact way the ritual is performed.

Architecture

The traditional architecture of shrines (**jinja**) is a primary expression of Shinto artistic expression. These structures seem to have begun as storehouses for grain and other foods, which were raised off the ground for protection from water and insects. These granaries functioned as the natural and comfortable homes of the gods who served as protectors of the stored foods. The original pattern of the shrine called for walls made of wood and roofs made of thatch, which would be renewed regularly. Roof beams often extended high above the roof, in a style that is also found in South Pacific island architecture. This feature of extended roof beams (*chigi*) and the fact that the construction materials seem to be appropriate for a warm climate lead many to think that the Shinto shrine originated possibly in Malaysia and islands farther south.

"Pure" Shinto style, with uncurving gabled thatch roofs, unpainted and uncarved wooden walls, and nailless construction, is most evident at Ise. Because the wood and thatch need to be replaced regularly in order to keep them bright and fresh, the maintenance of this style can be afforded at only a few sites.

The shrines of Ise, which are rebuilt every twenty years, are striking because of their extreme simplicity. They sit on a ground of white stones in the midst of tall cedar trees, and to reach the inner shrine, the visitor must cross a river. In the summer, the cicadas fill the air with cricketlike sounds, adding to the sense of primordial mystery.

The earliest torii, or ceremonial entryway, was probably made of three logs lashed together, though we don't know its exact origin. From this basic shape, many graceful variations emerged. The original torii were certainly made of unpainted wood, although today many are painted white, red, or orange. The torii usually signify sacred landmarks, but they can also be set in water. (The enormous orange torii standing in the ocean at Miyajima island near Hiroshima is the best-known example.)

Typical Shinto architecture is obvious at Itsukushima Shrine just off Japan's main island.

At some shrines, so many torii are set up as thanksgiving offerings that over many years they create a tunnel. Tied to the torii or to the front of a shrine is often a ceremonial rope (**shimenawa**), from which may be hung white paper streamers, particularly on festival days. Because kami are considered to reside in any place in nature that is awe-inspiring, shimenawa may also adorn exceptional trees and rocks.

Music and Dance

Shinto is also known for its distinctive music called **gagaku.** Originally played in the Chinese imperial court of the Tang and Song dynasties, gagaku was adapted by Shinto and so slowed down that it creates an impression of ancient solemnity. The instruments that are used make a flutelike, reedy sound that seems close yet faraway, timeless yet fresh and new. Gagaku is a perfect accompaniment to Shinto ritual.

One story in the Kojiki tells of how Amaterasu was lured out of a rock cave by music and dance. Shinto shrines often include dance at festival times to entertain the resident kami. Shrine dance eventually evolved into the stately **Noh** dance dramas, which tell the stories of people and their contacts with the spirits. The making of masks and exquisite robes for Noh performers has become a fine art.

SHINTO OFFSHOOTS: THE NEW RELIGIONS

The fact that Shinto is not a strongly institutionalized religion is both a weakness and a strength. It is a weakness because Shinto generally has not had the organizational structure necessary to make converts or spread the religion beyond Japan. Shinto shrines do belong to confederations, however, which help them with staffing; and many smaller shrines are affiliated with one of the old, large national shrines.

The relative weakness of institutional structure, though, can be a great benefit. Using rituals, symbols, and values derived from Shinto, people are able to create new forms of belief and practice that are more likely to resonate with contemporary society. Thus there has been a proliferation of sects, especially over the past two hundred years. Some sects are more traditional than others. Some worship all the major kami or focus on just one of them. Some borrow from Confucianism, Buddhism, or Christianity and speak of a divine parent (or parents) and of the human race as a single family. Some utilize traditions derived from mountain asceticism. Some emphasize healing. Some venerate a charismatic founder who is thought to be a kami and the recipient of a divine revelation. Offshoots that consider themselves separate religions are sometimes called the New Religions.

Japan, like Korea, has had a long history of shamanism; and in both countries the shamans are often female. We might recall that the shaman acts as an intermediary between the gods and human beings. The shaman helps bring physical and emotional healing. This openness to shamanism has helped produce the offshoots of Shinto that revere an inspired leader who was the recipient of a divine revelation. These offshoots illustrate the ability of Japanese religious traditions to take on new forms.

One of the New Religions is **Tenrikyo** ("heavenly reason teaching"), founded by Nakayama Miki (1798–1887), who discovered her religious abilities by accident. When Miki called in a shaman to perform rites to improve her unhappy life and miserable marriage, she intended only to act as the shaman's assistant. Instead, she went into a trance that lasted several days. During the trance a kami spoke through her, saying, "I am the True and Original God. . . . I have descended from Heaven to save all human beings, and I want to take Miki as the Shrine of God. . . ."[12] When Miki came out of the trance, she explained that many kami had spoken to her. The greatest, she said, was the parent kami (*Oya-gami*) of all human beings. The name of the kami was Tenri-o-no-mikoto ("Lord of divine wisdom"). This kami wished her to disseminate teachings to people about how to live properly so that they might have health and long life.

The notion that physical health comes from mental health is strong in Tenrikyo, which preaches healing by faith. This religion is exceptional for its institutional structure and other traditional religious elements that allow it to spread beyond Japan. It has sacred scripture—the poetry that Nakayama Miki wrote as a result of her revelations.[13] The sect has even created a city near Nara, called Tenri City, where its ideals are put into practice. Tenri City contains a university, library, and museum; religious services are offered twice daily in the main hall.

Another New Religion is called Omoto-kyo ("great origin teaching"), or simply **Omoto.** It was founded by Deguchi Nao (1836–1918), a woman who

A priest presents a symbolic offering of sake at the entrance to a haiden at Omoto headquarters in Kameoka, Japan.

experienced terrible poverty and misfortune. Of her eight children, three died and two suffered mental illness. Nao's husband died when she was 30, and she was reduced to selling rags. In her despair, she experienced a vision of the creation of a new, perfect world. Working with a man she adopted as her son, Deguchi Onisaburo, Nao established a religion that she hoped would begin the transformation of society.

Nao's vision grew out of the traditional Shinto view of earth as a heavenly realm of the spirits and its shamanistic trust in the spirits to bring healing to human life. Like many other New Religions, Omoto aims to better *this* world rather than accumulate rewards for an afterlife. It wishes to bring happiness to the individual and peace to society.

Omoto is of particular interest because it sees in the creation of art the essence of religious manifestation. For Omoto, all art is religious. To spread its belief about the connection between art and religion, Omoto began a school at its headquarters in Kameoka, near Kyoto, to teach traditional Japanese arts to non-Japanese. To encourage world peace, Omoto has promoted the study of Esperanto (a universal language) and sponsored contacts with members of other religions, such as Muslims and Christians. Omoto has even held services in New York's Cathedral of Saint John the Divine, where Shinto ritual objects remain on display.

Omoto has itself produced offshoots. One is the Church of World Messianity (Sekaikyusei-kyo). It was founded by Okada Mokichi (1882–1955), who was believed to be able to heal by means of a source of light within his body. He thought that he could share this healing light by writing the character for light (*hikari*) on pieces of paper, which he gave to his followers. Devotees work for the coming of a time on earth when the world will be free of war, poverty, and disease. Elements of Buddhism can be seen in this religion, for the supreme deity is called Miroku (the Japanese name of Maitreya, the Buddha expected to come in the future).

> Art is the mother of religion.
> —Omoto saying

Other Shinto offshoots include Seicho-no-Ie ("house of growth") and P. L. Kyodan ("perfect liberty community"), which emerged from Omoto, and Honmichi ("true road"), which emerged from Tenrikyo. The goals of all these groups are similar: harmony, beauty, health, happiness, and the creation of a paradise on earth.

The New Religions are the object of some interest for what they may foretell about the direction of religions. They tend to be practical, peace-oriented, and "this-worldly." Many value the contributions of women, and many esteem the arts. Borrowing valuable elements from other religions, they are moving in new directions.

SHINTO AND THE MODERN WORLD

Shinto could have died out as a result of the successful growth of Buddhism, or it could have easily faded away when Japan adopted Western science and technology. Yet Shinto is a unique example of an early nature religion that is still vital in the modern world.

Shinto is no longer confined to Japan. Here, the Reverend Barrish of Tsubaki America Shinto Shrine purifies a building in Seattle.

Though an ancient religion, Shinto is still relevant today. Having maintained its traditional emphasis on nature, it has much to teach the modern world about respect for the environment—for wood and stone, for flowers and fruits, and for the changing of the seasons. In its reverence for nature, Shinto is reminiscent of other indigenous religions. Many of Shinto's values also fit well with modern sensibilities. These values include low-key, non-judgmental moral views; inclusiveness; an emphasis on healing and living contentedly in this world; a positive view of the body; and the practice of esthetically pleasing rituals.

Shinto has gone wherever Japanese people have settled: Brazil, Peru, the United States (particularly Hawai`i, California, and the state of Washington). Some believers in Shinto see its potential as a universal religion of nature and would like to see it spread among non-Japanese people. But Shinto is not a missionary religion, nor does it generally have the institutional structure to do missionary work. It is possible, however, that some well-organized Shinto offshoot, such as Tenrikyo, will spread far beyond its country of origin.

It may be that traditional Shinto derives much of its vitality from the specific terrain, climate, and geographical isolation of Japan—from its mountains, waterfalls, thick forests, and myriad islands, all in continual change from the procession of the seasons. If so, then Shinto will remain restricted to that country. Nonetheless, it is easy at least to imagine the spread of traditional Shinto, especially to areas in which its special elements might take root in a welcoming, supportive community.

THE KOJIKI

According to the Kojiki, the primal parents, Izanami and Izanagi, together create the spirits of earth, wind, and fire. Unfortunately, Izanami, the first mother, is mortally burned while giving birth to the spirit of fire. The following description of the event shows the grief of Izanagi. After this passage, Izanagi resolves to find his wife's spirit in the underworld.

The process of procreation had . . . gone on happily, but at the birth of Kagutsuchi-no-Kami, the deity of fire, an unseen misfortune befell the divine mother, Izanami. During the course of her confinement, the goddess was so severely burned by the flaming child that she swooned away. . . . Her demise marks the intrusion of death into the world. Similarly the corruption of her body and the grief occasioned by her death were each the first of their kind.

By the death of his faithful spouse Izanagi was now quite alone in the world. In conjunction with her, and in accordance with the instructions of the Heavenly Gods, he had created and consolidated the Island Empire of Japan. In the fulfillment of their divine mission, he and his heavenly spouse had lived an ideal life of mutual love and cooperation. It is only natural, therefore, that her death should have dealt him a truly mortal blow.

He threw himself upon her prostrate form, crying: "Oh, my dearest wife, why art thou gone, to leave me thus alone? How could I ever exchange thee for even one child? Come back for the sake of the world. . . ." In a fit of uncontrollable grief, he stood sobbing at the head of the bier.[14]

TEST YOURSELF

1. The term *Shinto* comes from the Chinese *shen-dao* which means "_____."
   a. the way of the gods
   b. the path of the heroes
   c. the source of knowledge
   d. the walk through a torii

2. In the Shinto creation myth, primeval chaos became populated by several generations of deities, or spirits, called _____.
   a. *Meiji*
   b. *kami*
   c. *Ise*
   d. *kami-no-michi*

3. In Shinto mythology, the sun goddess Amaterasu sent her grandson to bring order to the islands of Japan. From her grandson came Jimmu, the first _____ of Japan.
   a. guru
   b. prophet
   c. emperor
   d. god

4. The entry of _____ into Japan forced Shinto to define itself. They preached that their deities were already being worshiped in Japan under Shinto names.
   a. Hindus
   b. Chinese
   c. Sikhs
   d. Buddhists

5. A turning point in Japanese history was the _____, named after the emperor who began a deliberate process of bringing Japan into the modern world in the late nineteenth century.
   a. Motoori Age
   b. Meiji Restoration
   c. Kamo Enlightenment
   d. Shinto Scholarly Revival

6. When _____ ended, the Occupation forces demanded that Japan become a secular country, and state Shinto was abolished.
   a. the Russo-Japanese War
   b. World War I
   c. World War II
   d. the Meiji Restoration

7. A visit to a shrine begins by passing under a *torii*, which looks like a ceremonial entrance or

gateway. After washing their hands and mouths with water, worshipers proceed to a courtyard building, called the _____, where the *kami* is worshiped.

a. *haiden*

b. *Nihongi*

c. *Kojiki*

d. *ema*

8. Shinto is known for its distinctive music, called _____, which uses instruments that make a flutelike, reedy sound that seems close yet far away, timeless yet fresh and new.

a. *kadomatsu*

b. *ozoni*

c. *gagaku*

d. *noh*

9. Daily Shinto worship occurs in the home, where a small shrine called the _____ is maintained.

a. *Kyoto*

b. *kamidana*

c. *misogi*

d. *ema*

10. One of the so-called New Religions, an offshoot of Shinto, is _____ ("heavenly reason teaching"), which preaches healing by faith. A central notion of this religion is that physical health comes from mental health.

a. Tenrikyo

b. Kameoka

c. Miroku

d. Eclecticism

11. Imagine you were to give a presentation in class on the most important aspects of Shinto. Explain how you would structure your discussion. Would you place greater emphasis on Shinto beliefs or on Shinto practices? Why?

12. Review the section on the Japanese New Religions Tenrikyo and Omoto. Why do you think these New Religions would be especially attractive to some people? Why do you think some people might find these New Religions to be unappealing?

RESOURCES

Books

Blacker, Carmen. *The Catalpa Bow*. New York: Japan Library, 1999. A literate study of Japanese shamanism.

Kasulis, Thomas P. *Shinto: The Way Home*. Honolulu: University of Hawai`i Press, 2004. An introduction to Shinto that emphasizes lived religious experience.

Llewellyn Evans, Ann. *Shinto Norito: A Book of Prayers*. Oxford: Trafford Publishers with Tenchi Press, 2004. A collection of ancient Japanese Shinto prayers.

Nelson, John. *Enduring Identities: The Guise of Shinto in Modern Japan*. Honolulu: University of Hawai`i Press, 2000. A study of Kamigamo Shrine in Kyoto—its buildings and grounds, its yearly rituals, and its people.

————. *A Year in the Life of a Shinto Shrine*. Seattle: University of Washington Press, 1996. A firsthand account of the rituals carried on during each of the four seasons at a shrine in Nagasaki.

Schnell, Scott. *The Rousing Drum*. Honolulu: University of Hawai`i Press, 1999. A description of the many phases of development and meaning of a raucous drum ritual in the town of Furukawa, Japan.

Smyers, Karen. *The Fox and the Jewel*. Honolulu: University of Hawai`i Press, 1998. An anthropological study of the worship of Inari, a Japanese deity often associated with the fox.

Yamakage, Motohisa. *The Essence of Shinto: Japan's Spiritual Heart*. Tokyo: Kodansha International, 2007. A book that makes the case for Shinto as a living religion, stressing its nondogmatic, nondoctrinal, and decentralized character.

Film/TV

The Essence of Being Japanese. (Films Media Group.) An examination of the kami and its influence in Japanese history and contemporary culture.

Kodo: The Drummers of Japan. (Director Jôji Ide; Image Entertainment.) A one-hour documentary of the world-famous Kodo drummers of Japan, as they perform at the Acropolis, Greece.

Princess Mononoke. (Director Hayao Miyazaki; Miramax.) Miyazaki's 1997 anime classic that chronicles the struggle between nature and civilization, drawing creative inspiration from Shinto belief in the kami of nature.

Spirits of the State: Japan's Yasukuni Shrine. (Films Media Group.) A look at Yasukuni Shrine, one of Shinto's most important and controversial shrines, dedicated to fallen soldiers.

Ugetsu Monogatari. (Director Kenji Mizoguchi; Criterion Collection.) A classic film in which two peasants follow different destinies, influenced by Shinto and Buddhist beliefs.

Woman in the Dunes. (Director Hiroshi Teshigahara; Image Entertainment.) A directorial masterpiece that examines the changing mental states of a biologist after he is imprisoned in a sand pit with a rural woman; notable for its depiction of the conflict between the modern Japanese person and traditional values tied intimately to nature.

Music/Audio

Festival of Japanese Music in Hawaii, vols. 1 and 2. (Smithsonian Folkways.) A recording of religious music accompanying Shinto festivals in Hawai`i.

The Japanese Koto. (Smithsonian Folkways.) A recording of traditional Japanese koto music.

Japanese Shinto Ritual Music. (Collectables Records.) A collection of traditional Shinto ritual music for invocations, dances, festivals, and purification ceremonies.

Religious Music of Asia. (Smithsonian Folkways.) A recording of Asian religious music, including Shinto processional and congregational chant.

Shakuhachi—The Japanese Flute. (Nonesuch.) A compilation of traditional Japanese flute music, some of which is closely associated with the Japanese imperial household.

Internet

Yasukuni Shrine: http://www.yasukuni.or.jp/english/. The official English language Web site of the controversial Shinto shrine in Tokyo dedicated to the kami of those who have died fighting in the service of the Japanese emperor.

The Internet Sacred Text Archive: http://www.sacred-texts.com/shi/index.htm. The "Shinto and Japanese Religions" page of the Internet Sacred Text Archive site, containing public-domain versions of Shinto texts, including the Kojiki and the Nihongi.

Kokugakuin University Encyclopedia of Shinto http://eos.kokugakuin.ac.jp/modules/xwords/. The most comprehensive Shinto reference database available online, including detailed information on kami, institutions, shrines, rites and festivals, belief and practice, and much more.

KEY TERMS

Amaterasu (*ah'-mah-te-rah'-soo*): "Shining in heaven"; goddess of the sun.

bushido (*boo'-shee-doh*): "Warrior knight way"; military devotion to a ruler, demanding loyalty, duty, and self-sacrifice; an ideal promoted by State Shinto.

gagaku (*gah'-ga-ku*): The stately ceremonial music of Shinto.

Ise (*ee'-say*): Location in southeastern Honshu of a major shrine to Amaterasu.

Izanagi (*ee-za-nah'-gee*): "Male who invites"; primordial male parent god.

Izanami (*ee-za-nah'-mee*): "Female who invites"; primordial female parent god.

jinja (*jin'-ja*): A Shinto shrine.

kami (*kah'-mee*): A spirit, god, or goddess of Shinto.

kamidana (*kah-mee-dah'-na*): A shelf or home altar for the veneration of kami.

kamikaze (*kah'-mee-kah'-zay*): "Spirit wind"; suicide fighter pilots of World War II.

Kojiki (*koh'-jee-kee*): The earliest chronicle of Japanese history.

misogi (*mee-soh'-gee*): A ritual of purification that involves standing under a waterfall.

Nihongi (*nee-hohn'-gee*): The second chronicle of Japanese history.

Noh: Dramas performed in mask and costume, associated with Shinto.

Omoto (*oh'-mo-to*): A New Religion, which stresses art and beauty.

samurai (*sah'-moo-rai*): Feudal soldier.

shimenawa (*shee-may-nah'-wa*)**:** Twisted rope, marking a sacred spot.

Tenrikyo (*ten'-ree-kyoh*): A New Religion devoted to human betterment.

torii (*to-ree'*): A gatelike structure that marks a Shinto sacred place.

Visit the Online Learning Center at www.mhhe.com/molloy5e for additional exercises and features, including "Religion beyond the Classroom" and "For Fuller Understanding."

Answers Key

Chapter 1

1. b., 2. c., 3. a., 4. b., 5. c., 6. d., 7. a., 8. d., 9. a., 10. c.

Chapter 2

1. c., 2. a., 3. d., 4. a., 5. b., 6. d., 7. b., 8. a., 9. c., 10. d.

Chapter 3

1. b., 2. c., 3. c., 4. b., 5. b., 6. d., 7. d., 8. c., 9. a., 10. b.

Chapter 4

1. b., 2. d., 3. c., 4. b., 5. a., 6. c., 7. a., 8. c., 9. d., 10. b.

Chapter 5

1. c., 2. d., 3. a., 4. a., 5. b., 6. d., 7. a., 8. c., 9. d., 10. c.

Chapter 6

1. b., 2. c., 3. a., 4. b., 5. b., 6. a., 7. a., 8. d., 9. b., 10. a.

Chapter 7

1. a., 2. b., 3. c., 4. d., 5. b., 6. c., 7. a., 8. c., 9. b., 10. a.

Notes

Chapter 1

1. *Webster's New World Dictionary,* 2d ed. (New York: William Collins, 1972). Other Latin roots are also possible.

2. *Cassell's New Latin Dictionary* (New York: Funk & Wagnalls, 1960).

3. Julian Huxley, *Religion Without Revelation* (New York: Mentor, c. 1957), p. 33.

4. Similar lists can be found, for example, in William Alston, "Religion," in *The Encyclopedia of Philosophy,* vol. 7 (New York: Macmillan, 1972), pp. 141–42; and Ninan Smart, *The Religious Experience,* 4th ed. (New York: Macmillan, 1991), pp. 6–10.

5. William James, *The Varieties of Religious Experience* (New York: Collier, 1961), p. 377.

6. Rudolf Otto, *The Idea of the Holy* (New York: Oxford University Press, 1963), p. 62.

7. Some have criticized Otto's notion of the *mysterium tremendum,* arguing that his theorizing was overinfluenced by Protestant Christianity, in which he was raised.

8. Carl Jung, *Memories, Dreams, Reflections* (London: Collins, 1972), p. 222.

9. "Between Mountain and Plain," *Time,* 20 October 1952, p. 33.

10. Alston, "Religion," 143–44.

11. Catholics touch the left shoulder first; Orthodox Christians touch the right shoulder first.

12. Kusan Sunim, *The Way of Korean Zen* (New York: Weatherhill, 1985), p. 168.

13. New Oxford Annotated Bible (New York: Oxford University Press, 1991).

14. Good News Bible (New York: American Bible Society, 1976). This version is a paraphrase.

15. For example, the Srimaladevisimhananda Sutra speaks of the enlightenment of a female lay ruler.

16. See Daniel Pals, *Eight Theories of Religion* (New York: Oxford University Press, 2007).

17. Martin Luther King Jr., *Strength to Love* (New York: Harper & Row, 1963), p. 3.

18. Carl Jung, *Memories, Dreams, Reflections.* (New York: Vintage, 1965), pp. 87–88.

Chapter 2

1. Nancy Parezo, "The Southwest," in *The Native Americans,* ed. Colin Taylor (New York: Salamander, 1991), p. 58.

2. Geoffrey Parrinder, *Religion in Africa* (New York: Praeger, 1969), pp. 18, 21.

3. Foreword to Peter Knudtson and David Suzuki, *Wisdom of the Elders* (Toronto: Stoddart, 1993), p. xxiv.

4. Gladys Reichard, *Navaho Religion* (Princeton: Bollingen, 1963), p. 286.

5. Frank Willet, *African Art* (London: Thames and Hudson, 1993), p. 35.

6. One entire room at the Gauguin Museum in Tahiti illustrates Gauguin's interest in discovering a "primary religion." It also shows the religious origin of much imagery in his paintings. A significant

collection of Gauguin's paintings and carvings can be seen at the Musée d'Orsay in Paris.

7. Florence Drake, *Civilization* (Norman: University of Oklahoma Press, 1936), quoted in John Collier, *Indians of the Americas* (New York: New American Library, 1947), p. 107.

8. Sword, Finger, One Star, and Tyon, recorded by J. R. Walker, in "Oglala Metaphysics," in *Teachings from the American Earth: Indian Religion and Philosophy*, ed. Dennis Tedlock and Barbara Tedlock (New York: Liveright, 1992), p. 206.

9. See Parrinder, *Religion in Africa*, pp. 47–59 for more detail.

10. Åke Hultkrantz, *Native Religions of North America* (San Francisco: Harper, 1987), p. 20, cited in *Ways of Being Religious*, ed. Gary Kessler (Mountain View, CA: Mayfield, 2000), p. 71.

11. Quoted in T. C. McLuhan, ed., *Touch the Earth* (New York: Promontory Press, 1971), p. 42.

12. McLuhan, *Touch the Earth*, p. 56.

13. Knudtson and Suzuki, *Wisdom of the Elders*, p. xxv.

14. Colin Turnbull, *The Forest People* (New York: Simon & Schuster, 1968), p. 14.

15. Knudtson and Suzuki, *Wisdom of the Elders*, p. 29.

16. Ibid., p. 27.

17. Parrinder, *Religion in Africa*, p. 43.

18. Ibid., p. 32.

19. Joseph Campbell, *The Power of Myth* (New York: Doubleday, 1988), p. 6.

20. Parrinder, *Religion in Africa*, pp. 80–81.

21. Collier, *Indians of the Americas*, p. 105.

22. Parrinder, *Religion in Africa*, p. 81.

23. For details, see William Sturtevant, "The Southeast," in Taylor, *The Native Americans*, pp. 17–21.

24. Sam Gill, *Native American Religions* (Belmont, CA: Wadsworth, 1982), p. 98.

25. Ibid.

26. Isabella Abbott, *La`au Hawai`i: Traditional Hawaiian Uses of Plants* (Honolulu: Bishop Museum Press, 1992), p. 37.

27. Ibid, p. 18. Four days were sacred to Ku, three to Kanaloa, two to Kane, and one day at the end of the month to Lono.

28. This is not unprecedented. In Samoa, universal claims were made for the god Tangaroa, possibly as early as 800 C.E. See John Charlot, *Chanting the Universe* (Hong Kong: Emphasis, 1983), p. 144.

29. John Charlot remarks that the first public Hawaiian temple service since 1819 was carried out by Samuel H. Lono on October 11, 1980. See ibid, p. 148.

30. From Florence Drake, *Civilization*, quoted in Collier, *Indians of the Americas*, p. 107.

31. See John Mbiti, *Introduction to African Religion* (London: Heinemann, 1986), pp. 143–44.

32. Joan Halifax, *Shaman: The Wounded Healer* (London: Thames and Hudson, 1994), p. 5.

33. Quoted in Knudtson and Suzuki, *Wisdom of the Elders*, p. 70.

34. Isaac Tens, recorded by Marius Barbeau, in *Medicine Men of the North Pacific Coast*, Bulletin 152 (Ottawa: National Museum of Man of the National Museum of Canada, 1958), found in Tedlock and Tedlock, *Teachings from the American Earth*, pp. 3–4.

35. Ibid.

36. For a detailed study of the religious use of peyote by Native Americans, see Omer C. Stewart, *Peyote Religion: A History* (Norman: University of Oklahoma Press, 1987).

37. John Fire/Lame Deer and Richard Erdoes, *Lame Deer: Seeker of Visions* (New York: Simon and Schuster, 1972), p. 220.

38. Mbiti, *Introduction to African Religion*, p. 165.

39. Ibid., p. 166.

40. These are the commonly used names; nomenclature is in a process of change for some Northwest tribes.

41. Pat Kramer, *Totem Poles* (Vancouver: Altitude, 1995), pp. 48–49.

42. Richard W. Hill Sr., "The Symbolism of Feathers," in *Creation's Journey* (Washington, DC: Smithsonian Institution Press, 1994), p. 88.

43. John C. Neihardt, *Black Elk Speaks* (New York: Pocket Books, 1972), pp. 18–19.

Note: The box on the Pueblo (in Chapter 2) has drawn on many sources, among which I especially recommend: Alph Secakuku, *Following the Sun and Moon: Hopi Kachina Tradition* (Flagstaff: Northland, 1995); Frank Waters, *Book of the Hopi* (New York: Penguin, 1977); Ronald McCoy, *Summoning the Gods* (Flagstaff: Museum of Northern Arizona, 1992); Tom Bahti, *Southwestern Indian Ceremonials* (Las Vegas, NV: KC Publications, 1992); John Collier and Ira Moskowitz, *Rites and Ceremonies of the Indians of the Southwest*, rev. ed. (New York: Barnes & Noble, 1993).

Chapter 3

1. Arthur Basham, *The Wonder That Was India* (New York: Grove, 1959), p. 16. Chapter 2 of Basham's book contains a detailed description of the Harappa culture.

2. Ibid., p. 23.

3. Also spelled *Rg Veda*. For representative prayers, see William T. deBary, ed., *Sources of Indian Tradition*, vol. 1 (New York: Columbia University Press, 1958), pp. 7–16.

4. Rig Veda 10:129, quoted in Basham, *The Wonder That Was India*, p. 16.

5. The same tendency toward philosophy existed in Greece at the time and a few centuries later in the Roman Empire.

6. The philosopher Shankara offered another interpretation—"to wear away completely."

7. These six notions are not fixed concepts in the Upanishads. They are more like centers around which speculation revolves, and there may be differences in how they are described, even within the same Upanishad. The notion of Brahman, for example, sometimes varies from that of a divine reality quite beyond the world to that of a spiritual reality that exists within the world.

8. Chandogya Upanishad 6:13, in *The Upanishads*, trans. Juan Mascaró (New York: Penguin, 1979), p. 118.

9. Shvetasvatara Upanishad, end of part 3, *The Upanishads*, pp. 90–91; emphasis added.

10. Ibid., part 4, p. 91.

11. Ibid.

12. See, for example, ibid., p. 92.

13. Ibid.

14. Brihadaranyaka Upanishad 2:4, *The Upanishads*, p. 132.

15. *Bhagavad-Gita: The Song of God*, trans. Swami Prabhavananda and Christopher Isherwood (New York: Mentor, 1972), chap. 5, p. 57.

16. Ibid., chap. 1, p. 34.

17. Ibid., chap. 18, p. 127.

18. Ibid., chap. 2, p. 38.

19. Rig Veda 10:90, as quoted in deBary, *Sources of Indian Tradition*, vol. 1, p. 14.

20. See chapter 2 of the Bhagavad Gita.

21. Sometimes the term *caste* is reserved for what I call here subcastes—the hundreds of occupation-based social divisions (*jati*).

22. I follow the common practice of using the word *brahmin* (priest)—rather than the Sanskrit term *brahman*—to avoid confusion with the term *Brahman* (spiritual essence of the world) with a capital *B*.

23. See, for example, the description of Gandhi's "fast unto death" for untouchables in Louis Fischer, *Gandhi* (New York: New American Library, 1954), pp. 116–19.

24. The six orthodox schools of Hindu philosophy all developed as systems of personal liberation but disagreed about the views and methods that would bring liberation. The six schools are Nyaya, Vaisheshika, Sankhya, Yoga, Mimamsa, and Vedanta. (The terms *Yoga* and *Vedanta*, when used to denote schools of philosophy, have a precise and different meaning than when used more generally.) Nyaya ("analysis") valued the insight that comes from clarity, reason, and logic. Vaisheshika ("individual characteristics") taught what it considered to be the correct way of understanding reality—seeing reality as essentially being composed of atoms. Sankhya ("count") was originally an atheistic philosophy that considered the universe to be made of two essential principles—soul and matter. Yoga ("union," "spiritual discipline") emphasized meditation and physical disciplines. Mimamsa ("investigation") defended the authority of the Vedas as a guide to salvation. Vedanta developed several subschools but tended to see a unifying principle—Brahman—at work behind the changing phenomena of everyday life; the individual can find salvation by attaining union with this principle.

25. Shankara's conception of Brahman is debated. For him, Brahman may have been a positive spiritual reality, or it may have been closer to the notion of emptiness found in Buddhism.

26. Shankara (attrib.), *Shankara's Crest-Jewel of Discrimination* (New York: Mentor, 1970), p. 72.

27. *Bhagavad-Gita*, chap. 2, p. 40.

28. Basham, *The Wonder That Was India*, chap. 18, p. 128.

29. Although these sutras are attributed to an ancient grammarian named Patanjali, who lived before the common era, they may have been written later, from about 200 C.E.

30. Basham, *The Wonder That Was India*, p. 326.

31. Heinrich Zimmer, *Myths and Symbols in Indian Art and Civilization* (Princeton: Princeton University Press, 1972), p. 153.

32. Basavaraja, quoted in *Sources of Indian Tradition*, vol. 1, p. 352. Basavaraja was a twelfth-century Indian government official who founded a religious order devoted to Shiva.

33. *The Gospel of Ramakrishna*, quoted in deBary, *Sources of Indian Tradition*, vol. 2, p. 86.

34. *The Upanishads*, trans. Swami Prabhavananda and Frederick Manchester (New York: Mentor, 1970), pp. 70–71.

35. The term *darshan* also extends to viewing images of deities in order to experience the divine presence that they mediate.

36. See Ainslie T. Embree, ed., *The Hindu Tradition* (New York: Vintage, 1972), p. 279.

37. Fischer, *Gandhi*, p. 11.

38. Quoted in Fischer, *Gandhi*, p. 18.

39. Gandhi compromised his position on nonviolence somewhat during World War I, when he urged Indians to join the war effort on the side of the British. Later, he said that this position had been a mistake.

40. *Bhagavad Gita*, chap. 2, lines 13–17, pp. 10–11.

Chapter 4

1. Arthur Basham put it nicely: "Much doubt now exists as to the real doctrines of the historical Buddha, as distinct from those of Buddhism." *The Wonder That Was India* (New York: Grove, 1959), p. 256.

2. The tree may have been a form of banyan, which today is called the *Ficus religiosa* ("religious fig") because of its supposed connection with the Buddha.

3. As quoted in William T. deBary, ed., *Sources of Indian Tradition* (New York: Columbia University Press, 1958), vol. 1, p. 110. The same word that is usually translated as "lamp" may also be translated as "island." The meaning remains that the disciple must make judgments that are independent of those of the ordinary world.

4. Some scholars think that the Reclining Buddha images may also depict the Buddha sleeping, sometimes with his cousin Ananda looking on protectively. It is often explained that those statues in which the Buddha's feet are joined represent him at the moment of death, while those that show his feet separated and relaxed represent the Buddha at rest.

5. Sometimes the term *Sangha* is used more widely to include devout laypersons.

6. See David Kalupahana, *Buddhist Philosophy: A Historical Analysis* (Honolulu: University Press of Hawaii, 1976), pp. 38–41.

7. *Buddhist Suttas*, trans. T. W. Rhys Davids (New York: Dover, 1969), p. 148.

8. *The Dhammapada: The Sayings of the Buddha*, trans. Thomas Byrom (New York: Vintage, 1976), chap. 15, p. 76.

9. From the *Sammanaphala Suttanta*, in *The Teachings of the Compassionate Buddha*, ed. E. A. Burtt (New York: New American Library, 1955), p. 104.

10. Sometimes the order is reversed, and the sutra is designated as the first basket, with the vinaya listed second.

11. The commonly accepted view about the introduction of form into Buddhist imagery has been questioned. See Stanley Abe, "Inside the Wonder House: Buddhist Art and the West, " in *Curators of the Buddha: The Study of Buddhism under Colonialism*, ed. Donald S. Lopez Jr. (Chicago: University of Chicago Press, 1995), pp. 63–106.

12. Hirakawa Akira, *A History of Indian Buddhism* (Honolulu: University of Hawaii Press, 1990), p. 258.

13. For details about the origins of Mahayana, see John Koller, *The Indian Way* (New York: Macmillan, 1983), p. 163.

14. For information about Buddhist schools of philosophy, see John Koller, "The Nature of Reality," in *Oriental Philosophies* (New York: Scribner's, 1970), pp. 146–79.

15. Kenneth Ch'en, *Buddhism in China* (Princeton, NJ: Princeton University Press, 1972), p. 385.

16. For more information see Richard Robinson and Willard Johnson, *The Buddhist Religion*, 4th ed. (Belmont, CA: Wadsworth, 1997), pp. 181ff.

17. Robert Buswell, *Tracing Back the Radiance: Chinul's Korean Way of Zen* (Honolulu: University of Hawaii Press, 1991), p. 5. See the introduction for a description of Korea's early Buddhist contacts with China and central Asia.

18. For a traveler's description of the monastery complex in the seventeenth century, see Li Chi, *The Travel Diaries of Hsü Hsia-k'o* (Hong Kong: The Chinese University of Hong Kong, 1974), pp. 29–42.

19. The meditation guidebook *Shikantaza: An Introduction to Zazen* (Kyoto: Kyoto Zen Center, 1990) contains instructions for zazen and a good selection of passages by Zen masters on the practice and effects of zazen.

20. See the story of Rinzai, who received a beating from his master Obaku as a koan-like response to his simple-minded questioning, in D. T. Suzuki, *Studies in Zen* (New York: Delta, 1955), pp. 68–70. Suzuki gives many examples of koan, with commentary. The actual use of the koan in Japanese monasteries over the last three centuries has become more formalized. Instead of working through a koan, a person in training (who hopes to take over his father's temple) now often refers to books for the appropriate answers.

21. For connections between Christianity and the tea ceremony, see Heinrich Dumoulin, *A History of Zen Buddhism* (Boston: Beacon, 1963), pp. 214–24.

22. *The Dhammapada*, chap. 1, pp. 3–4.

Chapter 5

1. Mahapurana 4:16; cited in William T. deBary, ed., *Sources of Indian Tradition,* vol. 1. (New York: Columbia University Press, 1958), p. 76.
2. Acaranga Sutra 1.6, 5, cited in deBary, *Sources of Indian Tradition,* vol. 1, p. 65.
3. See John Koller, *The Indian Way* (New York: Macmillan, 1982), pp. 114–15.
4. Selection from the Mul Mantra, cited in M. A. Macauliffe, *The Sikh Religion,* vol. 1 (Oxford: Oxford University Press, 1901), p. 195.
5. From Asa Ki Var, Mahala I. Cited in Macauliffe, *The Sikh Religion,* vol. 1, p. 221.
6. http://www.allaboutsikhs.com/sikhism-articles/quotations-from-adi-granth-about-women.html.

Chapter 6

1. See Livia Kohn, *God of the Dao* (University of Michigan at Ann Arbor: Center for Chinese Studies, 1998), p. 9, n. 6.
2. *Lao Tzu: Tao Te Ching,* trans. Robert Henricks (New York: Ballantine, 1989), p. 72.
3. *Tao Te Ching,* trans. Gia-fu Feng and Jane English (New York: Random House, 1972), chap. 8. This translation is used unless stated otherwise.
4. *The Wisdom of Laotse,* trans. Lin Yutang (New York: Modern Library, 1948), p. 76.
5. *Chuang Tzu: Basic Writings,* trans. Burton Watson (New York: Columbia University Press, 1964), p. 36 (sec. 2).
6. Ibid, p. 113 (sec. 18).
7. Ibid.
8. Cited in *The Way and Its Power,* trans. Arthur Waley (New York: Grove, 1958), p. 181.
9. Wing-Tsit Chan, "Man and Nature in the Chinese Garden" in *Chinese Houses and Gardens,* ed. Henry Inn and Shao Chang Lee (Honolulu: Fong Inn's Limited, 1940), pp. 35–36.
10. Ibid., p. 33.
11. *The Doctrine of the Mean* 20:18; in *Confucius: Confucian Analects, The Great Learning, and The Doctrine of the Mean,* trans. James Legge (New York: Dover, 1971), p. 413. (Legge's translation of the Four Books—the major Confucian books, which include the sayings of Confucius and Mencius—is used unless otherwise noted.) In the original translation, the word *right* is italicized and the word *way* is not. I have changed this to make my point clearer.

12. Ibid., 12:4.
13. *Analects* 5:25, 4.
14. Ibid., 2:4, 1–6.
15. R. D. Baird and Alfred Bloom, *Indian and Far Eastern Religious Traditions* (New York: Harper & Row, 1972), p. 169.
16. George Kates, *The Years That Were Fat* (Cambridge, MA: MIT Press, 1976), pp. 28–29.
17. See *The Doctrine of the Mean* 22:8 for a different order.
18. *Analects* 12:1, 1.
19. See *Analects* 12:1, 2; and *The Doctrine of the Mean* 13:3.
20. *The Doctrine of the Mean* 20:18; adapted.
21. *Analects* 4:16; trans. Arthur Waley (New York: Vintage, c. 1938), p. 105.
22. Ibid. 4:24.
23. *The Great Learning,* "Text of Confucius" verse 6.
24. *The Doctrine of the Mean* 1:1–2; adapted.
25. Ibid. 1:5.
26. *Mencius* 4:2, 12; trans. James Legge (New York: Dover, 1970); adapted.
27. See chapters 18–20 of the *Daodejing.*
28. See chapter 80 of the *Daodejing.*
29. *Mencius* 4:1, 9.2.
30. Ibid., 6:1.6.7.
31. Given in an introductory chapter of ibid., p. 81.
32. Cited in William T. deBary, ed., *Sources of Chinese Tradition,* vol. 1 (New York: Columbia University Press, 1960), pp. 45–46.
33. Ibid., vol. 1, p. 436.
34. *The Essential Confucius,* trans. Thomas Cleary (New York: Harper Collins, 1993), *passim.*

Chapter 7

1. This myth begins the Kojiki ("chronicle of ancient events"); see *Translation of Ko-ji-ki,* trans. Basil Hall Chamberlain, 2d ed. (Kobe: J. L. Thompson, 1932), pp. 17–23. The etymology of *kami* is debated.
2. Ibid., pp. 21–22. The same story, with many variants, appears at the beginning of another ancient work, the Nihongi.
3. Ibid., pp. 50–51.
4. Also called Shrine Shinto. For details, see H. Byron Earhart, *Religions of Japan* (New York: Harper & Row, 1984), pp. 43–45 and 93–100.
5. Sometimes a distinction is made between the spirits of nature and the spirits of the deceased. It is debated whether a belief in one type of spirit was the

origin of a belief in the other. See, for example, Carmen Blacker, *The Catalpa Bow* (London: Allen & Unwin, 1975), pp. 45–46.

6. For a translation, see *Nihongi*, trans. W. G. Aston (London: Allen & Unwin, 1956).

7. Such imagery was apparently much more common before Western influence—and its sense of decorum—entered Japan in the nineteenth century.

8. The sense that death is polluting and dangerous explains the regular rebuilding of some Shinto shrines and the destruction of the clothing and personal effects of a deceased person.

9. The torii is used as a gateway, but it can be placed anywhere to indicate the presence of kami.

10. See H. Byron Earhart, *Japanese Religion: Unity and Diversity*, 2d ed. (Encino, CA: Dickenson, 1974), p. 21.

11. Later, on a return journey to the temple, I discovered a Shinto shrine on a path just above the temple—another sign of the intermingling of Shinto and Buddhism. Dedicated to fertility and childbirth, Jishu Jinja is a place for worship of the protective kami that guards the temple.

12. Keiichi Nakayama, *Tenrikyo Kyoten Kowa* (Tenri: Tenrikyo, 1951), p. 3; cited in Harry Thomsen, *The New Religions of Japan* (Rutland, VT: Tuttle, 1963), p. 34.

13. A translation of Miki's poetic work, *Mikagura Uta*, can be found in Thomsen, *The New Religions of Japan*, pp. 41–48.

14. Genji Shibukawa, *Tales from the Kojiki*, trans. Yatchiro Isobe. http://www.wsu.edu:8080/~wldciv/world_civ_reader/world_civ_reader_1/kojiki.html.

Chapter 8

1. This theory is called the Documentary Hypothesis. For details, see Stephen Harris, *Understanding the Bible*, 3d ed. (London: Mayfield, 1992), pp. 53–59.

2. The Greek translation of the Hebrew Bible is commonly called the Septuagint. For details about the Septuagint translation, see Henry Jackson Flanders, Robert Wilson Crapps, and David Anthony Smith, *People of the Covenant*, 4th ed. (New York: Oxford University Press, 1996), p. 21.

3. Translation from *Tanakh—The Holy Scriptures* (Philadelphia: The Jewish Publication Society, 1985).

4. Emphasis added.

5. The New Oxford Annotated Bible (New York: Oxford University Press, 1991).

6. The translation by the Jewish Publication Society (1985) simply gives the Hebrew phrase "Ehyeh-

Asher-Ehyeh"; it adds a footnote, saying that the exact meaning of the Hebrew is uncertain but that a common translation is "I am who I am" (p. 88).

7. The words *Yahweh* and *Adonai* (also spelled *Adonay*) were ultimately blended to create the name *Jehovah*, used in English Bibles.

8. It is possible that the Book of Deuteronomy constitutes the first volume of a history about the Hebrews' entry into Canaan, which is continued in the Books of Joshua and Judges.

9. Exodus 20:2–17, from *Tanakh—the Holy Scriptures*.

10. The most famous is at Dura-Europos, in southern Syria.

11. Although today we might recoil at the thought of animal sacrifice, we must realize that it was common throughout the world of the time, even in India and China. It fulfilled several functions. Worshipers often thought the ritual of sharing a sacred meal would unite them with their deity. Punishment that might have fallen on human beings was thought to be transferred to the sacrificial animal. It was also a sign that the deity was in charge of all life.

12. The New Oxford Annotated Bible.

13. There are two long passages in Aramaic: Daniel 2:4–7:28 and Ezra 4:8–6:18. Short Aramaic passages also appear in Genesis (31:47) and Jeremiah (10:11).

14. Many other religious books were popular but were not finally accepted as canonical by Jews in Israel. A few additional books, however, were accepted as canonical by Jews living in Egypt, such as Sirach, the Wisdom of Solomon, and Maccabees. (Later, they were also accepted as canonical by Catholic and Eastern Orthodox Christians.)

15. The name *Sadducee* may derive from the name *Zadok* (or *Sadoc*), a priest at the time of King David.

16. The name *Pharisee* may derive from a Hebrew word meaning "separate"—referring to a ritual purity associated with the careful practice of religious laws.

17. It is possible that the dualistic worldview of the Essenes was influenced by the Persian religion of Zoroastrianism and that their semimonastic lifestyle was influenced by monastic ideals that had come from India to Egypt.

18. Union Prayerbook (New York, 1959), part 1, pp. 166–67.

19. A passage from the *Zohar*, quoted in *The Wisdom of the Kabbalah*, ed. Dagobert Runes (New York: Citadel, 1967), p. 172.

20. Quoted in Gershom Scholem, *On the Kabbalah and Its Symbolism* (New York: Schocken, 1969), p. 103.

21. The beginning of the movie *Yentl* illustrates the value put on the mystical interpretation of the Book of Genesis.

22. Martin Buber, the great Jewish writer, collected and published two volumes of Hasidic sayings. Many tales of the Baal Shem Tov appear in the first volume, *Tales of the Hasidim: Early Masters* (orig. pub. 1947; New York: Schocken, 1973).

23. Louis Newman, *Hasidic Anthology* (New York: Schocken, 1975), p. 148.

24. Ibid., p. 149.

25. Bella Chagall, *Burning Lights* (New York: Schocken, 1972). This book contains thirty-six drawings by Marc Chagall.

26. Anne Frank, *The Diary of a Young Girl* (New York: Pocket Books, 1959), p. 222.

27. Ibid., pp. 192–93.

28. Ibid., p. 233.

29. The origin of the Sabbath is uncertain. It may have been inspired by Babylonian culture, or perhaps it was unique to the Hebrews. It is logical, however, to divide a lunar month into four seven-day periods.

30. The literal truth of this story is doubtful. We might note that the names of Esther and Mordecai are suspiciously close to the names of the Babylonian divinities Ishtar and Marduk. As such, the festival may derive from a Babylonian fertility festival.

31. The fact that Passover occurs in the first month of the Jewish lunar calendar may be an indication that it was once the Jewish New Year.

32. It is also possible that pigs and shellfish were considered "imperfect" animals. Perfect land animals (such as sheep and goats) chewed a cud and had divided hooves; perfect sea animals had scales. All others were considered "less perfect."

33. Leo Trepp, *Judaism: Development and Life* (Belmont, CA: Dickenson Publishing, 1966), p. 75.

34. Ibid.

35. http://www.zeek.net/708environment/.

36. Chagall, Burning Lights, pp. 48–49.

Chapter 9

1. Jerusalem Bible (Garden City, NY: Doubleday, 1966).

2. American Bible Society translation, in *Good News Bible* (Nashville: Nelson, 1986).

3. Jerusalem Bible translation.

4. American Bible Society translation.

5. Jerusalem Bible translation.

6. See James Charlesworth, *Jesus and the Dead Sea Scrolls* (New York: Doubleday, 1992).

7. King James Version (Cambridge: Cambridge University Press, n.d.).

8. Acts 9:4, Revised Standard Version (RSV) (New York: New American Library, 1974).

9. RSV translation.

10. Jerusalem Bible translation.

11. RSV translation.

12. For more information on Christian Gnosticism, see Elaine Pagels's *The Gnostic Gospels* (New York: Random House, 1979) and *Adam, Eve, and the Serpent* (New York: Vintage, 1989).

13. Jerusalem Bible translation.

14. Earlier lists, such as the Muratorian Canon, differ from the present-day canonical list of New Testament books. The list, as we now have it, is mentioned in the *Festal Letter* of Athanasius of Alexandria, circulated in 367 C.E., and is the same list of books translated by Jerome into Latin. For further details, see Dennis Duling and Norman Perrin, *The New Testament* 3d ed. (New York: Harcourt Brace, 1994), p. 134.

15. Jerusalem Bible translation.

16. *The Confessions of St. Augustine*, trans. Rex Warner (New York: New American Library, 1963), pp. 182–83.

17. Jerusalem Bible translation.

18. See David Knowles, *Christian Monasticism* (New York: McGraw-Hill, 1972), which emphasizes the development of Benedictine monasticism.

19. *St. Benedict's Rule for Monasteries* (Collegeville, MN: Liturgical Press, 1948), chap. 1, pp. 2–3.

20. See Christopher Brooke, *Monasteries of the World* (New York: Crescent, 1982), for excellent maps, diagrams, and photographs.

21. Nikos Kazantzakis, author of *Zorba the Greek* and *Saint Francis*, lived for a time on Mount Athos and considered becoming a monk.

22. *The Disciplinary Decrees of the General Councils*, trans. H. J. Schroeder (St. Louis: B. Herder, 1937), p. 19; quoted in Colman Barry, ed., *Readings in Church History*, vol. 1 (Westminster, MD: Newman Press, 1960), p. 85.

23. Nicholas Gage, *Eleni* (New York: Ballantine Books, 1983), pp. 122–23.

24. For the mysticism of Gregory of Nyssa, see *From Glory to Glory: Texts from Gregory of Nyssa's Mystical Writings* (New York: Scribners, 1961), particularly the introduction by Jean Daniélou. For Augustine's

mysticism, see *The Essential Augustine* (New York: Mentor, 1964), pp. 127 and 148.

25. Origen, prologue to the "Commentary on the Song of Songs," in *Origen*, trans. Rowan Greer (New York: Paulist Press, 1979), p. 217.

26. From Sermon 6, in *Meister Eckhart*, trans. Raymond Blakney (New York: Harper, 1941), p. 131.

27. Julian of Norwich, *Revelations of Divine Love*, trans. Clifton Wolters (New York: Penguin, 1982), Chap. 59, p. 167.

28. Pamphlet, *Prayer of Saint Francis* (Columbus, OH: Christopher House, 1996), p. 4, adapted.

29. See Erik Erikson, *Young Man Luther: A Study in Psychoanalysis and History* (New York: Norton, 1962).

30. King James Version.

31. A similar development occurred in the Buddhist Pure Land movement. In Japan, Shinran concluded that only trust in Amida Buddha's grace was enough for the devotee.

32. J. Raboteau, "Afro-American Religions," in *World Religions* (New York: Simon and Schuster Macmillan, 1998), p. 18.

33. Bennetta Jules–Rosette, "African Religions," ibid., pp. 7–10.

34. The term *Mass* comes from the dismissal at the conclusion of this ceremony, when the priest said in Latin, *Ite missa est* ("Go, it is the dismissal").

35. Albert Schweitzer's classic study *J. S. Bach* (orig. pub. 1905 Neptune, NJ: Paganiniana, 1980) emphasizes the religious character of all of Bach's work.

36. Thomas Keating, interview with Kate Olson, in *Trinity News*, vol. 42 (1995), 4, pp. 8–11, cited at www.thecentering.org/therapy.html.

37. Ibid.

38. New International Version (Grand Rapids, MI: Zondervan, 1984).

Chapter 10

1. Also spelled *Mohammed*, although this spelling is now considered less accurate than *Muhammad*. We might also note that there is some disagreement about the details of Muhammad's life, particularly those regarding his early years.

2. John Esposito, *Islam: The Straight Path*, 3d ed. (New York: Oxford University Press, 1998), p. 3.

3. Also spelled *Kaaba, Ka'bah,* and *Kaba*.

4. For further details see Thomas Lippman, *Understanding Islam* (New York: New American Library, 1982), pp. 34–38.

5. Also commonly spelled *Khadija*.

6. It is possible that Khadijah was younger than this, given the fact that she gave birth to at least six children.

7. 96:1–19 passim; from *The Koran*, trans. N. J. Dawood (London: Penguin, 1993), p. 429. This translation is used unless otherwise noted.

8. Lippman, *Understanding Islam*, p. 44. Guides in Jerusalem sometimes point to marks in stone, which they say are footprints left by Muhammad. The account of Muhammad's journey may have influenced Dante's vision of paradise in the *Divine Comedy*.

9. 49:10.

10. In Islamic belief, punishment in hell is not necessarily eternal for all.

11. 2:163; from *Holy Qur'an*, trans. M. H. Shakir (Milton Keynes, England: Mihrab Publishers, 1986).

12. In Islam, a messenger is a prophet with a special call from God.

13. Some Shiite Muslims combine these into three periods of prayer.

14. Another translation is, "Allah is greater (than anything else)."

15. 2:144.

16. Although only Muslims may make the pilgrimage to Mecca, many films document the practice. See, for example, the classic film *Mecca: The Forbidden City*, by Iranfilms.

17. 2:158 (Shakir translation).

18. Muslims were originally permitted to drink wine, but later revelations to Muhammad prohibited it. There is, however, some variation in the keeping of this regulation. Countries that have experienced strong European influence (such as several in northern Africa—Morocco, Algeria, Tunisia) often produce wine, and countries that depend heavily on tourism usually allow the serving of alcohol in tourist hotels.

19. Female circumcision is sometimes said to be based on a hadith (a remembrance of Muhammad's early followers); see Annemarie Schimmel, *Islam: An Introduction* (Albany: State University of New York Press, 1992), p. 55.

20. An exception is made in some cases, such as the tombs of rulers and publicly recognized holy persons.

21. 4:34.

22. Although the early versions did not contain vowels or diacritical marks, later versions do; consequently, some differences exist between versions.

23. Esposito, *Islam: The Straight Path*, p. 6.

24. There is some disagreement over this matter among Sunni and Shiite Muslims.

25. 1:1–5.

26. Also called the Battle of Poitiers.

27. "The Nature of Islam in South-East Asia," *The Economist*, May 31, 2003, p. 37.

28. 2:115.

29. 50:16. See also John Williams, ed., *Islam* (New York: Washington Square, 1963), pp. 122–58.

30. 3:29 (Shakir translation). See A. J. Arberry, *Sufism* (New York: Harper, 1970), pp. 17–22.

31. Ibid., p. 28.

32. Ibid., p. 228.

33. Afkham Darbandi and Dick Davis, introduction to *The Conference of the Birds,* by Farid Ud-Din Attar (Hammondsworth, England: Penguin, 1984), p. 10.

34. Quoted in F. C. Happold, *Mysticism* (Baltimore: Penguin, 1963), p. 229.

35. Esposito, *Islam: The Straight Path,* pp. 105–106.

36. For representative samples of the writings of theologians, see the chapter "Kalam" in Williams, *Islam,* pp. 159–96.

37. Williams, *Islam,* pp. 138–41. Williams claims that al-Arabi influenced the Spanish mystics and poets John of the Cross and Ramón Lull and possibly Benedict de Spinoza, a Dutch philosopher.

38. Islamic influence on Christian architecture is almost certainly demonstrated by the use of these alternating lines of color, such as in the cathedrals of Siena, Pisa, and Florence.

39. See 2:25, 3:136, and 10:9.

40. See 2:25.

41. http://news.bbc.co.uk/2/hi/middle_east/1571144.stm.

42. Jon Basil Utley, http://www.mises.org/

43. fullstory.asp?control = 1313. I am grateful to this article for several points in this paragraph.

44. Lawrence Mamiya, "Malcolm X" in *World Religions* (New York: Simon and Schuster Macmillan, 1998), p. 19.

45. 6:95–99.

Chapter 11

1. See Leo Martello, *Witchcraft: The Old Religion* (New York: Citadel Press, 1991), chap. 5.

2. For further information, see Philip Shallcrass, "Druidry Today," in *Paganism Today* (London: Thorsons/HarperCollins, 1995), pp. 65–80.

3. See Raúl Canizares, *Cuban Santería* (Rochester, VT: Destiny Books), pp. 38–48.

4. For greater detail, see Migene González-Wippler, *Santería: The Religion* (St. Paul, MN: Llewellyn Publications, 1999), chap. 5.

5. *Theosophy* (Hudson, NY: Anthroposophic Press, 1989), p. 164.

6. "Rudolf Steiner," in *The Encyclopedia of Philosophy,* vol. 8 (New York: Macmillan, 1967), pp. 13–14.

7. *The Church of Scientology: An Introduction to Church Services* (n.p.: L. Ron Hubbard Library, 1999), p. 32.

8. King James Version.

9. Quoted in Leonard Barrett Sr., *The Rastafarians* (Boston: Beacon, 1997), p. 123.

10. *The Baha'is* (Oakham, UK: Baha'i Publishing Trust of the United Kingdom, 1994), p. 54.

11. For good sample illustrations and interpretations, see Leo Martello, *Reading the Tarot* (New York: Avery Publishing, 1990).

12. *The Gardnerian Book of Shadows,* by Gerald Gardner, at http://www.sacred-texts.com/pag/gbos/gbos36.htm.

Chapter 12

1. Robert Ellwood, *The History and Future of Faith* (New York: Crossroad, 1988), p. 137.

2. Ibid., p. 141.

3. "Which Humanism for the Third Millennium?" *Aizen* 16 (July–August 1997): 3.

4. Government in the United States, however, is not fully secular. We might note, for example, the use of prayer and chaplains in legislative houses, the mention of God in the Declaration of Independence, the use of the word *God* in court and on currency, and tax benefits given to churches and church property. See Ronald Thiemann, *Religion in Public Life* (Washington: Georgetown University Press, 1996), in which the author argues against the complete separation of church and state.

5. *Honolulu Advertiser,* 26 July 1997, sec. B, p. 3, adapted.

6. *Dhammapada,* chap. 10. *Dhammapada,* trans. Thomas Byrom (New York: Vintage, 1976), p. 49. The translation presents the material divided into stanzas.

7. *Tao Te Ching,* trans. Gia-Fu and Jane English (New York: Random House, 1972), chap. 30.

8. Ibid., chap. 31.

9. All biblical quotations here are taken from the New English Bible.

10. Dawood translation is used for the passages from the Qur'an. *The Koran* (London: Penguin, 1993).

11. For a good discussion of secularism in the modern world and its relation to religion, see Ellwood, *The History and Future of Faith,* chap. 5, pp. 96–117. Ellwood sees religions surviving in the future within a secular milieu but existing rather separately from it.

12. "Speech of the Very Rev. James Parks Morton at the Esperanto Conference, 1996, July 22, Prague," *Aizen* 16 (July–August 1997): 6.

13. See Maurice Tuchman, ed., *The Spiritual in Art: Abstract Painting 1890–1985* (New York: Abbeville Press, 1986) for many examples.

14. Philippe Gross and S. I. Shapiro, "Characteristics of the Taoist Sage in the *Chuang-tzu* and the Creative Photographer," *Journal of Transpersonal Psychology* 28:2 (1996), p. 181.

15. *Modern Photography,* October, 1988, p. 94; quoted in ibid., p. 177.

16. http://atheism.about.com/od/einsteingodreligion/tp/EinsteinMysteryReligion.htm.

Credits

Photo Credits

Frontmatter   p. xviii, Golden Temple: © Gaurav Sharma; p. xix, Native American elders drumming during Corn Dance ceremony in Santa Clara Pueblo, NM: © VisonsofAmerica/Jo Sohm/The Image Bank/Getty Images; p. xix, Man sitting on a rock overlooking fjord: © Raw File/Masterfile Chapter 1   p. 2, © Yoshinori Watabe/amana images/Getty Images;   p. 5, Digital Image © The Museum of Modern Art/Licensed by Scala/Art Resource, NY;   pp. 6, 8, 9, © Thomas Hilgers;   p. 10, © Royalty-Free/Corbis;   pp. 11, 16, 17, © Thomas Hilgers;   p. 18, © AP/Wide World Photos;   p. 20, © Kenneth Garrett/National Geographic/Getty Images;   p. 25, 29, © Thomas Hilgers Chapter 2   p. 34, © G. Brad Lewis/Science Faction/Corbis;   p. 39, © Wolfgang Kaehler/Corbis;   p. 40, © Corbis;   pp. 44, 46, 47, 50, © Thomas Hilgers;   p. 51, Reproduced by permission of University of Cambridge Museum of Archaeology and Anthropology (N.61395. GIJ);   pp. 55, 56, © Thomas Hilgers;   p. 58, © Reuters/Corbis; p. 60, © Thomas Hilgers;   p. 61, © Kenneth Garrett/National Geographic/Getty Images;   p. 63, © Thomas Hilgers;   p. 64, © Eyewire/PhotoDisc/PunchStock;   pp. 65, 66, © Thomas Hilgers Chapter 3   p. 74, © Mark Downey/Photographer's Choice/Getty Images;   pp. 83, 84, © Thomas Hilgers;   p. 89, © Réunion des Musées Nationaux/Art Resource, NY;   p. 95, © Pete Saloutos/zefa/Corbis;   pp. 97, 98, 99, 100, 102, 104, 108, 111, 112, © Thomas Hilgers;   p. 113, © AP/Wide World Photos;   pp. 118, 119, © Thomas Hilgers Chapter 4   p. 124, 127, 128, 130, 132, 137, 139, 144, 146, 148, 150, 152, 153, 156, 157, 158, 160, © Thomas Hilgers;   p. 161, Courtesy of the estate of David Kidd;   pp. 165, 167, © Thomas Hilgers;   p. 169, © Bloomimage/Corbis;   pp. 170, 171, 174, 175, 176, 177, © Thomas Hilgers;   p. 179, © AP/Wide World Photos;   p. 183, © Thomas Hilgers Chapter 5   p. 188, © Thomas Hilgers;   p. 193, © Liba Taylor/Corbis;   p. 197, © Paul Stepan/Photo Researchers, Inc.;   p. 201, Courtesy Adam Beroud;   p. 205, © AP/Wide World Photos;   p. 207, 209, © Thomas Hilgers Chapter 6   pp. 212, 216, © Thomas Hilgers;   p. 222, © Burstein Collection/Corbis;   p. 225, © Steven Vidler/Eurasia Press/Corbis;   p. 228, 229, © Thomas Hilgers;   p. 231, © National Palace Museum, Taipei, Republic of China;   p. 232, © Jerry Driendl/The Image Bank/Getty Images; pp. 233, 234, 236, 237, 239, 242, 244, © Thomas Hilgers;   p. 249, © The Art Archive/British Museum;   pp. 252, 253, 254, © Thomas Hilgers;   p. 257, © Wu hong/epa/Corbis Chapter 7   p. 262, © Alison Wright/National Geographic Stock;   pp. 269, 272, 274, © Thomas Hilgers;   p. 275, © Sisse Brimberg/National Geographic Stock;   p. 276, © Michael S. Yamashita/National Geographic Stock;   p. 278, © Thomas Hilgers;   p. 280, © Martin Gray/National Geographic Stock;   p. 282, © Thomas Hilgers;   p. 284, © Rev. Barrish/Tsubaki Grand Shrine of America Chapter 8   p. 288, © Richard Nowitz/National Geographic Stock;   p. 294, © A. Ramey/Woodfin Camp and Associates;   p. 297, *New Beginnings*, © Bruce David (www.davidart.com). Based on large stained glass window by the artist, part of a series of windows entitled "Covenants Dor L'Dor.";   p. 299, Photo © Réunion des Musées Nationaux/Art Resource, NY. © 2009 Artists Rights Society (ARS), New York/ADAGP, Paris;   p. 303, © The Art Archive/Ragab Papyrus Institute Cairo/Dagli Orti;   p. 310, © Erich Lessing/Art Resource, NY; p. 313, © David Boyer/National Geographic Stock;   p. 317, © Thomas Hilgers;   p. 320, © Raymond Depardon/Magnum;   p. 326, © Ted Spiegel/National Geographic Stock;   p. 328, © Tomasz Tomaszewski/National Geographic Stock;   p. 329, Photo © Scala/Art Resource, NY. © 2009 Artists Rights Society (ARS), New York/ADAGP, Paris;   p. 330, © Joel Gordon;   p. 331, © Thomas Hilgers; p. 334, © Rose Eichenbaum/Corbis;   p. 337, © Richard Nowitz/National Geographic Stock Chapter 9   pp. 342, 348, 350, © Thomas Hilgers;   p. 354, © Scala/Art Resource, NY;   p. 356, © A. Ramey/PhotoEdit;   pp. 359, 361, 365, 366, 367, 371, 374, © Thomas Hilgers;   p. 378, © James L. Stanfield/National Geographic Stock; p. 380, *St. Francis Receiving the Stigmata*, c.1295–1300 (tempera on panel), Giotto di Bondone/Louvre, Paris, France/The Bridgeman Art Library;   p. 385, © Scala/Art Resource, NY;   p. 389, © David Alan Harvey/National Geographic Stock;   p. 390, © Scott S. Warren/National Geographic Stock;   p. 394, *Martin Luther King of Georgia* by Br. Robert Lentz, OFM. Courtesy of Trinity Stores, www. trinitystores.com, 800-699-4482;   p. 396, © Richard Cummins/Corbis;   p. 399, © Ed Kashi/National Geographic Stock;   pp. 402, 404, © Thomas Hilgers;   p. 405, © Gordon Gahan/National Geographic Stock;   pp. 407, 408, © Thomas Hilgers;   p. 409, Used by permission of Crystal Cathedral Ministries;   p. 410, © Thomas Hilgers;   p. 411, Courtesy Vie de Jesus Mafa/jesusmafa.com;   p. 416, © Ed Kashi/National Geographic Stock Chapter 10   p. 422, © Thomas Hilgers;   p. 429, © AKG Images;   pp. 432, 433, © Thomas Hilgers; p. 435, © Nabeel Turner/Getty Images/Stone;   pp. 441, 442, 443, © Thomas Hilgers;   p. 445, Courtesy Adam Beroud;   p. 448, © AP/Wide World Photos;   p. 450, © Thomas Hilgers;   p. 455, © AP/Wide World Photos;   pp. 458, 460, 466, 468, 470, © Thomas Hilgers;   p. 471, © Nedra Westwater/Robert Harding;   pp. 473, 478, © Thomas Hilgers;   p. 479, © Bettmann/Corbis;   p. 480, © David Alan Harvey/Magnum Photos Chapter 11   p. 488, © Thomas

Hilgers; **p. 493,** © Rebecca McEntee/Corbis Sygma; **p. 497,** © Adam Woolfitt/Corbis; **p. 498,** © Reuters/Corbis; **p. 500,** © Steve Winter/National Geographic Stock; **p. 502T,** Courtesy Theosophical Library Center; **p. 502B,** © Corbis; **p. 504,** Courtesy Church of Scientology International; **p. 506,** © Reuters/Corbis; **p. 508,** © Thomas Hilgers; **p. 510,** © Willis D. Vaughn/National Geographic Stock; **p. 511,** © Daniel Lainé/Corbis; **p. 513,** © Pictorial Press Ltd/Alamy; **p. 516,** © James L. Stanfield/National Geographic Stock; **p. 519,** © Billy E. Barnes/PhotoEdit **Chapter 12   p. 526,** © Leland Bobbé/Corbis; **p. 530,** © Manfred Leiter; **p. 532,** © Craig Lovell/Eagle Visions Photography/Alamy; **p. 533,** © Thomas Hilgers; **p. 535,** © Reuters/Corbis; **p. 537,** © ESA and NASA/National Geographic Stock; **p. 545,** Courtesy NASA; **p. 547,** © James Forte/National Geographic Stock; **p. 548,** Courtesy Public Citizen (http://www.citizen.org); **p. 530,** © Ansel Adams Publishing Rights Trust/Corbis; **p. 552,** © Thomas Hilgers; **p. 555,** Georgia O'Keeffe 1887–1986. *Music—Pink and Blue II,* 1919. Oil on canvas, Overall: 35 × 29 1/8in. (88.9 × 74cm). Whitney Museum of American Art, New York; Gift of Emily Fisher Landau in honor of Tom Armstrong 91.90. Photography by Sheldan C. Collins. © 2009 Georgia O'Keeffe Museum/Artists Rights Society (ARS), New York; **p. 556,** Photo © Art Resource, NY. © 2009 Kate Rothko Prizel & Christopher Rothko/Artists Rights Society (ARS), New York; **p. 560,** © Karsh/Woodfin Camp and Associates.

Text Credits

Chapter 1,   p. 30: from *Memories, Dreams, Reflections,* by C. G. Jung, edited by Aniela Jaffe, translated by Richard and Clara Winston. Translation copyright © 1961, 1962, 1963 and renewed 1989, 1990, 1991 by Random House, Inc. Used by permission of Pantheon Books, a division of Random House, Inc. **Chapter 2,   p. 70:** from *Black Elk Speaks,* by John Neihardt. Copyright © 2008 SUNY Press. Used with permission. **Chapter 3,   p. 120:** from *The Bhagavad Gita,* translated by Juan Mascaró (Penguin Classics, 1962). Copyright © Juan Mascaró, 1962. Reprinted by permission. **Chapter 4,   p. 183:** from *The Dhammapada: The Sayings of Buddha,* translated by Thomas Byrom. Translation copyright © 1976 by Thomas Byrom. Used by permission of Vintage Books, a division of Random House, Inc. **Chapter 5, p. 209:** from *Siri Guru Granth Sahib.* Translation © Dr. Sant Singh Khalsa. Used with permission **Chapter 6,   p. 258:** from *The Essential Confucius,* translated by Thomas Cleary. Copyright © 1992 by Thomas Cleary. Reprinted by permission of HarperCollins Publishers. **Chapter 7,   p. 285:** *The Story of Ancient Japan or, Tales from the Kojiki,* by Yaichiro Isobe. Published 1929. **Chapter 8,   p. 307:** from *The New English Bible.* © Oxford University Press and Cambridge University Press, 1961, 1970. Used with permission. **Chapter 9, p. 418:** Scripture taken from the Holy Bible, NEW INTERNATIONAL VERSION®. Copyright © 1973, 1978, 1984 International Bible Society. All rights reserved throughout the world. Used by permission of International Bible Society. NEW INTERNATIONAL VERSION® and NIV® are registered trademarks of International Bible Society. Use of either trademark for the offering of goods or services requires the prior written consent of International Bible Society. **Chapter 10, p. 484:** from *The Koran,* translated by N. J. Dawood. Copyright © 1994. Reprinted by permission of Penguin Books Ltd. **Chapter 11,   p. 522:** from *The Book of Shadows,* by Gerald Gardner. Copyright © Gerald Gardner. **Chapter 12,   p. 561:** from "My Credo," Albert Einstein's speech to the German League of Human Rights, Berlin, Autumn 1932. Courtesy of the Albert Einstein Archives, Hebrew University of Jerusalem, Israel.

Index